Electric Indiana

Railroads Past & Present

H. Roger Grant and Thomas Hoback, *editors*

A list of books in the series appears at the end of this volume.

Electric Indiana

The Rise and Fall of the World's Greatest Interurban Railway Center, 1893–1941

Carlos Arnaldo Schwantes

Indiana University Press

This book is a publication of

Indiana University Press
Office of Scholarly Publishing
Herman B Wells Library 350
1320 East 10th Street
Bloomington, Indiana 47405 USA

iupress.org

Manufactured in the United States of America

First printing 2023

Cataloging information is available from the Library of Congress.

ISBN 978-0-253-06712-8 (hdbk.)
ISBN 978-0-253-06714-2 (web PDF)

Facing, Thomas G. Hoback founded the Indiana Rail Road in 1985 and served as its president from that year until he retired in 2016. In this 2018 image, Tom waits in Michigan City, Indiana, to board a Chicago-bound train of the historic but thoroughly modern South Shore Line/Northern Indiana Commuter Transportation District, the nation's last passenger-carrying interurban.

DEDICATED TO MY GOOD FRIEND,

Thomas G. Hoback

It would be hard to underestimate the effect of the interurban upon family, social, and business life in Indiana.

—*Indianapolis Star*, November 30, 1947

In a brilliant political move, Hugh McGowan located the Traction Terminal in the heart of Indianapolis adjacent to the Indiana capitol.

Unless Lafayette wants to be buried and heard of no more, it should get a grip on some interurbans at the earliest possible moment. The interurban means progress. Its absence means decadence.

—*Lafayette Journal*, as quoted in the *Republic* (Columbus, Indiana), July 17, 1902

There is little question that the interurban line has come to stay.

—*Electric Railway Review* (March 1908): 286

There is no disguising the fact that the farmers and villagers who once were the interurban's most profitable patrons now rely to a large extent on the automobile for transportation. They can whisk themselves to town as quickly and more cheaply than the interurban can carry them, and they are left to govern their departures by their own pleasure and convenience. The loss to interurbans from the automobile has been tremendous and it is highly probable that a number of the roads now operating in this state would never have been built had their promoters foreseen the coming of the auto age.

—*Fort Wayne Daily News*, November 29, 1915

Even so, though weeds now cover the rotting ties and nature will destroy the sturdy bridge structures, time will not erase the significant role the interurbans played in the social and economic development of Indiana.

—The *Republic* (Columbus, Indiana), June 23, 1942

First interurban into Seymour: in any Indiana community, the arrival of the inaugural car of a new electric interurban railway could always attract a large crowd of enthusiastic onlookers. After the line opened in late October 1907, the Indianapolis, Columbus and Southern Traction Company offered hourly service between Seymour and the capital city sixty miles away.

Contents

Acknowledgments xi

Introduction: Interurban versus Automobile 3
1. Memories and the Personal Discovery of Indiana's Interurban Era 19
2. The Promise of Electricity, The Peril of Gasoline 31
3. Investor's Dilemma: Interurban or Automobile? 49
4. Hoosier Hysteria; or, the Interurban Boom Years 64
5. Gas Belt Prosperity and Indiana's Interurban Pioneers 85
6. Hugh McGowan, Interurban Empire Builder 103
7. The Expansive Dozen Years 119
8. Growing Traffic, Going the Distance 144
9. Travel by Interurban 169
10. A Time for Sober Reflection 184
11. Jitney, the Emergence of a Disruptive Technology 199
12. Losing Traction, Rising Highway Competition 218
13. Deadly Delusion: The Comeback That Never Was 230

Conclusion: Remnants 252

Appendix: Who Really Coined the Word "Interurban"? 267
Notes 271
Suggested Further Reading 307
Index 311

Acknowledgments

To be honest, I never intended to write *Electric Indiana*. During the months of COVID-19 confinement that began in March 2020, I discovered that a new book project was a great way to occupy my time and structure my days. Trade journals detailing the rise and fall of the electric interurban railway were readily available online, and that meant I could complete the bulk of the research from home. The treasure trove of documents I found on the internet when combined with personal memories of the remnants of the interurban landscape I observed as a youth in Greenfield and Indianapolis provided the impetus for *Electric Indiana*. The topic gave me a welcome opportunity to revisit the landscapes I once knew and to make the historical connections I never perceived or understood back then. I felt a bit like a detective searching for clues that could explain the rapid rise and lengthy decline of a mode of transportation that provided Indiana and many other areas of the United States and Canada with a clean, quiet, and efficient mode of travel, the kind that many people wish existed today.[1]

Thus, I venture forth in this case study based on events in Indiana, the popularly acclaimed "world's greatest interurban center," to share with readers the story of the epic battle waged between the electric trolley and another new mode of transportation, the automobile, both of which emerged in the United States at much the same time in the same area—the Gas Belt, Indiana's greatest engine of prosperity in the 1890s. Early on, I realized that the histories of both modes of transportation from 1893 through 1941, the interurban's life span studied here, were as entwined as double-stranded DNA. It is impossible to account for the untimely demise of the interurban without noting the rise of a disruptive technology, the automobile, and how Indiana ranked with Detroit early on as a main center of production. Elwood Haynes, the acclaimed father of the American automobile, was based in Kokomo, and Charles L. Henry, the acclaimed father of the electric interurban railway, was based in Anderson, two Gas Belt cities less than forty miles apart as the crow flies. But if the crow flew at night in the 1890s, the flames from gas wells (flambeau)—a wasteful display because numerous "experts" believed (wrongly) that Indiana's underground reservoir of fuel was cheap and inexhaustible—would have lighted the bird's entire way.

Before I plunge into the intriguing story of Indiana's Interurban Era—a story of personal, technological, and financial hubris that ended badly for nearly all participants, I must hasten to give credit where credit is due. The person who did most to plant the seed that germinated into *Electric Indiana* during my COVID-19 confinement was Thomas G. Hoback, who encouraged me to write a journal article about a horrific 1924 interurban crash that had somehow escaped the attention of most scholars of electric railways.

Tom, the longtime head and now-retired founder of The Indiana Rail Road based in Indianapolis, even took time in November 2019 to drive me out to the crash site near Ingalls, Indiana, so that we could spend an afternoon doing some serious "history on the hoof." The exact location of the head-on collision that killed twenty-one riders is almost totally unrecognizable today, and evidence that fast-running trains of the Union Traction Company of Indiana once passed that way has been erased except for nearby bridge abutments along Lick Creek, the town hall of Ingalls that once served as one of the railway's electric substations, and a somewhat obscured historical marker in a park on the opposite side of the highway. In Anderson, the interurban's headquarters city, a long-abandoned bridge still spans the White River, and to the north stands the massive brick structure that once served as Union Traction's car shops. Eighty years after the railway ran its final interurban, the structure is still emblazoned with a UTC bas-relief logo.

Quite by accident, Tom and I discovered our mutual fascination with railroad history when we both served as directors of the Lexington Group, and our interests encompassed not just Tom's beloved Atchison, Topeka and Santa Fe Railway but also other steam railroads as well as interurbans. As luck would have it, Tom and I also shared an interest in the railway landscape of Great Britain, the nation that more than any other merits the term "mother of railways" because of its pioneering role and its inordinately large influence on the railway networks of other nations around the globe, including those of the United States and Canada. Every May from 2014 until the COVID-19 pandemic of 2020 knocked a hole in our travel plans, Tom and I traveled to Britain and used our fifteen-day BritRail passes to travel from one end of the United Kingdom to the other, literally from Land's End in Cornwall to John O'Groats in northern Scotland.

I often joked that Tom and I were like two twelve-year-old boys with a multiday pass to Disneyland, except that our Great Britain rail adventure cost each of us roughly $30 a day, far less than the price of a one-day pass to Disneyland. Tom and I have both remarked how enjoyable it would have been to indulge in the same kind of unlimited travel across our native Midwest during the heyday of the region's many interurban lines. So, Tom's suggestion that I write an article somehow took flight and resulted in the book you hold in your hands, and the "mission creep" was also due to Tom's encouragement. It is appropriate that I dedicate this book to him.

It is impossible to hang around my fellow Lexington directors and not feel energized by their continuing passion for transportation history. In addition to Tom, I want to acknowledge fellow professors H. Roger Grant of Clemson University, Albert Churella of Kennesaw State University, and Don Hofsommer, now retired from St. Cloud State University. Peter Hansen, editor of *Railroad History*, was a coauthor with me and Don of a book-length history of Missouri railroads, and I regard both as good friends and respected colleagues. Alas, I must now refer to Pete in the past tense because he passed away suddenly in May 2020, but his unfailing optimism continues to inspire me.

Collectively, these five individuals have written or edited so many books and articles that they would fill a large shelf—many large shelves—in the library. I am indebted to their collective scholarship. Likewise, Gregg Ames, former curator of the John W. Barriger III National Railroad Library housed in the Saint Louis Mercantile Library, is a walking encyclopedia of railroad history and where to find it. In fact, it was Gregg who introduced me to the wealth of trade journals and various other rail publications now easily accessible to researchers via the internet. Ed Nolan, Head of Special Collections at the Washington State Historical Society, provided me with a similar introduction to the world of railroad ephemera, examples of which I am delighted to display as "visual text" on the pages that follow. Likewise, Gregg's successor at the Barriger Library, Nick Fry, graciously provided help whenever I requested it. For their research assistance I also thank Leigh Anne Johnson of the Indiana State Library and Amy Vedra of the Indiana Historical Society and their colleagues at both Indianapolis institutions. Norman Carlson, a keen student of electric railways and editor of *First & Fastest*, the quarterly journal of the Shore Line Interurban Historical Society, helped me track down some elusive historical material.

Finally, when dealing with the technical and financial topics that will inevitably arise in a book of this sort, I found myself needing to explain complex matters in ways that I and all general readers could easily understand. Fortunately, help was as close at hand as my iPhone and an internet connection that enabled me to tap into my son Matthew's expertise even though he is now based on the opposite side of the world

If we were to define an interurban railway we might describe it as a high-speed electric railroad, having nearly all its mileage outside the limits of municipalities and running, as the name implies, between cities.

—Joseph A. McGowan, treasurer of the Terre Haute, Indianapolis and Eastern Traction Company, in *AERA* (August 1924): 54

Above, Union Traction of Indiana operated numerous interurban cars such as Number 298, all beautifully crafted from a variety of hardwoods. It later supplemented these with steel cars, but the company's long-serving president, Arthur Brady, was not fond of metal rollingstock because, in the event of a serious accident, he feared steel might conduct hundreds of volts of electricity to the onboard passengers.

in Singapore. Fortunately for me, Matt holds a master's degree in electrical engineering from The University of Michigan and an MBA from the Melbourne School of Business, a graduate school in the University of Melbourne in Australia. My other son, Benjamin, holds a history doctorate from the University of Delaware with a specialization in the history of technology. So, Ben, the former managing editor of the *JANNAF Journal of Propulsion and Energetics* published by Johns Hopkins University in Baltimore, served as a valuable (and convenient) sounding board for some of my ideas. Thanks, guys!

Railroad history (and the subfield of interurban history) is a data-intensive field of study. If in my research and writing I have made any errors of fact (entirely possible) or errors of judgment (also entirely possible), I blame only myself. The risk is well worth the reward that came from researching and writing this admittedly personal study of the Interurban Era. Likewise, it is a pleasure to use as illustrations throughout *Electric Indiana* the many pieces of trolley and interurban ephemera I collected over the years. All these images come from the Schwantes-Greever-Nolan Collection of Travel and Transportation Ephemera.

Carlos A. Schwantes, Saint Louis Mercantile Library
Professor of History Emeritus

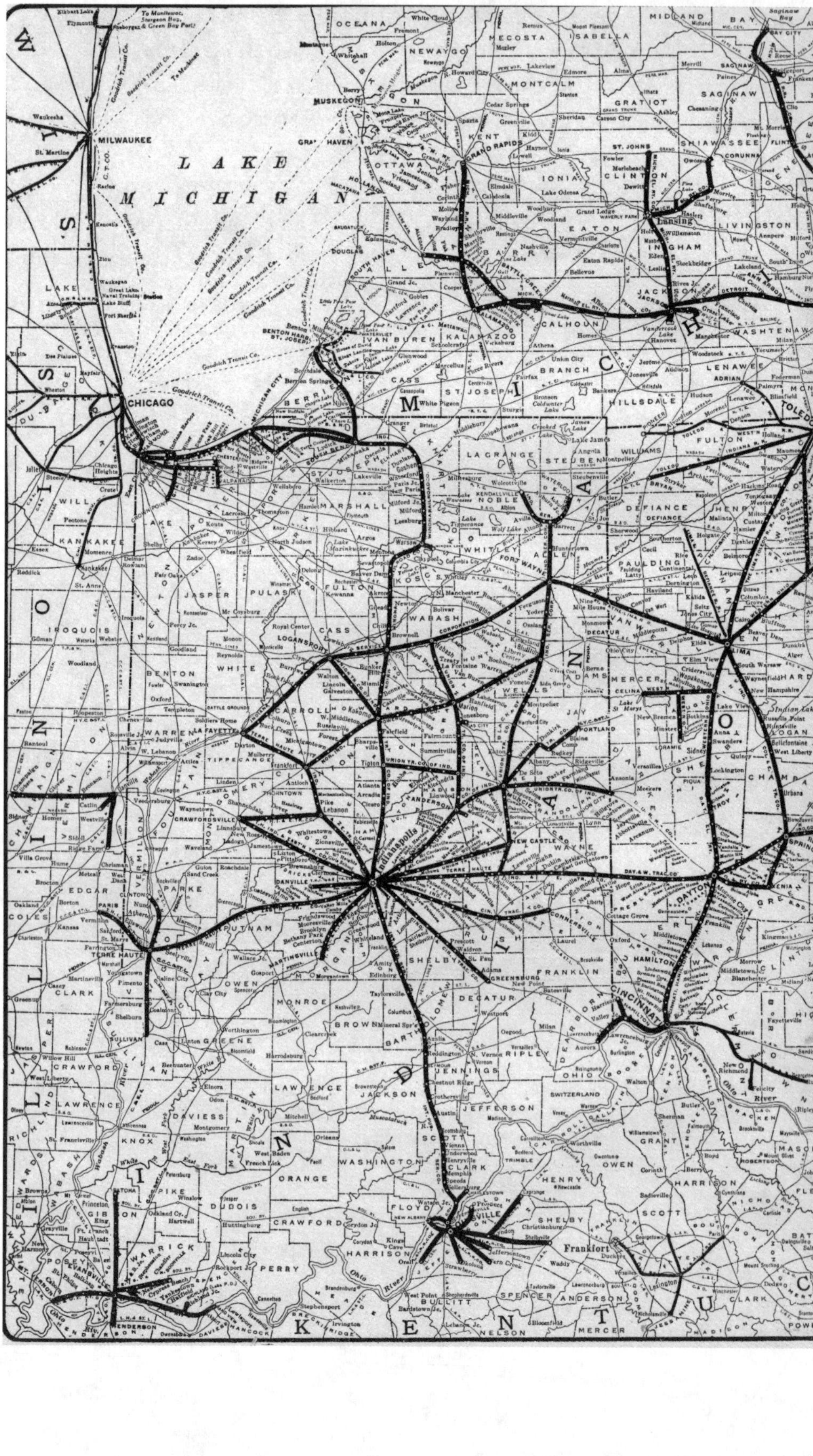

LAKE MICHIGAN
MILWAUKEE
CHICAGO
MUSKEGON
GRAND RAPIDS
KALAMAZOO
JACKSON
Lansing
TOLEDO
FORT WAYNE
LOGANSPORT
LA FAYETTE
Indianapolis
TERRE HAUTE
DAYTON
CINCINNATI
EVANSVILLE
HENDERSON
Frankfort
LIMA

Ohio has considerably more electric railroad mileage than any other State in the Union, and Pennsylvania, New York, Illinois, and Massachusetts follow in the order named, although the race between Illinois and Massachusetts is so close that the precedence varies from year to year. Indiana comes next, and yet the interurban lines in that State may fairly be said to be more important than the interurban lines in any equal area in the world. Not including the lines in towns and cities, there are 1,539 miles of interurban road in Indiana, and no other state is served so thoroughly by its through trolley lines.

—*Electric Railway Section, Commercial & Financial Chronicle*, September 26, 1908, p. 1.

Facing, Indiana's sprawling interurban network, which at its peak numbered nearly two thousand miles, was still largely intact at the time this map was published in the mid-1920s.

Cars of the Marion, Bluffton and Eastern pause in Warren, Indiana. The interurban line extended thirty-two miles to link its two namesake cities, but the "eastern" portion of its name represented wishful thinking.

Electric Indiana

Crawfordsville: The Indianapolis, Crawfordsville and Western was nicknamed the "Ben Hur Route" because the illustrious Hoosier author Lew Wallace called Crawfordsville home. His novel *Ben-Hur: A Tale of the Christ* was published in 1880 and became one of America's all-time bestsellers.

Introduction

Interurban versus Automobile

> Interurban lines have been a great convenience in the past for both passenger traffic and local freight service. The inventors of automobiles in the first stages of their development little dreamed of the economic effect motor vehicles—passenger and truck—would have on the economic condition of the nation. First to succumb were the livery stables and blacksmith shops, then came curtailment of steam railroad service, and now the abandonment of interurban lines as conditions warrant.
>
> —*Brownstown* [Indiana] *Banner*, August 16, 1939

At the dawn of the twentieth century, the electric interurban railroad seemed like the ideal mode of transportation. The cars, comfortable, quiet-running, and clean, offered riders a noticeable contrast to the smoke, cinders, and heavy puffing of a coal-burning steam locomotive. Interurbans ran at frequent intervals, often once an hour, and could easily stop almost anywhere to board or discharge passengers. This was a convenience that encouraged farmers to donate land for a right-of-way so that they and their families could enjoy the new door-to-door link between rural and urban America. Interurban enthusiasm was contagious and resulted in the construction of nearly two thousand miles of electric railways across Indiana alone. The state's press warned in 1901 that in the years ahead, a city without interurban service would be a "graveyard of business."[1]

So many different interurban lines intersected in the massive Traction Terminal opened in downtown Indianapolis in 1904 that the Indiana capital became known as the "world's greatest interurban center," a term that boosters soon applied to the entire state. The sale of interurban securities was brisk, and a lucrative return seemed ensured for years to come. A few investors, notably the Philadelphians who bankrolled many of the Midwest's early interurban companies, did enhance their personal fortunes. But despite the high hopes of many an Indiana farmer, teacher, lawyer, and doctor, the typical small-time investor did not fare so well. The Interurban Era proved exciting, at least initially, but it was unexpectedly short-lived because another new mode of transportation, the automobile, soon emerged as the ultimate disruptive technology. By the 1930s, it was no longer meaningful to brag that Indianapolis or any other place was the "world's greatest interurban center."

By late 1922, Indiana could already claim that it supported a four-thousand-mile system of hard-surface highways, a grid at least twice the size of its interurban network. The state's taxpayer-funded roadways grew ever more extensive and better built during the rest of the decade, much to the delight of motorists. The result was highlighted by the *Indianapolis News* in 1930 when it called the modern highway to Danville, Indiana, a "Frankenstein Monster" that had devoured the adjacent interurban line. "Because former passengers have taken to automobile travel over the hard-surface highway that parallels the traction line, the interurban managers asserted the electric line can no longer be made to pay expenses, not to mention taxes on its property. Only a few years ago the traction line made fair-sized profits from hauling the materials from which the highway was built." Now the only thing that made economic sense to its owners was to abandon an interurban line constructed in 1906 with every confidence in its long-term profitability. The same scenario played out all over Indiana.[2]

Sherman Minton, an Indiana attorney destined to become a justice of the US Supreme Court, served in 1933 as counselor to the Public Service Commission. One day, after listening to a litany of woes voiced by electric interurban railway executives who had petitioned regulators to reduce or abandon service between Indianapolis and Louisville because the formerly promising connection had lost riders and bled red ink during each of the past five years, Minton was inspired to quip: "Abandon all hope ye who enter the interurban business."[3]

Listeners laughed at the allusion to Dante's *Inferno*, but Minton stated an undeniable truth. During the Great Depression of the early 1930s, Indiana's interurbans were locked in a deadly embrace with economic reality from which there was no escape and no reason to hope that industry fortunes might ever improve. All its leaders could do was slow the steadily downward trend until, in late 1941, shortly before Pearl Harbor plunged Americans into World War II, a final car departed downtown Indianapolis. Just three decades earlier, nearly six hundred interurban cars had begun or ended their journeys in the cavernous Traction Terminal each day, and millions of travelers passed through its portals each year. The rise of the private automobile and other forms of highway competition took the electric industry by surprise and relentlessly diminished the popular appeal of all that the interurbans had been able to offer—fast, frequent, and inexpensive passenger travel and the rapid delivery of freight and express.

Cutting-edge technologies of the recent past, hopes for a promising and prosperous future, and personal investments large and small were fast disappearing during the 1930s along with the interurban network that once had been the pride of Indiana and

In this popular postcard image, a Union Traction interurban car crosses a lengthy trestle near Logansport, part of the once-extensive infrastructure that all but vanished after 1941.

made it a world leader worth emulating. Observers in former years had come from as far away as Germany and Japan to see how the electric interurban railways of the Hoosier State showcased the new mode of transportation.[4]

When the first interurban cars entered an Indiana community, residents were fascinated by the new technology. "Of course, in a small place like Rushville, the new trolley car is the wonder of wonders, and it is not surprising that people bring their dinners and stand along the track to watch it go by, hour after hour." At the dawn of the twentieth century, interurban cars proved equally fascinating to residents of Greenfield, Greentown, Greensburg, Greencastle, and a multitude of other Hoosier communities now connected for the first time by rapid transit to hub cities like Indianapolis, Fort Wayne, South Bend, and Evansville. The interurban redefined spatial relationships and quickened the tempo of daily life across Indiana and the Midwest.[5]

The electric interurban railway was exciting not just because it offered a convenient new mode of transportation. It did that, of course, but its arrival invariably conferred many additional benefits. Not only did it signify modernity to communities large and small; it also greatly increased the range of everyday economic and social options available to city dwellers, and even more impressive were the tangible blessings it conferred on the once semi-isolated residents of rural and small-town Indiana. A trip to the big city of Indianapolis for a day of shopping, for example, no longer entailed the expense and inconvenience of an overnight stay because steam trains on many rail lines serving the lightly populated countryside that typified much of the southern half of the state ran only once or twice a day.

The interurban, both the vehicle and the industry, represented the convergence of several exciting developments that took place in the United States in the late nineteenth and early twentieth centuries. Foremost was the dawn of the electrical age, which gave rise to all kinds of useful innovations, from electric fans to "bottled sunlight," a term J. P. Morgan used to describe the light bulbs that Thomas Edison installed to illuminate the formerly gloomy chambers of Morgan's Wall Street banking empire. Electricity, unlike steam that powered all the great railroads of the United States, enabled interurban railways to run single-car trains as inexpensively as multicar ones and to do so at closely timed intervals. Onboard electric motors enabled interurban cars to start or stop quickly, unlike the ponderous trains of the steam railroads, and this feature made it easy for them to accommodate passengers almost anywhere—at the front gate of any farm that abutted the tracks or along the main streets of countless cities and villages.

The interurban car, which superficially resembled a streetcar but was larger, faster, and far more comfortable, was not just a convenient vehicle. Wherever tracks ran, interurban railways opened the door to all kinds of new spatial arrangements that contributed to the transformation of America from a rural to an urban nation between 1890 and 1920.

When, for example, a last rail was spiked into place in mid-1903, the residents of Knightstown were thrilled to be connected by the electric cars not just to Indianapolis but also to distant locations across central Ohio. The local newspaper highlighted the newly forged spatial relationship on its front page by noting that Knightstown was now situated along the world's longest interurban line and that its residents were privileged to enjoy a continuous trolley ride of 250 miles. Laying a final spike to connect Indianapolis with Dayton, Columbus, and Newark, Ohio, the paper asserted, "is to the electric world somewhat as the completion of the first transcontinental line was to the railway world for it marks the realization of long-distance travel by electricity."[6]

In its early years, the "people's railway" thrilled riders and investors alike, and scarcely a week passed between 1897 and 1907 without some new project grabbing the local newspaper headlines. That was especially true in Indiana, the Hoosier State, which had embraced the interurban with such unreserved passion that it emerged as the industry's premier role model, and not just for the Midwest or the United State and Canada but even for distant parts of the world. "There was a time not so many years ago when the interurban electric or traction lines were the very last word in handy transport," recalled a Lafayette newspaper in 1932. "It was Indiana's part to adopt with enthusiasm the interurban line idea."[7]

Why Indiana? Until the coming of the automobile, electric interurban railways compensated for the lack of navigable waterways in the Hoosier State. Landlocked Indianapolis lacked the transportation advantages that nature conferred on Chicago, Saint Louis, Detroit, Cleveland, Toledo, Cincinnati, and Louisville, all great port cities of the Midwest that Indianapolis aspired to emulate. The northern half of Indiana was flat and conducive to the construction of a network of tracks, and the spatial arrangement of Muncie, Anderson, Kokomo, and other cities of the state's prosperous Gas Belt of the 1890s provided an environment that nurtured the growth of interurban railways. The first lines reached Indianapolis in 1900; after that, there seemed to be no end to additional interurban projects. A popular phrase often used to describe the frenzy of construction activity was to "make the dirt fly."[8]

Indiana's interurban network at its peak of approximately eighteen hundred miles ranked second only to Ohio in the United States.[9] Even more remarkable than the mileage statistics was the inordinately great influence that individuals and innovations in Indiana had on the entire electric railway industry in the United States and Canada. It was no accident that many prominent individuals tasked with overseeing complex urban transportation systems in Baltimore, New York City, Saint Louis, and other large cities during the 1920s were Hoosiers who first learned to run interurban passenger and freight trains across the corn and bean fields of Indiana. No other state or Canadian province could claim a similar succession of national industry leaders during the decades from the early twentieth century through the 1930s. In fact, so many Indiana interurban executives rose to leadership positions within North America's numerous electric railway professional associations that newspapers could correctly describe their prominence as the "Hoosier cabal."[10]

Finally, the interurban can also serve as a metaphor for life itself: its birth, maturity, and death all took place within the typical span of a human life of sixty or seventy years. That is, some of the same people whose entrepreneurial and technical talents gave birth to the industry were still around to witness its demise. Thus, with *Electric Indiana,* I offer a cautionary tale, a case study that seeks to describe in detail how plans and expectations for a rosy future could easily be upended by the unexpected emergence of a new technology. In this case, the disruptor was the private automobile and its highway allies, the intercity bus and truck lines, which emerged as potent competitors during the 1920s. Even as late as middecade, it was impossible for most industry leaders to imagine that an enterprise worth billions could ever be consigned to history's scrap heap. Joseph A. McGowan, a respected industry authority who for a quarter of a century held top-level positions on several Indiana interurbans, assured his fellow executives across the Midwest in 1924 that "rubber tires can never supersede steel rails in the carrying of passengers and freight, as a whole. Rival methods of transportation may last for a while but they can never supplant interurban railways."[11]

The interurban occupied the middle ground between horse-drawn conveyances limited to local use in city and country and the almighty steam railroads that dominated intercity transportation. Also occupying the same middle ground was the automobile, which emerged in North America at roughly the same time as the interurban, in 1893 or 1994. The two modes of transportation coexisted peacefully until 1914 or 1915 when automobiles noticeably and rudely began to elbow streetcars and interurbans aside. The steady improvement of internal combustion engines and the popular crusade for better roads and highways converged during those years to enable motor vehicles to do everything the electric railways did, only better. The interurban that "in its day was the acme of convenience became a back number when the more convenient motor cars congested the highways." In the following chapters, I recount the story of the generally forgotten yet still instructive contest between the interurban and the automobile.[12]

After half a century of teaching American history, all of it at universities west of the Mississippi River, it gave me great pleasure in recent years to travel east to revisit my Indiana roots and to explore in detail a question that had long fascinated me: what accounted for the rapid rise and lengthy decline of the electric interurban railway across North America? Seldom, if ever, has a transportation technology that showed so much promise, solved so many everyday logistical problems, and created so many new travel possibilities for ordinary people been consigned so quickly to the dustbin of history. The Interurban Era lasted barely forty years. Of the 15,580 miles of interurban track in the United States at the industry's peak in 1916, only a ninety-mile-long segment across northwestern Indiana remains in place and is still operating today.[13]

There can be only one explanation: a parallel technology, a personal mobility module known as the automobile, rose inexorably to prominence during the boom times of the electric interurban railway. Instead of faltering as the interurban industry did around 1916 before it entered its lengthy terminal decline, the automobile only continued to grow in popularity. America's well-documented love affair with private automobiles and public highways contributed more than anything else to the death of the interurban. The intertwined history of these transportation technologies is the subject I wish to explore by occasionally adding a personal perspective. In *Electric Indiana,* I will trace how one disruptive technology could upend the best projections and expert calculations of another, such as our familiar cell phones did in recent times to landline telephone networks dependent on metal wires, cables, and fiber optics.[14]

Cars of the Cincinnati, Lawrenceburg and Aurora crossed into Ohio to connect Aurora with the outskirts of Cincinnati. The southeast corner of Indiana, like the Evansville area in the southwest, remained an outlier never linked by electric interurban railways with the network of tracks that crisscrossed central and northern portions of the state.

When I was a graduate student at the University of Michigan in the late 1960s and early 1970s, my professors admonished all young historians-in-training to avoid injecting personal observations into the scholarly books and essays we were expected to write to become tenured professors. Now that I am retired after having earned tenure at three separate universities, it gives me a profound sense of personal freedom to break the scholarly rules and conventions once so important to me. Part of what I wish to do in *Electric Indiana* is to share with readers my behind-the-scenes search for the historical evidence that forms the foundation for this book.

While the central theme of this book, the Interurban Era, enabled me to roam across North America in search of historical evidence (mostly via the internet), I feel confident that the most important features of the lengthy contest between interurban and automobile can best be revealed by focusing on Indiana. Neighboring Ohio can claim to have had the most miles of interurban line in the United States, but Indiana was widely recognized by contemporaries as the state that offered the most congenial home to the promising new transportation technology.[15]

In the Hoosier State itself, the interurban modernized life, and it is there that a ninety-mile remnant of a vast network of tracks continues to offer a defiant alternative to the automobile. Moreover, before Detroit emerged as the "Motor City," Indiana was home to an astonishing number of automakers, including Haynes, the first successful brand sold in the United States. Thus, the Hoosier State provides a perfect location in which to explore one particularly dramatic case of a disruptive technology in action.

During the 1940s and at least through the 1990s when columnists still retained personal memories of the Interurban Era, Indiana newspapers published numerous nostalgic accounts of riding the electric railways and how they changed Hoosier lives for the better. Frequently running interurban cars enabled isolated farm families to connect to urban centers as they never could have done in horse-and-buggy days or been able to afford to do when traveling aboard a steam passenger train. "Such a life was not possible for these people ten years ago [in 1897]." Local trains operated by steam railroads did not permit a quick and easily affordable trip to town and back. In fact, the interurban offered medium- and low-income Americans from all walks of life access to an unprecedented world of travel pleasures. For example, a journey aboard one of the interurban cars that dashed between Rushville and Indianapolis and covered the distance of forty-one miles in a mere ninety minutes cost sixty cents when the line opened in 1905.[16]

A farm wagon plodding along the rutted pathways that passed for roads in Indiana in those days would have required at least two days to make the round-trip journey and necessitated an overnight stay in the Hoosier capital. Years earlier, a steam railroad had been completed between the same two cities, but its passenger trains ran only a few times each day, and tickets cost several dollars—no small consideration when the average American worker earned approximately $500 a year. Passengers riding the electric cars noted how clean and quiet the ride was. Seated at an open window and enjoying a refreshing breeze on a hot and sticky summer's afternoon, they experienced a special intimacy with the rapidly passing countryside without having to endure the coal smoke and grit blown back by a galloping steam locomotive.

The same transportation miracle redefined spatial relationships across Indiana and the Midwest by expanding the outreach and influence of the region's largest cities in a way that nothing, not even the many steam railroads, had done before. When the first interurbans commenced regular service out of Indianapolis in January 1900, a local newspaper commented that they would be a benefit not only to the Hoosier capital but also to "towns along the line, and to all that live in the neighborhood thereof. Here at a man's door will come this trolley railroad, stopping easily and quickly at any place—a rural streetcar to carry him to and fro at will." In short, it had the potential to transform everyday life across Indiana.[17]

Until the automobile proved itself to be a practical and reliable vehicle, it was impossible for Hoosiers to envision an alternative to the interurban. "It is difficult to conceive the practical effects which would result if every mile of interurban railway throughout Indiana were suddenly torn from place, the operation of cars, both freight and passenger, abandoned, and the public compelled to resort again to the primitive methods of transportation in vogue years ago." This comment appeared in an editorial published in the *Indianapolis Star* in 1912, but the alternative to the interurban by that date would not be the horse and buggy of yesterday but the ever-improving automobile of the near future. Contrary to the expectations voiced in 1912, nearly every mile of Indiana's once-vast interurban system was, indeed, to be "torn from place" not suddenly but by the slow dismemberment that took place mainly during a dozen years beginning in the late 1920s.[18]

While I had long enjoyed reading everything I could possibly find on the history of electric interurban railways, I never expected to add anything of significance to the many informative studies already in print or, most notably, to the books written by George Hilton and John Due, William D. Middleton, and H. Roger Grant. Nonetheless, it occurred to me that there was room for a book that was fundamentally a biography of what Middleton had labeled the "Interurban Era," a term I borrow throughout *Electric Indiana*.[19]

There are countless additional books devoted to the histories of individual interurban lines and to the array of equipment they used. Though the details differ, their authors tell of an industry that rose rapidly to prominence between 1894 and 1907, the recession year that tamed the runaway enthusiasm that animated the pioneer interurban builders. Nonetheless, the industry continued to grow after 1907 but at a much more measured pace. Shortly after another recession year, 1914, the interurban network attained its greatest extent and importance before entering its long period of terminal decline.

If any specific time in the early twentieth century witnessed milestone events in the history of American transportation, the years 1914 and 1915 would easily qualify. This short period marked the peak of the Interurban Era, though few people at the time recognized this. The recession of 1914, brief though it was, reminded steam railroads how much transportation had evolved in recent years because of the huge number of once-healthy companies that needed to be resuscitated financially. Many railroads in receivership were not relatively insignificant short lines but giants of the industry. Also, in 1914, the Panama Canal opened to ships carrying nonperishable freight between the coastal United States that might previously have traveled by rail. Finally, Henry Ford's introduction of a moving assembly line greatly lowered the price of his incredibly popular Model T automobiles. At one time, half the motorists in America drove a Ford. The increasing number of auto owners forced Congress to do something about the abominable condition of the nation's roads and highways. In too many locations, crosscountry motorists were forced to run a gauntlet of axle-deep mud, sand traps, and indistinct traces across an unfamiliar landscape that made getting lost a virtual certainty. Two years later, in 1916, Congress appropriated money for the first federal highway construction program since the 1830s when Conestoga wagons lumbered across the Midwest on the National Road.

One additional noteworthy event of 1914–15 largely forgotten today was the phenomenal and seemingly overnight rise of the "jitney." These private automobiles were at the center of a chaotic but potent urban mass protest directed at the street railway industry but also had worrisome implications for interurban railways. Even the steam-powered railroads that dominated intercity passenger transportation across the United States at the time were affected by the jitney phenomenon—and I can think of no better word than "phenomenon" to describe the nemesis that arose seemingly in a single night and proved absurd, frightening, or exhilarating, depending on a person's perspective. The jitney was absurd in the simplicity of its origins, frightening in how rapidly it spread like a financial virus to impact America's big-city street railway systems, and exhilarating to the many urban dwellers who had never known the thrill of riding in an automobile on rubber tires, a form of sensory deprivation unthinkable today.

Nearly forty years ago, I wrote an article about the jitney, but research for *Electric Indiana* has convinced me that the phenomenon was even more disruptive than I had originally thought because the street railway industry in places like Muncie, Indiana, continued to battle the ubiquitous "jitney plague" well into the 1920s. So important was the jitney as a component of the constellation of landmark events occurring in 1914–15 that in a later chapter I will explore its devastating impact on electric railways. I will also note how it served as an ominous portent of the kind of ruthless competition for passengers that both the interurban and steam railroads experienced during the 1920s.

In many ways, the rapid rise and premature death of the electric interurban railway between 1894 and 1924 can be seen as a cautionary tale—a case of misplaced technological pride as well as misdirected investment capital. But things are not so simple, as I hope to explain. No one connected with the interurban industry during its most optimistic years before 1907 could have foreseen the rise of a disruptive technology, the automobile and other forms of highway competition, and how easily the new modes of transportation made a mockery of their expectations of a prosperous future for the interurban. One need only read the pages of the *Street Railway Journal*, the *Street Railway Gazette*, the *Street Railway Review*, *Electric Traction*, and many other trade publications devoted to all things electric to see how with logic, precise calculations, and elaborate mathematical formulations a generation of engineers and financiers confidently planned for the interurban to enjoy a long and financially robust future. Every mile of track was spiked into place with the optimistic expectation that electric railways were a modern marvel built to accommodate travelers and freight for decades and possibly centuries to come and would return a reasonable and steady income to investors.

The highlight of the year for the electric railway industry was the big fall conference intended to showcase the latest products of its many manufacturers and suppliers. Because the typical interurban line originated as a small-scale and locally oriented enterprise that seldom ran a line of tracks longer than fifty miles, the annual gatherings brought industry leaders together from all parts of the United States and Canada. These conferences performed a vital educational function, both formally and informally, by facilitating the exchange of information among the geographically scattered members.

Ever since its founding in Boston in 1884 as the American Street Railway Association, the industry's annual conference had provided a convenient forum for public presentations devoted to a host of technical topics. During the association's first decade, the topics related mainly to horse and cable railways, but electricity gained an increasingly respectful hearing after 1888. The electric interurban railway emerged in the late 1890s during the same years as the first American automobiles, but conference speakers only rarely gave any serious thought to the possibility of highway competitors until forced to do so by the disruptive events of 1914 and 1915, and especially by the abrupt rise of an army of jitney drivers who used their private automobiles to steal tens of thousands of passengers who formerly rode the streetcars. The jitney freebooters impacted the electric railways of the United States and Canada as nothing had ever done before and cost them millions, but one of the industry's most respected spokesmen, Indiana's Charles L. Henry, dismissed the jitney "fad" in a 1916 speech and confidently asserted that soon "the interurbans will carry their old-time allotment of passengers."[20]

Henry, who was exceptionally well positioned to assess where the industry had been and would likely be headed in the future, was frequently labeled the "father of the interurban." The two-term Indiana congressman easily qualified as the dean of electric railway executives nationwide. In his always friendly and approachable manner, he delighted in sharing with fellow executives across the United States and Canada lessons learned from his constructing two of the Hoosier State's most significant interurban railways. It was Henry's fate to serve as president of the American Electric Railway Association (1915–16) during a time of unprecedented hand-wringing throughout the industry he had helped launch in the late 1890s. Ever the optimist, he always did his utmost to encourage fellow industry leaders to be positive about the future, a sunny perspective he had exhibited ever since the 1890s when he oversaw construction of the state's first large interurban enterprise, the Union Traction Company of Indiana, an industry role model that attracted interest from across North America. Union Traction was at one time the single largest electric interurban railway in the world.

Henry was always quick to note that the interurban industry had many fathers, yet it was he who had indisputably fathered the Union Traction line that opened in early 1901 to link Anderson and Indianapolis. As was often the case during the Interurban Era, industry pioneers like Henry were still around to witness its grim devolution starting in the 1920s.

Let me borrow a popular financial term to affirm that the "bottom line" for me is that the history of the Interurban Era is highly instructive in how it illustrates the power of a disruptive technology to not just upset an industry's confident predictions of its prospects in the years ahead but also to make obsolete what were once cutting-edge ideas and innovations. Electric railway industry publications featured running dialogues on how best to improve interurban cars, to cite one example, but many of the most sought-after improvements proved technological dead-ends during the industry's slow-motion demise. The same was true for innovations that suppliers like General Electric and Westinghouse once proudly showcased at the annual electric railway conventions. The industry served as a fertile field for inventors, so much so that each issue of its weekly or monthly trade journals often listed a full page or more of newly patented ideas. Perhaps the hubris of the electric railway industry serves today as a useful cautionary tale as we ponder our present and future technologies and their potential for unexpected obsolescence.

As my research and writing progressed, I came to see ever more clearly that a primary purpose of *Electric Indiana* was to give a complex story a human face. It was the same for the concept of the supposedly "soulless" corporation, a common term used to condemn big business in the early twentieth century. People made decisions, good or bad, that resulted in the wreck of a train and the consequent loss of life—or the wreck of an entire industry, as in the interurban's losing battle with the automobile. There are many reasons for the success or failure of an enterprise, or even of an entire industry, and I hope to explore the human dimension that accounts for the turns and twists of any narrative of the Interurban Era. On the following pages, I introduce readers to key actors in the drama of *Electric Indiana*, most notably Charles L. Henry and Arthur W. Brady. Hundreds of noteworthy individuals contributed in one way or another to interurban history, but Henry and Brady warrant close attention because both emerged in the early twentieth century to dominate the industry in Indiana and soon thereafter became national spokesmen for the cause that was to dominate the most productive years of their lives.[21]

At a less serious level, writing about this topic was for me an inexplicably nostalgic experience. Nostalgia as a motivating influence is not so inexplicable, except that over the years I have observed that professional historians often appeared loath, even embarrassed, to admit that nostalgia might shape their thinking. I offer no apologies for wishing to return, at least mentally, to an era defined by the golden years of interurban transportation that just happened to coincide with the last years of American innocence before the unspeakable carnage of World War I. The interurban conjures up for me ragtime music, an extensive network of first-rate railroad passenger trains, and a bucolic America in which urban dwellers could still enjoy warm evenings in a public park singing "In the Good Old Summertime" or listening to a brass band provided by the local trolley or interurban company.[22]

A favorite quotation of my late father was: "You know you are growing old when you feel increasingly alienated from the present." Now in my late seventies, I realize that he spoke a profound truth, and in my own increasing alienation from the present, I found a welcome escape by revisiting the Interurban Era and indulging in nostalgia for a time and place innocent of so many troubling issues that defy easy solutions today. I wrote this book not just to study why transportation technologies succeed or fail but because the process of researching and writing also offered me a welcome chance to revisit at will a simpler time and place (and during much of the years 2020 and 2021 to stay sane during home confinement and to escape the depressing barrage of COVID-19 news).

I would be the first to admit that I indulge in an illusion—that in many ways, the "good old days" were terrible. Those years were free of the random and inexplicable cases of fatal road rage and the opioid crisis that afflicts modern America, but drug abuse and personal violence simply took other forms, and there is no hiding from the ugliness of lynching and racial and ethnic discrimination. Popular culture was replete with crude jokes and demeaning visual stereotypes. But while acknowledging that the fabric of American society during the Interurban Era contained imperfections, I much prefer to dwell on the positive attributes of that bygone time in an America full of self-confidence and positive about its future.[23]

"The World's Greatest Interurban Center"

If some readers think I'm prone to unpardonable exaggeration to use this phrase as the subtitle for *Electric Indiana,* let me say that those exact words appeared numerous times in newspapers across the Hoosier State, and, after 1906, the American press spread the claim nationwide. That is largely attributable to the Traction Terminal erected in downtown Indianapolis and to its inspiration, Hugh J. McGowan. Both the monumental building and one of Indiana's most remarkable "Trolley Kings," the

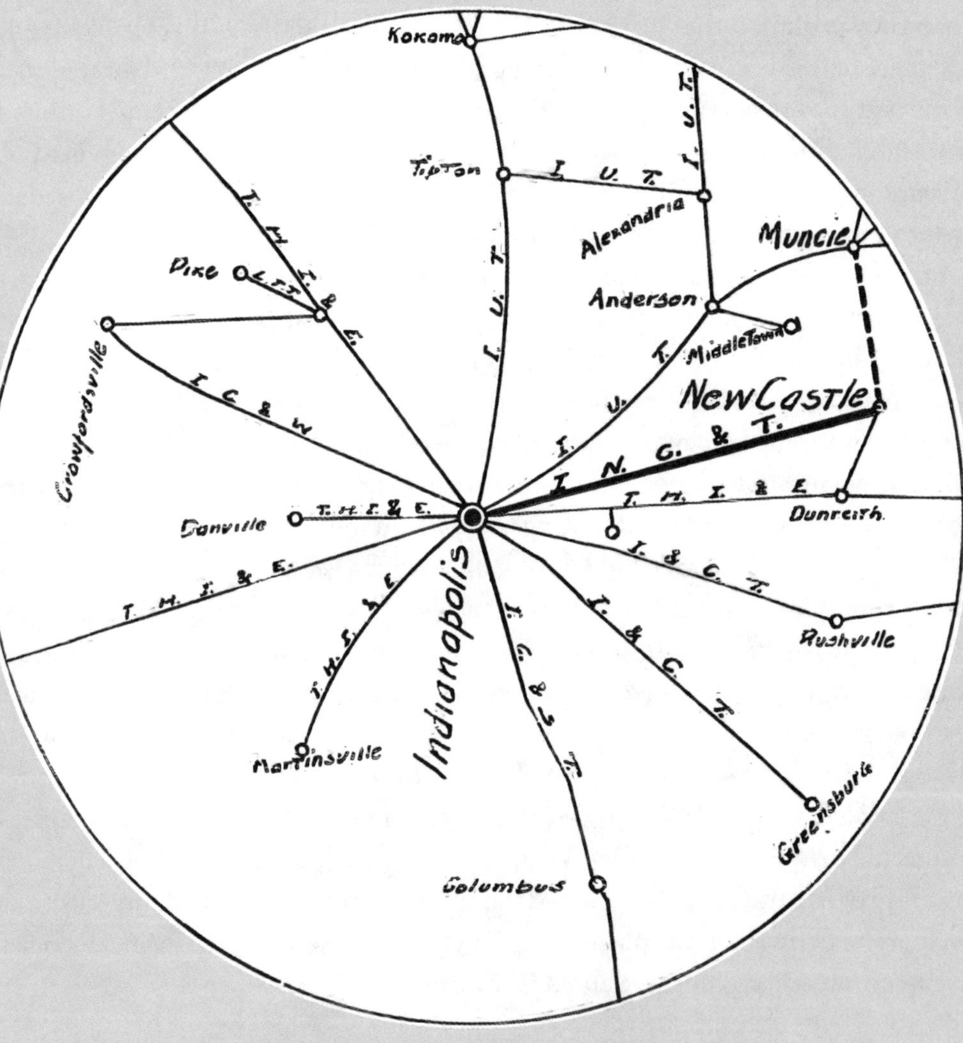

Indianapolis, the Traction Hub

As this 1911 graphic emphasizes, Indianapolis functioned as the hub for numerous interurban lines.

human dynamo responsible for its construction, inspired awe in contemporary observers. Even when he paused for a rare interview, McGowan could barely contain his energy. Both the man and his building receive considerable attention on the pages that follow.

Helping to amplify Indiana's boundless pride in its interurban network were the nearly four hundred members of the National Editorial Association who assembled in Indianapolis during June 1906 for their twenty-first annual convention. "Indianapolis is well prepared to receive and entertain the newspaper men who will be here from all parts of the United States. She will give them every welcome." The generous measure of Hoosier hospitality shown to the nation's influential wordsmiths during their visit to Indianapolis likely included a tour of the city's Traction Terminal. Because their conference took place in the Claypool Hotel just a block away from McGowan's interurban edifice, any attendee could easily have walked to it for a personal inspection.[24]

The June gathering was a great success, and, not coincidentally, many daily and weekly newspapers nationwide subsequently amplified the claim that Indiana and its capital city constituted the world's greatest interurban center. One enthusiastic Kansas editor returned home to the town of Hiawatha to inform his readers that "the street car service in Indianapolis is perfect. An ex-Kansas City man, Hugh McGowan, is in command of it. The electric railway has reached its highest development in this city. It has a great traction depot, probably the only one of its kind in the world."[25]

Likewise, when Iowa newspaper mogul Alfred Wilson Lee described his experience at the recent editors' conference, he lavished praise on the Indiana capital and its interurbans. "Indianapolis: The Heart of Civilization" read the banner headline that introduced his lengthy feature story. "Everybody in Indianapolis talks interurban," and Lee affirmed for subscribers to his several Iowa newspapers that the city "is today the greatest interurban center on the globe, all the lines terminating at a magnificent traction terminal building in the heart of the city, and which is said to be the only exclusive interurban station in the world."[26]

The only pushback to Indiana's claim to fame came from Southern California partisans who insisted that their sprawling Pacific Electric Railway was the world's greatest interurban. In truth, both assertions were valid. Nonetheless, the *Sacramento Star* highlighted the historic rivalry between Northern and Southern California when it reported that a vocal group of city residents much preferred to emulate the Indianapolis model as they promoted construction of a new union interurban depot. In the words of their spokesman, "It is the proper thing to have all these roads use the same depot and terminal, as they do in Indianapolis, and Sacramento too would become the great city that Indianapolis is."[27]

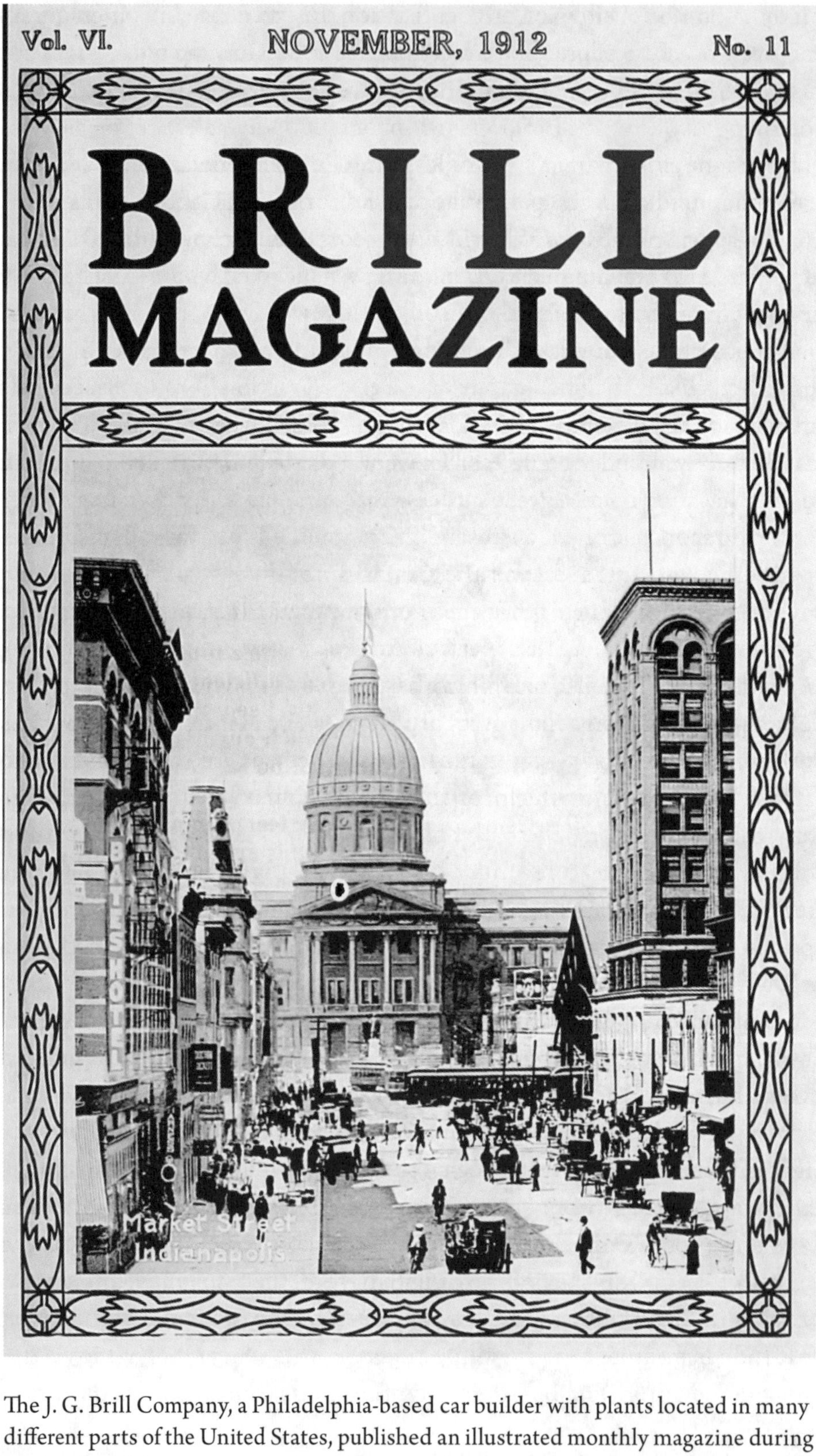

The J. G. Brill Company, a Philadelphia-based car builder with plants located in many different parts of the United States, published an illustrated monthly magazine during the heyday of the interurban. The publication chose a familiar image for its November 1912 cover to salute Indianapolis and the "world's greatest interurban center."

1

Memories and the Personal Discovery of Indiana's Interurban Era

> Indiana has the greatest group of electric railway lines in the world and Indianapolis is the largest interurban railway center in the United States. This is a distinction of which every Hoosier should justly be proud.
>
> —*Indianapolis Star*, November 4, 1912

As a schoolboy in 1950s Greenfield, I grew up surrounded by evidence of the interurban railway network that had previously blanketed Indiana and other Midwest states. I failed to recognize until many years later, however, my good fortune of having been born four years after the last interurban car departed nearby Indianapolis. Four times a day during my first six grades of school, I trudged past the slatted gate that barred entrance to the dark and seemingly empty interior of a garage-like building that fronted Main Street. I seldom, if ever, gave the long-unused structure any thought. My main goal as a schoolboy was to get safely past the Hancock County Courthouse a block away.

The Romanesque hulk was not just spooky. In the words of geographer Yi-Fu Tuan, it was the centerpiece of a "landscape of fear."[1] For reasons I can no longer recall, I was always too scared to enter the grim building or even to trespass on its grassy lawn. Six decades later, I finally summoned up enough courage to open the front door of the courthouse and look inside. To my great surprise, I discovered a wealth of architectural beauty I never could have imagined or appreciated in the early 1950s. I had also been blissfully unaware of some significant events in Hancock County history that mirrored on a smaller scale milestones in American transportation history. For starters, the gated space I barely noticed on my way to and from elementary school was, in fact, the long-disused Greenfield depot of the Terre Haute, Indianapolis and Eastern line! A final interurban car had departed Greenfield in early January 1932 when the line east of Indianapolis was abandoned and the tracks were removed or paved over

An interurban car trundles along West Main Street in downtown Greenfield, Indiana. In this early twentieth-century image, the electric car has the thoroughfare, the former National Road, entirely to itself.

to make way for a widened portion of US 40. The recently formed Indiana Railroad continued to run daily interurban trains between Indianapolis and Richmond, but those trains now bypassed Greenfield and followed a roundabout route through the city of New Castle and across a more northerly rural portion of Hancock County.[2]

In the Greenfield of my youth, Highway 40 had obliterated all but a few traces of the interurban tracks that in the early twentieth century had run alongside the rutted dirt roadway that led west to Indianapolis or east to Richmond and into Ohio. Motorists in the 1930s and 1940s would have considered the highway upgrade across eastern Indiana an example of progress. A century earlier, this had been the route of the National Road, a significant infrastructure improvement funded by the federal government that citizens of the new American republic viewed with justifiable pride because it served as their nation's main transportation corridor to the Great West. Also known as the Cumberland Road, the transportation showpiece sought to forge a link between tidewater Maryland and Saint Louis, the great inland port on the Mississippi River that was the gateway to the nation's farthest frontier. But the Panic of 1837

The Hancock County Courthouse was an imposing structure, one of many that highlighted the prosperity enjoyed by Indiana in the late nineteenth century. Interurban cars passed the front of the building, offering a measure of convenience to residents needing to transact legal business.

dried up funds and halted construction in Vandalia, a village that enjoyed temporary status as the capital of Illinois. There, the National Road remained eighty miles short of its Missouri goal. Not until 1916 would Uncle Sam formally resume funding the construction of a national system of all-weather highways. Between 1837 and 1916, an ever-expanding matrix of steam railroad tracks had come to define inland transportation across the United States, and highway corridors, including the National Road, had declined in importance until they amounted to little more than dirt paths all but impassable in wet weather. During such times, many Indiana farms were as isolated as if they were on an island in the middle of the Pacific Ocean.[3]

The informal contest between two remarkable transportation technologies, the electric interurban and the automobile, would end after four decades (1893–1933) with a whimper and not a bang as mile after mile of once-busy interurban track was quietly abandoned, and, as was true for US 40 in the Greenfield area, the construction of all-weather highways obliterated the former right-of-way. The imposing steel web formed by Indiana's electric railways disappeared strand by strand until a single ninety-mile snippet remained. The South Shore Line still carries commuters between Chicago and South Bend and is the sole survivor of hundreds of electric railway companies that collectively constructed nearly sixteen thousand miles of interurban lines across the United States.[4]

In the early years, every mile of track, every powerhouse and electric substation, and every interurban car represented cutting-edge technology—modernity in motion—and an optimistic vision of the future shared by thousands of inventors, investors, and entrepreneurs. An industry with an estimated value of nearly $90 billion in today's inflated currency subsequently vanished. Only odd remnants like the ghostly interurban station in Greenfield remained, and today, even it is gone.[5]

The interurban's rise and fall spanned barely two generations: some of the same motormen and conductors who ran Indiana's first interurban trains in the late 1890s were still around to ride some of the last ones to depart Indianapolis in early 1941. A conductor named Hadley Clifford, who in 1898 worked aboard one of Indiana's first interurban cars as it bobbed along the twelve-mile stretch of newly laid track linking Anderson to Alexandria, was a guest aboard the car that forty-three years later made a final journey from Indianapolis to Anderson before the line shut down and scrappers removed the unused track and overhead wire.[6]

Growing up in Greenfield in the 1950s, I remained blissfully unaware of central Indiana's multilayered transportation history, the details of which made for compelling reading in my retirement years. Through a combination of online research and visits to the Indiana State Library in 2019 and 2020 to sift through government documents and newspaper volumes not available online, many things I had observed and experienced growing up but never really understood came into sharp focus. By casting a wide historical net, I understood more clearly the context that accounted for the rise of Indiana's most prominent interurban line, Union Traction, the Gas Belt brainchild of Congressman Charles L. Henry. I was also intrigued by the runaway enthusiasm that greeted the first electric railway cars. For many Hoosiers, the convenient new mode of transportation must have seemed like a gift from heaven.

My single biggest surprise, however, was discovering the importance of Indiana's natural gas boom of the 1880s and 1890s. My sixth-grade class in Indiana history never mentioned it, though my teacher at the James Whitcomb Riley School, Ruby Reeves, did inspire a lifelong interest in the state's past. Likewise, she never mentioned interurban railways or connected them to Greenfield's history, though her husband, Robert,

New Castle in the early twentieth century was linked to Indianapolis by the Indianapolis and Eastern Traction Company. The interurban, which originated as the Indianapolis and Greenfield Rapid Transit, formed the eastern portion of the gangling Terre Haute, Indianapolis and Eastern cobbled together in 1907. This postcard image features an interurban car on the left and a city open trolley on the right.

The Interurban Identity Crisis

Ostensibly, an interurban was a streetcar-like vehicle powered by electricity. In the eyes of the law, however, nothing was quite so simple. Classifying an interurban electric railway as an actual railroad or an oversized street railway made a huge difference to government tax collectors, regulators, and legislators. Based on appearance and function, it was easy to think of the larger and more imposing interurban lines as closely related to the steam railroads of the day. But because early interurban lines had originated in the 1890s as an outgrowth of urban trolley systems, it was equally easy to classify them with street railways. Individual states and municipalities could never agree, and so the industry kept lawyers busy for decades wrangling over how to define an interurban so as to regulate and tax it. Fortunately for electric railways based in Indiana, the state's two most prominent interurban executives and the most tenacious defenders of the industry, Charles L. Henry and Arthur W. Brady, were attorneys. Both men became national spokesmen and regularly journeyed from Indiana to Capitol Hill whenever members of Congress discussed bills relating to the interurban industry.

as the city attorney had waged a heroic but losing battle in the early 1930s with Chicago utility mogul Samuel Insull and his legion of lawyers to prevent the interurban from leaving town. I discovered Greenfield's plucky battle decades later as I researched newspapers for this book.[7]

With the same sense of surprise I learned how the natural gas boom inspired Indiana interurban pioneers like Charles L. Henry and interested Philadelphia grandee Randal Morgan, a gas industry executive, in financing many of Indiana's early lines. It became common for Indiana interurban builders to travel first to Pennsylvania to consult with Morgan before they engaged in any expansion or acquisition projects. In years to come, Henry became the acclaimed "father of the interurban," a title that newspapers from coast to coast repeated in his obituary in 1927. Morgan, the real power behind many of Indiana's largest electric railways, should have been recognized as the "godfather" of the industry, but he preferred to maintain a low profile because of the criticism "outside money" inspired in Indiana. His Philadelphia obituary in 1926 emphasized his local philanthropy and his role as chair of the regents of the University of Pennsylvania. It said not a word about his significance in Indiana interurban history, nor did it note how his natural gas connections contributed to the meteoric rise of Morgan's Golden Boy in Indianapolis, Hugh McGowan. Fleeing life on a hardscrabble Missouri farm, McGowan rose to become one of Indiana's wealthiest citizens, thanks to his patron in Philadelphia and his own skill in building the electric railway empire he based at the Traction Terminal in downtown Indianapolis in 1904. Both McGowan and Morgan loom large (along with Charles Henry) in the story told by *Electric Indiana*.

Indiana's natural gas boom dated from the early 1880s. Not only did the inexpensive (and supposedly inexhaustible) supply of fuel promote the industrial development and urban growth in the eleven-county area of east-central Indiana centering on Anderson, Muncie, Marion, and Kokomo; gas-boom prosperity also nurtured the rise of the interurban railways that interconnected these four cities as well as many smaller communities and linked them all to Indianapolis. My discovery of the importance of the gas boom also cleared up a lifelong mystery.[8]

During the years our family lived in Greenfield, my neighborhood friend Louis and I would occasionally crawl through a concrete culvert beneath the busy New York–Saint Louis main line of the Pennsylvania Railroad that ran just behind our rental home. On occasion, we stayed inside the culvert while a heavy freight pounded along the tracks above our heads just to prove how brave we were. The culvert provided a shortcut to the heavily wooded area that defined the banks of Brandywine Creek. Acclaimed Hoosier poet James Whitcomb Riley, himself a Greenfield native, had in the

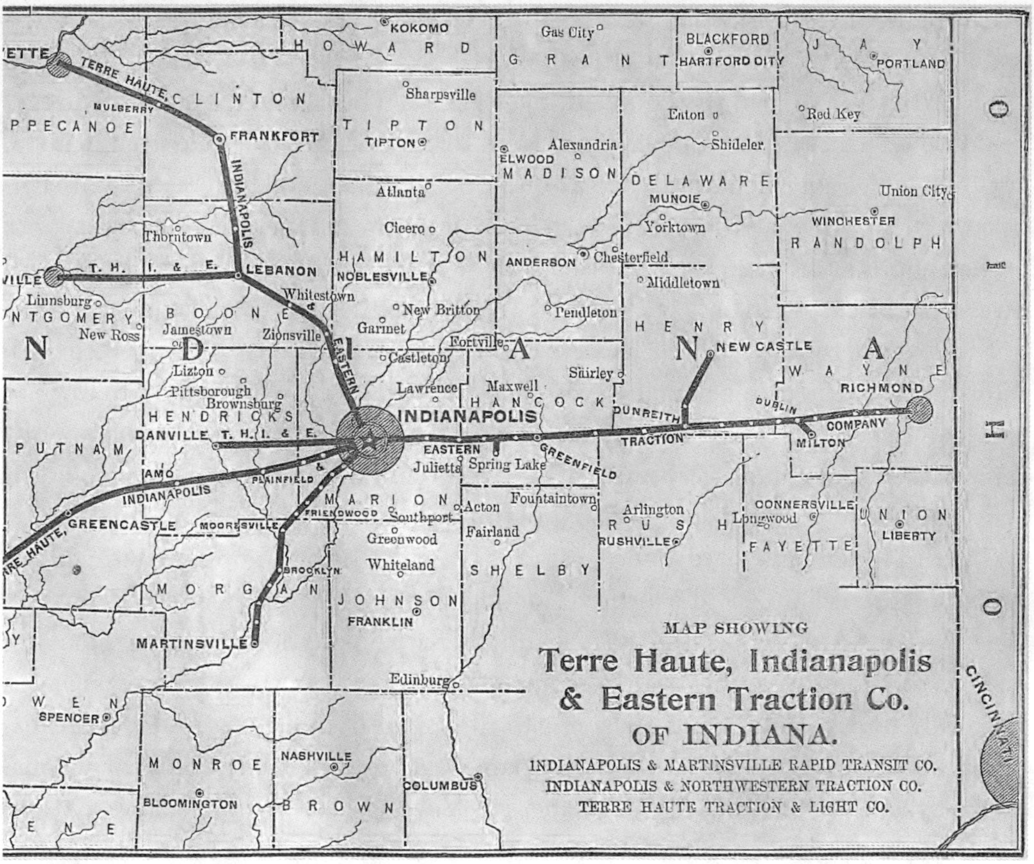

This segment of a map published by the Terre Haute, Indianapolis and Eastern in 1911 illustrates the portion of the interurban line that paralleled the historic National Road across eastern Indiana.

early 1880s written a well-known poem called "The Old Swimmin' Hole," a location somewhere farther upstream from where Louis and I liked to explore.

The odd thing about our seemingly remote patch of field and forest were the numerous fist-sized chunks of green glass that lay strewn about in the weeds. We pretended they were pieces of jade. I never realized until I recently read a massive history of Hancock County published early in the twentieth century that Greenfield had benefited at least briefly from its location near the southern edge of Indiana's Gas Belt. Entrepreneurs located a glass-making plant alongside Brandywine Creek, but the "inexhaustible" supply of natural gas did not last long, and their factory failed. The Ball brothers purchased the unused machinery and moved it north to their huge glass jar manufactory in Muncie, one of several Gas Belt cities grown prosperous and that formed a spatially ideal location for the state's first network of interurban lines. All that remained in Greenfield some fifty years later were the chunks of "jade" that Louis and I had found.[9]

So, during research for this book, things I had seen but ignored as a boy in Greenfield or a teenager in Indianapolis coalesced to tell a fascinating tale. Remnants of concrete bridge abutments along US 40 and long-ago abandoned depots and carbarns became silent witnesses that recalled the Interurban Era and the electric cars that once dashed hourly across the corn and bean fields of Hancock County and along the Main Street that bisected Greenfield. As was true for many Indiana towns, the interurban line was routed to pass within a few feet of the county courthouse, so it enabled rural dwellers for the first time to enjoy a fast and easy way to travel from farm to town to transact legal business and to shop in the nearby stores, and then return home the same day. Or they could easily ride the interurban cars all the way to Indianapolis, the state capital and Indiana's largest and most important city.[10]

The word "remnant" hardly does justice to the single-most impressive reminder of Indiana's Interurban Era, the former Traction Terminal in Indianapolis. In my day, the cavernous structure served as the main intercity bus station. Though its massive and somewhat intimidating train shed no longer sheltered any interurban cars, it was filled with buses coming from and going to all corners of Indiana as well as more distant destinations. Greyhound was the big name, but I recall a colorful array of regional bus lines such as A. B. C. Coach, Indianapolis-Vincennes Coach, and Indiana Motor Bus Company. I would not have thought back then to distinguish a bus made by General Motors from one made by Flxible or ACF-Brill. The constant parade of intercity coaches through the hanger-like terminal offered excitement enough.

One day, as my mother, little brother Dave, and I were about to board our Central Swallow coach to return home to Greenfield, I glanced down and was puzzled to see a patch of asphalt that bus tires had worn away to reveal the shiny top of a piece of rail. I could not make sense of it then, but I know now that hidden beneath the veneer of asphalt were remnants of the nine tracks and eighteen rails once used by a dozen different electric railway companies.

Where bus after bus rolled across the asphalt pavement in the 1950s, more than six hundred interurban trains burnished those rails daily during the industry's golden years before World War I. The Traction Terminal served as the hub of a giant wheel with metallic spokes extending outward in all directions to connect Indianapolis with in-state destinations as far distant as Fort Wayne, Terre Haute, Connersville, Crawfordsville, Jeffersonville, Martinsville, and Richmond, and with hundreds of towns and villages in between. Interurban cars ran between Indianapolis and Dayton for the first time in 1903, and soon a chain of interurban lines extended across Ohio and as far as Upstate New York to form an interconnected web of tracks that even as late as 1930 was ten thousand miles long.[11]

All a Hoosier farmer had to do was stand alongside the tracks and wave a white handkerchief or set fire to a piece of newspaper after dark, and the fast-approaching interurban car would pause to transport him and any family members almost magically to their destination, which, on less serious occasions, might be an amusement park, a popular new form of entertainment pioneered by trolley and interurban companies. South Bend merchants promoted an annual "Interurban Day" that stoked the same desire to take advantage of sales as Black Friday did a century later. As early as 1904, it was possible for one industry observer to write that frequent service and low fares "have wrought such a change in farm life that wherever these interurban roads have been built there can hardly be said to be any country at all, but that the whole region has become transformed into a great though scattering city. The farmer along the line of one of these roads enjoys at the cost of 15 or 20 minutes in time and a few cents in fare almost every convenience of the dweller in the city. He can go to town for business or pleasure at any hour of the day."[12]

The interurban greatly enlarged the influence of the city in many other ways, including the delivery of metropolitan newspapers to surrounding towns and villages. "The Union Traction Co. of Indiana has been carrying papers for some time, and this traffic is growing so heavy that it could not be handled on the regular cars." Union Traction trains delivered Indianapolis newspapers to the Gas Belt cities of Anderson, Muncie, Marion, and Elwood within hours of their daily press runs.[13]

As an agent of profound change, the expanding network of interurban lines also aroused some people's fears. Would the rural dweller's now convenient access to the county seat and the state's large cities doom village and small-town merchants? Would it enable urban vice to seep outward and corrupt an "innocent" countryside?[14]

This much was certain: in just two or three hours at most, one of the fast and frequent interurban cars could whisk residents of the central third of Indiana to the state capitol in Indianapolis. The Traction Terminal itself was conveniently located in the heart of Indianapolis: half a block east of the state's capitol, just across Market Street from William H. Block's big department store and a block west of Monument Circle, the city's iconic tribute to the nation's soldiers and sailors. In terms of convenience, the Traction Terminal was far better situated than the city's venerable Union Station, which in my day was used by passenger trains of the Pennsylvania, New York Central, and Monon Railroads. In fact, it was there in 1957 that I first discovered another prized but now-vanished transportation artifact: the railroad timetable.[15]

Indianapolis was the first in the United States to implement the concept of a union station (in 1853) that conveniently united under a single roof the passenger trains of all railroads serving the city. A massive Romanesque Union Station replaced the original building in 1888, and it remains today even though Amtrak trains make little use of the structure apart from a gloomy portion that still covers the tracks. Sadly, the equally

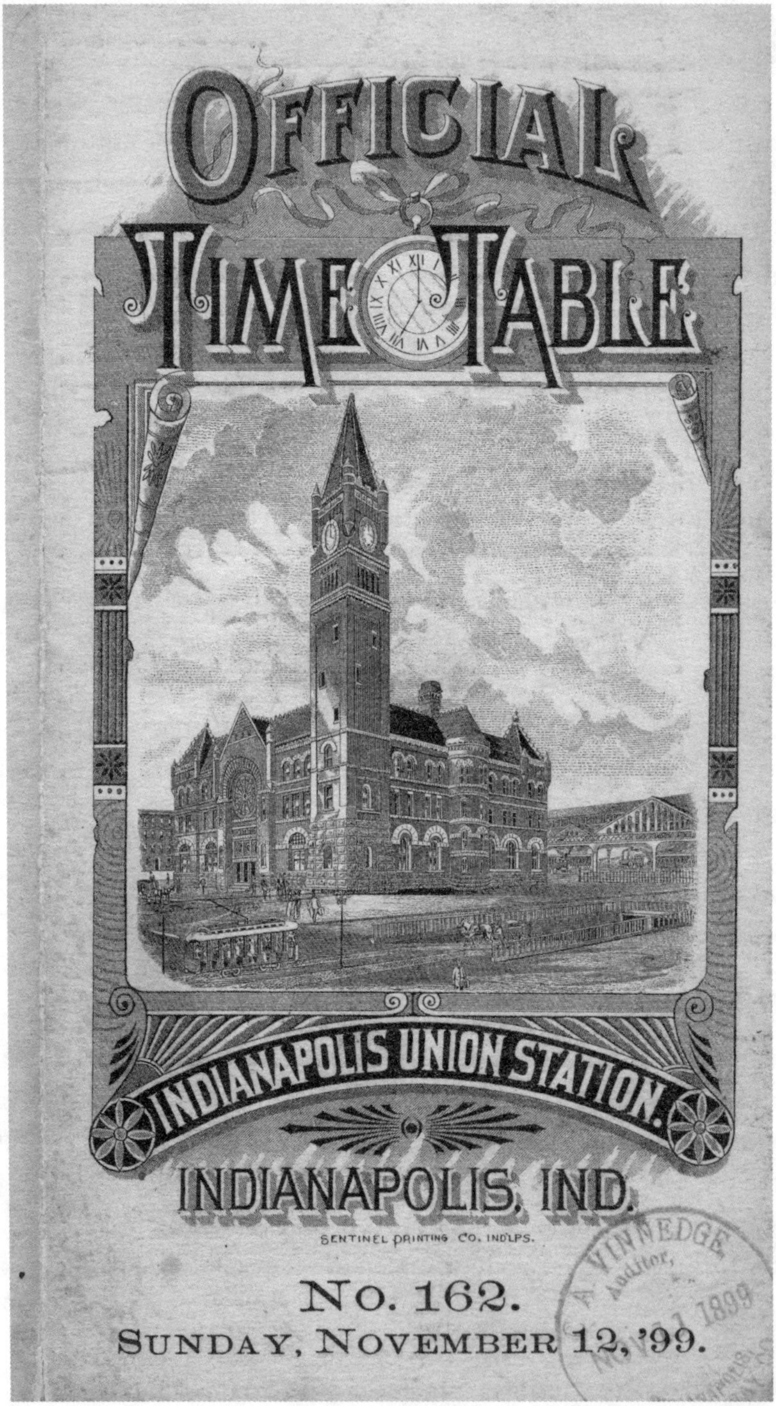

So many steam railroad passenger trains used the Indianapolis Union Station that it published its own timetable in 1899 and for many years thereafter.

imposing Traction Terminal that once implemented the same unifying principle for a dozen interurban lines vanished in piecemeal fashion between 1968 and 1972. The Hilton Hotel that stands in its place does not even acknowledge its historic predecessor with a picture in its lobby, even though one of America's most renowned architects, Daniel Burnham, designed the Traction Terminal complex that opened for business on the site in September 1904.[16]

Given that in the early twentieth century electric interurban railways across Indiana and the Midwest generated a measure of popular enthusiasm that could accurately be described as "almost beyond belief," and given that many Hoosiers welcomed the "people's railways" heralding the dawn of modernity, why did the interurban disappear so completely? The disruptive technology never envisioned during the boom years before 1907 was the automobile, which offered the same convenience as the interurbans, only more so because the time of its comings and goings was infinite, as was its service area. Indiana's Hancock County, for example, was fully endowed in terms of rail transportation: four interurban lines crossed it, as did the tracks of four steam railroads, but all eight carriers ran east to west with centrally located Indianapolis as their place of convergence. Not a single rail line of either type ever crossed Hancock County from north to south. Such obvious spatial anomalies were not at all unusual for counties across the Midwest, but they had profound implications for rail carriers after the coming of the automobile.[17]

As efficient as the trains of Union Traction were at whisking patrons from the villages of northern Hancock County to the big cities of Anderson or Indianapolis, they fell woefully short in facilitating easy travel to the county seat of Greenfield. That journey required a traveler to ride one of Union Traction's interurbans southwest to the Traction Terminal in Indianapolis and there change to one of the trains operated by the Terre Haute, Indianapolis and Eastern. A farm buggy was likely a better option in terms of time, and certainly an automobile offered by far the best option.

When, for example, popular public speaker and frequent Democratic presidential candidate William Jennings Bryan visited Indiana in October 1906 on a speaking tour intended to energize his faithful followers, he traveled around the Gas Belt aboard a special interurban car provided by his fellow Democrat Arthur Brady. To cover the fourteen miles separating Fortville and Greenfield, he rode in a chauffeured auto provided by one of his many admirers in Hancock County. The terrible condition of rural roads in those days offered Bryan a bumpy and often dusty thirty-minute ride in exchange for spatial convenience.[18]

The example of Fortville and Greenfield, two relatively close communities as the crow flies, yet miles apart in terms of good public transportation during the decades before all-weather roads, was repeated in an almost infinite number of places across the Midwest, even in those areas well served by a dense network of interurban and steam railroad lines.[19]

The rail passengers most directly impacted by these numerous gaps were the "drummers" or "knights of the grip," two once-popular nicknames given to traveling salesmen. Not without reason were traveling salesmen among the most frequent users of interurban trains, but, ironically perhaps, they were also among the early purchasers of private automobiles. They could easily carry heavy sample cases with them in an automobile instead of checking them aboard a railroad baggage car; they could drive overland and ignore the numerous gaps in the public transportation networks, and they could escape what was popularly called the "tyranny of the timetable." That is, a traveling salesman could travel at a time that best suited his needs and not just at times set by companies like the Big Four or Union Traction.

That said, in terms of their long-term transformative impact, it would be a mistake to insist that the once-popular electric railways simply vanished because of the ever-growing popularity of the automobile. Indiana was a very different state because of the impact of the interurban. "They have extended the city well into the country and have brought the country into the city." An industry insider based in Indianapolis at the city's landmark Traction Terminal estimated that as late as 1923, nearly a decade after mileage and ridership numbers had peaked nationwide, "250,000,000 passengers traveled on interurban railways in the Middle West states during the past year, while about 5,000,000 tons of freight were hauled." Optimists hailed such statistics as solid evidence that the interurban was experiencing a comeback during the early 1920s from the dark days that followed World War I and was now destined once again to enjoy a bright future in the years ahead.[20]

It was not to be. Brief though the Interurban Era was, it nonetheless left its mark on the state as an agent of modernization, and its passing left plenty of artifacts, if only I as a youngster had had the eyes to see.

2

The Promise of Electricity, The Peril of Gasoline

> The street railway interest has nothing to fear, in our judgment, from competition of the horseless carriage. At the present time, its use is more of a pastime for a few wealthy persons who are forming automobile clubs, and for transient service in two or three large cities, than any well-organized system of passenger transportation.
>
> —*Street Railway Review* (February 1900)

The claim often made is that Indiana's Charles L. Henry originated the term "interurban" and was the father of the industry across North America. An important industry pioneer he truly was, but regarding his neologism, history suggests that it is an "interurban legend." He is supposed to have coined the word in 1897 or 1898 to describe the twelve-mile-long electric railway he completed from his hometown of Anderson to nearby Alexandria. A careful search through the pages of the *Street Railway Journal* and the *Street Railway Review*, however, confirms that the word "interurban" enjoyed widespread use significantly earlier, though it was often hyphenated as "inter-urban." Not to take anything away from the widely respected Henry, it appears he did more to popularize the term than to originate it. (For an in-depth account of the word's true origin, see the appendix.)

As if to suggest how slippery it is for historians to ascribe the origin of a technology or a new word to any one person, the ever-polite and genial Henry simply ceased correcting people and later in life seems to have accepted the accolade himself. It would have been easy for him to believe the legend because it was reprinted so often in newspapers from coast to coast. Henry even invented his own interurban creation myth—two of them, in fact.

According to one version, in the early 1890s, Henry visited the lead belt of southwest Missouri during a hunting trip to the Ozark Plateau. While there, he observed the construction of an intercity electric railway system extending from Joplin to several small urban centers that dotted the interstate mining region that included Kansas

Electric City was one of the many magazines spawned by popular enthusiasm for all things electric—from electric transportation to the supposed curative powers of a variety of electric medical devices.

This line drawing of Charles L. Henry dates from the 1890s, when he was a rising star among Indiana politicians and nurturer of the state's infant interurban lines.

and Oklahoma. From "intercity" he derived the word "interurban." In another, perhaps more plausible version, he claimed to have coined the word after a visit to the World's Columbian Exposition in Chicago in 1893 and was inspired by the "intramural" electric railway that hauled visitors to different parts of the sprawling fairgrounds.

Without doubt, the World's Columbian Exposition served as a magnet to attract anyone who had time and money enough for a visit, and millions of people did visit the greatest extravaganza of the age. The fair was at one level a coming-out party intended to showcase the meteoric growth of the nation's second-largest city, Chicago, which had been little more than a lakeside marsh just seventy years earlier. The 1893 fair also put on public display the greatest and latest technological wonders of the age, and some of the most impressive displays used transportation to emphasize how much progress had taken place in recent years. One large building was devoted entirely to transportation, a topic that in one way or another touched the lives of every fairgoer. Grand displays by the largest steam railroads of the United States dominated the transportation exhibits and mirrored how completely the industry influenced the everyday life of millions of Americans.[1]

If the railroad exhibits collectively underscored the technological prowess of the nation's single biggest business, the many bicycles on display spoke to the era's most popular fad. Conspicuously missing in 1893 was the automobile, although Karl Benz did feature his Velocipede, a self-propelled internal combustion vehicle based on a concept he had pioneered in Germany in 1886. Neither Benz's Velocipede nor an electric vehicle invented in Des Moines, Iowa, merited serious mention in the official exhibition catalog. Because so many exhibits at the Chicago fair could accurately be described as huge or hulking, the diminutive Benz vehicle would have been lost in the crowd, and its future significance wholly ignored by fairgoers. In fact, nothing at the World's Columbian Exposition, including these two odd vehicles, hinted that America's *first successful automobile brand* would soon originate in Elwood Haynes's humble workshop located 160 miles south of Chicago in Kokomo, Indiana.[2]

ELWOOD HAYNES, M.E.

An early twentieth-century portrait of Elwood Haynes, the Indiana father of America's first successful automobile brand.

Although Haynes and Henry never met one another as they strolled the exposition grounds and gazed in wonder at the myriad displays scattered among the halls of transportation, electricity, and mechanics, both men were no doubt influenced by what they observed at Chicago's 1893 fair. In other words, the World's Columbian Exposition deserves recognition as the common ground occupied at least temporarily by these two "fathers" of the world's emerging transportation technologies, though that would become obvious only with the benefit of hindsight. Moreover, like the biblical brothers Cain and Able, both forms of transportation grew up together, but one, the automobile, would eventually slay the other, the interurban.

Haynes revealed an early automobile to his Kokomo neighbors in mid-1894, a few months before the publication of America's first automotive magazine, *The Horseless Age*. From late 1895 until its final issue during World War I in 1918, the magazine chronicled the rise and fall of literally thousands of automakers as well as featured numerous advertisements for the latest Haynes models. Initially, the magazine barely took note of another Midwestern inventor associated with a tiny firm called the Detroit Automobile Company. He became much better known after 1903, the year he created a new enterprise using his name: the Ford Motor Company.

If the word "interurban" is of disputed origin, so is the technology itself. Some people assert that the first example of an electric railway meriting the term "interurban" opened between Portland and nearby Oregon City in early 1893. But history records that an even earlier "inter-urban" linked the twin cities of Minneapolis and St. Paul. Only this is certain: the interurban industry that took shape during the 1890s was the latest iteration of the horse-drawn "city railroads" that first grew popular in the United States during the 1850s.[3]

Urban transportation was once just as fruitful a field for inventors (and investors) as computer hardware and software, cell phones, and attendant electronic devices became in the early twenty-first century. For "city railroads," the process of invention began in earnest during the late 1850s with the growing realization that a horse-drawn vehicle commonly called an "omnibus" might operate more efficiently along a smooth surface of iron rails instead of bumping along over the uneven dirt and mud surfaces that in those days typified the main streets even of America's largest cities. A set of rails was easily embedded in a street, and horsecars were inexpensive and quick to provide a reasonable return on investment.

As simple as this application of common sense may sound, it opened the door wide for creative minds. For another eighty years, inventors continued to improve the shape of the rails and to develop new ways to embed tracks in the increasingly busy city streets. Just the quest to take the irritating squeal out of streetcar wheels running along metal surfaces resulted in the introduction of a host of promising new soundproofing technologies.

The horse proved a faithful servant in urban transportation, as it had been for centuries on the farms and ranches of rural America, but animal power was not without its drawbacks when it came to a city railroad. A rapidly spreading equine sickness, often termed an "epizootic," might afflict a whole stable of horses and thus hobble a city's entire fleet of horse-drawn cars. Moreover, the biological waste that tens of thousands of horses produced in an urban environment grew increasingly worrisome as the nineteenth century progressed. The search for some sort of fully mechanical alternative to the horse inspired inventive minds.[4]

Andrew Hallidie demonstrated a more reliable and efficient form of "horse power" when in the 1870s he successfully installed a cable system that overcame the steep hills of San Francisco, his hometown. He claimed his invention was inspired by the sickening sight of a team of horses struggling to pull a loaded car uphill. When one horse slipped and fell on a stretch of wet pavement, the weight of the car and its many occupants dragged the helpless animals downhill for several blocks and severely injured them all.

Hallidie's invention featured an underground cable that ran along a slot embedded in the pavement to pull small vehicles that resembled the horse-drawn cars. For obvious reasons, these became known as "cable cars." Like the motive power that horses provided, the moving cable had its share of drawbacks. First, it took a powerhouse and a considerable amount of energy to maintain in motion the hefty cable required to move the cars, which themselves were light compared to the many tons of underground cable. Second, the cable system was mechanically complex and prone to

This photograph from Brownstown dates from 1910, the end of Indiana's horsecar era.

The Streetcar Mule

Charles L. Henry is supposed to have gotten his start as the dean of Indiana interurban transportation in 1891 when he purchased a mule-powered street railway line in Anderson that he converted the next year to electricity. It is possible to interpret his purchase as a woebegone property, but the humble mule (and not the horse) was the favored motive power for street railways all across Indiana until the industry switched to electricity. Moreover, mule power should not imply shoddy construction or a street railway in decline. Mule cars prevailed in Indianapolis until 1894, and Indiana's final equine line ceased running only in the early twentieth century. Electric streetcars, on the other hand, represented modernity, but the mule did not disappear without evoking a sigh of nostalgia from the *Indianapolis Journal*: "The jingle of the mule bell is heard no more, the electric gong has taken its place, and the maddening whirr of the wires is substituted for the click of the little hoofs on the pavement. The mule has passed to other fields."[5]

Most of Indiana's thousand or more streetcar mules were purchased in Saint Louis, "which is considered the best mule market in the United States. They are bought by the car-load, there being generally twenty-four to the car." The nation's fourth-largest city not only served as the mule capital; it also emerged during the 1890s as one of North America's great centers for streetcar and interurban manufacturing. Like the Missouri mule, Saint Louis–made vehicles of all types were familiar to riders of Indiana's electric railways. Finally, despite the widespread use of mule power, all such animal-drawn vehicles were popularly referred to as "horsecars."[6]

The complex workings of a cable car powerhouse made this mode of urban transportation prohibitively expensive outside America's largest cities.

breakdowns. Buried beneath the city streets were numerous pulleys, and the system grew even more complex and troublesome at cross streets where two cable lines passed atop one another. Because a cable could move in only one direction, the individual cars were unable to back up. Although promoted as an improvement over horses and mules, cable systems were in their own way inefficient, inflexible, and maintenance-intensive. They were so expensive to install and maintain that they made financial sense only in America's largest and most densely populated cities like New York, Saint Louis, and San Francisco. Cable cars did provide a mechanical solution to the public health concern of how best to dispose of animal waste.[7]

Cars powered by electricity, as an ever-increasing number of the city cars were in the late 1880s and 1890s, were called "streetcars" or "trolleys." The latter name derived from the pickup device, or troller, that ran along the underside of the overhead wire used to transmit power to the vehicle's onboard electric motors. Outside North America, the common term was "tram." The streetcars of the late 1880s were very similar in design and appearance to their predecessors, the cable cars and the horsecars. All cars in those early days were fashioned from wood, and often the same car-building companies and the same skilled artisans crafted all three types. Compared with the later interurban cars, the streetcar was smaller and lighter because of its origin as a horse-drawn vehicle. A horse or mule, or even a pair of animals, could not pull large and heavily loaded cars without risk of injury. Street railway journals during the 1880s devoted many pages to the proper care and feeding of horses and mules, the most valuable assets the early urban railroads possessed.[8]

"This is the electrical age as well as the age of steam. We cannot put any limit to the uses of electricity." During the dawning decades of electrification, the 1880s and 1890s, inventors of many different backgrounds and educational attainments—from self-trained tinkerers to a new class of university-educated engineers—discovered innovative ways to illuminate and power the world. Thomas Edison gained fame for his "invention" of the incandescent light bulb, but lesser-known individuals invented the light switch and a host of other necessary but largely unsung devices that made artificial illumination a household necessity.[9]

It was the same story for inventors who sought to use electricity to power machinery, and that included developing an electric motor strong enough and reliable enough to run a trolley fully loaded with passengers, and to do it through the heat of summer and the slush of winter without burning out. No less important were inventors who discovered how best to generate electricity and then how to transmit it efficiently from a central power station to any location it was desired. At first, the distance over which electricity could be transmitted without a significant loss of power was quite small, a matter of a few city blocks at most, but inventive minds during the early 1890s solved the riddle of how to transmit electric power across ever greater distances.

In the early 1880s, however, the market was for horse- and cable-powered cars only. The electric side of the street railway industry seemed unimpressive. Initially, it seemed to stumble hesitantly along, and so it was not yet obvious to most people that the future of urban transportation belonged to the trolley. Many Americans and Canadians feared the lethal potential of electricity, and journalists who were technologically ignorant or given to sensationalism only served to stoke public concern about the "mysterious" properties of electricity and the danger of electrocution.

The takeoff occurred only after Frank Sprague successfully installed a twelve-mile electric streetcar system in Richmond, Virginia, in 1888 that worked as well as its youthful inventor had promised. The electric streetcar finally had its poster child, and numerous cities large and small across North America hastened to emulate Richmond's well-publicized success. In contrast to cable railways, which because of the complexity of their infrastructure cost five or six times more per mile than an electric one, electric trolley lines could turn a profit even in communities of only a few thousand residents.

The five years from 1888 through 1893 saw one streetcar system after another energized by electricity, and the ubiquitous cars clanged noisily along the streets of every community that aspired to municipal greatness. The electric streetcar became, in fact, the symbol of modernity, an elusive quality to which every would-be metropolis aspired if it cared at all about its future. Inspired by the examples of Sprague, Edison, and others, inventors of all things electric inundated the US Patent Office with their applications. In 1899, the office issued more than five hundred patents for automatic trolley wire switches alone, "a device essential in railway systems using electricity as their motive power." As of that date, however, only one overhead switch worked as promised.[10]

After Sprague's Richmond triumph, installing a successful municipal trolley system was no longer a major technological challenge fraught with unknowns. But why stop at the city's edge? Why not link suburbs to city or even reach farther afield into the surrounding countryside to connect to a nearby city? The key to building a successful intercity electric railway was being able to transmit enough power from a central power plant to distant points along the line to keep the cars running smoothly. That remained a serious challenge until the year 1893, when among the steady stream of new inventions that dazzled investors in the electric industry came a breakthrough in the long-distance transmission of electric power. Here was the secret that did the most to make the interurban railway possible. This feat untethered the urban trolley from the technological bonds that had limited the reach of street railroads since the early days of horsecars and freed it to evolve into the electric interurban. In this way, the interurban railway offered many new and exciting spatial possibilities.

As noted earlier, there are several claimants to the title of the first interurban railway, but as the *Street Railway Journal* explained in 1896, it was impossible to validate any one claim: "The extension of city electric railways to suburban towns has been naturally followed by the construction of electric lines for an exclusively interurban business. This enlargement of the field of electric railroading was so logical and gradual that it is difficult to draw a definite line between what should be regarded as interurban and what [are] city lines, and most roads partake of both characters."[11]

Only this is certain: as was true years later for interurbans and automobiles, two distinct technologies initially conjoined in terms of their American origins in the mid-1890s, so it was for streetcars and interurbans also. One pundit distinguished the two modes of transportation simply as "urban" and "interurban," and that word pairing nicely sums up their common origins and distinct differences. Nonetheless, throughout their lengthy history, both modes were often grouped together as "electric railways." Street railways and interurbans, for instance, always belonged to the same national professional association, which made no distinction between officers chosen annually from either side of the industry. However, in the 1920s, the cordial alliance proved detrimental to the interurban railways because the use of a common set of economic statistics tended to obscure how sick that segment of the electric railway industry had become.

As interurban railways emerged from municipal streetcar systems, their vehicles evolved to meet the distinctive needs of the new mode of transportation. Only slight variations distinguished the first generation of interurban cars from streetcars: they were larger, often included a separate space for a limited amount of baggage or express, and typically rode on two sets of wheels, or trucks, instead of one. Over time, the finest interurban cars featured comfortable seats, luxurious interior appointments, and even onboard restrooms. Every year—almost every month, in fact—inventors offered new and improved designs for virtually every feature of an interurban car and its support structure.

Something so basic and yet unnoticed by the daily millions of electric railway riders was the trolley "harp," the deceptively simple metal assembly required to hold a small rotating wheel in contact with the overhead wire to power the cars. One favorite challenge for creative minds was to improve the design of the harp and the wheel (or later a shoe) required to maintain contact with the overhead wire so that interurban cars could attain speeds of seventy miles per hour or more—and to do so even when ice coated portions of the trolley wire. Trolley wheels also needed to be tough enough to withstand the destructive power of the occasional electric arc that resulted when the pickup device momentarily lost contact with the overhead wire.

The same was true for the cohort of inventors in search of ways to improve the undercarriage wheel assemblies, or trucks, on which car bodies rode, to better the shape and metallurgy of rails embedded in city streets and even to find the best design for the metal hand punch that conductors used to validate tickets. Entire industries might rise or fall with the introduction of an improved version of car ventilators, for example, or a better quality of varnish to protect a car's wooden exterior.

It is almost mind-boggling today to realize how many different manufacturers and suppliers, both large and small, prospered during the Interurban Era in addition to the car builders and electric railway companies. Many ancillary enterprises dated back to the horse railways of the 1850s and had evolved during the late 1880s and early 1890s as the industry switched to electricity as its primary motive power and as interurban railways emerged from among the trolley companies and multiplied rapidly after 1893. A cedar pole to support overhead copper wires, for example, was basically the same product whether used by trolleys or interurbans, but an inventor might patent a metal or concrete support pole that worked better and lasted longer than the familiar wooden ones.

The trolley wheel represented the vital point of contact between interurban cars and the railway's complex infrastructure. Also finding favor with the industry were trolley shoes that slid along the energized wire. Either device, while seemingly simple, inspired a generation of inventors determined to develop an improved design.

Despite their glowing initial prospects, over the long haul, most interurban companies fared less well financially than many of the enterprises that grew prosperous selling them everything from steam boilers for their power plants to electric headlights to enable night operation of their cars. Emerging industry giants like General Electric and Westinghouse became household words during the Interurban Era. The paints and varnishes supplied by Sherwin-Williams and DuPont kept wooden car bodies attractive and protected in sun and rain. Industry suppliers numbering in the hundreds displayed their latest products at the electric railway industry's annual conventions, and their advertisements added interest and considerable bulk to the trade journals.

Among the most visible of the suppliers were the carmakers. Some, like the John Stephenson Car Company, dated back to the early horsecar era, while others, like the St. Louis Car Company and the J. G. Brill Company of Philadelphia, came later and profited handsomely from the runaway enthusiasm for electric trolleys after 1888. North America's single largest concentration of carmakers was in the Missouri metropolis of Saint Louis. Its products were sold to operators around the world, but the city also enjoyed a competitive edge within the United States west of the Mississippi River, because in that vast region, there were no other significant carmakers.[12]

East of the Mississippi River where North America's largest cities were located, competitors to the Saint Louis carmakers were eager to supply trolley and interurban rollingstock to the rapidly expanding electric railway industry both in the United

Many of the Hoosier State's trolley and interurban cars originated in the Missouri metropolis. In fact, the finest car ever to burnish the rails of Indiana's electric railways, the Union Traction's Martha, was crafted by the Saint Louis Car Company.

States and Canada and around the globe. Dominant among these manufacturers was the venerable Philadelphia firm of J. G. Brill. Its corporate history spanned a century from horsecars to intercity buses. At the dawn of the twentieth century, Brill gained added prominence when it acquired several other car manufacturers, including two former competitors in the Saint Louis area. But because Brill chose not to consolidate its enlarged holdings under a single banner or group them all in Philadelphia, the location of Brill's massive street railway manufactory, Saint Louis, remained prominent in industry circles not just for the construction of quality rollingstock but also as a major supplier of wheels, brake shoes, and even the heavy leather belting required to spin the electric generators inside power plants.[13]

In the late 1850s when rail-guided vehicles first gained popularity along the streets of urban North America, the favored term was "city railroad." Only in later years did the preferred term become "street railway." Initially, the trade journals ostensibly devoted to steam railroads also carried news of the evolving city railroads. In the eyes of many observers, the fact that both modes of transportation ran cars along rails made them technological brothers—or at least first cousins. Despite their superficial similarities, it soon became obvious that the steam and electric roads were in most ways very different. With few exceptions, they operated in two separate spheres, and when their tracks did need to intersect, the result in the early days was conflict, if not an outright war waged by steam railroads intent on thwarting a pesky competitor.

Each industry held its own conventions, developed its own set of trade journals, used terms that were foreign to outsiders, and developed a distinct cadre of luminaries to serve as industry spokesmen. There were exceptions, of course, and employees in both rail-based industries knew what "frogs" and "block signals" and "turnouts" were, but who outside the electric railway industry knew the purpose of trolley harps or interurban fenders? Perhaps, the greatest exception to their many distinctions was the use by most (but certainly not all) electric and steam carriers of the same standard-gauge tracks, which made possible the interchange of freight cars in later years between steam railroads (often reluctantly) and some forward-thinking interurban lines.[14]

By the early 1890s, the city railroads had matured into an industry large and robust enough to support three entirely new trade publications, the *Street Railway Journal* (first published in 1884), the *Street Railway Review* (first published in 1891), and the *Street Railway Gazette* (first published in 1886), not one of which was closely related to the numerous journals devoted to steam railroads, a much older and much larger industry that dated back to the mid-1820s. Likewise, in 1882, the little fellows grew confident enough to convene in Boston to form a professional association of their own that encompassed city railroads powered by horse, mule, and cable, but with the addition of the electric streetcars a few years later. Nearly every autumn since it was founded in 1882, the American Street Railway Association held its yearly conference in a North American city that showcased the best in street railways, the term increasingly favored throughout the industry. During the decades from 1882 and 1904, the annual conferences took place in major cities around the United States and Canada, such as New York, Chicago, and Montreal, but no city during those early years offered a more favorable site for the industry's big annual gathering than Saint Louis, the Missouri metropolis that played host to conferences in 1885, 1896, and 1904. The city had "always" been, in the words of one of the industry's leading trade journals, "in the front rank" of electric railway matters.[15]

Apart from its status as the nation's fourth-largest city or its role as one of the world's premier manufactories of rail rollingstock, Saint Louis enthralled the movers and shakers of North America's street railway industry for another compelling reason:

the city's busy boulevards and avenues simultaneously featured all three main forms of street railway motive power in daily operation. An interested observer could ride a horsecar in the morning, a cable car at noon, and relax aboard the latest model electric streetcar in the evening. Moreover, it was easy to travel aboard cars operated by at least a dozen independent street railway companies. No other city in North America better illustrated how the evolution of street railway motive power during the second half of the nineteenth century was not nearly as linear or sequential as it might at first appear. City governments often franchised companies to operate along a single street only, and so within a single municipality like Saint Louis during the 1880s and 1890s, one company might prefer to stick with living horsepower, a proven and relatively inexpensive technology, while another dared to take a chance on electricity.

As a convention bonus, whenever street railway executives met in Saint Louis, they could enjoy a personal tour of the sprawling St. Louis Car Company complex in full production, no doubt an impressive sight. Company advertisements proclaimed that its streetcar manufactory was the largest in the world. For convention delegates responsible for running transit systems large and small across North America, here was an opportunity to "kick the wheels" of the latest trolley models and to talk shop with their builders—not just at the St. Louis Car Company but also at the manufacturing plants of several other of the nation's largest streetcar makers that called Missouri home during the 1880s and 1890s. Whereas Indiana emerged as the most congenial home to interurban lines, its many electric railways still needed to buy cars mainly from out-of-state manufacturers or to build their own, which Union Traction occasionally did in its massive Anderson shops. Another exception of note was American Car and Foundry's plant located in Jeffersonville.[16]

Trolley or interurban, the possibilities for improvement seemed endless during the late nineteenth and early twentieth centuries, and a generation of inventive minds responded to the challenges. A clever tinkerer could make money from just one successful invention—often a considerable amount of money. Fortune and fame were always powerful lures. The accomplishments of electrical wizard Thomas Edison inspired other would-be electrical wizards. Edison was simply the best known of the many inventors and entrepreneurs who prospered along with the electric railway industry. George Westinghouse and Nikola Tesla, his resident genius, built a huge industry devoted to all things electrical; Frank J. Sprague and Elihu Thomson did likewise by developing the first workable street railway system, which then spread like wildfire to cities across the United States and Canada.[17]

A canny investor might reap a personal fortune by backing a successful inventor or by bankrolling a successful interurban company or even by figuring out a better way to organize the rapidly expanding but badly fractured electrical industry, as Samuel Insull, a former associate of Edison, did. Or one might corrupt city officials to secure the lucrative franchises required to construct street railways, as did Chicago magnate Charles Yerkes, a man popularly demonized in life and death as a malevolent "Trolley Baron."[18]

The money-making possibilities associated with street railways and interurbans seemed almost limitless during the fifteen boom years from 1893 through 1907. Copies of the weekly *Street Railway Journal* and its several competitors showcased the runaway enthusiasm of the Interurban Era. All such publications, whether issued monthly or weekly, grew bulky as they added dozens of pages of industry advertisements, many of them visually stunning in layout and design. The advertising bonanza mirrored the enthusiasm of everyone involved with interurbans and their unshakable conviction that North America's latest mode of transportation was destined to enjoy a long and prosperous future.

Interurban railways were initially focused on serving a limited geographical area. The reach of even the largest companies seldom extended more than fifty miles, and industry executives gave little, if any, thought to the possibility of interconnecting with other interurban railways to form a regional network. As years passed, however, some enthusiasts dared to dream of large interurban systems that in their geographic reach would rival the much older steam railroads or possibly even outdistance them. That expansive vision seemed ever more attainable because each month the industry's trade journals listed dozens of newly incorporated interurban companies. Investors almost literally threw money at any project that seemed promising, and at numerous projects, too, that detachment and reason suggested held no real promise of any return on investment. The optimism was contagious. Investors large and small confidently expected to reap large personal fortunes from their interurban investments. Especially during the runaway enthusiasm that characterized the decade from 1897 to 1907, it was wholly unthinkable that a disruptive transportation technology might someday emerge to upend their expectations of imminent wealth.[19]

Working largely out of sight during the latter half of the 1890s was another earnest cadre of inventors who were willing to devote time and talents to perfecting a balky personal mobility vehicle variously labeled a "horseless carriage, a "motor car," or an "automobile." In the early years, "horseless carriage" was clearly the preferred term because it was the most accurate description of a vehicle that featured wheels as narrow and spindly as those of a lightweight buggy, had a center of gravity located as dangerously high as that of a heavy farm wagon, and used a tiller as a substitute for a horse's reins. Something so fundamental as a steering wheel had yet to be invented in the 1890s. *The Horseless Age* was, in fact, an appropriate name for America's pioneer automotive journal, the first issue of which appeared in November 1895.[20]

As with the invention of the word "automobile" or even the word "interurban" to describe the intercity electric railway, no commonly accepted term yet applied in the mid-1890s to the petroleum blend used to fuel internal combustion engines. What the world commonly recognizes today as "gasoline" went by a variety of names in the early 1890s, such as "petrol" or "motor spirits." Moreover, if an internal combustion engine were used to propel a horseless carriage, the vehicle could easily be as temperamental as a high-strung horse, or maybe worse. Alfred P. Sloan, Mr. General Motors, once quipped that his first automobile "taught me how to swear."[21]

When popular publications explained to readers that internal combustion engines attained their motive power by means of a continuous series of small gasoline explosions within the cylinders, the realization that highly volatile gasoline and the resulting explosions took place near an automobile driver's backside did frighten some people. Newspapers of the day were, in fact, filled with accounts of gasoline lamps and heating stoves that exploded without warning and immolated homeowners. When *The Horseless Age* devoted special issues in 1900 to each of the major forms of propulsion, it did little to instill popular confidence in gasoline-powered automobiles when it labeled the issue devoted to internal combustion its "Explosive Motor Number." No wonder it required an act of Congress and the signature of President William McKinley before the ferryboat captains plying the waterways of New York City permitted gasoline-powered cars aboard their vessels, and then only if the auto engine and its fuel supply were both shut completely off. Thus, during the 1890s, it was impossible for anyone apart from a dedicated band of tinkerers to regard the gasoline-powered horseless carriage—in truth, all horseless carriages whether gasoline, electric, or steam models—as anything other than a novelty or a fair-weather plaything of the idle rich that with the arrival of winter would need to be stored for several months in large public garages.[22]

The *Street Railway Review* observed in February 1900 that "the various vapor [gasoline] motors have not yet been brought to any such degree of perfection as to warrant the establishment of large numbers of these vehicles on certain routes with specific schedules." Obviously, the editor of the *Street Railway Review,* like the industry he represented, could not envision that the sputtering gasoline buggy might mature one day into a motor bus that could compete successfully with electric trolleys or interurban cars.[23]

Held in even lower esteem than the much-cussed internal combustion engine were the dirt paths that in the early twentieth century passed for rural roadways in much of the United States. Hoosier automaker Elwood Haynes set a new American record in July 1899 when he and his Kokomo business partner Edgar Apperson successfully

An interurban car was a prominent feature of this postcard image of Portland, the Indiana Gas Belt community that was once home to Elwood Haynes.

drove one of their handcrafted mechanical creations, a single-seat gasoline buggy, from central Indiana to a customer in Brooklyn, New York. Haynes and Apperson required a full twenty days to complete their journey of slightly more than a thousand miles. The Hoosiers' pioneer road trip was newsworthy, but it confirmed the prevailing skepticism of traction operators.

The initial leg of the journey to Brooklyn was from Kokomo to the Haynes hometown of Portland, the site of the discovery of Indiana's first gas well in 1886. The intrepid pair needed nearly seven hours to complete the day's drive of seventy miles because of the daunting condition of the muddy pathways that typified Indiana roads in those days. They reached Portland with fully fifty pounds of Hoosier mud clinging to the wheel spokes of the little vehicle that for lack of a better name Haynes called a "motorcycle."[24]

No one in the mid-1890s could possibly foresee what the future held, but if either the automobile or interurban, or both, was to emerge as a compelling new technology, it would require a major infusion of investment capital. Fortunately for inventors, both industries by 1900 had investors lining up to provide the money each needed to boost its growth. The main question for canny investors to ponder was which of the era's latest transportation innovations represented the better financial bet.

Hemingray originated in Kentucky but soon built a large plant in Indiana's Gas Belt. This design was marketed as the "Muncie" insulator.

3

Investor's Dilemma

Interurban or Automobile?

> The automobile was in its earliest days of development, and only a few enthusiasts thought it would ever become anything more than a rich man's toy, so that interurban railroads were greeted most heartily by the public which they undertook to serve, and as the first railroads built in the choicest spots were to all appearances at least, largely successful from a financial standpoint, the capital was easily found to go into the interurban business, and even considerable amounts of capital would be raised locally for that purpose.
>
> —*AERA* (October 1918): 334

"The city piled itself high in the center, tower upon tower for a nucleus and spread itself out over the plain, mile after mile," wrote Newton Booth Tarkington in his 1915 novel, *The Turmoil*. The Indianapolis native was almost certainly describing the rapid transformation of his formerly bucolic hometown into a Midwestern metropolis of consequence. Tarkington detested the city's headlong quest for "bigness" for the sake of ever greater bigness. Electric interurban railways enabled the spatial outreach of its department stores, banks, newspapers, stockyards, and all other enterprises, at least initially, and then the automobile further amplified the city's quest for "bigness."

Tarkington observed Indianapolis as the heyday of the interurban overlapped with the rise of automobile ownership throughout Indiana. He voiced strong opinions about both modes of transportation, and each served as literary vehicles in his novels. In *The Magnificent Ambersons* (1918), the automobile functions as a transformative force for individual betterment, while in *The Turmoil*, the debasing of local interurban securities by clever East Coast financiers propels one of the city's "first families" into genteel poverty and provides the novel's primary motif. Perhaps Tarkington himself enjoyed dividend income from Indiana interurban securities—a good many Hoosiers did—and had experienced firsthand the pain of loss resulting from the "holding company" schemes crafted by Philadelphia financiers like Randal Morgan, a name that figured prominently in the rise and fall of Indiana's once magnificent interurban network.[1]

Indianapolis architecture was beginning its reach for the sky at the beginning of the twentieth century. Here, at the corner of Washington and Illinois Streets, just a block from the Traction Terminal and the Indiana capitol, was the site of Edward Fay Claypool's new hotel, which hosted many a gathering of Midwest interurban executives.

There are always canny individuals seeking to make money from the next big thing. Imagine an investor gazing out the window of one of the tall office buildings rapidly redefining the downtown skyline of Indianapolis in the fall of 1904, perhaps gazing from the newly completed nine-story office tower that formed a prominent part of the Traction Terminal complex that opened there in September. From this lofty promontory, a person could easily observe on the streets below a bustling mix of trolley and interurban cars. Occasionally an automobile dashed by. It dodged nimbly around the electric railway vehicles confined to their fixed rails, but if an automobile were a gasoline-powered model, it was noisy and left a light trail of smoke that was a telltale sign at that time of the inefficient internal combustion engine. Tarkington immortalized the cacophony in his aptly titled book *The Turmoil*: "Trolley-cars and long interurban cars, built to split the wind like torpedo-boats, clanged and shrieked their way round swarming corners; motor-cars of every kind and shape known to man babbled frightful warnings and frantic demands."

As recently as 1900, about a third of the motor vehicles in the United States had been powered by gasoline, another third by electric storage batteries, and a final

Randal Morgan, whose hand the Indiana press perceived in every major interurban transaction, was based in Philadelphia, where he oversaw a myriad of business interests. In his later years, he chaired the board of trustees of the University of Pennsylvania.

third by steam. Four years later, the balance had begun to tip in favor of internal combustion models. At the New York auto show held in early 1904, gasoline-powered cars clearly predominated. Electrics ranked second, and steam cars had dropped to a distant third, although their advocates claimed it was far too early to dismiss steam from the mix.[2]

Automobiles on Indianapolis streets no longer caused heads to turn in 1904 as they had done just four or five years earlier, but they did turn the heads of investors and cause them to open their pocketbooks wide. "The 'automobile' has, almost in a day, emerged from comparative obscurity to a position of utmost importance in the world of transportation," observed the *Street Railway Journal* in early 1899. It warned readers that capital was "rushing into these new fields with ardor and enthusiasm" and that disappointments might await overly enthusiastic investors. Trade in automobile securities became commonplace as the self-propelled vehicles grew familiar. Likewise, by 1904, a short automobile jaunt was no longer newsworthy, as it had been as recently as 1901 when the *Muncie Star Press* printed an article about local resident Mary Moore's brief motor outing under the headline "Rode in Automobile." The motor-car outing, apparently her first, "embraced a run of eight miles and at the end Mrs. Moore said that it almost took her breath away. It was quite different from the old method of transportation."[3]

In 1904, a surprising number of automobile brands would be made close at hand in Indianapolis or in a number of smaller manufacturing communities scattered across the Hoosier landscape, such as Connersville, Union City, Elkhart, Kokomo, Anderson, and Auburn. Detroit was by no means synonymous with the automobile in 1904: the cities of Indianapolis, Saint Louis, and Cleveland each had the potential to emerge as the automobile capital of the United States. Regardless of which place might ultimately claim to be the "greatest automobile center in the world," investors were already lining up to place their bets. But should they purchase stocks or bonds in auto companies that made gasoline, electric, or steam models? Perhaps they should simply hedge their bets by investing in all three types. They could invest in Studebaker Automobile Company, a South Bend firm long renowned for the quality of its farm wagons that in the early twentieth century manufactured both gasoline and electric cars.[4]

What to do? In many ways, the rapidly expanding interurban industry represented an equally appealing investment opportunity. Even more than the automobile, it represented the union of several technologies that had advanced well beyond the experimental stage and proven beyond a doubt their practical value. Apart from a few eccentric inventors who promoted compressed air or storage batteries, by 1904, electricity seemed to be the best way to power street and interurban railways. Horsecars were yesterday's technology, as were cable cars. By the turn of the century, electricity had vanquished all former rivals. Looking to the future, it seemed certain that electric railways would prosper. Despite an increasing number of automobiles sharing city streets, the electric railway seemed invulnerable because its hundreds of well-established streetcar systems were vital to daily life in urban America, and every year brought new interurban lines to extend the reach of hub cities.

To encourage interurban investors, the *Street Railway Review* in September 1901 published a lengthy article detailing reasons for confidence in the financial prospects of the industry. Nationally recognized analyst Guy Morrison Walker, himself a Hoosier, admitted that most bankers at the time remained indifferent to interurban securities despite the many advantages the new mode of transportation offered. "The earnings of interurban lines are not so quickly nor so severely affected in times of industrial depression as are the earnings of steam roads," claimed Walker. Moreover, until the early twentieth century, no one gave serious thought to any potentially lucrative revenue stream other than that of carrying passengers.[5]

On the opposite side of the city's iconic Monument Circle and just a few blocks east on Market Street from the Traction Terminal was the Indianapolis Stock Exchange, little more than a year old in 1904. Located on the ninth floor of the Union Trust Building, it made a statement just as compelling as the city's new high-rise Traction Terminal Building about the rapid transformation of turn-of-the-century Indianapolis from an oversized country town into a Midwestern metropolis worthy of note. A dense web of electric interurban railways radiating from the city center was widely regarded as a primary engine of growth. "Fast interurban trolley lines have made it easy for the people of a circle of 250 miles in diameter to visit Indianapolis," observed a Saint Louis newspaper in 1915. "In the streets of the capital, the man from Fort Wayne rubs elbows with the man from Terre Haute. A shopper from Columbus meets her old school friend

The Indianapolis and Greenfield Rapid Transit extended an interurban line west from the Hancock County seat into Indianapolis. The tracks followed the edge of the National Road, an economic measure that made sense in 1900 but later brought debilitating highway competition.

from Logansport. A trolley map of Indiana looks like the spokes of a wheel whose hub is the city of Indianapolis"[6]

Trade in Indiana's electric railway securities was brisk, and on many days, the buying and selling of Union Traction common stock and bonds dominated the local financial news. Another securities newsmaker was the Indianapolis Traction and Terminal Company. "Traction Terminal stock went to another high record at the session of the local Stock Exchange, ten shares selling for 90 1/2, an advance of 1 1/2 over the previous high bid," reported the *Indianapolis News* in early 1906. Both local traction enterprises, like the interurban industry nationally, seemed destined only to rise as the still-youthful enterprise further expanded its web of tracks and increased its passenger and freight business. Electric railroad securities "represented one of the best utility investments on the Exchange," recalled a newspaper article in 1935, but by that time, the glory days had long ago departed. "A lot of investors had faith in the large issue of securities based on the enduring character of the interurban scheme of transport." Originally, the interurban (still frequently referred to as the "country trolley" in the early twentieth century) had thought only of growing its passenger traffic, but in 1904, the profit-making potential of freight had begun to bedazzle executives and investors alike.[7]

No one knows how many people invested in electric railway securities. There were certainly Hoosiers who mortgaged homes and businesses to buy shares of Union Traction, Indianapolis and Eastern, and the several other interurban companies listed on the local stock exchange. By working with respected hometown bankers like John Franklin Wild, Indiana investors gained confidence in interurban securities and in the honest values the elaborately engraved stock certificates supposedly represented. But working quietly in 1903 and then more openly and brazenly after 1910, utility financiers located primarily in Philadelphia crafted interurban holding companies and syndicates that enriched their creators but diminished the value of Hoosier holdings and left many local investors feeling shorn like sheep.[8]

It was increasingly common for the Indiana press to report the big changes that seemed to inevitably result after local interurban executives journeyed to Philadelphia to confer with Randal Morgan and his associates and then returned home to implement a financial scheme crafted by the utility moguls of Chestnut Hill or Rittenhouse Square. One primary example of their collaboration was the Terre Haute, Indianapolis and Eastern Traction Company, a rickety holding company set afloat in March 1907 on a sea of watered stock. In the acerbic words of Tarkington's *The Turmoil,* "three servitors of Bigness in Philadelphia took greedy counsel with four fellow-worshipers from New York, and not long after that there were no more dividends for Mr. Vertrees." The novel's old-money Hoosier was laid low by the new financial realities. "In fact, there was nothing for Mr. Vertrees because the 'traction stock' henceforth was no stock at all, and he had mortgaged his house long ago to help 'manage somehow' according to his conception of his 'position in life'—one of his old-fashioned phrases." Worth noting is that Tarkington's Hoosier-based indictment of conspicuous moneygrubbing became America's bestselling novel in 1915 and was further serialized in numerous daily newspapers across the nation.[9]

Dissent from the popular conviction that interurban investments were certain to grow personal wealth was neither common nor especially popular during the electric railway industry's growth decade after 1897. Yet, some words of caution were voiced in newspapers as early as 1897. "There are two kinds of trolleys—those that are built to carry passengers and those that are built to sell bonds and to sell machinery too. They may look alike at first, but in time the difference becomes very apparent and there are obvious dangers in multiplying the latter variety." Newspaper dissenters warned readers of an unhappy scenario that was, in fact, played out numerous times across Indiana during the coming years. "The farmer who takes his savings bank deposit to help build a trolley that is to pass his door, may mortgage his home next to keep the road running, and eventually may see the service stopped and the house sold." It was a knowledgeable dissenter who asserted that "one must search long to find a single cross-country trolley [interurban] that pays. Be that as it may, it is obvious that a good many are projected that cannot pay, and it is equally true that eventually the line that doesn't pay will come to grief." This dire assessment was in many ways too optimistic because it assumed that even interurbans that had no hope of providing a return on investment would nonetheless get built. During the boom years in Indiana, at least two hundred electric railway projects took investors' money but never managed to get any tracks on the ground. For good reason, these dubious, if not blatantly fraudulent, enterprises were disparaged as "paper interurbans" or "hot-air lines."[10]

The year 1904 witnessed only the beginning of Indiana's roller-coaster romance with interurban securities, the value of the stocks and bonds climbing rapidly until the Panic of 1907 and then bobbling along for at least another fifteen years before entering a downward trending series of financial loop the loops. An uptick during the early 1920s was hailed as evidence of an industry "comeback," but it was short-lived. There would be no long-term return to prosperity. The entire roller-coaster ride lasted forty years before it finally ground to an inglorious halt in 1941. Interurban stock certificates currently trade on eBay, but they are valuable only to collectors who prize the artistic engravings. Each one serves as a reminder of the popular enthusiasm that greeted interurban enterprises during the decade of frenzied finance from 1897 through 1907.[11]

The *Street Railway Journal* published a detailed description in 1901 of how interurban promotion worked in Ohio, but the same frenzied enthusiasm applied to neighboring Indiana and other states across the Midwest. In some Ohio counties, electric railway promoters were "thicker than flies in summer these days, and they appear to have entirely superseded the lightning rod agents of former days. The progressive farmers in these parts all have special rooms set for conferences with railway promoters, and hardly a day passes but they are called into use." The faddish sale of lightning rods to gullible Midwestern farmers had become widely regarded in 1901 as a borderline fraud, and the intensity of interurban promotion seemed to be almost in the same category. "A well-dressed stranger drives up and the farmer at once ushers him into the conference room where paper and pen are kept. The right of way through farm or along highway is signed, and the promoter passes on to the next with neatness and dispatch. Thus far nothing has been seen of cars hereabouts, but if the farmers keep on granting rights of way, it is hoped that someday the real thing will materialize."[12]

Numerous groups prospered as a result of the introduction and rocket-like ascent of the interurban industry: promoters, builders, inventors, suppliers, and investors. A person with money to invest could look at hundreds of advertisements that appeared in the special convention issues published annually by the *Street Railway Journal* or the *Street Railway Review* and select a promising enterprise. Even better were the several annual guides that provided investors with detailed financial information about every electric railway in the United States.[13]

In addition to the stocks and bonds of the interurban companies, there was money to be made by investing in everything from forest products—support poles for overhead wires and the wooden bodies of trolley and interurban cars, all fashioned from wood—to metals of all types. Copper, an excellent conductor of electricity, became synonymous with the new age of illumination and power. Big companies like Anaconda and Phelps Dodge extracted tons of the seemingly magic red metal from mines in Montana and Arizona, while processors like Ohio Brass fabricated it into overhead trolley wire and other accessories. Endless miles of copper wires and cables were required to meet the demands of a young and vigorous industry that grew exponentially greater with each passing year. Iron and steel were essential for rails, car fittings, and wheels. Whether it was trolley wire and steel rails or paint and varnish, investment opportunities abounded.

As was equally true for the infant automobile industry, a person could bet on a prosperous future for the interurban industry in a multitude of ways—in the electric interurban railways themselves, in the utilities that supplied power to the interurban companies that did not generate their own electricity, and in companies that made the various appliances needed to craft the big wooden cars—everything from electric motors and brake shoes to window glass and headlights. Each offered investors a chance to make money.

Steam was the oldest of all technologies that enabled the interurban to emerge in the 1890s as a viable mode of transportation. Herein lies an irony: it was common to treat electric and steam railroads as two separate categories, which in many ways they were, but in 1900, both derived their motive power mainly from steam. The difference lay in the application. The railroad locomotive was a self-contained vehicle powered by an onboard steam boiler, while an interurban car depended on a chain of connections that began with the coal used to raise steam in a powerhouse to run the generators that sent electric energy to the cars. There was one often-noted difference: unlike trains of the typical steam railroad, an interurban car could pause to pick up a farmer at his front gate and then accelerate rapidly to full speed thanks to the dynamics of its onboard electric motors. The downside was that a break in the trolley wire could immobilize cars for several miles in each direction. Even worse was that any serious problem, such as a lightning bolt from a thunderstorm, could trigger a powerhouse outage that might last for minutes or even hours. Yes, there was money to be made, too, by the inventor of a reliable lightning arrestor that protected both electric railway rollingstock and its support structure.

By the turn of the century, so much was already known about steam and its many practical uses. The American railroad industry had used steam to power its freight and passenger trains since the 1830s; steamboats had used it even before the railroads; and the coal and metal mines of England had used large and lumbering steam-powered pumps even earlier to keep seawater from flooding underground diggings near the coast. Much more recently, engineers had adapted steam (along with a small but growing amount of hydropower) to generate electricity for the railways.

In short, based on long-term familiarity, steam would win hands down over any internal combustion engine, and electricity as generated by steam had, by the late 1890s, evolved from a poorly understood novelty into the most reliable and useful servant of the age. Even if an investor declined to buy stock in electric railways or in their several carmakers, a person could still profit from the industry's growth by buying into Babcock and Wilcox. This company was not a household name like Westinghouse or General Electric, but it was one of several companies that made money by making the gigantic steam boilers used in power plants. Electric railway journals frequently devoted more ink to discussing each new generating station as it came online—always illustrating their stories with numerous line drawings and photographs—than to the interurban cars or any other feature of the electric railway.[14]

The list of technological advantages that heralded a bright future for the interurban industry went on and on. Rails made from steel and spiked into place atop wooden ties represented track technology now well perfected by the steam railroads and easily adapted to the needs of the interurban newcomers. The same was true of the construction techniques used to build interurban cars. Freight and passenger cars used by steam railroads during the 1890s were universally constructed from wood, and the carpentry skills used to build them could easily be adapted to making streetcars and interurbans. Thus, a canny investor would risk little money by betting on one of the up-and-coming manufacturers of vehicles for city and interurban railways.[15]

The first interurban line into Indianapolis ran north from Greenwood into Indianapolis in early 1900. The ten-mile "Greenwood Line," as it was popularly labeled, proved to be a gold mine from the start, and not too many months later its owners pushed the tracks farther south to Franklin and then to Columbus, Indiana. If a ten-mile line paid well, then a forty-mile line should pay still better. Soon to join the ranks of the capital city's pioneer interurbans were the Greenfield Line, the Plainfield

Line, the Martinsville Line, the Rushville Line, the Danville Line, and several more carriers that during the expansive decade before 1907 multiplied and extended out from Indianapolis like the spokes of a wheel. A company's official title was often a long-winded and cumbersome statement of geographical aspirations. So, in popular parlance, the Indianapolis and Cincinnati Traction Company was shortened to the "Rushville Line" or the "Henry Line," and the Indianapolis, Columbus and Southern Traction Company became the "Greenwood Line." It was also known as the "Irwin Line," a nickname that referenced the remarkable father-and-son team from Columbus, Indiana, who oversaw what was likely the most lucrative and certainly the longest-lived electric interurban railway serving Indianapolis. The city's first interurban line was also its last.[16]

Any interurban line well positioned geographically seemed likely to make money for investors during the industry's boom decade. The car builders thrived, too, as the industry continued to expand—so rapidly and with such runaway zeal that it grew increasingly obvious to industry insiders even before the threat of automobile competition that many early interurban projects had been launched with too much enthusiasm and too little financial common sense. During the boom times, even villages like Thorntown, Indiana, home to only 1,511 residents in 1900, willingly succumbed to the temptation to construct a short interurban line of their own. Again, the last thing true believers in a bright future for the interurban industry could have imagined in the late 1890s and early twentieth century was that within two decades, the automobile would erode and then annihilate investments in the once-promising mode of transportation.[17]

Only the most optimistic investor in 1904 was likely to bet his personal fortune on the automobile when electric interurban railways seemed far more certain to offer a reasonable return on investment. Admittedly, some interurban companies looked financially shaky from the outset, but in 1904, after a trial-and-error decade, there was much that was comfortingly familiar about all facets of the electrical industry. That said, automobile manufacturers continued to pop up in cities all across Indiana during the first two decades of the twentieth century, and the continued glamor of the new industry, if not the staying power of individual brands, suggests that automakers did not lack for investment capital despite the many risks. Indeed, some of them produced automobiles merely for a few months before exiting the business. The same was true, however, for the many automakers based in Detroit, Saint Louis, and elsewhere. Some entrepreneurs even made a profitable business out of repeatedly liquidating auto company assets or by finding new entrepreneurs willing to try their luck at auto building by purchasing an idle factory and its array of tools and fabricating equipment. The

The Electric Railway as a Cash Cow

Timing was everything in terms of investments in the electric railway industry. For approximately a quarter century—from the 1880s until about 1910—it was a cash cow for canny investors like Charles Yerkes, the Chicago transit mogul. It is amazing to consider that great fortunes like his were enlarged one nickel at a time but multiplied by hundreds of thousands of nickels deposited daily by streetcar patrons.

Yerkes was a Philadelphia Quaker who made his fortune in Chicago, which is ironic because several other notable Philadelphians made their fortunes from street railways located in their home city. One of the wealthiest Americans of all time was Peter A. B. Widener, who worked with another Philadelphian, William L. Elkins, to build the city's street railway system. Widener invested his rapidly growing fortune in the Chicago enterprises of Yerkes and was a founding member of United States Steel and American Tobacco.[18]

Another wealthy Philadelphian of note was Randal Morgan, whose name or that of his son, Marshall, appeared frequently among the directors of Indiana's interurban railways. Charles L. Henry may have distinguished himself as the "father of the interurban," but the title derived mainly from his organizing skills. He did not invent any of the technologies employed on his Union Traction Company of Indiana, and it is probably not even appropriate to describe the enterprise as "his" because much of the initial investment capital came from others, most notably from a small group of wealthy Philadelphians that included Morgan. In Indiana as across the United States after 1900, real control of the first generation of interurban companies increasingly gravitated from local investors into the hands of money barons like Morgan who added to their riches by organizing syndicates or holding companies, clever financial schemes that left many Hoosier investors feeling resentful. "The reason for this at first was usually the lack of funds to replace worn-out apparatus or to purchase additional equipment necessary to serve a growing community," and soon the locus of power moved from Indiana to New York's Wall Street and the mansions of Philadelphia's Chestnut Hill and Rittenhouse Square.[19]

Bets placed on interurban companies did not always turn out as well for most investors as they usually did for Yerkes, Widener, and Morgan. Moreover, timing was

The interurban line connecting Lebanon with Thorntown was among the shortest in Indiana.

everything. One of the industry's most astute observers, Dr. Thomas Conway Jr., of the prestigious Wharton School of Finance and Commerce in Philadelphia, published an article in early 1911 on urban street railway investments in which he claimed, "There is no industry in which the public exhibit a livelier or keener interest." The securities of street railways "have become a favorite field for conservative investors"—actually, for "uncounted thousands" of investors of all types. The title of Conway's article, "The Decreasing Financial Returns upon Urban Street Railway Properties," suggests that after more than a decade of unprecedented boom years, by 1911, the bloom was off the investment rose. The obvious question for Conway was whether interurban railway investments would follow a similar pattern of prosperity and then decline—as the street railways had—and if so, when?[20]

Increasingly after 1910, electric railway enterprises both of the urban and interurban varieties ran short of money and chose receivership as a way to forestall creditors. Especially after 1914 or 1915, the interurban industry represented such a poor investment prospect that it grew exceedingly difficult, if not impossible, for most executives to raise the money they desperately needed to purchase modern rollingstock to replace road-weary cars that often dated back to the late 1890s, to upgrade their aging support structure, or even to maintain that structure in working condition. Canny investors no longer found viable cash cows among the electric railways of Indiana or elsewhere, and so they redirected their money to the lucrative opportunities that abounded in the rapidly expanding automobile industry. Back in 1904, however, it was the automobile industry that looked like the less promising prospect.

auto plants, however, did not include any type of assembly line until Ford invented one in 1913.

Before the age of automakers like Ford, bicycle makers had prospered during the craze that swept across the United States during the 1880s and 1890s, but few of them made the successful transition to making automobiles, though many tried. Even if most American bicycle makers failed as automobile manufacturers, the growing legion of bicycle riders in the 1880s and 1890s did impact the future of both the motor car and the interurban by promoting improved country roads for their bicycle outings. Bike riders, like their auto counterparts a few years later, desired good roads, and so when they formed the League of American Wheelmen in 1880, they laid a foundation for the improvements to come. The organization's main purpose was to pressure state and federal lawmakers into funding better roads and highways. Initially, however, very little changed. The League of American Wheelmen (LAW) was less a false start than a delayed one. A few years later, it launched a modest publication called the *L. A. W. Magazine*, which during the 1890s evolved into a national journal called the *Good Roads Magazine*. As a result of the rapidly growing number of bicycle riders during that decade, the magazine's circulation grew to a million readers from all walks of life, and all of them became advocates for good roads.

Their next logical step was to form the National Good Roads Association. Despite the high hopes of good roads advocates, success in those early years proved elusive. Nonetheless, articles in *Good Roads Magazine* with titles like "Value of Good Roads for Dairy Farmers" no doubt planted seeds that bore fruit a few years later when even major steam railroads like the Southern, Illinois Central, and the St. Louis-San Francisco joined the crusade to build all-weather farm-to-market roads to benefit agrarians and those who carried their products to market. These three railroads and others ran "Good Roads Trains," which featured public demonstrations intended to show people who lived along the tracks how best to construct improved roads and highways. The railroads expected to benefit from better farm-to-market roads that would enable agrarians to move crops to railheads regardless of inclement weather. Rail executives never imagined that they were helping to create a nationwide highway network that would offer an alternative to their own rail network—and also to the one the interurbans had created.

Bicycle racing became the rage with one leader of the sport being an African American man named Major Taylor. Bicycle races, including their specially constructed tracks called velodromes, foreshadowed the popularity of auto racing. Other bicyclists relished the challenge of not only getting out of the city into the nearby countryside but also of long-distance pedaling that functioned as a forerunner to the long-distance road trip by automobile. A favorite outing for central Indiana bicyclists was a multiday ride through the rural countryside and scenic hills along the way between Indianapolis

In this postcard image of downtown Marion, the interurban and the automobile appear to coexist peaceably. Marion was the home of Phil Matter, who loaned Charles L. Henry the initial capital required to launch the Union Traction Company of Indiana.

and Cincinnati. The challenges bicyclists faced on rutted farm lanes highlighted why they were early converts to the gospel of good roads.

Given the importance that advocates placed on improved roads to benefit farmers, and with the United States still a predominately rural nation in the early twentieth century, it is perhaps not surprising that federal interest in good roads, modest though it initially was, first found a congenial home within the Department of Agriculture. There, the Office of Road Inquiry opened in 1893, though its work was formally limited to research that helped to educate Americans about the best road-building practices. For another two decades, the federal government provided no money to support actual construction of better roads.

Though the *Good Roads Magazine* was published in Cleveland and then in New York, the movement's main hub of activity in the early twentieth century emerged in Saint Louis, which, ironically, was best known as the home of many manufactories supported by both steam and electric railroads. Since the 1890s, Missouri's largest city had served as the headquarters of the National Good Roads Association. In 1903, the city hosted an important national congress devoted to better roads. Many national luminaries attended, including President Theodore Roosevelt, who in characteristic fashion energetically thumped the podium for emphasis during his oration in support of better roads.

Interestingly, the movement initiated by bicyclists in the early 1880s enjoyed its greatest successes a third of a century later, when Congress in 1916 and 1921 finally voted to help fund a national network of all-weather highways. But by the 1920s, the long-envisioned network was far more likely to benefit the rapidly growing number of automobile owners than bicyclists, and it created serious competition that interurban lines could not hope to match.[21]

An interurban car trundles past the Kosciusko County Courthouse in Warsaw, Indiana, an important stop on the Winona interurban line that connected Goshen and Peru to form the only link between the northern and central Indiana interurban networks.

4

Hoosier Hysteria; or, The Interurban Boom Years

> In 1904 3,275,000 interurban passengers were carried into and out of Indianapolis. During 1905 old lines were extended and new lines were built so that at the end of the year 10 roads entered the city. They carried approximately 4,000,000 passengers in and out and this number was increased to nearly 4,600,000 in 1906 and exceeded 5,000,000 in 1907.
>
> —Joseph A. M'Gowan, Secretary and Treasurer, Terre Haute, Indianapolis and Eastern Traction Company (1911)

"I wonder if they are not overdoing this interurban railroad business just a trifle," Indiana's secretary of state worried aloud in 1901 as he oversaw the latest frenzied round of incorporations. His fees were nominal, which meant anyone of modest means but unbounded hopes could become an interurban promoter.[1]

During the first seven years of the twentieth century, Indiana's interest in all things interurban grew so frenetic with weekly news stories of additional lines projected, existing ones extended, and new traffic developed that the burst of enthusiasm could aptly be described as "Hoosier Hysteria." I recall that in my youth, the term applied to the annual statewide basketball tournament held every March in Indianapolis. Back then, teams from high schools large and small competed against one another for the honor of emerging in triumph as that year's state champions. The size of the student body did not matter, so, in 1954, when a team from the tiny southern Indiana town of Milan defeated teams from far larger high schools to become the state champions, it was a dramatic event. The 1986 movie *Hoosiers* starring Gene Hackman and Barbara Hershey is loosely based on the "Milan Miracle." The dynamic was much the same for the earlier spasm of "Hoosier Hysteria" that energized the state's Interurban Era at least through 1907, a landmark year when an economic panic finally tamed the runaway enthusiasm.[2]

When interurbans commenced running between Richmond and Cambridge City in late 1902, a link in the chain that would soon connect the capital cities of Indiana and Ohio, local residents attracted by the thrill of a new experience crowded aboard the first electric cars. Veteran employee Matt Boswell recalled that "country people drove in from miles each way. They would put up their horses at the little towns or with farmer friends. They would then ride on the cars." More importantly, Boswell recalled, those early electric cars generated an enormous amount of cash: "It was a very common thing to collect $75, $125, or $150 in 10 hours," real money in years before our inflated dollars. During the first Fourth of July holiday that followed commencement of local interurban service in late 1902, Boswell "collected $250.15 and sold about 900 tickets between Richmond and Cambridge City," an impressive haul considering that the distance each way was a mere fifteen miles. "The work was very hard. The last two rounds I was too tired even to register my fares," Boswell recollected.[3]

Investors took note of cash flows such as this. Helping to stoke their often irrational exuberance before 1907 was the frequently repeated claim that electric interurban railways "are in their infancy. It is impossible to anticipate the development of such roads within the next ten years." One result of this overly expansive thinking was an investment bubble that grew large and then deflated with disappointing results. Given the irrational exuberance that early interurban projects generated, Indiana-born Guy Morrison Walker warned in his 1904 booklet that "reckless promoters and unthinking investors have built many such lines in communities not yet sufficiently developed to support them, and now find that they have made an investment which not only yields them no income, but that the traffic in many instances does not yield enough to pay even operating expenses, and they are threatened with the loss of their principal." Nonetheless, a common attitude across the state at this time was perhaps best exemplified by the city of Marion, "which wants all the interurbans she can get, no matter where they come from or who builds them. The more we have the better Marion will be." In total, Indiana witnessed the launch of at least two hundred operating electric railways plus an additional two hundred and fifty "paper interurbans" proposed but never built. In many cases of "popular subscription," tracks never arrived, money simply vanished into a promoter's pockets, and communities never reaped any benefit from their interurban investment.[4]

Already by 1900 more than a thousand miles of interurban roads were planned or under construction across Indiana. Every important community within fifty miles of Indianapolis was eager to grant a franchise to encourage the new mode of transportation. The Indiana legislature gave the promotion of interurban railways a significant boost by enacting a law that granted them the same right of eminent domain enjoyed by the state's steam railroads. This enabled the electric newcomers to survey and condemn land for a right of way despite the objections of stubborn or greedy landowners.

Freed from the need to lay tracks along public roadways, builders could strike out across the Indiana landscape and fashion dedicated corridors conducive to speeds of sixty or seventy miles per hour. In sum, the rapid pace of interurban construction across Indiana benefited from state and local encouragement; favorable topography; the commercial ties already in place between Indianapolis and the several prosperous cities of the Gas Belt; and the expansive vision, determination, and enterprise of a pioneering generation of promoters, builders, and managers.

At the top of the list of reasons for the Hoosier love affair with the interurban in the early twentieth century was possibly the state's topography, which in many ways was Indiana's destiny in terms of its unbounded enthusiasm for electric railways. The relatively flat and prosperous northern half of the state was a landscape ready-made for interurban construction and operation, and its population was receptive to the numerous advantages that electric railways could be expected to confer.

Lawmakers had relocated the capital from Corydon to the center of the state in Indianapolis in 1825 to serve as a hub equally accessible from all parts of Indiana. But therein lay a problem in terms of transportation. Corydon as the state capital had been positioned in extreme southern Indiana, but it was close to the Ohio River, which before the dawn of the Railroad Age in the late 1840s formed one of the Midwest's greatest river highways, a corridor that connected the Indiana capital to Cincinnati, Louisville, Saint Louis, and other vibrant cities of the region. By contrast, Indianapolis benefited from its central location at the junction between the east-west National Road and the north-south Michigan Road, but unlike many sister cities across the heartland, it was not located along a navigable body of water, a major disadvantage before the coming of steam railroads to Indiana in the 1840s and 1850s. In fact, even a century later, in the 1950s when I was growing up in Indiana, Indianapolis could still claim to be the largest city in the United States situated along a nonnavigable body of water.[5]

The White River coursed along the north and west sides of Indianapolis as it flowed southwest to join the Wabash, the languid waterway immortalized in the state song composed by Paul Dresser. Interestingly, Dresser's brother was Indiana-born novelist Theodore Dreiser, who successfully demonized traction magnate Charles Yerkes and by extension the entire electric railway industry. Upstream from Indianapolis lay Anderson and Muncie, and had the White River been navigable, Charles L. Henry might have had far less incentive to inaugurate interurban service between Indianapolis and the Gas Belt cities in January 1901. The expanding network of interurban lines, like the dense network of steam railroad lines spiked into place across the Hoosier heartland between the 1850s and the 1890s, enabled Indianapolis and its surrounding hinterland to compensate for Indiana's noticeable lack of navigable waterways apart from Lake

Michigan and the Ohio River that formed the state's northern and southern "coasts" and the Wabash and Erie Canal completed across Indiana in 1843. Along the 468-mile canal corridor, the longest in the United States, commerce flowed between Toledo on Lake Erie and Evansville on the Ohio River to give an economic boost to Fort Wayne, Lafayette, and Terre Haute, all major centers of commerce by the dawn of the Interurban Era. As vital as Indiana's most significant artificial waterway was in fostering urban prosperity and growth, it bypassed Indianapolis by a considerable distance.[6]

In contrast to landlocked Indianapolis, the cities of Saint Louis, Cincinnati, and Louisville all benefited from and were interconnected by fleets of steamboats that plied the Ohio and Mississippi Rivers, which together with the Illinois, Tennessee, and other navigable waterways formed the Midwest's greatest transportation network during the first half of the nineteenth century. The Great Lakes formed an equally impressive water highway interconnecting the cities of Buffalo, Cleveland, Toledo, Detroit, Milwaukee, and Chicago. What nature did not provide, human ingenuity did by constructing a trio of canals across Ohio and Indiana to link Lake Erie with the Ohio River. In the late 1840s, the Illinois and Michigan Canal opened yet another important water highway across the Midwest. The line used the Illinois River to link the youthful economic system of Lake Michigan with a much older one based in Saint Louis and spread along the Mississippi River and its numerous navigable tributaries. By rearranging the existing spatial relationships in this way, the canal heightened the developing rivalry between two great cities each determined to dominate commerce across the Midwest—between the young and aggressive lakeside entrepot of Chicago and the old and proud capital of the inland river system, Saint Louis. The rivalry between the two giants, both ranking among the five largest centers of population in the United States in the late nineteenth century, grew increasingly intense (and bitter) after railroads dramatically upset the heartland's existing metropolitan hierarchy.[7]

During the 1850s, the Midwest experienced a rail-building boom unlike anything that had preceded it. New railroads crisscrossed Illinois, Indiana, and Ohio, and construction continued at a more measured pace for several more decades. By the 1890s, the posh passenger trains of no fewer than five major railroads raced across northern Indiana on their daily journeys between New York and Chicago. Through passenger trains of another three steam railroads crossed central and southern Indiana to connect cities of the East Coast with Saint Louis. Likewise, the trains of four separate railroads steamed north-south between Louisville, Cincinnati, and Chicago. With more main lines running across Indiana between Saint Louis and Detroit, Toledo, and Cleveland, and the many branch lines of all these railroads, the state was blanketed by steam railroad tracks and trains at the dawn of the Interurban Era in the late 1890s. Electric railways nonetheless found a profitable niche within the matrix formed by the existing steam-powered carriers.[8]

Because of the steam railroads, many Midwestern communities enjoyed far better public transportation in the early twentieth century than they do today. Consider the example of Warsaw, the northern Indiana community that is home to some fourteen thousand residents. Its current claim to fame is that it is the bioengineering capital of the United States, if not the world. The same Indiana-designed artificial shoulder and hip joints that orthopedic surgeons implant in their American and Canadian patients are also implanted in patients in China, Thailand, Australia, and numerous countries around the globe. In 1900, for example, when the medical miracle of a hip replacement was the stuff of science fiction, a Warsaw resident could board one of the Pennsylvania Railroad's several daily trains that raced across northern Indiana and be whisked in comfort and style west to Chicago or east to Pittsburgh, Philadelphia, Baltimore, Washington, or New York.

Several passenger trains of the Big Four, a subsidiary of the New York Central, followed tracks oriented north and south through Warsaw, and though these branch line locals were slow and unimpressive compared to the Pennsylvania's fleet of posh expresses, they did connect with the finest trains of the New York Central at Goshen, twenty-five miles north of Warsaw, or a bit farther away at Elkhart. In either place, a Warsaw resident could board luxurious trains bound not just for Chicago or New York but also for Toledo, Cleveland, Buffalo, and Erie, several Great Lakes cities not served directly by the fleet of Pennsylvania trains that thundered along the railroad's main line through Warsaw.[9]

When Billy Sunday, the most celebrated evangelist of the first two decades of the twentieth century, chose Warsaw's near neighbor, the pleasant retreat of Winona Lake, as his home base in 1911 (an appropriate term for a former National League baseball player), the area's excellent rail connections were without doubt a major asset as he traveled to destinations around the United States to hold one of his "old-time-religion" evangelistic crusades.[10]

As valuable as steam railroad connections were to Warsaw residents or to the residents of any American or Canadian community, they nonetheless imposed certain restrictions on every traveler arriving or leaving by train. Foremost, there was the "tyranny of the timetable." Apart from the expensive option of chartering a special train, all travelers were forced to conform their comings and goings to times dictated by the railroads and so stated in their latest public timetables. In addition, their passenger trains operated along fixed linear corridors that permitted absolutely no deviation to serve towns located off a railroad's right-of-way or from the station stops listed in geographical succession in its timetables. Only in an emergency, and most often only if it suffered a derailment, would a steam passenger train end up stopped at a farmer's front gate instead of continuing its highly programmed journey along the

The station at Peru formed the link between Union Traction and Winona interurban trains, but it was also unusual in that it included the steam-powered Chesapeake and Ohio of Indiana.

"metropolitan corridor." It picked up and discharged passengers only at stations built specifically for that purpose in towns the railroads served.

As functional as steam railroads were, the convenience of public transportation increased noticeably for Warsaw residents after the Winona Interurban Railway began running frequent trains north to Goshen and south to Peru, where they continued via a Union Traction connection into downtown Indianapolis. The hope was that through cars would entice passengers to travel between Indianapolis and South Bend, but often it was necessary to change trains in Goshen to do that. By making additional connections with the South Shore Line in South Bend, a traveler could ride interurban cars the full distance between Indianapolis and Chicago.[11]

Perhaps it mattered little that only a person obsessed with interurban travel was likely to cover the distance separating Indianapolis and Chicago aboard a succession of electric cars. Not only must a traveler trace a roundabout route but through passengers were required to change trains at least twice along the way. Dollars saved were more than offset by the inconvenience of making these connections and enduring the extra hours the full journey required. Moreover, three highly competitive steam railroads—the Pennsylvania, Big Four, and Monon—already ran a fleet of direct and convenient passenger trains daily between Indianapolis and Chicago.

One early peculiarity of the Winona Interurban Railway was that it refused to run its cars on Sunday, an important and lucrative travel day for other electric railways. The reason was that many of its investors, including its president, H. J. Heinz, the Pittsburgh pickle potentate, were religious conservatives who adamantly opposed such frivolity as a Sunday interurban outing into the countryside or to one of the many parks owned and operated by the electric railway companies.

So why construct the Winona Interurban Railroad? One answer is that it benefited local travelers who found that the extant steam railroads failed to address their needs. Here was the primary justification for interurban lines constructed across the Midwest. Before the coming of the automobile and good roads, and in areas located inconveniently far from the nearest steam railroad station (a distance often of no more than a dozen miles), the alternative to travel aboard an interurban car had been a horse-drawn buggy or farm wagon over marginally passible rural roads, a ride by horseback, or a journey by foot. Compared to these time-consuming and often unpleasant modes of transportation, the interurban must have seemed like an answer to a prayer—except to those pious souls who feared that interurban outings degraded proper Sunday-keeping. Religious issues aside, the Winona Interurban Railroad was unusual in that it originated as a single, purpose-built line that connected the communities of Goshen and Peru via Warsaw, and that was all it ever did during its entire life span.[12]

By contrast, the big three interurban companies of central Indiana—Union Traction; Interstate Public Service; and Terre Haute, Indianapolis and Eastern—all originated as locally oriented enterprises that grew significantly larger during the first dozen years of the twentieth century by extending tracks to new destinations and through the acquisition of smaller interurban lines. The process of construction and consolidation enabled each carrier to reach its maximum mileage by the time the United States joined the Great War in April 1917.

Union Traction properties at that time included three separate lines into Indianapolis as well as streetcar systems serving Anderson, Elwood, Marion, and Muncie, four prosperous manufacturing centers in Indiana's northeast quadrant, or Gas Belt. The ongoing prosperity of the Gas Belt cities contributed to the "financially robust" status of Union Traction.[13]

To describe any interurban company in 1917 as "financially robust" was quite a compliment. Some Midwest electric railways never qualified as financially sound even on the day they first turned a wheel. It often appeared that runaway enthusiasm to implement the new interurban technology during the 1890s and early twentieth century had trumped financial common sense. The word "weak" attached itself early on to the state's other big interurban operator, the Terre Haute, Indianapolis and Eastern, and it remained financially precarious throughout its quarter-century life span. Other words often used to describe smaller interurban companies serving Indiana communities at one time or another were "optimistic," "plucky," "community spirited," "threadbare," "destitute," and "moribund." The most elusive word of all was "successful."

As for the Winona Interurban Railroad, it remained small by comparison to the big three traction companies of central Indiana, but the seventy-one-mile line formed the only link ever forged between the network of interurban lines that took shape in central Indiana and the state's second large network that emerged in Indiana's far northern counties between South Bend and Chicago.

The Winona link between Indiana's two largest interurban networks was completed only in 1910, thus making it a latecomer compared to Union Traction or the Terre Haute, Indianapolis and Eastern. The timing was important nonetheless because the late date of Indiana's vital north-south connection illustrated how industry thinking had evolved since the 1890s. During the early years of the Interurban Era, an intense localism had shaped the outlook of the interurban builders. That is, "interurban lines were primarily built for the purpose of handling local traffic, but with the widespread increase of trackage during the last few years some of our more energetic traffic men have been promoting long-distance travel, and from present indications through train service will become popular with the general public." Most of the industry's pioneers had thought only in terms of a very modest service area. The length even of the largest interurban companies was seldom more than fifty miles and encompassed terrain that extended out about three miles on either side of the tracks, the distance farmers could reasonably be expected to walk to catch a train.[14]

Most industry pioneers gave little thought to interconnections with other rail carriers, electric or steam, and or even to adding freight and express to a business that had as its primary purpose the transport of local passengers. The limited horizons that prevailed during the early years were without doubt a result of the interurbans' street railway origins. A service so basic as transporting passenger luggage occasioned considerable debate, especially in the Midwest where industry leaders wondered aloud whether interurbans should haul it for free, charge a fee, or not accommodate it at all. On steam railroads, hauling a reasonable amount of luggage free for passengers was an accepted practice, but not for city trolleys or, initially, for their interurban progeny.

The result of the prevailing localism was a noticeable lack of standardization of everything from operating rules and rollingstock to powerhouses and the infrastructure required to deliver electricity to the cars. One carrier might choose a 600-volt direct current system while a nearby one preferred a 3,300-volt alternating current system. In many cases, the interchange of cars among companies was impossible. Even securing agreement on a common set of operating rules within a single state proved a daunting task. It required years and numerous national and regional conferences for managers to agree on a system (more or less) of uniform operating rules because of the industry's early local orientation. "The primary object of these meetings is to exchange ideas for the general betterment of the service." That included not just hammering out a uniform set of operating rules but also agreeing on something as fundamental as track gauge.[15]

While most interurban track was spaced four feet by 8 and a half inches between the rails, the same standard that prevailed on steam railroads, a few local variations prevailed during the early years of electric railways. Before the Winona completed its vital link between the interurban networks of northern and central Indiana, it had sought in 1907 to run through cars between Warsaw and Elkhart in partnership with the Chicago, South Bend and Northern Indiana. The initial interline arrangement failed, however, because Winona rails at the time were set one-half inch closer than standard. The company had standardized its idiosyncratic gauge by the time it extended tracks into Peru because it subsequently promoted through service between Indianapolis and South Bend via its connections with two other interurban companies. The Midwest's best example of the headaches created by incompatible gauges was Cincinnati, where an oddball distance between the rails of its streetcar tracks prevented half of the ten interurban lines that reached the city's outskirts from accessing the downtown business district. Travelers endured the inconvenience of changing between interurban and trolley cars at stations located at the city's edge. This discombobulation remained a curse throughout the era of electric railways. Experts sought to unsnarl the mess Cincinnati's broad-gauge tracks created, but a workable fix defied the industry's best minds.[16]

A map of Indiana interurban lines in 1910 when the statewide network of interurban lines neared its final configuration—though even the industry's best minds were unable to recognize in 1910 how close to final it was—illustrates the odd spatial pattern that resulted from localism. There were logical patterns of tracks scattered here and there across Indiana, such as prevailed among the cities of the Gas Belt or in the urban northwest counties tributary to Chicago, but the shape of the state network was inexplicable except in terms of Indiana geography and the fact that builders originally constructed their interurban lines to serve local transportation needs only. In fact, any intersection of tracks between two separate companies in the early years was purely fortuitous. As builders filled in obvious gaps, it became possible to merge the local lines to create a pattern of interurban systems and even to facilitate the interline exchange of freight and passenger traffic, but because of the local origins of the interurban and thus the lack of any overall planning, the map of Indiana interurban lines in

The Curse of Localism and Its Impact on Indiana Interurbans

Two peculiarities became noticeable as I studied industry journals to trace the historical trajectory of Indiana interurbans. Interurban executives seemed addicted to reading news of their industry, and hence over the years, their enthusiasm supported the publication of numerous trade journals. Even more noteworthy was their personal commitment to attend numerous industry conferences held throughout the year. These gatherings included the American Electric Railway Association's (AERA) annual conference as well as the several smaller meetings it sponsored each year. At times, it seemed that busy executives had barely concluded one regional conclave before they raced off to a national one, or vice versa.

The intense craving for industry news and the personal commitment to attend meetings of all types were yet another result of the interurban's local origins. During the late nineteenth century, and at least until 1905, each newly formed carrier adopted the technologies and operating rules it alone thought best. Only after the formation of the Indiana Electric Railway Association in late 1904 did leaders of the state's independent-minded interurban lines seek to create a more-or-less uniform set of operating rules as well as use some common technologies. Success often proved elusive. Before the creation of the Interstate Public Service Company in 1912, three separate and nominally independent interurban companies formed a through route between Indianapolis and Louisville. Even here, the middle link in the 117-mile-long chain adopted a different standard featuring much higher voltage than its two partners. Cars could run between their Indiana and Kentucky terminal cities only because they featured a switch that enabled motormen to change back-and-forth conveniently from the Indianapolis and Louisville Traction Company's 1,200-volt direct current system to the lower voltage of its two neighbors. The forty-one-mile southern Indiana line was first in the United States, incidentally, to adopt the higher direct current voltage, which, like the 3,300-volt single-phase alternating current infrastructure that Charles L. Henry pioneered on his Indianapolis and Cincinnati line, was a technological novelty that forced the industry to focus national and international attention on two

Indiana interurban lines that dared to be different. Whether the oddball technologies succeeded or failed, they highlighted the industry's prevailing localism.[17]

With greater standardization, it became possible for industry movers and shakers to launch interline and long-distance travel among several independent carriers, an unanticipated outcome of the interurban building boom of the early twentieth century that surprised pioneers like Charles L. Henry when, without any advanced planning, the tracks of two locally oriented companies serendipitously happened to intersect. The intense localism of the industry's early years continued to be reflected in the odd shape of the network of interurban network that eventually did emerge in Indiana. Even the *concept* of a statewide "network" of tracks developed only slowly in the minds of early interurban executives.

To implement any form of standardization, industry leaders benefited from the detailed articles that described what others were doing as well as from the face-to-face exchange of ideas at their frequent meetings. In 1911, Arthur Brady, the president of Indiana's largest and wealthiest interurban company, Union Traction, completed his one-year term as leader of the AERA. His successor was Thomas N. McCarter, a fellow attorney who for thirty-six years headed the Public Service Corporation of New Jersey, one of the largest urban transportation networks in the United States. During his term as president, McCarter suggested a novel way to undercut the industry's prevailing localism. By organizing a six-week rail tour of all US regions in 1912, he and any executives who cared to join him could meet face-to-face with other interurban and street railway executives and observe their operations in action. Not many of McCarter's peers could afford the time needed to complete the entire transcontinental circuit, but numerous electric railway executives did join the entourage for a portion of the multistate odyssey. Welcoming McCarter and his travel companions to Indianapolis were Charles L. Henry, Indiana's now-legendary "father of the interurban" and young Robert I. Todd, a newcomer who represented the next generation of Indiana interurban executives. The Hoosiers treated their out-of-town guests to an auto tour of the city that included a trip to the speedway to watch cars being tuned for the upcoming 500 Mile Race, only the second one ever held, and concluded with another Indiana favorite, a hearty dinner of fried chicken.[18]

Brady met McCarter's group in Indianapolis and again in Cleveland, but he chose not to join their roundabout odyssey through Ohio. This trip featured a visit with Midwest traction magnate Kesley Schoepf—another of Randal Morgan's Midwestern minions—and a group of fellow Cincinnati luminaries that included Charles Phelps Taft, owner of two Major League baseball teams, the Philadelphia Phillies and the Chicago Cubs, and brother to the current occupant of the White House, William Howard Taft. The national journey was historic, but how much it accomplished to overcome the industry's prevailing localism is difficult to say.[19]

1910 resembled a lopsided web woven by a drunken spider or two. Also worth noting, the concept of a "web" of interconnected tracks applied mainly to the northern half of the state. While a majority of the state's interurban lines eventually connected to Indianapolis, sometimes in a roundabout way, significant portions of Indiana were never joined to the electric web that extended the reach of the state's capital city and largest population center.

South of Indianapolis, the curse of localism was most visible. Across the entire southern half of the state, only the Indianapolis-Louisville line that operated under the Interstate Public Service Company banner qualified as a through route between two major population centers. Geographical challenges and a diffuse pattern of settlement across southern Indiana complicated the task of visionaries who dared to imagine an interurban network that interconnected all of Indiana's large cities, served most of the state's ninety-two county seats, and offered fast and efficient transportation to Chicago, Cincinnati, and Toledo, each an interurban hub of significance.

Terre Haute, Indianapolis and Eastern tracks that extended across the state's midriff from Terre Haute to Richmond via Indianapolis traced the economic dividing line between the two Indianas. The northern half of the state, thanks in large measure to its Gas Belt and a fertile expanse of farmland that extended from the Ohio to Illinois borders, grew ever more prosperous between the end of the Civil War in 1865 and 1900. By contrast, southern Indiana lagged far behind economically. There, much of the land was uplifted into hills offering scenic vistas, especially during the season of fall colors, but areas of good farmland tended to be scattered, in contrast to the Corn Belt that stretched across the generally level northern counties. Hence, most Indiana interurban lines followed the money and built where booming businesses and population growth were most pronounced and were certain to ensure a reasonable return to investors.

So although Indianapolis at one time served as the hub for at least a dozen different electric railway companies, the resulting "wheel" formed by the interurban spokes was strangely lopsided. Far more of the spokes extended north and northeast into the quadrant defined by Indianapolis, Richmond, Kokomo, and Fort Wayne than anywhere else. South of the capital city, it was a different story. There, the map of interurban lines contained numerous blank spaces. Boosters and builders advanced numerous proposals during the years of runaway enthusiasm to fill these gaps to create a fully integrated statewide network that linked Indianapolis with electric railways to all corners of the Hoosier State.

That was the expectation that motivated Hugh McGowan to open the world's largest interurban station in downtown Indianapolis in September 1904. Perhaps more than any of his Hoosier peers, he thought in terms of a large network that broke entirely free of the constraints imposed by localism. To fully appreciate McGowan's remarkable achievement, we must look back to the final months of 1903 when 306 interurban cars arrived and departed downtown Indianapolis each day, a total of nearly 112,000 cars annually. These cars transported approximately two and a half million travelers in 1903.[20]

As impressive as these figures were, and the numbers in each category were climbing rapidly, there was a problem that McGowan determined to solve. Any travelers seeking to pass *through* Indianapolis to reach a destination in the opposite direction from the hub city needed to change stations as well as cars. Individual interurban companies maintained separate waiting areas that often amounted to nothing more than storefronts. McGowan planned to build a union depot that put all interurban cars and their many passengers under one roof. Not only was it to be the grandest interurban edifice the world had yet seen, or would ever see, but it was to occupy perhaps the single-most desirable parcel of real estate available in downtown Indianapolis: one block west of Monument Circle, the iconic heart of the city, and only half a block east of the Indiana state capitol. Thus, McGowan's Traction Terminal was intended to be far more than an imposing building.

The site was formerly famous as the city's Cyclorama, a moving panoramic painting show that, before it went bankrupt in 1890, provided public entertainment in the era before true motion pictures. One of its most popular features was titled "The Battle of Atlanta." During the 1890s, the large Cyclorama building, minus its once-popular picture show, housed a bicycle riding academy, a roller-skating rink, a zoo, boxing tournaments, and a small-scale roller coaster, a sequence of failed ventures that caused the structure to be known as the "House of Fads." In 1902, the building housed the capital city's first annual automobile and bicycle show with numerous displays of the latest horseless carriages to wow the crowd of onlookers. At that time, the site was also home to the Fisher Automobile Company, a sales agency launched by Carl Graham Fisher, a local motor enthusiast who in 1909 was one the founders of the Indianapolis Motor Speedway (and years later of Miami Beach). During the summer of 1903, a wrecking ball and a large charge of dynamite obliterated the worse-for-wear Market Street landmark, and teams of workmen immediately launched construction of McGowan's interurban masterpiece.[21]

The Traction Terminal opened its doors in September 1904, and in rapid succession during the next twelve months, there followed the expansion of the Indiana Electric Railway Association and publication in Indianapolis of the *Interurban Railway Journal*, which swiftly gained a national readership. With its offices housed in the Traction Terminal, it is perhaps not surprising that the new publication's introductory issue in

November 1905 opened with a feature story on McGowan that included a full-page portrait of the "trolley king" fast emerging as the Hoosier embodiment of the electric railway industry's boundless expectations.

By any measure, McGowan was a big man who made big plans, and he always got his projects completed promptly, which impressed his several Philadelphia patrons. This historically significant group of investors emerged in the late nineteenth century and served as the financial dynamo that energized interurban projects all across central Indiana. They provided the money that supported McGowan's remarkable rise from a humble farm in western Missouri to Indiana electric railway mogul, and through their web of behind-the-scenes connections across the Midwest, they made themselves and McGowan fabulously rich.

McGowan, whose friends often quipped that his hobby was his work, refused to tolerate half-pint projects of any type, as was illustrated by his personal commitment to build the largest interurban terminal ever constructed and to situate it on prime real estate in downtown Indianapolis. The complex of buildings McGowan envisioned was not just physically imposing; by locating them next door to the state capitol, he intended them to loom large in the business and political affairs of Indiana. No other city offered a precedent for what McGowan had in mind. Early interurban companies were typically low-budget enterprises and had little money for building any structure out of the ordinary. The twenty-mile line that connected Indianapolis and Greenfield, for example, acquired discarded trolley bodies to serve as its trackside way stations.

Indianapolis had no formal station structures for its electric railways before construction of the Traction Terminal. When interurban cars first entered the capital city in 1900, their own company tracks ended at the edge of town. To access locations downtown that served as their modest first stations, the city's initial three interurban lines each paid McGowan's street railway company four cents per passenger to use its tracks. Cars serving Greenfield, for example, originally ran no farther into metropolitan Indianapolis than its far east-side suburb of Irvington where passengers transferred to one of McGowan's city trolleys to continue their journey downtown. The problem was that Greenfield's new and imposing cars, a source of considerable local pride because the small community had literally bootstrapped its way into the Interurban Era, proved too wide to clear a line of lampposts positioned in the center of busy Washington Street, the main east-west thoroughfare across Indianapolis. That was one of several startup problems that McGowan solved with dispatch.

Similar arrangements prevailed in cities across the United States, unless the local street railway company refused to allow the heavy interurban cars to pound along its lightweight trolley tracks, an understandable objection. Conversely, some interurban companies complained that the slotted design of trolley tracks crimped the wheels of their rolling stock. McGowan remained open-minded on the matter of interurban use of his Indianapolis trolley tracks so long as his company collected a fee for every incoming car. After hammering out a complex agreement that permitted interurban lines to access the central city, his next step was to eliminate the ad hoc station arrangement that originally prevailed in Indianapolis, which was especially inconvenient for long-distance travelers who desired to connect between interurban lines. The extravagance represented by a dedicated interurban station at a downtown location, especially one as commodious as McGowan had in mind, was foreign to the pinchpenny thinking of most electric railway executives in 1902, the year during which McGowan first publicly floated the idea of his Traction Terminal. Indianapolis had pioneered the concept of a union station serving all steam railroads, and now McGowan intended to provide Indianapolis interurban travelers with the same convenience, but with an added touch of architectural grandeur unknown on electric railways.

The Ohio cities of Cleveland, Toledo, and Cincinnati were the first to discuss the idea of a union interurban station, but McGowan's project was so much larger in scale that it dwarfed all other proposals. No electric railway executive before McGowan had hired an architect with Daniel Burnham's national stature to design a structure of any kind for an interurban line. Burnham is famous for his imposing union station worthy of the nation's capital, a true cathedral of commerce still used by Amtrak, but his Indianapolis Traction Terminal antedated his masterpiece in Washington, DC, by four years.[22]

When McGowan initially revealed plans for the gargantuan structure he intended to add to the built environment of downtown Indianapolis, no one mentioned Burnham's now-famous dictum to "make no small plans" for one obvious reason: the architect had not yet stood before the Chicago city council and admonished politicians to make big plans that would impress onlookers for generations to come.

Small plans were not part of McGowan's thinking; though not tall, he was stout and physically imposing. The Missouri farm boy and former Kansas City policeman would never have been successful in Indianapolis or anywhere else had he been timid about his plans for the future. The editor of industry-leading publication the *Street Railway Review* was so astonished by McGowan's architectural daring that he summed up his thoughts by describing the Indianapolis Traction Terminal as "epoch-making."[23]

Indeed, it was epochal because nothing before McGowan's Traction Terminal had focused the national spotlight on Indiana interurban activities. The industry's leading trade journals had published a few feature articles on Indiana interurbans before 1904, but these accounts were invariably overshadowed by the attention that editors lavished on mass transit projects in the big cities of Philadelphia, New York, Chicago, and Boston. After the Traction Terminal was completed, the journal editors could no longer ignore events in Indiana. By the same token, during the coming years, so many people with Indiana connections rose to national leadership positions in the electric

Whether featured in black-and-white or as a hand-tinted postcard image, the Traction Terminal was always impressive when filled with interurban cars.

railway industry that one Indianapolis newspaper dared use the term "Hoosier Cabal" to describe the state's rapidly rising men of influence. Eventually, Charles Gordon, an electrical engineer and wordsmith who fondly recalled his Rushville, Indiana, roots would edit the *Electric Railway Journal*, the oldest and most prestigious publication in North America devoted to electric railways.

During the two years required to construct the Traction Terminal complex, industry leaders devoted more and more time to discussing the nature and purpose of the interurban. Was it a glorified streetcar system, or was it a scaled-down version of a steam railroad? The answer made was important because in many states the laws that applied to urban streetcar systems were very different from those that governed steam railroads. McGowan left no doubt where he stood: his plans both for his Traction Terminal complex and the several central Indiana interurban properties with which he was financially involved confirmed that, as much as possible, he intended to see them all run in the same way as a first-class steam railroad.

The Traction Terminal complex opened its doors to travelers in September 1904. Burnham's grand combination of a nine-track train shed, waiting room, nine-story office building, and several freight houses was next door to the state capitol, and it was clear that McGowan was looking to the future regarding both the imposing design of the Traction Terminal and of his choice of a location intended to make a conspicuous statement about political power and influence. A traveler, perhaps a state legislator, could literally walk from an interurban car to the Indiana governor's office or to the senate and house chambers across Capitol Avenue in less than five minutes. It had no doubt occurred to McGowan that the location he chose for his Traction Terminal was far better situated than the Indianapolis Union Station several blocks south of the state capitol. Indianapolis always remained Indiana's premier interurban hub, and a trip through the city's cavernous Traction Terminal became a familiar feature of interurban travel around the midriff of the Hoosier State.

No other city in the world ever came close to matching the size of the Traction Terminal complex, but McGowan's daring concept of a single imposing station serving multiple interurban companies did inspire emulators who needed only to visit Indianapolis to be impressed by what he had accomplished, and many did. McGowan delighted in hosting industry executives from around the United States who had traveled to Indianapolis to examine and be inspired by his architectural wonder. One guest in early 1905 was Henry Everett, the Cleveland head of a Midwestern traction syndicate, who planned to construct interurban terminals in Toledo and Detroit. "There is nothing like it in the country," exclaimed a suitably awed Everett. Likewise, a staff correspondent for the *Chicago Tribune* who styled himself simply as "Raymond" was impressed in 1907 by the mass of humanity the capacious structure handled annually: "The traction depot in Indianapolis is as busy a center as any steam railroad depot in Chicago and the estimate of 6,000,000 passengers handled by the electric roads running into the traction station in Indianapolis is well within the mark of absolute accuracy." He believed that in terms of its architecture and importance in the daily life of the city, the Traction Terminal was "as recognized an institution as the courthouse or the statehouse itself."[24]

No location constructed a more obvious copy of the original Traction Terminal than Muncie, where Union Traction erected a scaled-down version that included an overarching train shed modeled after the Indianapolis original. Oddly, no other Midwestern metropolis was ever able to create a comparable interurban edifice in design and function, although Akron, Ohio, did construct an imposing structure to serve its several electric railways. That city's terminus opened its doors only in 1919, very late in the Interurban Era.

Burnham's expansive vision could well have applied to Indiana's interurban industry during its boom years, when McGowan's outsize influence on the construction and operation of several of the state's largest companies grew ever more noticeable and impressive. In addition to the Traction Terminal Building, McGowan controlled the street railways of Indianapolis and served as a director of several large interurban companies, including the Union Traction Company of Indiana and the Terre Haute,

The Muncie interurban depot was modeled after the Traction Terminal in Indianapolis.

Indianapolis and Eastern. His business interests were by no means limited to electric railways. He simultaneously presided over a gas utility in Kansas City and regularly commuted by Pullman cars between the two locations. By his early forties, McGowan, with the aid of his Philadelphia patrons, emerged as one of Indiana's richest men, and his mansion on the near north side of Indianapolis was a wonder to behold.

A Cincinnati study published in 1912 wistfully saluted the genius of McGowan as it assessed the interurban muddle that prevailed in the Ohio metropolis. Unlike Indianapolis, no downtown union station existed in Cincinnati, and prospects for a single interurban terminus remained remote because its broad-gauge trolley tracks remained incompatible with the standard gauge favored by the largest and most important electric railways that reached the city's outskirts but could not proceed downtown. None of Ohio's largest population centers had built union interurban stations in the central city as of 1912. This was no doubt one reason why the several interurban companies using McGowan's Traction Terminal earned two-thirds more money per mile of track than those serving Cincinnati.[25]

Apart from differences in gauge, another obstacle impeding interurban travel to the center of some metropolitan areas was that tracks intended solely for lightweight trolley cars could not support the weight of the much-heavier interurban cars. It was also possible that their wheels simply did not align well with the grooved design typical of trolley rails or with the way they were embedded in street pavement. Hadley Clifford, the motorman who made the inaugural run from Anderson to Alexandria in 1898, recalled that the wheel assembly of his interurban car hung up on the brick pavement into which Alexandria's streetcar tracks were set, and so he had to reverse course and back his car all the way to Anderson.

Finally, the challenge of interurban cars accessing the heart of a city might have had a political dimension. When the trolley company serving Toledo, Ohio, failed to resolve a long-running franchise dispute with the mayor and city council, municipal officials forced it to close temporarily in late 1919. During the streetcar shutdown, interurban cars had no way to reach downtown Toledo, and so they had to halt at its outskirts and transfer passengers to whatever motor vehicles happened to show up.

In the early twentieth century, when interurban companies first addressed how best to access city centers, motor traffic was not a serious problem. As an increasing number of automobiles crowded city streets, interurban cars wasted precious minutes as they crept through downtown traffic. The several interurban companies that served Indianapolis debated building elevated structures to speed their access to the Traction Terminal, but nothing ever came of the idea.

When Hugh McGowan grew too busy running numerous gas and electric enterprises in addition to his traction empire, he brought his cousin, Joseph McGowan, to Indiana from Maine in 1903 to lend him a hand with day-to-day management chores. The immense size of the Traction Terminal spoke to the expectations of both McGowans and other industry pioneers that Indiana interurban companies would continue to multiply and be long-lasting. The years of growth illustrated the vital role that creative and bold individuals, and a few eccentrics, played in creating Indiana's Interurban Era. There was nothing "soulless" about these enterprises. The only dark cloud on the horizon for Hugh McGowan was a personal one: his various businesses easily weathered the Panic of 1907 (though the financial storm battered several major steam railroads), but there was growing public concern about his well-being. Electric railway trade journals on several occasions published cryptic news briefs that referred to his return to Indianapolis from a European holiday or a vacation trip to Hot Springs, Arkansas, with his health much improved. On one occasion, an industry publication used the term "dangerously ill" to describe the state of McGowan's health in early 1908. What exactly did that mean?

Were Philadelphia patrons like Randal Morgan demanding ever greater returns from their Golden Boy? McGowan never explained his close relationship with Morgan, nor did he ever complain in print, but the Philadelphian's shadowy presence, his increasingly visible monetary machinations, and his ever-tightening grip over several of the largest interurban railway companies in Indiana and Ohio began to alarm

Fort Wayne, like Indianapolis, was one of Indiana's major interurban hubs.

Hoosier investors and no doubt placed increased stress on McGowan. As early as 1905, the *Indianapolis News* referred to Morgan as "the bogy man from Philadelphia who has gobbled up" a number of Indiana interurban lines "and is alleged to have designs" on several more. Hoosier hostility to Morgan's outside control peaked in 1912 with a concerted effort by dissident Hoosier shareholders "to eliminate the Randal Morgan control of the Indianapolis Street Railway Company" at the company's upcoming annual meeting. Their effort to "retire" Morgan was unsuccessful.[26]

Rising concern in Indiana about Morgan's absentee control of the state's largest electric railway systems and the "high-handed" financial machinations that he and his fellow Philadelphia money barons used to forge their monopolistic holding companies eventually resulted in Indiana lawsuits and court action. Thus, the public spotlight shone as never before during the industry's formative years on the outsized role that a few key individuals played in shaping the state's Interurban Era.

5

Gas Belt Prosperity and Indiana's Interurban Pioneers

> There are various reasons why a plan which might have failed a few years ago is now a success. The large increase in the population of north-central Indiana since the discovery of natural gas, the manufacturing industries supplying wages which enable the workingmen to enjoy the luxuries of life have preceded the increase in population, and the recent discoveries and inventions in the line of electricity have all added their part to the cause of the inter-urban railway in Indiana.
>
> —*Pharos-Tribune* (Lafayette), June 24, 1899

The typical interurban rider cared little about who ran the company as long as the ride was comfortable and everything ran according to the timetable. The financial arrangements that paid for the cars, track, and power delivery meant little. The details were of no concern to most passengers, but in this chapter and the next, I offer a biographical portrait of the movers and shakers responsible for launching Indiana's largest electric interurban railways.

The Interurban Era never produced a towering personality who in the eyes of the world represented the embodiment of the industry, as Edison did for basic electrical innovations or as Cornelius Vanderbilt, James J. Hill, and Edward H. Harriman did for the steam railroads. Nonetheless, at the state level, several notable personalities did emerge during the early years of the Interurban Era, a few of whom went on to become industry leaders respected throughout North America.

In the early twentieth century, Henry Edwards Huntington built the world's single-largest interurban company in his Los Angeles–based Pacific Electric Railway. William Brown McKinley was only a few steps behind Huntington in constructing his large and generally successful Illinois Traction system. Huntington seemed content to focus his entrepreneurial energy on the development of Southern California, so he never played an active role in promoting electric railways outside his home state, nor

The built environment of Anderson, Indiana, showcased the prosperity of the Gas Belt Era. Headquarters of Union Traction were on the top floor of the six-story building to the right.

did he ever become actively involved with industry groups like the American Electric Railway Association.[1]

Likewise, McKinley concentrated on expanding his interurban empire in Illinois and his utility holdings in neighboring states. He remained only nominally active in the industry's main professional association. Apart from enlarging his Midwestern empire, his primary interest lay in national politics. McKinley (a distant cousin of President William McKinley) served Illinois both in the US House of Representatives (1905–13 and 1915–21) and in the US Senate (1921–26).

Two Indiana pioneers, Charles Lewis Henry and Arthur Wolfe Brady, remained doggedly committed to their state's interurban industry from its earliest boom days until it entered its terminal decline during the latter half of the 1920s. In addition, both men achieved national prominence, each serving a term as president of the American Electric Railway Association. Both men were lawyers who gave liberally of their time to defend the electric railway industry before Congress and various federal regulatory bodies like the Interstate Commerce Commission (ICC). To prevent regulatory overreach in 1914, both Brady and Henry hastened to Capitol Hill to dissuade Congress from adding federal oversight of interurban lines to the ICC's seemingly endless accretion of power and expanding range of responsibilities. Brady, ever the diplomatic scion of Yale University, tactfully asserted that less than 1 percent of the industry's business truly qualified as interstate commerce, that few interurban companies exceeded fifty miles in length, and that most of their business was purely local. Henry underscored Brady's objections and insisted that Indiana regulators provided sufficient oversight. Thus, national leadership must be added to the list of reasons why Indiana came to represent the very epitome of the Interurban Era. It ranked second to Ohio in terms of mileage, but the Hoosier State yielded to nowhere else in its impressive interurban terminal in Indianapolis, its enthusiastic embrace of interurban railways, and the quality of its industry leaders.[2]

The state was, however, a latecomer to national prominence as an interurban showcase. A sprinkling of Hoosiers attended the annual conferences of the American Street Railway Association during the organization's first two decades, 1882–1902, but none ranked among its movers and shakers. Records of the annual proceedings suggest that they did not even speak aloud or participate in any discussions. Just weeks after he founded the Union Traction Company of Indiana in September 1897, Charles L. Henry apparently traveled to Niagara Falls to explore what the electric railway industry's big annual conference had to offer. I must say "apparently" because although the official program lists him as a delegate from Anderson, he uttered not a word during several days of proceedings. If he did attend, he was unimpressed by what he saw and heard because he allowed Union Traction membership to lapse the next year. Henry departed the House of Representatives with the expiration of his second term in early 1899. He had declined to run for another term because he wanted more time to pursue a growing passion for electric interurban railways as well as several other business opportunities in the Anderson area that ranged from creating a new cemetery to overseeing a chain of men's clothing stores.

The national industry took little note of anything Henry, Brady, or any other Hoosier interurban pioneer did in the opening years of the twentieth century until the state gained unprecedented national prominence with the mid-September opening of Hugh McGowan's monumental Traction Terminal in downtown Indianapolis in September 1904. Industry trade journals published multipage and copiously illustrated feature stories on Indiana's newest landmark. The country trolley that emerged with so little fanfare that no one could agree on its place or date of origin seemed now to boldly flex its muscles to prove it was a bona fide railroad.

Just a few months later, Henry provided an additional reason for the entire industry to stand in awe of the accomplishments of the gentlemen from Indiana. He did that by making a bold commitment to cutting-edge electrical technology to power his second great interurban railway project, the Indianapolis and Cincinnati Traction Company. Only recently had Westinghouse developed a new and radically different delivery system for electrical energy, and even before it was fully perfected, Henry took a considerable risk, both personal and financial, by being the first in North America to use "single-phase alternating current" technology. Having learned the basics by building the Union Traction Company, he was determined now to create the finest interurban line in Indiana and possibly in all of North America.

Most of Henry's industry peers did not understand the concept of single-phase alternating current or the advantages it was supposed to confer, but the revolutionary new technology became the talk of the industry in 1905 and 1906. Almost overnight, it became the topic of numerous papers delivered at professional meetings, much hallway chitchat among executives, and onsite visits to Henry's latest Indiana enterprise by curious individuals and delegations of electrical engineers from places as far away as Germany and Japan. The cutting-edge interurban technology that Henry unveiled in rural Indiana, of all places, so greatly impressed the New York–based editor of *Scientific American* that he labeled the concept "the most important step that has yet occurred in the introduction of single phase alternating current traction in this country." He further noted that "there has been an absence of troubles from sparking and overheating, while the sliding contact bow trolley on the high-speed line has, contrary to expectations, given but very little trouble in the nine months of its operation." During the watershed months from 1904 through 1905, Henry, McGowan, and their Hoosier peers emerged from the shadows to gain national recognition as significant movers and shakers of the electric railway industry.[3]

Charles L. Henry was born into modest circumstances in 1849 on a farm eight miles north of Greenfield in rural Hancock County, Indiana. As a boy, he relocated to the nearby community of Pendleton with his parents and attended public school there. Pendleton was a station stop along the busy Big Four main line linking Indianapolis and Cleveland, and just as in countless other communities, the local railroad station served as the portal to a larger world for ambitious youth like Henry. Unlike many young men of his day, Henry left his modest but comfortable surroundings to pursue a college degree, still a rarity in the 1860s and 1870s. He first journeyed west from Pendleton to Greencastle for his undergraduate education at a predecessor school to DePauw University, then headed south to Bloomington for a law degree. After graduating from Indiana University in 1872, the young attorney returned to Pendleton to practice law. Three years later, he relocated to nearby Anderson, the new center of Indiana's Gas Belt prosperity. Henry remained restless, however, and apart from his

Role Model Indiana

Before 1900, the electric railway industry regarded interurban activity in Indiana as little more than a sideshow. The focus of its several journals and the American Street Railway Association's annual conference was on significant events taking place on big-city transit systems that moved the masses in Philadelphia, Chicago, and several other metropolitan areas. Elevated railways and subways (frequently called "subterranean railroads") were important features of the industry's focus on mass transit. By contrast, apart from a prominent industry pioneer like Union Traction, the interurbans of Indiana rarely rated more than a two- or three-line mention in industry trade journals. They were ignored in matters of technology, finance, and leadership.

The perception changed in 1906 when Indiana gained unprecedented recognition in the nation's press. Helping to burnish the state's reputation as the "world's greatest interurban center" among American newspaper readers at large, and not just among industry insiders, was the fortuitous scheduling of the National Editorial Association's national convention in Indianapolis in June 1906, which, as noted in the introduction, shone a public spotlight as never before on developments in Indiana that during the previous two years had transformed its interurban industry into a worldwide role model.[4]

These developments included Hugh McGowan's massive Traction Terminal that opened to travelers in September 1904; Charles L. Henry's technological daring of being the first in North America in 1905 to adopt a revolutionary technology to electrify his Indianapolis and Cincinnati Traction Company; and the expansion that same year of the Indiana Electric Railway Association, which gave Hoosiers a huge boost in terms of the industry's heightened awareness of their cutting-edge interurban technology and bold leadership.

When this formal portrait of Charles Lewis Henry appeared in 1915, the Greenfield, Indiana, native was president of the electric railway industry's top North American organization, a career move that further solidified his reputation as the "father of the interurban."

Further heightening the visibility of Indianapolis was the merger in early 1906 of Indiana and Ohio trade groups to create the Central Electric Railway Association, the headquarters of which were in McGowan's Traction Terminal building. The regional body enabled Hoosiers to confer with industry peers several additional times each year in cities in Indiana and nearby states. Furthermore, when the two states with the most extensive and interconnected network of interurban lines launched a single regional association, they created the second-most powerful professional group in the electric railway industry, one that elevated to prominence the rising cohort of Hoosier interurban executives soon to become industry leaders in North America.

Finally, the Saint Louis World's Fair of 1904 initiated a series of ongoing scientific evaluations of interurban car physics, a subject of great interest to managers of the still-young mode of transportation and one that attracted widespread coverage in its trade journals. After the Missouri extravaganza closed its doors late that year, engineers at Purdue University continued their measurements and analysis through 1905 aboard a special test car furnished by Arthur Brady and the Union Traction Company. This was another of the noteworthy events occurring between 1904 and 1906 to focus widespread attention on Indiana interurban executives and their achievements. The June 1906 convention of the National Editorial Association in Indianapolis was thus timed perfectly, if unintentionally, to spread the word of Hoosier accomplishments to a broad audience of newspaper readers.

law practice, he spent time exploring several local business opportunities and another one not so local that he embraced with enthusiasm for the rest of his life.[5]

That was the result of a hunting trip Henry made with a relative to southwest Missouri in 1892. In his brief memoir deposited at the Indiana Historical Society, he never mentions if he bagged any game, but he discusses at length his infatuation with the new mode of transportation he saw taking shape there. In fact, he was so captivated by the potential of the intercity electric railway, apparently the first "interurban" project Henry had ever considered, that for the next several months, he attempted to purchase a share of the still-unfolding enterprise. Although owners of what became the Southwest Missouri Electric Railway declined his offer, the railway project that Henry witnessed emerging in the Joplin area forever changed the second half of his life.[6]

Back home in Anderson, he had recently converted a short mule car line to electricity, but his hunting trip to the Show-Me State greatly enlarged his horizons: Henry, now a successful Gas Belt lawyer and entrepreneur still in his early forties, had seen for himself an exciting and innovative spatial application of the familiar trolley technology. Electric streetcars no longer needed to be tethered to their horse car antecedents or limited to conveying riders within a single community. The little electric railway that impressed Henry prospered because it linked several towns in the tristate lead and zinc region, a natural-resource-rich area that straddled the borders of Missouri, Kansas, and Oklahoma. Perhaps, reasoned Henry, Anderson, Muncie, Tipton, and several other booming cities nearby offered a similar money-making possibility to anyone innovative enough to construct an electric railway to interconnect them. As he recalled in his brief memoir, "I took up the idea of interurban service between what were known as the Gas Belt Cities in Indiana."[7]

The pioneer interurban builders of Missouri and Indiana realized intuitively the spatial relationships that made for success. As Henry's highly capable counterpart in Illinois, William B. McKinley, once explained to a group of engineering students, hands-on experience had taught him that "the best passenger feeders for interurban roads are where there is a medium sized town next to a large one." This was the case for Illinois Traction and the cities of Indiana's Gas Belt. Additional personal experience convinced McKinley that the typical rural area across which so many interurbans extended their tracks would furnish only a piffling 7 percent of any company's overall passenger traffic. In other words, interurban lines that depended too heavily on rural traffic were likely doomed to an early death once automobile ownership grew common among farm families. In the interurban business, urban geography clearly determined a company's destiny.[8]

During the 1890s, when Henry first began to assemble the components that became the Union Traction Company of Indiana, the northeast quadrant of Indiana had gained fame as the Gas Belt because drillers in the 1880s and 1890s easily tapped into an extensive but rather shallow underground deposit of natural gas. Because the fuel was so cheap and seemingly so abundant, glass manufacturers gravitated to the youthful cities of Kokomo, Anderson, and Muncie, where the five Ball brothers relocated from Buffalo, New York. They soon dominated the national market by producing the glass jars favored for home canning in an America still largely rural and still growing much of its own food. Locating yet another massive manufactory in Muncie was the Hemingray Glass Company, the world's largest producer of the electric insulators that formed a key component of the interurban railway infrastructure. Like Ball, Hemingray also made glass jars. Was it any wonder that the local baseball team at the turn of the century was named the Muncie Fruit Jars!

Indiana's natural gas bonanza proved not nearly as plentiful as the "experts" had predicted, but even after the last gas had vanished into thin air in the early twentieth century, much of it having been foolishly wasted, a firm foundation was in place to support a robust manufacturing economy in the cities around the region, including in future years a variety of large and small enterprises that served the rising automobile industry. According to the capital city's former mayor, Charles Bookwalter, "Two factors have been prominent in the development of Indianapolis since 1890." Initially, he explained, "the city rode on the wave of manufacturing prosperity during the days of natural gas. When natural gas failed, another influence came—the interurban railway."[9]

Fortunately for Union Traction, its tracks (or, more accurately, those of its several predecessor companies) were already in place when Indiana's gas boom flickered out, and its trains continued for the next three decades to serve a prosperous area that mixed manufacturing enterprise with some of the best farmland in Indiana.

In Anderson, the city that could accurately be described as the "buckle" of the Gas Belt, Henry found an outlet for his restlessness in the area's nascent electric railroads and through reengagement with Republican politics. A decade earlier, Henry had journeyed to Indianapolis to serve as a state senator (1880–81, 1883), and not long after he returned to Indiana from his life-changing hunting trip to Missouri, his neighbors elected the rising street railway entrepreneur to the US House of Representatives in 1894 and again in 1896. He remained closely involved with Anderson's electric railroads, and after he extended one streetcar line twelve miles beyond its city limits to the community of Alexandria, he is supposed to have dubbed his bold venture an "interurban." One must wonder what emotions Henry felt or what his former Pendleton neighbors thought of the hometown boy who made good when in early January 1901 his Union Traction trains rolled through town on the first of their frequent runs between Anderson and Indianapolis.[10]

For reasons never made clear, Henry abruptly severed his ties with Union Traction in late February 1901, a mere two months after Union Traction's triumphal entry into

This postcard image showcases the imposing building that Charles L. Henry had erected in downtown Anderson, one of his several enterprises apart from interurban railways. Union Traction's train dispatching center was on the sixth floor along with other company offices.

Indianapolis. No fanfare accompanied his departure, unlike when Kesley Schoepf left as head of the Pittsburgh trolley system to devote more time to his expanding interurban empire in Ohio and Indiana, an enterprise soon to become known as the "Schoepf-McGowan Syndicate." Schoepf was given a proper send-off at a huge banquet with a band playing "Hail to the Chief." Henry, by contrast, rated exactly two lines in an industry trade journal that noted in passing that he, his wife, and their several children were soon to sail for Europe. His interurban and real estate investments in the Gas Belt during the 1890s had made him a wealthy man by 1901, and with wealth came many new options, but it is also possible that Henry was uncertain about his future career moves when he left Union Traction. Curiously, he always deflected the subject whenever asked during the many interviews he willingly gave to the press. The only public reason Henry ever gave for his abrupt departure was that he was physically tired as a result of his intense devotion to Union Traction business and now wanted simply to enjoy more time with his family.[11]

Lengthy news features complete with full-page portraits typically saluted the leaders of the dynamic transit systems based in Boston, New York, Philadelphia, and Chicago—cities that defined the electric railway industry during the latter half of the nineteenth century. Philadelphia in 1897 was home to the world's largest transit system with a value of more than $100 million. From a national perspective, all Indiana interurban companies combined did not amount to much in 1901, compared with these giants of the industry. According to the latest federal census, the state of Indiana at the time had slightly more than 2.5 million residents, while Philadelphia claimed half as many. The Quaker City's several mass transit systems also served sizeable suburban communities in both Pennsylvania and New Jersey. By comparison, Indiana seemed like a backwater with nothing to offer those who oversaw the sprawling and heavily used metropolitan systems that often included both elevated and subway trains, neither of which ever appeared in Indiana. Not surprisingly, Hoosiers were not among the leaders of the American Street Railway Association during the two decades that followed its formation in 1882. In fact, only a handful of individuals from Indiana even bothered to attend its annual conferences during those twenty years.

At the time of Henry's 1901 retirement, no one in Indiana or elsewhere saluted him as the "father of the interurban," and he expressed no public regrets about leaving the industry he had done so much to pioneer. When he returned home to Indianapolis the following October, after his family's six-month sojourn abroad, no national trade publications took note of it. Henry was fifty-two, and it was anyone's guess what he intended to do, if anything, during the coming years.

Some observers in Indiana speculated that after a few months touring Europe and the Holy Land, Henry would re-enter the familiar political arena, perhaps to once again seek his former seat in Congress. Republicans were especially eager to see their popular, well-spoken, and always approachable "Charlie" Henry run for Congress again or for the US Senate should Charles Warren Fairbanks step aside before the 1904 election, as the Indiana senator had done when he agreed to join Theodore Roosevelt as his vice-presidential running mate. Or maybe Henry should run for governor.

If during his months of rest and reflection he remained undecided about a return to the political arena, he could always hedge his bets by purchasing a newspaper—and not just any newspaper. When Henry bought the *Indianapolis Journal* in 1903, the state's oldest newspaper still in business and the official voice of the Indiana Republican Party, he certainly lent credence to ongoing political speculation. In fact, it seemed clear that with his resignation from Union Traction in early 1901, the interurban phase of Henry's multifaceted career had reached its terminus.

Henry's immediate successor at the railway was Muncie businessman George McCulloch. Herein lies an intriguing interlude involving both Henry and McCulloch. When Henry left Union Traction, it was with a bundle of money. Most reports say one million dollars (and a few newspapers even claim ten million dollars), a real fortune in 1901 and especially in Indiana. The financial bonanza came mainly from McCulloch, who purchased Henry's investment in Union Traction. With his sudden wealth, Henry acquired a newspaper, erected the tallest and most imposing building in

Anderson, and became the largest shareholder in Anderson's recently opened Maplewood Cemetery.

When Henry acquired the *Indianapolis Journal*, his silent financial ally in the deal was rumored to be Charles Warren Fairbanks, Indiana senator and soon-to-be-elected vice president of the United States. However, shortly before this was to happen, the Republican Party's Indiana mouthpiece, the *Indianapolis Journal*, proved such a financial fizzle that Fairbanks apparently withdrew his money.

Henry's commitment to the venerable but now clearly languishing newspaper lasted about a year and might have drained his newly acquired fortune had not a financial angel come to his rescue in 1904 to purchase the publication, which he promptly folded into the *Indianapolis Star* he had founded the previous year. Indiana's would-be media mogul, now the owner of the "Star chain" of newspapers published in Indianapolis, Terre Haute, and Muncie, was none other than George McCulloch, Henry's former boss and immediate successor at Union Traction. When Henry left Union Traction, some journalists had speculated that it was the result of a monumental disagreement with McCulloch over the future direction of the interurban company, but the fact that McCulloch bailed Henry out two years later seems to undercut that claim.[12]

Even if Henry's journalism career ended abruptly, he was able to defy the common assertion that there are no second acts in life. During his several months of enforced rest abroad, he came to realize that he missed the excitement of building a new interurban line. So, in early 1902, at least a year before his disastrous detour into journalism, he quietly returned to the interurban industry, and it soon became clear that electric railways had become the true love of his lengthy business career. He remained devoted to the Indianapolis and Cincinnati Traction Company until the day he died in 1927. His faith in the industry was complete and unshakable, a form of financial myopia that caused him to ignore all signs of its decline during the 1920s and thereby greatly diminish his original fortune by investing heavily to renovate his beloved southern Indiana interurban line during a supposed industry comeback. It was only during Henry's second engagement with the industry that he gained widespread public acclaim as the "father of the interurban" and a generous measure of national prominence.

During his initial involvement with the interurban industry, he had remained focused on enterprise in Indiana, while during his second career, he became increasingly involved with regional and national trade organizations with which he served as president as well as numerous support roles. After he declined to seek reelection, he would sometimes visit former colleagues on the floor of the House of Representatives and be warmly welcomed. For good reason, Henry was for several years the industry's top representative on Capitol Hill, where his formal training as a lawyer and four years of experience as a congressman enabled him to skillfully navigate the murky halls of power.

Not long after Henry returned home to Indianapolis from his 1901 trip abroad, a group of Hoosier businessmen intent on building an interurban between Indianapolis and Cincinnati sought his help. Adding to the challenge were two other projects proposing to do the same thing. Henry soon outmaneuvered the would-be competitors and folded these potential rivals into his Indianapolis and Cincinnati Traction Company. Exactly how Henry intended to use this modest new interurban property—exceedingly modest when compared to Union Traction—to engineer a career comeback was anyone's guess. But come back he did in spectacular fashion.[13]

In contrast to his former restlessness, Henry made this enterprise the focus of the next twenty-three years of his life. From a personal office in Hugh McGowan's Traction Terminal tower, he had only to walk a few feet to the adjacent train shed to be inspired by the sights and sounds of hundreds of interurban cars arriving and departing each day. From his office in Indianapolis and company headquarters in Rushville, he addressed his interurban's many financial challenges, and never once did he depart from his dogged determination (his obsession, some labeled it) to extend a set of double tracks across rural Indiana to Cincinnati. Not only that, but Henry also intended to build on his experience gained at Union Traction to create an interurban that could run high-speed trains across the breadth of Indiana to link Indianapolis with *both* Cincinnati and Chicago. He would do so with the finest interurban rolling-stock made in America, the handiwork of the St. Louis Car Company, an enterprise that Henry admired for its exquisite craftsmanship.[14]

Henry's successor at Union Traction, George McCulloch, did not remain at the interurban's helm for very long. One reason for his abrupt department was no doubt the untimely death of his wife from breast cancer. Another was that his newspaper ventures were not going well. Finally, the Muncie businessman seems to have harbored a desire to become a big-time financier like his Philadelphia associate, Randal Morgan. McCulloch resigned from Union Traction management in 1904 in favor of his brother-in-law, Arthur Brady, who guided the company for the next three decades.[15]

McCulloch left Indiana abruptly and relocated to New Jersey where he positioned himself much closer to the levers of big-time financial power and a nationwide web of financial connections that extended outward from New York's Wall Street and the Philadelphia-based United Gas Improvement Company. The gas trust was the principal conduit Randal Morgan and his associates used to finance Indiana interurbans.

Natural gas never furnished onboard power for Indiana interurban cars in a literal sense. It did, however, serve to open the money pipeline that linked several central Indiana interurban companies with their Philadelphia financiers. During the twenty-three years Charles L. Henry presided over the ups and downs of the Indianapolis and Cincinnati Traction Company, his principal backers were nearly all Hoosiers, and he bragged publicly of that fact. But they lacked the deep pockets of the Philadelphians. As a result, Henry's interurban, despite its grand intentions, ran short of money on at least two occasions and ended up in receivership, just one step short of bankruptcy. The company's first bout of insolvency occurred in 1906 shortly before Indiana's best-built interurban finished laying tracks to Connersville. In desperate need of funds to pay for an extension that would place them one step closer to Cincinnati, the company directors headed to court to ask for a receiver "so that money might be raised on the original bonds." When Henry, now the court-appointed receiver, sought to raise money from outside Indiana, he conspicuously avoided the Philadelphians in favor of Wall Street capitalists.[16]

A line drawing of George F. McCulloch, the Muncie-based interurban and newspaper baron and occasional Republican Party kingmaker in Indiana.

Arthur W. Brady was in many ways Henry's capable understudy. Both names frequently appeared together in news stories and feature articles about the interurban industry. Both Henry and Brady had central Indiana roots, both were uncommonly well educated for their time, and both emerged as nationally recognized luminaries of the interurban industry during the first three decades of the twentieth century. This remarkable duo functioned as a team of co-equals even after Henry died in early May 1927—Brady served as a pallbearer and even arranged for a special Union Traction business car to take Henry's body to its final resting place in Anderson's Maplewood Cemetery. For a quarter of a century, from the interurban's rapid rise to its subsequent demise, the two men supported one another as if they were blood brothers.

Brady and Henry likely met in February 1901 at the annual meeting of the Indiana State Board of Commerce in Indianapolis. They may have rubbed shoulders at the

Arthur Brady was elected mayor of Muncie in the early 1890s, the youngest in the city's history, before serving as Union Traction's attorney and then its president from 1904 to 1930.

Commercial Club gathering when Brady presented a report on his passion at the time, municipal charter legislation, and Henry later agreed to speak extemporaneously on his current passion, "interurban electric railways." Because the carriers were still quite a curiosity, he began a presentation that one reporter called "entertaining as well as instructive" by explaining the difference between suburban and interurban electric railroads. It is impossible to say whether Brady was among the audience members entertained and instructed by former Congressman Henry's little stump speech. At that time, Henry was still the general superintendent of Union Traction, and Muncie's ex-mayor Brady had no idea that in three years he would be running the company or that he might profit from Henry's experience.[17]

Brady was born in Muncie in 1865, and apart from time spent earning a bachelor's degree at Yale University and a law degree at The University of Michigan, from which he graduated in 1889, he maintained lifelong ties to Muncie. He joined Union Traction in 1902 as its general counsel, and he became president of the interurban company two years later, a position he held for nearly thirty years. He sold the railway to Midland Utilities in the mid-1930s, and the interurban subsequently formed a cornerstone of Samuel Insull's emerging Indiana Railroad edifice. In the early 1890s, the personable young lawyer was elected mayor of Muncie, the youngest in the city's history, but whereas Henry was a staunch Republican, Brady was a loyal Democrat.[18]

Obviously, the interurban's promise of prosperity and modernity to all who embraced the young industry transcended political labels. Partisan politics made little difference to these two men because when it came to their beloved interurbans, they functioned as a single nonpartisan team. When, for example, Brady served as president of the American Electric Railway Association (1910–11), he appointed Henry to important committees and made certain that in addition to his presidential address opening the organization's 1911 convention in Atlantic City, his fellow Hoosier would follow later in the week with a talk called "The Interurban."

One highlight of the 1911 conference was to have been a presentation by a rising industry star, William G. McAdoo, on his recent and much-celebrated feat of railway engineering that connected Newark and Hoboken, New Jersey, with New York's Lower Manhattan via tunnels laid beneath the Hudson River. Some sort of last-minute conflict prevented McAdoo from speaking to the large gathering of eager listeners. What Brady did next was entirely predictable: without a moment's hesitation, he asked Henry to move his talk on "The Interurban" to the prime-time evening slot vacated by McAdoo. The change of plans provided Henry maximum exposure to the organization's several hundred members. It is probably not coincidental that only two days later, the nominating committee selected him as the organization's fourth vice president, a plum assignment that would serve as a stepping stone for another Hoosier president of the American Electric Railway Association four years later.[19]

Brady almost certainly had a hand in Henry's nomination. The *Indianapolis News* was sufficiently impressed by the Hoosier team that it saluted both Brady and Henry in a story headlined "Indiana Fares Well." With a generous measure of hometown pride, the *News* specifically took note of the fact that "many other states had not yet received recognition in the distribution of offices." Likewise, during his term as president of the American Electric Railway Association (1915–16), Henry made certain to involve Brady in special ways. The dynamic duo operated in much the same reciprocal way during their two decades of involvement in the Central Electric Railway Association. Because trade journals published news of its frequent meetings and reprinted members' groundbreaking technical presentations, many an up-and-coming Hoosier was in this way catapulted to national prominence.[20]

When Governor Thomas Riley Marshall wanted to know the reason for a series of horrific interurban crashes that took place in Indiana and also in neighboring Illinois during the fall of 1910, he summoned Henry, Brady, and other industry executives to Indianapolis. They discussed what safety measures could be implemented to silence a rising chorus of criticism, with the most extreme voices calling for the interurban industry to shut down because of its supposedly dangerous methods of operation. The statehouse gathering was cordial, no doubt because Marshall and Brady were both moderate Democrats, and the Indiana governor and future vice president of the United States was known for his homespun and self-deprecating sense of humor in the style of Abraham Lincoln, on whose lap he had once sat as a boy.[21]

Among the most significant of Indiana's interurban pioneers were two other families, the Irwins of Columbus and the Murdocks of Lafayette, both having acquired the money needed to launch electric railways by investing initially in one or more of the Gas Belt's many wealth-generating enterprises. Moreover, in both of these families, the father successfully transmitted his interest in electric railways to the next generation.

After industrialist Joseph Ireland Irwin (1824–1910) and his dutiful son William Glanton Irwin (1866–1943) sold their successful venture in the Gas Belt's booming tinplate industry in 1898, they reinvested the family money in the Indianapolis, Greenwood and Franklin interurban line, an electric railway its original promoters had incorporated in 1894 but failed to push much beyond the status of a paper enterprise. The Irwins bought the moribund company in June 1899, and little more than six months later, they ran an interurban car into Indianapolis. They thus achieved a historic first among the capital city's dozen interurban lines. In another year, they had completed tracks to Franklin, and after changing the name to the Indianapolis, Columbus and Southern, they announced their intention to extend the electric railway to their home base of Columbus, which they reached on their quest to run tracks ever farther south.[22]

The Irwins seemed to earn a profit with each mile of track they added. They reached Seymour, fifty-seven miles from Indianapolis, in 1907, but here they met the northbound tracks of a separate company, the Indianapolis and Louisville. It made good sense for the two independent companies to operate a through interurban route rather than for the Irwins to continue a competing line south another fifty miles into Louisville. The interurban companies of Indiana rarely ran their tracks parallel to one another, although they did not hesitate to parallel the steam railroads already in operation. So, until construction of a north-south highway, the main competition for traffic between the two largest population centers in Indiana and Kentucky came from the Pennsylvania Railroad.[23]

Joseph Irwin died in 1910, but Will remained involved with the interurban in various ways until the company ran its last car in September 1941—or, more accurately, when its remaining interurban car crashed head-on into a work car near Seymour to bring an abrupt end to the Interurban Era in Indiana (apart from the ongoing South Shore Line). The Irwins' interurban enterprise, while historically significant, served as but a prelude to the globe-girdling business known today as Cummins, Inc. This multifaceted enterprise was founded in 1919 and is now perhaps most widely recognized for its diesel engines that power numerous semitrucks along the roadways of North America. Will died in 1943, but the Irwin family legacy is still on display in Columbus, Indiana, which gained widespread fame through numerous world-class architectural wonders funded by the heirs of Joseph and Will Irwin.

While the Irwins focused narrowly on the interurban lines serving just one part of Indiana, the Murdock family took the opposite approach by acquiring interurban and trolley properties scattered literally from one end of the state to the other. In a quiet way, Irish-born Lafayette businessman James Murdock (1837–1908) amassed one of the most impressive financial empires in Indiana. A self-made man, he was elected sheriff of Tippecanoe County, an office in law enforcement that functioned as a useful stepping stone to his twelve-year career as warden of the Indiana State Prison in Michigan City. During the natural gas boom of the late 1880s, he seized an investment opportunity that would forever change the course of his life. Murdock built his initial fortune by acquiring natural gas properties across the Indiana Gas Belt.

Like George McCulloch in Muncie, Joseph I. Irwin became a leading businessman of Columbus, Indiana. Both entrepreneurs enjoyed prosperity because of their early Gas Belt investments.

His "Midas touch" included a Lafayette bank that he and several others organized. During the 1890s, he grasped yet another alluring investment prospect in the new technology of electric railways, and through a series of winning bets placed on Indiana trolley and interurban properties, he further enlarged his family's fortune.[24]

Wisely, Murdock kept his holdings outside the orbit of the powerful Schoepf-McGowan Syndicate that dominated central and northeast Indiana lines and concentrated instead on electric railways located mainly along the state's periphery, notably in Richmond, South Bend, and Evansville. He nonetheless respected Hugh McGowan, a fellow Irish Catholic, and did not hesitate to invest in his several Indiana properties or to serve on their boards of directors. Unlike McGowan, Murdock never combined his scattered trolley and interurban properties into one large system as exemplified by McGowan's brainchild, the Terre Haute, Indianapolis and Eastern. As Murdock's electric railway holdings multiplied, Indiana newspapers frequently referred to the "Murdock Syndicate."

When the elder Murdock died suddenly in 1908 of heart failure, his two sons, Samuel T. and Charles Michael, continued to operate the family's business empire for several more years until both brothers died during the 1920s. Among the largest of the Murdock electric utility and interurban properties was the Chicago, South Bend

An interurban car of the Chicago, South Bend and Northern Indiana pauses at the depot in Michigan City. This property was part of the electric railway portfolio of James Murdock, who, with a touch of irony, perhaps, got his start as the warden of the Indiana state penitentiary in Michigan City before he, too, benefited from Gas Belt investments.

and Northern Indiana Railway, which the Murdock family began operating on January 1, 1907.[25]

The generation of interurban pioneers profiled in this chapter excelled at launching new projects at a time when the industry was still evolving from its street railway origins. They made mistakes, as Charles L. Henry readily admitted in his public talks, because they had little precedence to guide them. Over time, the builders learned to be good managers of their respective interurban properties. The next step was for an organizer of grand vision to show the industry how several small and locally focused companies might work together to create an Indiana interurban network—and, ultimately, a Midwestern network, That contribution would be yet another product of Hugh McGowan's nonstop mind.

McGowan saw the advantage of combining several scattered and locally focused interurban lines to create a geographically imposing network centered in the Traction Terminal he erected in downtown Indianapolis. He confidently expected his terminal to serve as a hub not just for electric railway tracks already in place in 1904 but also for hundreds of additional miles he expected to see constructed during coming decades.

6

Hugh McGowan, Interurban Empire Builder

> Hugh McGowan had a genius for organization, for management, for seeing straight into the heart of things.
>
> —*Kansas City Star*, December 20, 1911

On August 3, 1907, "Jumbo" died. The landmark news, essentially an obituary for Indiana's once-fabulous Gas Belt, made front-page headlines. "The last chapter in the life of 'Jumbo,' the strongest gas well ever located in the Indiana natural gas field is being written and within a few hours the final curtain will have fallen." At the time of its discovery, its flames flared for six weeks, and local lore claimed that because of the continual illumination, the chickens never went to roost. "Excursions were run daily to Fairmount from all parts of Indiana, as well as other states." Sightseers were dutifully impressed—as were investors.[1]

Cheap fuel propelled the rise of an impressive array of new enterprises across the Gas Belt, including the National Tinplate Company, which erected a big mill in Anderson in 1894. Here was the source of the investment capital that enabled Joseph and Will Irwin to purchase their first interurban in 1899. Another National Tinplate investor was Philip Matter of Marion, who lent Charles L. Henry the initial $100,000 he needed to launch the Union Traction Company of Indiana. When George McCulloch sought to force the local trolley company and Indianapolis politicians to allow Union Traction trains to access the center of the city, he boasted that Union Traction was "ready to dump the gas belt of Indiana upon Washington Street," the city's main east-west thoroughfare. By promising Indianapolis an opportunity to benefit from the state's greatest economic engine, he cleverly steamrollered opponents who tried to block his heavy Union Traction cars from using local trolley tracks. So important was interurban access to downtown Indianapolis that one local newspaper served public notice on local politicians who appeared to be angling for personal gain in exchange for the required franchise, that "there should be no playing of peanut politics or display of

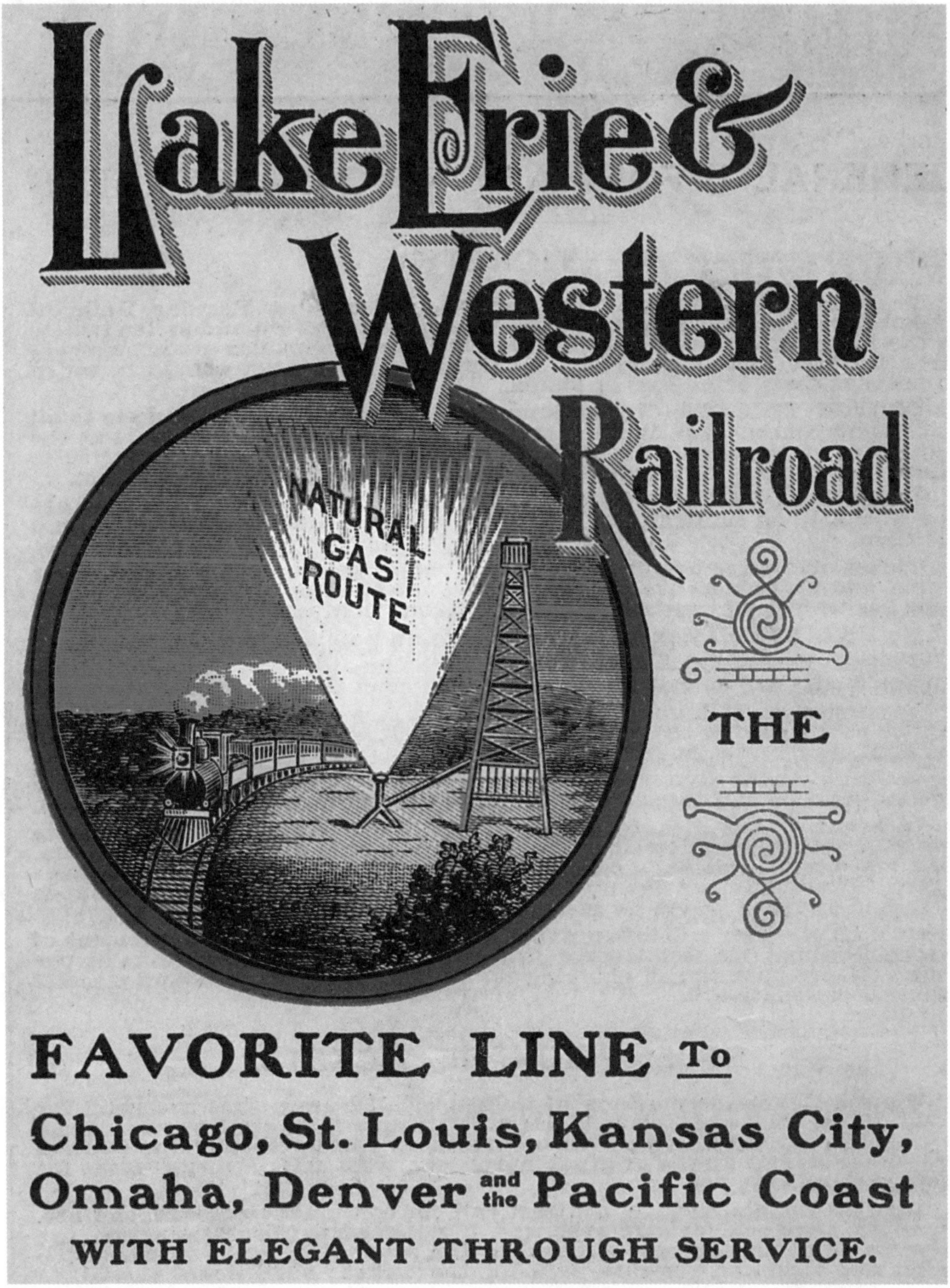

The Lake Erie and Western, a hardscrabble steam railroad that crossed northern Indiana, used the front cover of its public timetables to salute the Gas Belt.

small demagoguery. Indianapolis needs the interurban traffic; therefore, encourage the interurban lines."[2]

It took most of 1901 to resolve the impasse that required Union Traction passengers to connect at the city limits with local trolley cars. One stumbling block was that politicians and bureaucrats who held absolute power over franchise matters found it difficult to distinguish between the needs of urban trolleys and the city's interurban newcomers. Union Traction had reached the outskirts of Indianapolis in early January, but eight months later, it still lacked the franchise required for intercity cars to proceed to a downtown terminal. The same was true for cars of the Greenwood and Greenfield lines. Coming or going, early interurban travelers had to use local streetcars to initiate or conclude their journeys. McCulloch, the new boss of Union Traction, was clearly frustrated when in October 1901 he complained to regulators that the "three companies which have been foolish enough to build their roads are at your mercy." The Muncie entrepreneur insisted that Union Traction "would not have built to Indianapolis had we known there would have been such a delay and controversy in getting a franchise." In the end, the city's desire to attract additional interurban lines prevailed over its initial display of bureaucratic intransigence, and McCulloch was able to infuse downtown Indianapolis with Gas Belt prosperity.[3]

The franchise imbroglio dragged on for two years and was finally resolved in the summer of 1902. As a result, Hugh McGowan committed to building the freight and passenger facility that opened in September 1904 as the Traction Terminal, a union depot for ten interurban lines then serving the capital city and the many more lines expected during the years to come. Each company agreed to pay the Indianapolis Traction and Terminal Company four cents per car entering the city for the next eleven years with the rate rising slightly at fixed intervals during the following two decades. The city would receive one cent for each car during the thirty-year life of the franchise and would retain the right to severely limit freight traffic along its streets. One additional provision granted the local streetcar company the right to build a double-track beltway around the perimeter of the central city to remove interurbans from congested streets and speed up their running times in Indianapolis. This, however, was never fulfilled, which was unfortunate because it could have addressed a multitude of problems unforeseen in 1902. Later, as private automobiles clogged arterial corridors, an interurban car could spend more time fighting city traffic than completing its run through the Hoosier countryside to reach a destination a few dozen miles away.[4]

In the years following 1902, interurban railways serving Indianapolis did multiply, as McCulloch claimed they would once the franchise impasse was unsnarled and the rapidly expanding network of tracks gave the city an ever-growing trade area. Both the Hoosier metropolis and its hinterland prospered, as did the electric railways and their many investors. However, in 1907, the natural gas that transformed the Gas Belt into a money-making machine flickered to a finish.[5]

The year 1907 proved to be a watershed for other reasons as well. During the previous year, thirty-two electric railways were operating in Indiana, with many more miles under construction. "Today, when the announcement is made that a new interurban is to be built, all the towns along the proposed route manifest the keenest sort of enthusiasm. For them it means more business, more business, more money." With its repetition of the words "more business," the *Indianapolis Star* was no doubt trying to underscore the prosperity that followed almost magically with the coming of a new interurban railway. "The liberal use of paint is usually the first sign that the interurban is having an effect on the pride of the people. The owner of a little home along the traction line finds that hundreds of people are being carried past his place every day. Instinctively almost this fact awakens in him a desire to show off his place to the best advantage. He paints the house and the barn, then he builds a new fence, tears down or moves far to the rear some of the unsightly little outhouses on the place." The Interurban Era in mid-1907 was synonymous with "hustle and bustle and prosperity everywhere."[6]

During the first two-thirds of 1907, the interurban boom times roared ahead as they had for the past decade, and most industry observers saw no sign of the financial storm just over the horizon. That March, for example, Hugh McGowan presided over the greatest electric railway combination in Indiana history before the creation of the Indiana Railroad in 1930. He publicly boasted that his imposing financial edifice, the Terre Haute, Indianapolis and Eastern, was but a stepping stone toward his ultimate goal of forging an interurban line that reached west all the way to Saint Louis. Working with his Ohio counterpart, Kesley Schoepf, he envisioned continuing east to Pittsburgh, with sleeping cars traveling overnight across the Midwest to offer a luxury class of service between those two great cities. As with the Traction Terminal complex he opened in Indianapolis in 1904, McGowan continued to loathe small plans.

McGowan, Indiana's newest interurban empire builder, regularly grabbed newspaper headlines across the state in 1907, while the first generation of interurban pioneers seemed quietly content to run the electric railway companies they already had in place. Charles Henry's bold plan to build the nation's most technologically advanced interurban showpiece through the hills of southern Indiana and into Cincinnati was temporarily put on hold in 1907 while, as the court-appointed receiver, he struggled to reconcile his grand ambitions with his company's embarrassing financial shortfall. In the state's former Gas Belt, Arthur Brady seemed pleased to preside over the well-oiled machine called Union Traction, the interurban version of a fine Swiss watch.

Other, lesser entrepreneurs, and a few clever swindlers, continued to announce bold new projects. Perhaps some of the better-funded and wholly honest endeavors would have successfully enlarged Indiana's network of electric railways if not for the Panic of 1907. The investment capital required to build new lines dried up, at least temporarily, and so many grand proposals fizzled that in the coming years, the terms "promoter" and "paper interurban" became synonymous with deceit. Hugh McGowan, however, attained the status of Indiana folk hero because he still got things done and usually did so in a grand manner that impressed the skeptics. The *Indianapolis Sun* issued a public confession in early 1903: "We, here in Indianapolis have considered Mr. McGowan simply as the chief officer of a soulless corporation. As such we have damned him and convinced ourselves that we were happy in doing so." This was the typical newspaper response to traction magnates across the United States at that time. McGowan came to Indianapolis in 1899 as an outsider and was initially viewed as little more than a puppet of Philadelphia finance. His tireless boosting of Indianapolis and numerous contributions of money and time to a variety of local charities turned that negative perception on its head. "Hugh McGowan is not the sordid, grasping, greedy corporationist he has been pictured," emphasized the *Sun* in its reassessment.[7]

This formal portrait of Hugh McGowan makes a not-so-subtle statement about the physical and intellectual prowess of Indiana's "big man" of electric railways.

In an *Indianapolis Star* interview published in 1906, the reporter noted that during his brief visit with McGowan in his office high atop the Traction Terminal Building, "several men of prominence were waiting in the adjacent room" to talk with Indiana's "Traction King." One secret of the former Missouri farm boy's astounding rags-to-riches success, McGowan confessed, was that "a man must be interested in his work to enjoy it. You don't have to put this down, but I work from fifteen to eighteen hours a day." The interviewer described his subject as "a short, sturdy man," who looked remarkably healthy and "showed no sign of fatigue on his face" despite his punishing hours of work. However, hidden from view—and its seriousness perhaps not even fully recognized by McGowan himself—was his family predisposition to heart failure. The heavy workload did take its toll.[8]

Buried among the numerous and often lengthy news stories devoted to McGowan, his interurban projects, and his public-spirited activity, however, were occasional brief mentions of some sort of ongoing health problem. The *Richmond Item*, which had been among McGowan's most acerbic foes, ran a news brief in 1908 under the headline "Hugh J. McGowan Very Sick." The story noted that McGowan "will leave soon for a European trip. He will spend most of his time in Germany and be away three months." In an age before medicine provided quick relief from stress and anxiety, it was not unusual for harried executives to take weeks away from the office for a period of rest or to pay an extended visit to a hot spring or sanitarium in search of relief from various forms of ill health caused by overwork. News accounts of McGowan's occasional bouts of ill health did not seem particularly worrisome except possibly to his Philadelphia patron, Randal Morgan, who was heavily dependent on his Midwestern wunderkind.[9]

In almost every way, Morgan and McGowan were polar opposites, and yet their unusual relationship formed the keystone of Indiana's interurban edifice. By working together, the moneyed patrician from high-society Philadelphia and the self-made man from the prairies of western Missouri achieved a synergy of purpose that defies easy explanation. So, who were these two individuals, and how did Morgan's capital enable McGowan to become an Indiana empire builder?

McGowan was a Missouri farm boy who hated the farm. In 1875, a grasshopper plague of biblical proportions, one of many that occasionally cursed the homesteads of Kansas and western Missouri, prompted him to walk abruptly away from the family farm near Liberty, a community north of Kansas City. The cloud of hungry grasshoppers descended on a warm summer day as young Hugh worked with his father to plow weeds growing among the rows of corn. It took just moments for the ravenous insects to eat their fill and leave the McGowan field bare of every blade of green. The younger man quietly unhitched his team of horses and started to walk away.

> "What are you going to do?" his father asked.
>
> "Quit farming," replied his son. With just $4.75 in his pocket he headed south to Kansas City.[10]

In Missouri's young and booming western metropolis, he landed one of the dirtiest jobs imaginable: he labored under steam locomotives of the Wabash Railroad to rake hot ashes from their fireboxes and then wipe clean the sooty iron horses to prepare them for their next runs. Experience gained working with live horses on the McGowan family farm soon landed him a slightly better job at a Kansas City street railway. His personal introduction to the industry that later made him a fortune began literally at the bottom as a stable boy hired to groom the mules. Soon he was driving a pair of mules and an attached car along street railway tracks through Kansas City. During the coming years, McGowan bootstrapped his way to success by working a succession of jobs, seventeen- and eighteen-hour days, if necessary. He worked for six years as a Kansas City policeman, a job for which his strong build and outgoing personality served him well.

Unlike Henry or Brady, McGowan never had the opportunity to study at a world-class university, although in his relentless climb upward, he did come to see that education could open doors for him, so he pursued a two-year course at a business college in Kansas City. He was also a keen student of the world around him, which included marrying well and finding a patron with money to support his business ventures. McGowan, in short, had an uncanny ability to connect with the right people, who saw him as a man of ideas with the ability to deliver results.

McGowan's most important patron was Randal Morgan, the Philadelphia blueblood whose primary interest was the gas industry. He also had plenty of money to invest in another utility: the emergent electric railways of the Midwest. Morgan preferred to operate in the shadows, but his name appeared frequently as a director or officer of interurban lines in Indiana and Ohio, and he probably provided McGowan much of the money needed to erect the million-dollar Traction Terminal in Indianapolis.

McGowan, who was handsome and possessed a generous measure of Irish charm (and good luck), had first impressed Morgan in Kansas City. It was Morgan and his fellow Philadelphia venture capitalists who dispatched their fair-haired boy to Indianapolis in early 1899 to remedy the all-around mess that was the city's street railway company. Former executives of the traction company were at loggerheads both with their workers and with city officials over the politicians' heavy-handed attempt to cap streetcar fares at three cents a ride. McGowan, a master at cultivating good relations with others, soon proved he was the right man for the job and was able to set the company on a positive course. He charmed city officials, employees, and investors alike.

When McGowan relocated to Indianapolis in 1899, he confided to a Kansas City friend that he felt a premonition of sudden death. His fear was well founded: his father had died several years earlier when he fell from a farm wagon, and a fatal heart attack felled his mother only months before Philadelphia patrons sent her son to rescue their traction investments in Indiana. Perhaps fear of sudden death is what drove him to work long hours while still in his thirties and forties.[11]

As part of his punishing schedule, he commuted regularly by train between Indianapolis and Kansas City to oversee a variety of enterprises in both places. On October 31, 1904, as the crush of the Saint Louis World's Fair passenger traffic pushed the region's steam railroads to their limits and beyond, his Missouri Pacific train to Kansas City was rear-ended by a closely following second section when the headlight beam from an oncoming train temporarily blinded its engineer, or so he later claimed. McGowan escaped without a scratch from his drawing room in the nearly demolished Pullman car, but three other passengers died and twenty-one suffered serious injuries. His time had not yet come.[12]

Until his untimely death in his early fifties from a heart attack in late December 1911, McGowan was the Philadelphia investors' trusted front man in Indiana. Though he became one of the wealthiest citizens of Indianapolis, his good fortune remained untainted by the stench of corruption, unlike that of Charles Yerkes of Chicago. Even as he increased in wealth and gained fame across the Midwest, McGowan never forgot his humble roots. He remained approachable and generous both to his employees and to the many local charities he supported. Even during the so-called Progressive Era when an ever-relentless cohort of muckrakers delighted in demonizing street railway executives like Yerkes, McGowan remained a much-beloved figure, the embodiment of the American dream of success.

The natural gas connection led Randal Morgan to Hugh McGowan in Kansas City, and it was a primary reason why McGowan relocated to Indianapolis in 1899 to save the Philadelphians' investment in the city's street railways. The same group of Quaker City capitalists provided the money to extend interurban lines across the Gas Belt, and they helped to finance McGowan's Traction Terminal complex and his 1907 creation of the Terre Haute, Indianapolis and Eastern. McGowan's Ohio partner, Kesley Schoepf, invited Morgan's son, Marshall, to move to Cincinnati for three months of personal tutoring in all things related to electric railways by one of the acknowledged masters of the profession. Once again, the United Gas Improvement Company served as a convenient conduit through which Philadelphia financiers channeled their money *and their increasing influence* into the heartland.

Hoosiers initially welcomed the outside money needed to build their electric railways. As time went on, however, the East Coast capitalists grew bolder. Trusts had been outlawed by 1904, but that did nothing to prevent a group of clever industry insiders from creating a holding company that same year called Indiana Union Traction to manage its several electric railway operating companies, including Union Traction of Indiana. Some Hoosier investors grew convinced that this and other complex financial schemes enriched the Philadelphians but left locals feeling shorn of their investments.

The result was rising resentment within Indiana, increasingly negative newspaper publicity, and pushback in the form of lawsuits.

Turn-of-the-century Indiana prided itself on its unpretentious lifestyle. Of course, the state had its rich families, even snobby ones such as those that Hoosier author Booth Tarkington immortalized in his 1918 novel *The Magnificent Ambersons*. But Randal Morgan and his colleagues represented a level of wealth, social sophistication, and influential connections unknown in Indiana. The Morgan mansion in upscale Chestnut Hill was among the finest in Philadelphia, and the Morgans were fully the equals of the Biddles, Stotesburys, and others among the Quaker City's first families. In Philadelphia, Edward T. Stotesbury functioned as the right-hand man of New York financial titan John Pierpont Morgan. Indiana journalists would on occasion confuse the two Morgans, who may have been cousins. It was rumored during the Panic of 1907 that the two financiers consulted together in New York on how to tame the financial whirlwind.[13]

In any case, when the Philadelphia Morgans wanted to inspect their far-flung investments or to socialize with their super-wealthy peers in Palm Beach, they traveled to Florida in style aboard their private railway car or their sea-going yacht, the *Waturus*. Morgan had purchased his steam-powered maritime palace from an archduke of the Hapsburg Empire, and it was among his most ostentatious possessions. On one notable occasion that he immortalized in a privately printed book given to each of his guests as a souvenir, he used his capacious yacht to carry wealthy associates across the Atlantic for a Grand Tour of Europe.[14]

As was often typical of a person of old-money wealth, Morgan remained comfortably positioned as a vice president of the United Gas Improvement Company, a Philadelphia-based utility holding company, but he typically left the demanding job of president to others while he dealt with investment matters, both the company's and his own. As the years passed, Morgan began to treat local investors in the many Indiana interurban properties he controlled as "Hoosier Hicks," a term the Philadelphian did not use, but one I occasionally heard voiced in Indiana to push back against an outsider who held the state and its residents in low esteem.

As resentment built, a group of angry Hoosiers determined to oust the Philadelphia grandee in favor of local control. In one acerbic account of the lengthy legal fight, the *Indianapolis News* in 1913 went so far as to label members of the Indiana opposition as "suckers" and referred to the city's street railway as a "cow" to be milked by the "Randal Morgan crowd."[15]

In future years, Indiana newspapers would praise Charles L. Henry for his refusal to engage in any funny money schemes at the expense of his Hoosier investors. Earlier, as a congressman from Indiana, his honesty had endeared him to Republicans and

Kesley Schoepf (pictured) in Ohio and Hugh McGowan in Indiana made a formidable team popularly known as the Schoepf-McGowan Syndicate. Neither man was as closely allied with their Illinois counterpart, William B. McKinley.

earned grudging respect from many Democrats as well. The public record strongly hints, but never explicitly confirms, that Henry abruptly departed Union Traction in 1901 because he resented the growing intrusion of the "Randal Morgan crowd."[16]

During an after-dinner talk Henry gave in 1906, he offered a subtle clue to his thinking during his earlier career transition. Union Traction in its formative years was clearly the embodiment of Henry's dreams and the focus of his midlife energy, but he never really could be said to have owned it. He essentially managed the budding enterprise for moneyed individuals (venture capitalists in today's terms) like Randal Morgan, who was in turn allied with Kesley Schoepf of Cincinnati and Hugh McGowan of Indianapolis. Their cozy investment alliance was frequently referred to as the "Schoepf-Morgan-McGowan Syndicate" or simply the "Schoepf-McGowan Syndicate." Henry rotated among a variety of job titles during his years at Union Traction, but his name was never added to the financial syndicate that provided the money he needed to grow the interurban line.

Unlike the close working relationship Henry maintained for a quarter of a century with Arthur W. Brady, there is nothing to suggest that he developed a similarly close relationship with Hugh McGowan or with his dutiful cousin Joseph McGowan, who embodied the family connections at the Terre Haute, Indianapolis and Eastern. But neither is there anything to suggest that Henry and the McGowans or his Union Traction boss, George F. McCulloch, were hostile to one another.

During his 1906 after-dinner talk, Henry felt comfortable enough in the presence of his fellow industry executives to open up for the first time publicly about how he became an interurban pioneer and even to drop a few tantalizing clues about why he quit Union Traction. "Much has been said about outside capital, and much credit is due to outside capital in the development of our state, but I take pleasure in calling attention to the fact that Indiana men first loaned Indiana money to commence the development of Indiana interurban railroads." It should be noted that the interurban Henry headed at the time of his talk, the Indianapolis and Cincinnati Traction Company, had a board of directors composed of four men from Indianapolis, one each from Greenfield, Rushville, and Muncie, and not a single Philadelphian or anyone else from outside Indiana.[17]

Henry was determined to avoid entanglement with Philadelphia finance. Underscoring this was his proposal to build his interurban line with local money and use it to connect two large terminal cities in which streetcar systems were controlled by Hugh McGowan in Indianapolis and Kesley Schoepf in Cincinnati, with both men beholden to Randal Morgan. Adding Henry's interurban connection would have been a logical next move for the acquisitive Schoepf-McGowan Syndicate, and, together with Morgan, they could have found the money to complete the project in a matter of months. Henry, by contrast, waged a two-decade struggle to open the local money spigot to fund the interurban link across southeastern Indiana that he and fellow Hoosiers had launched.

The first annual meeting of the recently formed Indiana Electric Railway Association took place in Indianapolis in January 1906. Arthur Brady conducted the business portion of the gathering, then introduced the banquet speaker, Charles Henry, who used the occasion to give his most complete public account of how he came to launch Indiana's first large interurban railway. During his after-dinner talk, he also embraced fully and publicly for the first time the assertion that he had coined the word "interurban." Yet, if Henry was henceforth referred to as the "father of the interurban" at numerous public events, his 1906 after-dinner recounting of how he launched the Union Traction Company made clear that the Indiana industry's "godfather" was Philadelphian Randal Morgan.

For Henry's first twelve-mile line between Anderson and Alexandria, he relied entirely on Indiana investors, and he was proud of that fact. But as Henry's plans grew ever more ambitious and hence more expensive, Hugh McGowan introduced him to Randal Morgan, his own Philadelphia financier. Few Americans understood the gas industry better than Morgan, and the fact that Henry's interurban proposed to link cities of the Indiana Gas Belt with Indianapolis no doubt encouraged Morgan to open his purse.

Morgan proved helpful to Henry as he sought to combine several streetcar lines and a pint-sized interurban to create the much more imposing Union Traction Company of Indiana, which, probably because of the Morgan connection, bore the same name as the Union Traction Company of Philadelphia. (The same name appeared in Chicago, incidentally, where it was used for the traction holdings the Philadelphia financiers purchased from Charles Yerkes.). In terms of his formal job title, Henry never served as president of the interurban company he did so much to create. He was its general manager and held a seat on its board of directors, but others held the more impressive titles. Similarly, when he left Union Traction to create the Indianapolis and Cincinnati Traction Company, he served first as its general manager but soon became the interurban company's long-time president. Clearly, the big East Coast investors were calling the shots at Union Traction, and Henry, like Hugh McGowan, had profited handsomely from the good work he did for them.

Though Henry never publicly stated his reason for leaving the enterprise he had founded or for joining a far less impressive enterprise, the primary lure of a leadership position at the Indianapolis and Cincinnati Traction Company may have been that he did not have Morgan and other East Coast financiers looking over his shoulders as he built and managed the new interurban enterprise. Nor would he remain the outsider among a family clan that included Henry's former boss, McCulloch; Muncie's hardest-charging entrepreneur and now president of Union Traction, McCulloch's successor and brother-in-law, Arthur Brady; and the powerful Ball family into which Brady's sister had married.[18]

McGowan's death while still in his early fifties raises the question of what else might have happened had he lived as long as Charles Henry into his seventies or Arthur Brady into his late sixties. Both Henry and Brady did not achieve prominence as interurban pioneers until their forties. McGowan exited the stage of history in 1911, James Murdock did so in 1908, and Joseph Irwin in 1910. Succeeding these three, all of them having achieved a measure of fame as pioneer interurban builders, was the following generation best described as managers of the properties their fathers had built: Will Irwin and Samuel and Charles Murdock.

Perhaps most prominent among the managerial generation was Harry Reid, an innovative thinker much needed by the interurban industry during the 1920s to respond to the rising tide of highway competition. Reid defied the industry's initially negative opinion of bus and truck lines by embracing both new modes of transportation and used Indiana's public highways to funnel passenger and freight traffic onto the trains of the Interstate Public Service Company. In this way, he became a prominent and outspoken innovator among his traction-focused peers. Reed, who was equally at home in the electric utility industry, served as one of the primary conduits for Samuel Insull's growing involvement with Indiana interurban and electric utility properties, which eventually led to the formation of the Indiana Railroad.

Like McGowan, Reid was not a native Hoosier. McGowan had departed the stage of history six years before Reid stepped into the limelight in 1917 when he relocated to Indiana to head the Interstate Public Service Company. This union of three formerly independent interurban railways would conveniently link Indianapolis and Louisville as well as some important Indiana cities along the way. Always an innovative thinker, Reid soon reinvented the Interstate Public Service Company as one of America's most forward-looking electric railways and one of a handful of interurbans that operated overnight sleeping cars between their terminal cities. He left Indiana in the early 1930s for a utility industry job, but Reid must have made a good impression on Hoosiers with his innovative thinking. During World War II, an influential group invited him to return to Indianapolis to run its streetcar lines. As might be expected, he did not hesitate to replace the capital city's money-losing trolleys with the latest motor buses.

All the personalities profiled in this chapter and the previous one qualify as the primary movers and shakers responsible for the evolution of Indiana's Interurban Era. The electric railway industry also had its crooks and cranks, the latter term being very popular in the 1890s to describe an eccentric, even obsessive person. Wellington Adams's obsessive promotion of a high-speed interurban line between Chicago and Saint Louis during the 1890s might qualify him as both crank and crook. He issued a beautiful brochure in 1892 to promote his visionary project and to attract money from investors, but in the end, the most impressive result of Adams's promotion was undoubtedly the visually attractive brochure itself. When Adams kept begging his long-suffering investors to provide more money for his pet project even though it had not yet placed a single mile of track on the ground, the *Street Railway Review* dismissed Adams's Chicago-St. Louis interurban scheme as "99 percent hot air."[19]

Flitting around Indiana's Gas Belt during the 1890s and occasionally crossing paths with Charles L. Henry was an interurban gadfly named Noah Jasper Clodfelter, an eccentric man forever promoting interurban lines but never getting even so much as a mile of track in operation. "A few years ago," recalled a Muncie newspaper, "nearly every street electric project in this part of Indiana had Noah Clodfelter's name attached to it in some way." Like cranks who patented wildly impractical inventions—variations on the perpetual motion machine—Clodfelter grew obsessed with the concept of the interurban and squandered his fortune (real or imagined) on constructing fantasy projects that never managed to rise above the level of poetic license—or above a graded roadbed and a few rails spiked into place. In fact, Clodfelter thought himself to be a poet and writer fully equal in reputation to Indiana's favorite poet, James Whitcomb Riley, and for a time he was part of a circle of creative individuals that included Riley himself. Clodfelter's poetic application of the English language and his promotion of larger-than-life projects attracted support from a surprising number of admirers who referred to him as the "dreamer," but to others, he became a laughingstock. Some of his literary fellow travelers even claimed that Clodfelter and not Henry deserved to be recognized as the true "father of the interurban."

All through the mid- to late-1890s, the Clodfelter name and short news accounts of his many interurban schemes appeared more frequently in print than did news of Charles L. Henry's on-the-ground accomplishments. But there was something curiously manic about Clodfelter's intensity; at a meeting in Richmond, he insisted that local newspapers introduce him as the "father of the interurban." During the state's intense love affair with the interurban, that seemed a title worth coveting. One newspaper editor, exasperated by the assorted interurban projects never completed, referred to him sarcastically as "Noah Jonah Clodfelter," the biblical name "Jonah" being synonymous with a person whose presence invariably brought bad luck to any enterprise.

Noah Clodfelter was an enigmatic character whose pursuit of a Gas Belt interurban was cut short by Charles L. Henry, according to his partisans who also boldly claimed that Clodfelter was the true "father of the interurban."

Increasingly out of touch with reality, Clodfelter was committed to the recently opened Central State Hospital for the Insane in Indianapolis. He died there two years later in 1901 at age forty-nine. For all the hot air Clodfelter generated, the "dreamer" did play an important, if backhanded, role in the interurban industry by goading Henry to organize the Union Traction Company of Indiana and inaugurate interurban service between Anderson and Indianapolis, a project first proposed by Clodfelter in the mid-1890s.[20]

Anderson can claim credit as the place where Henry supposedly coined the term "interurban," while Kokomo can legitimately promote itself as the home of Elwood Haynes, the man widely acclaimed to be the inventor of the first *successful* automobile brand made in America. Indiana's Interurban Era cannot be understood without at least a brief mention of Haynes, who along with his many auto-industry peers hastened its demise.

During 1893, the year the first electric railway car made its way up the Willamette Valley from Portland to Oregon City—an event that to many people represented the debut of the Interurban Era—brothers Charles and Frank Duryea ran their first automobile invention along the streets of Springfield, Massachusetts. Haynes did likewise in Kokomo, Indiana, in 1894. Whether the credit for creating the first *successful* American automobile brand should go to Haynes or the Duryea brothers depends less on the date of their respective inventions than on the word "successful." The Haynes Automobile Company (initially Haynes-Apperson) produced automobiles in Kokomo from 1896 until it went bankrupt in 1924. Haynes is also credited with opening the nation's first automobile dealership to sell his brand of automobiles. The Duryea brothers launched the Duryea Motor Wagon Company in Springfield in 1895, but after a bitter argument over finances, they separated a few years later to each form their own automobile companies, but neither brother's enterprise enjoyed long-term success.[21]

Haynes came from Portland, Indiana, about fifty miles north of Henry's Anderson. The two cities would eventually be linked by Union Traction's fast and frequent interurban cars, the tracks of which at their greatest mileage would literally crisscross Indiana's Gas Belt. Like Henry and Brady, Haynes was an uncommonly well-educated man for his time. He studied at Worcester Polytechnic University and Johns Hopkins University, and after he returned to Indiana, it appeared for a time that he would make his mark either as a metallurgist or a professor of chemistry in Muncie at the predecessor school of Ball State University, where he headed the chemistry department.

The discovery of natural gas lured Haynes into the booming industry, and he oversaw construction of the first gas pipeline built for the Indiana Natural Gas and Oil Company of Chicago. A deeply religious man, Haynes was shocked and dismayed to discover that one of the businessmen behind Indiana Natural Gas and Oil was none other than Chicago's trolley magnate Charles Yerkes. A former inmate of Pennsylvania's infamous Eastern State penitentiary because of his participation in a funny-money scheme in Philadelphia, Yerkes enhanced his unsavory reputation through his widespread use of bribes to wrangle street railway franchises from the equally corrupt Chicago politicians who eagerly accepted them. Haynes quit the pipeline company.

The mid-1890s, particularly the years 1893 and 1894, witnessed a series of landmark events that would forever change the travel habits of Americans. Though the history of the two transportation industries, interurban and automobile, were entwined for the next three decades, they also differed in profound ways that are not completely obvious but are critical to understanding why the auto industry continues to thrive today and the interurban is but a distant memory.

Hugh McGowan's opulent residence in Indianapolis was the setting Orson Welles hoped to use for his 1940s movie adaptation of Booth Tarkington's *The Magnificent Ambersons*. McGowan's widow sold the home to the Knights of Columbus for a nominal sum, but several years later after the Knights found the large structure a burden to heat, it was razed.

7

The Expansive Dozen Years

> The development of interurban roads is one of the most interesting and promising studies of the day, both sociologically and physically; by it the farm life is relieved of many of the disadvantages which belong to isolation. The new electric construction is on a healthy basis. Practical street railway men who are now interested in street railway properties are quietly looking about and planning interurban lines, which, if they build—judging from past experiences, will soon become paying properties.
>
> —G. T. Rogers, president of the Street Railway Association of the State of New York, as quoted in the *Street Railway Review* (November 15, 1899): 570

For companies large or small, the growth years of the Interurban Era—the time during which nearly every mile of Indiana's electric railway network was spiked into place—lasted from 1897 through 1907, with a construction postscript continuing through 1910. Compared with America's steam railroads, which continued to grow their web of tracks from 1826 until 1916, maturation of the interurban took place in the blink of an eye. As previously noted, Gas Belt prosperity had fostered the creation of the Union Traction Company of Indiana, the industry model that played an inordinately large role in North America, but the seductive idea of launching an interurban company animated promoters and organizers in all corners of the Hoosier State. In the hilly and less populated half of the state south of Indianapolis, the obstacles to success were more formidable, but even there, the money-making possibilities were alluring to industry pioneers like Charles L. Henry.

At the dawn of the twentieth century, two separate groups of entrepreneurs launched interurban projects intended to link Indianapolis with some of the small manufacturing centers in southeastern Indiana. The groups also intended to push their tracks through to Cincinnati, but neither project got very far before it ran into serious financial trouble. The Indianapolis, Shelbyville and Southeastern Traction Company built a twenty-eight-mile line that featured steel and concrete bridges solid enough to carry the interurban equivalent of a steam railroad. As was typical

Preparing to continue its daily sprint south from Indianapolis to Louisville, the Dixie Flyer paused in downtown Columbus. The car dominates the interurban landscape on a wintry day in 1911 or 1912. The Dixie Flyer linked Indianapolis and Louisville via the three-company interchange that became the Interstate Public Service.

elsewhere in Indiana, its officers planned to run parallel to steam railroad tracks, the Big Four's main line between Indianapolis and Cincinnati, in their quest to construct an electric railway ultimately expected to reach and profit from traffic generated by Ohio's second-largest metropolis (after Cleveland). The Shelbyville Line carried its first paying passengers in late September 1902, but almost immediately thereafter, its march to Cincinnati stalled.

Slightly farther north, the backers of the Indianapolis, Morristown and Rushville line planned to run tracks parallel to the Cincinnati, Hamilton and Dayton, a financially troubled steam railroad that the Baltimore and Ohio would acquire in 1917. Existing competition was of no concern to directors of the Rushville Line because they were confident their electric railway when completed "would take care of the traffic" between Indianapolis and Cincinnati "in a more satisfactory way than is now done by the steam roads."[1]

Despite its proponents' lofty ambitions, the Indianapolis, Morristown and Rushville interurban made little discernible headway. It was still mainly a paper enterprise in 1902, but that year a third entrant in the race to reach Cincinnati acquired an asset that only one other of the state's electric railways could claim. Its backers coaxed out of retirement Indiana's premier interurban builder, Charles L. Henry, in the hope that a man of his experience could rescue their struggling enterprise (reincorporated as the Indianapolis and Cincinnati Traction Company on February 4, 1903). The company's new manager welcomed the opportunity to rejoin the industry he had grown to love and embraced his assignment with enthusiasm. One of the first things he did was spend several days walking much of the proposed right-of-way from Indianapolis to Rushville, a distance of forty miles, to assess the construction challenges that lay ahead as well as the traffic potential of the surrounding countryside. Henry seemed genuinely energized by the prospect of building an interurban line once again.[2]

Perhaps it was during Henry's two-day reconnaissance of the proposed route that he mentally formulated his business plan. We cannot be certain about his thinking during this time of transition because if he ever committed his thoughts to paper, the document is lost to history. Nonetheless, amazing things soon began to happen. To protect his flanks from any interurban competitors, Henry acquired both the unbuilt Rushville line and the Shelbyville line, which was intent on building to Cincinnati by way of Greensburg and Batesville. He combined the three electric railways as the Indianapolis and Cincinnati Traction Company, which on an Indiana map resembled the letter "V" turned on its side. Further, in Henry's quest to extend interurban tracks across southeastern Indiana, the president and general manager of the Indianapolis and Cincinnati Traction Company chose to march to a decidedly different drummer.

Henry made the risky decision to be the first in North America to electrify his interurban line with cutting-edge technology only recently developed—in fact, still being perfected—by Westinghouse in its Pittsburgh laboratories. If, however, the radically different single-phase alternating current system worked as well as Westinghouse promised, its installation would catapult Henry and his modest Indiana interurban onto the world stage and attract industry visitors from far and near to witness his railway in operation. Most people, even many interurban executives, had no idea what the term "single-phase" meant or what advantages it might offer. Henry, as noted earlier, was a lawyer by training, but his keen mind did not hesitate to explore complex matters of electrical engineering. When he became president of the American Electric Railway Association in 1915, *Brill Magazine* saluted his achievement by publishing a special biographical sketch that emphasized Henry's abiding interest in electrical engineering matters.[3]

That interest and aptitude were first displayed in the late 1890s when Henry nixed the idea of using several small powerhouses spaced at intervals along the tracks of Union Traction. Instead, he built a single large generating facility in North Anderson and employed half a dozen substations to maintain steady voltage along every mile of the railway. It was typical of Henry's way of doing things that the power plant he built for Union Traction was not just large but gargantuan—the largest in the United States apart from the even larger and world-famous installation at Niagara Falls, (He

Charles L. Henry's Indianapolis and Cincinnati Traction Company was as much an extension of one man's aspirations as any interurban in Indiana. As part of Henry's determination to make it the premier interurban line in the United States, it marched to a decidedly different drummer in terms of the high quality of its infrastructure, which included an unusual bow pickup device to transmit high-voltage alternating current to its cars.

likely toured the facility if—as its official program claims—he actually attended the 1897 annual meeting of the American Street Railway Association in the nearby city of Niagara Falls.) His massive Union Traction power plant attracted some press attention, but not nearly as much as his daring implementation of a single-phase alternating current system on his Indianapolis and Cincinnati line a few years later.[4]

By using single-phase technology, Henry's generating plant in Rushville could send alternating current pulsing along the cables and wires of the distribution system at enormously high and efficient voltages to transformers that stepped it down to 3,300 volts, still an abundance of energy compared with the 600 volts of direct current that prevailed on most other interurban railroads. One great advantage of single-phase technology was that it gave Henry ample power for the present and into the foreseeable future to send an ever-growing fleet of high-speed trains racing along the two segments of his Indianapolis and Cincinnati Traction system. So impressed was the *Electrical Review* that the respected New York City–based technical journal devoted six pages of its February 18, 1905, issue to Henry's latest feat of daring.[5]

Indiana's Most Famous Interurban

During the golden age of Indiana's several dozen interurban companies, three enterprises attracted the greatest national and international attention. These three are the Chicago South Shore and South Bend because it outlasted all its North American peers; Union Traction, which, in the early twentieth century, ranked as the largest interurban railway system in the world and was an industry role model; and the Indianapolis and Cincinnati Traction Company, high-profile innovator that became the talk of the industry in 1905 and for years to come.

At the big annual conference held in Philadelphia in 1905, many of the usual technical papers read aloud and the hallway conversations were devoted to single-phase electrification. When talk was not enough, individuals and delegations from as far away as Europe and Asia traveled to rural Indiana to see what the excitement was about. As much as anything, Charles L. Henry gained fame for his repeated feats of technological daring, and not just for the two interurban lines he constructed. When he was between interurban assignments and flush with investment capital, he built the Union Building in downtown Anderson, a six-story "skyscraper" that was the tallest in Indiana north of Indianapolis and the talk of the Gas Belt. The building, incidentally, housed the headquarters of Union Traction on its top floor, along with the interurban railway's always vital train dispatching office.

As for the South Shore Line, it managed to stumble along in an unimpressive manner until 1925, when Samuel Insull acquired the bankrupt railway and thoroughly modernized it. The Chicago magnate thus saved it from the fate of all other interurban companies.

The *Electrical Review* heaped praise on Henry as someone who has "always been in the front ranks of electric railway progress," adding that "the honor due the pioneer" in this "notable" technical advance belonged to him and his consulting engineers. The firm of consulting engineers, Sergeant and Lundy of Chicago, was the same one Henry had used to construct his first interurban line completed in 1898 between Anderson and Alexandria. In yet another skilled maneuver the *Electrical Review* found praiseworthy, Henry and the Indianapolis and Cincinnati Traction Company successfully negotiated the best franchise terms in all of Indiana, which included the right to carry freight, express, and mail "so that the company confidently expects a large income from this source." By contrast, in New England states, many franchises had expressly forbidden interurbans from becoming freight haulers. To complement his newsworthy support structure, Henry purchased the finest set of interurban rollingstock crafted by the St. Louis Car Company.[6]

No matter how newsworthy Henry's technological daring was, his expensive installation was, in truth, far better suited to a densely populated urban portion of the United States than to rural southern Indiana. Unless he could soon link the two bookend cities that gave his interurban its name, his company could not possibly earn enough money from local traffic to cover its expenses. Time and again, Henry promised to extend interurban tracks into Cincinnati, a necessary move to earn enough money to repay his company's large debt to Westinghouse. Short of that goal, his much-praised enterprise would experience humiliating financial embarrassment, and Henry's reputation would be tarnished. The clock was ticking. Indianapolis's population in 1910 was 233,650, and Cincinnati's was 363,591, numbers that compelled Henry to rapidly implement plans to extend tracks beyond their two present endpoints, Connersville and Greensburg with populations in 1910 of 7,738 and 5,420, respectively. Even combined, these numbers were a drop in the bucket compared with Cincinnati's population.

Henry's interurban venture was even more expensive (and impressive) because, instead of implementing the industry standard of a single track with turnouts at intervals to permit two approaching cars to pass one another safely—an arrangement typical of the state's other interurbans, including Union Traction's main line between Indianapolis and Anderson, the fastest and busiest stretch of track in Indiana—he proposed to install two parallel tracks to handle the expected volume of traffic, and he built substantial bridges with that future in mind. For his biggest bridges, Henry was also a pioneer in the use of reinforced concrete. He was clearly building with the expectation of centuries of use. Few interurbans in the Midwest (apart from a handful of heavily trafficked electric railways serving Chicago) were constructed to such high standards.

It often seemed that whenever Indiana newspapers experienced a slow news day, a reporter would hurriedly type up a feature article speculating about Henry's completion of his interurban line from Greensburg through Batesville and on to the Ohio metropolis. Or maybe it would run from Connersville to Cincinnati by way of Hamilton, Ohio. Or maybe its tracks would divert south through Brookville to connect with the Cincinnati, Lawrenceburg and Aurora Electric Street Railroad that extended a short distance west of the state line to tiny Aurora, Indiana, on the Ohio River. Rumormongering and incessant chitchat in print that newspapers dignified under the heading "traction gossip" were notable features of Indiana's Interurban Era.[7]

Between Indianapolis and both Connersville and Greenburg, the interurban's tracks traversed some of the most prosperous farmland in southern Indiana, but just beyond both communities, the landscape changed abruptly. By whatever route, the gap that Henry had to cross to access Cincinnati was tantalizingly short, a distance of less than sixty miles, but the intervening countryside was hilly, heavily wooded, and lightly populated, which made construction expensive and any return on investment highly problematic should the line fall short of its Cincinnati goal.

Regardless of the route he chose, Henry faced stiff competition from two long-established steam railroads for through traffic across Indiana. Every weekday, when he formally opened his state-of-the-art interurban route in 1905, at least seven Big Four passenger trains steamed each way along tracks that closely paralleled the lower segment of Henry's intended Ohio connection if constructed via Shelbyville and Greensburg, while six Cincinnati, Hamilton and Dayton passenger trains ran in each direction along tracks adjacent to the interurban's upper segment via Rushville and Connersville. In other words, should Henry's dream ever be realized, it faced immediate competition from at least thirteen daily steam trains already offering the same through service between Indianapolis and Cincinnati.[8]

The final hurdle Henry had to surmount was a well-publicized one that bedeviled the best minds in the industry: how to access downtown Cincinnati despite the headache created years earlier when local streetcar lines adopted nonstandard broad-gauge tracks. For high-speed interurban cars to have maximum appeal, they needed to continue to downtown Cincinnati, as Henry's steam railroad competitors did. But accessing the Fountain Square area, the financial heart of the Ohio metropolis, posed a significant challenge. Arthur Brady in a 1909 speech hosted by the Engineers' Club of Cincinnati commended the Indianapolis model that gave interurban lines access to the downtown Traction Terminal as an ideal arrangement. "Many of you remember the Indianapolis of 15 years ago before a single interurban railroad entered its boundaries. It was not a modern city—it was rather an overgrown country town. It was backward in every respect." Converging interurban lines transformed Indianapolis by bringing modernity to the city and greatly enlarging its trade territory to encompass fifty-two of the state's ninety-two counties, or nearly 40 percent of the area of Indiana. None of this could have happened, asserted Brady, without access to downtown Indianapolis, but lack of rapid access to central Cincinnati would inconvenience travelers and stunt the growth of the city's interurban traffic.[9]

Ten separate interurban companies served the Ohio metropolis in 1917, the year Cincinnati residents finally determined to address their interurban muddle. At that time, half of the ten electric railways—the less significant half—used broad-gauge tracks and accessed the central city by means of existing streetcar lines, but interurban cars still experienced frequent delays when stuck behind a slow-moving trolley that blocked the tracks ahead. On the other hand, tracks of the five standard-gauge interurban lines, which collectively covered a much greater portion of Ohio than their broad-gauge peers, dead-ended at separate depots at the outer edge of the city. Travelers transferred to local street cars to continue to downtown Cincinnati, an inconvenient arrangement at best.[10]

The *Electric Railway Journal* noted in 1917 that "although the territory around Cincinnati is well covered by existing and proposed interurban electric railways, the city has not benefitted from interurban traffic like Indianapolis, Cleveland, Toledo, etc." because the gauge differences restricted traffic and the city lacked downtown terminal facilities. That April, local voters approved a far-reaching rapid transit plan intended to resolve Cincinnati's long-standing traction discombobulation.

Here was the opening, literally, that Charles L. Henry required to avoid the expense of laying track along a street not already occupied by Cincinnati's 222 miles of trolley lines or else constructing several miles of dual-gauge track. So compelling was Henry's perceived wizardry that his Hoosier backers never lost faith in his ability to overcome every obstacle no matter how formidable it might appear to others. Alas for Henry and his financial backers, just ten days before Cincinnati voters removed the last roadblock preventing speedy interurban access to their city's downtown, the United States formally declared war on Germany and joined the conflict then raging across Europe. The Great War and the unprecedented financial upheaval that followed on its heels in 1919 once again thwarted Henry's Cincinnati ambitions.[11]

The Indianapolis and Cincinnati Traction Company commenced regular service between Indianapolis and Rushville in January 1905 with an interurban car equipped with four of the revolutionary single-phase electric motors. No one, especially the road's acclaimed president, could imagine the many struggles that lay ahead on the road to Cincinnati.

Henry located both the interurban's shop complex and operating offices in Rushville near the company's large powerhouse, but he also maintained an executive office in Indianapolis. Even though his anticipated connection to Cincinnati was not yet in place, Henry delighted in impressing fellow executives with whirlwind tours of his state-of-the-art property. In late 1905, for instance, he treated fifty-two fellow members of the recently formed Indiana Electric Railway Association to a thrilling ride between Indianapolis and Rushville. "While no great effort was made to do fast running, one of the cars made several sprints of speed and once or twice went at the rate of sixty-three miles an hour." An additional attraction for Henry's guests was the chance to view for themselves the radically different single-phase infrastructure.[12]

Henry was always delighted to showcase the railway he considered to be the first interurban reinvented to address the industry's early mistakes. During the early years, as he explained to listeners in 1907, "we regarded traction lines merely as the extension into the suburbs of local lines. As such the construction, equipment and rolling stock was on a corresponding plane. Later developments brought the through business—the more substantial business. Our whole scheme of construction had to be changed, and that was a very expensive mistake."[13]

Before 1905, Henry had shown absolutely no interest in any form of industry leadership other than running the Union Traction Company and subsequently implementing cutting-edge technology at the Indianapolis and Cincinnati Traction Company. He appeared indifferent to any form of personal advancement in the world of electric railways outside Indiana.

A significant turning point in Henry's life was the formation in late 1904 of the Indiana Electric Railway Association. When the *Street Railway Journal* published news of the new organization, its editor took mild exception to the name the Hoosiers had chosen. Nowhere in the state was there a great urban transit system comparable to those operating in New York or Chicago, the so-called Big Tractions, but Indiana was, insisted the editor, the nation's foremost "interurban state" and a name that Hoosiers chose for their new organization should have boldly acknowledged that fact. The *Street Railway Journal* further observed that Union Traction's status as the largest interurban company in the world provided an additional reason for the new Indiana organization to reference the word "interurban" in its formal title.[14]

In any case, when members convened the following January 1905 to formalize their new association, they met in the office portion of Hugh McGowan's new Traction Terminal Building. They kept the organization's original name and honored Charles L. Henry by electing him their first president. It appears entirely likely that another of the several dozen charter members, Arthur Brady, quietly engineered Henry's election as a way to recognize his predecessor's role in creating Indiana's pioneer interurban. A large contingent of Union Traction managers had accompanied him to the Indianapolis gathering, and several additional employees from Henry's Indianapolis and

Cincinnati Traction Company increased Brady's behind-the-scenes leverage. One can infer this election dynamic because, as noted earlier, Brady during the coming decades frequently pushed Henry onto the public stage. Union Traction's president admired Henry, the man he would henceforth insist on introducing as the "father of the interurban."

Beginning with Brady in 1911, the Hoosiers were remarkably successful over the next fifteen years in electing four of their own to the prestigious office of president of the American Electric Railway Association, the industry's premier North American organization. For a relatively small state like Indiana, that was an impressive feat, but during the same period, the Hoosier state was remarkably successful in getting its politicians, both Republicans and Democrats, elected vice president of the United States. Hoosier politics, which had occasionally embodied the complex calculations of a game of chess combined with mud wrestling, had apparently imparted valuable lessons in the art of winning friends and impressing people.[15]

There were two other members of the so-called Hoosier cabal who served terms at the helm of the American Electric Railway Association. Robert I. Todd worked closely with Hugh McGowan, and after McGowan's death in 1911, he became his obvious successor to preside over the Traction Terminal, the street railways of Indianapolis, and the Terre Haute, Indianapolis and Eastern. Charles D. Emmons headed the transit system in Baltimore at the time of his election but was a bona fide Hoosier, a native of Lafayette, who in earlier years had been a close associate of the industry's several other prominent gentlemen from Indiana. Emmons was, in fact, general manager of the Fort Wayne and Wabash Valley at the time of its crash at Kingsland in 1910, the bloodiest in interurban history. None of his peers blamed him for the poor judgment of his motorman, and Emmons's career trajectory continued upward.[16]

At the Indianapolis meeting in early 1905 that elected Henry president of the Indiana Electric Railway Association, he was relaxed enough in the company of his fellow Hoosiers to publicly discuss his current and future plans for the Indianapolis and Cincinnati Traction Company, something the self-effacing executive had never been inclined to do previously. Henry was not bragging when he revealed the details of his historic leap of faith as the first electric railway president in North America to adopt single-phase alternating current technology to run its interurban cars.

At that time, Henry's Rushville line operated exactly one car, which shuttled along fourteen miles of track that linked Rushville, the seat of Rush County, with the nearby village of Morristown. That arrangement was financially unsustainable, of course, unless the interurban company could rapidly extend track in both directions to Indianapolis *and* Cincinnati, the two great population centers that Henry expected to generate most of the passenger and freight revenue he needed to pay for the interurban line of his dreams. Its full dimensions, as Henry carefully revealed them, must have amazed his listeners. The expensive power-delivery system was intended to energize the double-track line that Henry envisioned as laden with the rapidly swelling volume of traffic the heavy-duty infrastructure warranted. No one ever accused Henry of timidity as he planned aloud for future growth, and he exuded total confidence as he promised fellow executives that in the days and months ahead, they would witness great accomplishments from the Indianapolis and Cincinnati Traction Company

Robert I. Todd, a gifted electrical engineer trained at Johns Hopkins University, served as an understudy to both Kesley Schoepf and Hugh McGowan. On the latter man's death in late 1911, Todd succeeded him as head of the Traction Terminal and McGowan's stable of streetcar and interurban lines.

The company's only interurban car to date featured two ways to access electric current, a traditional trolley device to be used for direct current along the streets of Indianapolis and a bow-like device intended for the single-phase alternating current outside the city limits. Henry, who seemed comfortable accepting a high degree of risk, freely admitted he was not sure how well the bow pickup would work in practice, but he was confident that engineers could overcome any electrical challenges. He seemed to understand that his interurban line, whether single-phase technology proved a success or failure, served as an electrical engineering guinea pig for the entire industry.

Indeed, even before Henry had statistics in hand to evaluate his technological leap of faith, the single-phase concept had already bolted out of central Indiana and was applied to interurban railways poised to launch construction elsewhere in the Midwest and on the Atlantic and Pacific coasts. It found favor, too, with the engineers working to reequip busy stretches of steam railroads with heavy-duty electric installations, most notably the New Haven's busy tracks outside New York City.

Despite its several triumphs and favored status among Indiana interurbans, the Indianapolis and Cincinnati Traction Company struggled for the better part of two

Current Wars, Hoosier-Style

Ever since its early days, and as a result of its origins in a thousand different communities, America's electric railway industry had devoted considerable time and thought to matters of standardization. Its quest encompassed everything from the standardization of track gauges to facilitate the seamless interchange of cars between different interurban companies to the implementation of a standard set of operating rules, a pursuit that lasted for years and met with only a modest measure of success. No less fundamental was the industry's long-term effort to design the most efficient powerhouse. Despite the lofty goal, industry experts never could agree on what worked best. The result was that every powerhouse, while appearing to be superficially similar structurally, ended as a one-of-a-kind design. Nor could industry leaders agree on how best to engineer the infrastructure needed to deliver electricity along the tracks. Finally, industry experts never agreed on whether alternating or direct current worked best, or whether to adopt single or polyphase technology.

It turned out that even Charles L. Henry's bold commitment in 1904 to pioneer single-phase alternating current technology on his Indianapolis and Cincinnati Traction Company did not turn out as well as he had hoped. First, until it could complete its line into Cincinnati, the interurban had to rely on local traffic to pay its bills. That did not generate enough money to repay Westinghouse the cost of the single-phase installation, and the shortfall pushed Henry's interurban to the brink of bankruptcy in 1906.

Twenty years later, Henry admitted that he had backed the wrong horse in 1904 when he chose single-phase alternating current, or at least the steady improvements to direct current technology during the intervening two decades made him think so. After operating the Indianapolis and Cincinnati Traction Company for twenty years with an electrical infrastructure far more robust than the volume of traffic ever warranted, the father of the interurban made the equally bold decision—or the certainly very puzzling decision to some industry observers—to scrap the once-state-of-the-art single-phase installation in 1923 and rebuild his interurban line from the ground up using a more conventional direct current system to power its cars. He had to borrow considerable money to pay for the expensive changeover. Given the noticeably downward trend of the industry by that time, Henry's commitment to reengineer his entire railway represented an even bigger financial gamble than his decision to pioneer single-phase alternating current two decades earlier. The result was a financial and personal disaster that I will discuss in a later chapter.

decades to close the gap between its namesake cities. Time and again, the seemingly magic touch of Charles L. Henry fell short when it came to financing both his cutting-edge technology and tracks to Cincinnati in defiance of the topographical obstacles that nature placed in his way across southeastern Indiana. Twice, the company could not pay its bills and was forced into receivership, with Henry serving on both occasions as its court-appointed receiver. It is tempting to think of Henry as a better visionary and industry booster than a successful day-to-day businessman.

Three other interurban companies joined forces to forge a corridor of steel that successfully linked Indianapolis and Louisville, the larger of the two cities, with through trains. Admittedly, the topography that provided a channel between the hills of southern Indiana was far more favorable to the enterprise's success than it was to the Indianapolis and Cincinnati's ongoing quest to place those two large cities at opposite ends of its lines. The Interstate Public Service Company gained fame as Indiana's only interurban line to run sleeping cars, which it did nightly between its two terminal cities. Kentucky's largest city, Louisville had a population of 223,928 in 1910, slightly more than that of Indianapolis, which helped to make Interstate's sleeping-car operation a multiyear success—at least until the Great Depression years.[17]

Indiana's southwest quadrant—the area from the Interstate's north-south corridor of tracks to the Illinois border—remained comparatively empty of interurban railways apart from a short line that ran south from Terre Haute to Sullivan, and another that connected Indianapolis with Martinsville. Both properties became part of the gangling assemblage of companies that Hugh McGowan and his associates cobbled together in 1907 to form the Terre Haute, Indianapolis and Eastern Traction Company.

Finally, in the extreme southwest, a collection of interurban lines reached out in separate directions from Evansville, Indiana's third-largest city in 1910. In what was without doubt Indiana's most unusual interurban operation, in 1912, the Evansville, Henderson and Owensboro Railway Company commenced running nine daily round trips across the Ohio River to Henderson, Kentucky, using the state's only interurban ferry.[18]

Evansville was also Indiana's most isolated population center in terms of the state's interurban network. During the boom years, interurban promoters repeatedly promised to link Evansville's interurbans with Indianapolis, but their bold proposals invariably stalled out following optimistic proclamations about having surveyed the necessary right-of-way or hired the contractors needed to launch construction. Given that Evansville did not even enjoy good steam railroad connections to Indiana's capital city, forging an interurban connection would have been a logical move. However, any electric railway that linked Evansville and Indianapolis would need to thread its tracks through the hills of southwestern Indiana and, apart from its two endpoints,

Evansville was an Indiana outlier not just in terms of its geography but also in its use of a ferry to run interurban cars across the Ohio River to Henderson, Kentucky. In the United States, the only other interurban ferry plied the waters of San Francisco Bay.

serve no population center larger than Bloomington, with 8,838 residents in 1910 plus students attending Indiana University. As for natural resources, the area featured scattered areas of farmland and valuable seams of coal. South of Terre Haute and Brazil lay numerous productive coal mines, but even collectively they could not compare with the wealth-generating capabilities of the state's Gas Belt.[19]

Northwestern Indiana witnessed the rise of several interurban lines serving the South Bend area. But because so many steam railroads already provided convenient connections to Chicago, the South Shore Line remained something of an anomaly, both in its hesitant origins and its halting progress west from South Bend into Chicago instead of reaching outward from Chicago into its hinterland, as some of the Windy City's other interurban lines did. In fact, the progress of the original Chicago, Lake Shore and South Bend tracks toward the nation's second-largest city across an area of heavy industry exemplified by the steel mills of Gary and the oil refineries of Whiting was excruciatingly slow, and the completion of a through connection came surprisingly late in Indiana's Interurban Era.

The area's second major interurban was the Chicago, South Bend and Northern Indiana, a Murdock Syndicate property that formed an important link between South Bend and Elkhart and the Winona Interurban Railroad at Goshen. One of its most

Spatial Anomalies: The Case of French Lick and West Baden Springs

Few Indiana locations, and none with populations so small, were mentioned more often by electric railway promoters than the twin resort communities of French Lick and West Baden, yet not even one of their many paper interurbans ever got built.

During the railroad era, southwestern Indiana was a spatial anomaly that enjoyed far better rail connections with Chicago and Louisville than with Indianapolis or the cities of the Gas Belt. French Lick's population in 1910 was 1,803, and West Baden Springs' was 746. Connecting the two small communities was a mile-long trolley line sometimes dignified as an interurban.

The formal name of the Monon, the Chicago, Indianapolis, and Louisville, suggests more than the Hoosier railroad delivered. It did connect all three cities, but it did not link communities along its tracks through southwestern Indiana with Indianapolis in any direct or convenient fashion. It did, however, provide West Baden Springs and French Lick with an excellent connection to the Midwest's largest city, and in 1906 and 1911, the Chicago Cubs held their spring training camp at the West Baden Springs Resort. At the time, the Cubs dominated baseball's National League and participated in three consecutive World Series. Some people claimed that the team's remarkable success resulted from the mineral waters players drank at West Baden Springs. Perhaps that was why the Pittsburgh Pirates also trained at the same Indiana location. The popular local elixir was called Pluto Water, and its slogan was "When nature won't, Pluto will." The claim refers not to the increased prowess of baseball players but to the water's properties as a strong laxative.

The resort's location three hundred miles from Chicago is supposed to have provided Al Capone with a convenient getaway when the heat grew too intense for the nation's best-known gangster of the 1920s. Indeed, he could easily board a Monon sleeping car in Chicago's Dearborn Station and be whisked overnight to the West Baden Springs Hotel. Alas, local historians cannot find conclusive proof that the Capone connection actually existed.

Equally elusive are documents that might explain why the area was such a magnet for promoters of paper interurbans. My guess is that sales agents discovered that many residents of the isolated area were too easily impressed by clever outsiders. News stories in industry journals tell of individuals and communities that committed precious dollars to support one of the many interurban projects, all of which featured impressive-sounding names and equally impressive geographical reach. One of these was the New Albany and French Lick Valley Traction Company, which promised to not only build a sixty-mile main line but also to extend branches north to Mooresville and south to Corydon, the former state capital. Conferring a measure of legitimacy on the proposal was the interurban's endorsement by the Louisville Commercial Club.[20]

The first car of the Gary and Interurban line attracted the usual crowd of enthusiasts in 1908.

lucrative lines ran north from South Bend to St. Joseph, Michigan, where trains met the steamships plying Lake Michigan. The commodity that made the line prosperous was Michigan fruit shipped fresh by the carload to markets in central Indiana.[21]

No traction company ever forged a direct route between South Bend and Fort Wayne, northern Indiana's two largest cities, though the Winona Interurban Railway and other companies proposed to do so, and none built a direct route from South Bend to Indianapolis. And, as logical as it may have seemed, no interurban company ever completed a direct route between Indianapolis and Chicago, though rumors circulated for years that Union Traction or some other company was about to do so. A feature writer for the *Chicago Tribune* called it a "painful discovery" to learn that no interurban line yet linked these two great Midwestern cities.[22]

That was in 1908. Over the years, interurban lines built northwest from Indianapolis and for a time appeared headed for Chicago, but their tracks were pushed no farther toward Chicago than Crawfordsville, Lafayette, or Logansport. This left a hundred-mile expanse of fertile farmland untouched by interurban tracks all the way to Lake County, an area that was densely populated and had the greatest concentration of heavy industry in Indiana. Just as Hoosiers often claim that Evansville in the state's extreme southwest corner was more connected to Kentucky than to Indiana, the same could be said of Gary, Hammond, and the other cities of northwest Indiana that were part of Chicago's vast hinterland.[23]

The first interurban cars to roll along the brick and cobblestone streets of downtown Indianapolis belonged to companies that served as the nuclei of central Indiana's three largest electric railways. Of these, only Union Traction entered Indianapolis under its own name. The city's other big interurban companies all came later and, unlike Union Traction, had originated as combinations of smaller companies. The Indianapolis, Greenwood and Franklin Railroad, predecessor of the Interstate Public Service Company made history in January 1900 when it ran the first interurban car into the capital city. Cars of the Indianapolis and Greenfield Rapid Transit reached Indianapolis a few months later, followed in January 1901 by the city's third interurban, Union Traction from Anderson.

The Terre Haute, Indianapolis and Eastern originated in 1907 when the Schoepf-Morgan-McGowan Syndicate combined Terre Haute and Richmond trolley lines with several additional interurban properties it controlled across central Indiana. The syndicate then filled the short remaining gaps that separated these properties until it had extended a line of interurban tracks across the middle of Indiana from Terre Haute, near the Illinois border, east through Indianapolis and then to Richmond at the Ohio border. To its cross-state main line the company added branches extending from its Terre Haute and Indianapolis hubs mainly by purchasing several already-existing interurban companies. As impressive as the new combination was—in mileage, it ranked second only to Union Traction in Indiana—an appropriate term to describe what the syndicate had achieved might be "jerry-built." Although the edifice was imposing, its various parts failed to form a harmonious structure, and it rested on a shaky financial foundation.

Terre Haute, Indianapolis and Eastern competition in 1907 was Pennsylvania Railroad trains that also connected Indianapolis and Richmond. The interurban faced even greater competition between Indianapolis and Terre Haute, where the addition of Pennsylvania and Big Four trains gave travelers three separate options. Twenty years later, these rail options remained in place, but because the Terre Haute, Indianapolis and Eastern main line tracks clung tenuously to the shoulders of newly designated US 40, it faced additional competition from a rapidly growing number of intercity buses, trucks, and private automobiles. Its large and fast-running cars proved intimidating to motorists on the adjacent roadway, and it became the target of public criticism whenever one of its interurban cars tangled, often fatally, with a highway vehicle. The Terre Haute, Indianapolis and Eastern tracks stood in the way of motor-minded Hoosiers who in the late 1920s wanted to widen US 40.[24]

The Interstate Public Service Company faced the same competitive dynamic along its route between Indianapolis and Louisville. When the holding company was formed in 1912 as an end-to-end combination of three smaller interurban lines, its main competitor was the Pennsylvania Railroad. By 1927, newly designated US 31 also paralleled its tracks from Indianapolis to Louisville and greatly intensified the competition—not just for traffic between the largest cities in Indiana and Kentucky but also for the businesses of Greenwood, Franklin, Columbus, Seymour, and some smaller communities on its line. Just as soon as the interurban line ceased operation in late 1941, the ever-eager highway builders paved over or removed the tracks to widen US 31, just as they had done during the 1930s to interurban tracks along US 40.[25]

In terms of mileage in 1910, Union Traction Company of Indiana was the state's largest interurban, and in the words of the *Street Railway Journal*, it was its "most pretentious." Presumably, the editor meant that term as a compliment because Union Traction did aspire to steam railroad standards. Whether run by Charles L. Henry or Arthur W. Brady, the company made no small plans. As previously noted, its Anderson power plant was one of the nation's largest, and its interurban cars were the finest that money could buy. The company's history during its first twenty-five years was a record of one success after another—until the head-on collision of two interurban cars in February 1924 sent it spinning into receivership at year's end.[26]

Shortly after Union Traction completed its important interurban line between Anderson, the company's headquarters city, and Indianapolis in early 1901 to access Indiana's largest population center, it gained a second entrance to Indianapolis when it acquired control of the Indianapolis Northern, an interurban company that extended tracks north from the Hoosier capital to the Gas Belt manufacturing center of Kokomo. By means of a connection farther north in Peru with the Fort Wayne and Wabash Valley Traction Company, it ran through trains between Indianapolis and Fort Wayne either via Anderson and Muncie or Kokomo and Peru. Union Traction interchanged freight and passengers at Peru with the Winona Interurban Railway, which extended north to Goshen where its trains connected with the electric railways that served Elkhart, South Bend, and southwestern Michigan.

Union Traction gained a third and final entrance into Indianapolis in October 1912 when it acquired the oddly nicknamed "Honey Bee and Wild Flower Line," a hard-luck enterprise formally titled the Indianapolis, New Castle and Toledo Traction Company. Because no Indiana interurban offers a better example of a line that should never had been built but that somehow made sense to its backers during the height of interurban enthusiasm before 1907, I will discuss its many shortcomings in a later chapter.

During the coming years, although the pace of construction slowed noticeably, promoters and entrepreneurs still added track to the interurban network across Indiana until it reached its maximum mileage in 1912. Of approximately eighteen hundred miles of track on the ground, 65 percent belonged to the large interurban companies centering on Indianapolis. With two conspicuous exceptions, Henry's Indianapolis and Cincinnati Traction Company and the Irwins' largely self-financed Indianapolis, Columbus and Southern line, most of these miles had been constructed with capital provided by the Philadelphia financiers. In contrast to the impeccable timing of this early group of investors who amassed fortunes during the dozen best years of the Interurban Era, numerous local investors and overly eager small communities joined the rush to support new interurban projects just as most honest-to-goodness construction stopped and the paper interurban boosters enjoyed their brief and shameful heyday. The promoters, whether they were honest individuals who met with unexpected setbacks or slick-talking thieves who dressed in stylish three-piece suits and wore kid gloves to impress their gullible victims, left the naive investor with little more than a colorfully engraved stock certificate and empty pockets. All too often, many months of marketing puffery were followed by the ominous sound of silence as dishonest promoters took the money and slipped quietly out of Indiana.[27]

This phase of interurban "construction" grew so common that the editor of the *Electric Railway Journal* felt it necessary to "sound a note of warning against the vice of overconfidence" in 1903. Much had been mentioned "about the promoter of the Hot Air Line, and perhaps the public is sufficiently acquainted with his devious, not to say crooked ways." In addition, there were "rash enterprises undertaken in wholly good faith but with quite insufficient caution." Finally, one expert explained the many failed projects by noting: "Engineering locations and surveys are amateurish and bad, and the notes and records so inadequate that no one can tell whether the field work is correct or not." Not surprisingly, the result often amounted to nothing more than a "scheme, a dream, utterly impractical from the standpoint of the man or financial institution that might be interested in an investment." Whatever the cause, the number of failed projects filled an impressive "graveyard" in Indiana alone, and they continued to do so during the boom years of the Interurban Era.[28]

After the recession year of 1907, interurban enthusiasm across the Midwest gradually diminished from the frenzied state that prevailed during the previous decade. Major projects continued to be proposed throughout Indiana, such as additional interurban lines to link Indianapolis and Evansville or to reach across state borders to connect the ends of lines at Crawfordsville, Indiana, and Danville, Illinois, to form a through route between Indianapolis and Saint Louis. In fact, many hundreds of such paper projects were publicly proposed by promoters. One must wonder, however, if such late-term projects marked the resurgence of the pre-1907 enthusiasm but failed to recognize how the world of the interurban had changed after that year's Wall Street

The Interurban Rumor Mill

During the boom years, the newspapers of Indiana delighted in reporting details of every rumored interurban project, and reader interest no doubt encouraged them to pursue any possible lead. Charles L. Henry's forever quest to connect Indianapolis with Cincinnati was one popular topic, but so were newspaper interpretations of the sometimes-stealthy activity of Muncie interurban entrepreneurs like George McCulloch. A local newspaper claimed that when McCulloch, Brady of Union Traction, and George A. Ball of the Muncie and Portland Traction company were seen in conference together, their collective presence in New York "excited the curiosity of the Eastern traction magnates greatly, and opinion ran rife as to what would be done." The *Muncie Star Press* warily noted on another occasion that the news "grapevine" reported the sale of the Muncie and Portland line to Union Traction "for about the forty-sixth consecutive time." Episodes of interurban intrigue such as this had the reader appeal of a first-class soap opera.[29]

Indiana's Paper Interurbans

The popular term used to describe a steam railroad that looked promising on paper but somehow never got built was "paper railroad." As previously noted, the same term applied to a variety of interurban projects. Some of the industry's most appealing prospects on paper were interurban companies that repeatedly promised to connect Indiana's largest cities. The 1910 census recorded that Indianapolis and Evansville ranked as Indiana's first- and second-largest cities in terms of population, while South Bend ranked fifth after Fort Wayne and Terre Haute (see table 7.1). Of the state's Big Five cities during the Interurban Era, Evansville, in the far southwestern corner of Indiana along the Ohio River, was the most isolated geographically, but because it was remote from the state capital, it was perhaps the most tempting plum for the many interurban frauds who repeatedly promised to connect it to Indianapolis.

An article in the *Interurban Railway Journal* published shortly after its 1905 founding in Indianapolis was headlined "Why Forty-Nine Projected Electric Roads Fail and the Fiftieth Succeeds." The author provided at least three dozen reasons for the many paper projects that languished in every corner of Indiana, but he spared hurried readers from having to ponder each of his many explanations (or excuses) by opening his essay with the general observation that "many a project is buried beneath an avalanche of mistakes long before the announcement of its birth reaches the ears of the financial world." Anyone could purchase a franchise from the secretary of state's office for a nominal sum, and temptation to join the interurban "game" with its potential for a financial windfall was as compelling as any roll of the dice or purchase of a lottery ticket today. However, so many pitfalls awaited interurban builders and their often-gullible investors—at least thirty-nine, according to the author's way of reckoning them—that it was a wonder any tracks ever got on the ground. Successful role models like Charles Henry, Hugh McGowan, and Joseph and Will Irwin were rare, but their achievements as headlined in many Hoosier newspapers no doubt inspired many less capable or less well-informed individuals to take the plunge.[30]

Table 7.1. Interurban-era populations of Indiana cities

	1900	1910	1920
Indianapolis	169,164	233,650	314,194
Evansville	59,007	69,647	85,265
Fort Wayne	45,115	63,933	86,265
South Bend	35,999	53,684	70,983
Terre Haute	36,673	58,157	66,083

For every honest and well-intentioned interurban builder, there was probably an equal if not greater number of frauds, or "fakers" in the lingo of the day. Some would-be builders probably began a project with the best of intentions but ran headlong into one of the thirty-nine (or more) pitfalls that awaited the unwary, and then quietly gave up.

Among the most promising of Indiana's some two hundred paper interurbans was the impressively titled Grand Central Traction Company, which proposed to extend a line of tracks across the state's southwest quadrant from Indianapolis to Evansville, with added branches either to Terre Haute or Bloomington, depending on which route its main line followed. Logically, this should have been a successful venture across a portion of the state largely devoid of electric and steam rail competitors. Industry trade journals during 1907 and 1908 published accounts of numerous franchises the company had secured from city officials in Vincennes, Bloomington, and elsewhere to further its quest, but somehow Grand Central's tracks never materialized. Southwest Indiana proved to be a veritable graveyard of paper interurban projects because in no other part of the state were so many new interurban lines proposed but never built.

During the dozen boom years of interurban construction, promoters announced various plans to complete a direct interurban link between Indianapolis and South Bend or even between Indianapolis and Chicago, which, with a population of 2,185,283 in 1910, was the Midwest's grand prize in terms of generating interurban traffic. As with the Grand Central's projected line to Evansville, nothing concrete developed from the numerous paper proposals across the portion of Indiana between Lafayette and the greater Chicago area.

An industry journal denounced as an outright fraud a proposal to link Seattle and Saint Paul by an interurban line. That was not a difficult assessment given the sparsely settled northern tier states and the fact that two steam railroads already connected Seattle and Saint Paul, and a third steam railroad link would be completed between them in 1909. No such denunciation was forthcoming to describe the numerous paper interurbans of Indiana, and perhaps that was because some promoters were quick to sue their detractors. To be fair, it was probably difficult for industry observers to distinguish between the intentionally fraudulent schemes and those that lacked a sound financial foundation and were unable to implement bold plans after the financial whirlwind that was the Panic of 1907.

"Crawfordsville is the greatest interurban center in Indiana—on paper," quipped the local press earlier that year. "We may console ourselves, however, with the thought that where there is so much smoke there must be some fire and so hope that out of the great number of projected roads a few will be constructed." If all the new companies proposed during the frenzied years of 1906 and 1907, and even in postrecession 1908, had been built, Indiana would probably have doubled its approximately eighteen hundred miles of interurban line.[31]

panic, or whether they were intended mainly to transfer ill-gained money to the canny promoters.

Following incorporation, many promised interurban lines made a big show of securing the necessary municipal franchises, and a few companies even graded a right-of-way and spiked down a few miles of track. Promoters announced bold plans in the electric railway publications and local newspaper for the construction of power plants and carbarns, but typically such announcements were followed by inaction as the latest cohort of interurban promoters collected investors' money and then skedaddled for parts unknown.

Many features of the interurban network completed across Indiana made good sense, such as Charles L. Henry's original quest to interconnect the prosperous cities of the Gas Belt and then to link them to the state's capital. Likewise, it made sense for the interurban builders to avoid hilly and lightly populated areas of limited agricultural potential, such as typified many areas in southern Indiana. But the lack of interurban tracks across the fertile swath of farmland in northwestern Indiana or their failure to connect Fort Wayne with South Bend speaks to the local origins of the industry and the lack of any grand strategy. The desire of most early interurban builders was to connect two population centers for the sake of convenience, like Greenfield's interurban builders did to link their county seat to the big-city pleasures and opportunities in nearby Indianapolis. It was inevitable that as more interurban companies built into or out from major population centers, their tracks would intersect and a more encompassing regional vision would replace the industry's original local orientation.

Even so, only gradually and mainly during the years of consolidation beginning most noticeably in 1906 or 1907 did industry luminaries grasp all the benefits to be derived from creating larger systems by merging several smaller companies and then filling in the gaps. If the boom times had lasted beyond 1907, it is likely that industry leaders would have built tracks across many, if not all, the obvious gaps to forge an encompassing interurban network across Indiana. Already in 1905, the phenomenal growth of a Midwest interurban network inspired industry executives to boast "that within a short period it will be possible to travel from St. Louis to New York by trolley." Just how much larger a Midwestern interurban network might have grown in future years was anyone's guess. Especially during the building boom before the Panic of 1907, anything seemed possible.[32]

One of the boldest interurban proposals to impact Indiana was the Chicago–New York Electric Air Line Railroad. This multistate venture promised to construct and operate an arrow-straight, high-speed interurban connection between America's two largest cities. Its proposed route of approximately 750 miles would have been at least 150 miles shorter than the main lines of either the New York Central or Pennsylvania railroads and would have offered them serious competition. A clever entrepreneur, or perhaps scoundrel, raised enough initial capital to launch the project, and though it was never a clear-cut case of taking money from gullible investors and then absconding, only about twenty miles of the proposed route were completed in northwestern Indiana in the Gary area before the project collapsed.[33]

The project was a complete fizzle, much like the first such bold adventure, the 250-mile Chicago-St. Louis electric railway line that Wellington Adams announced in 1892. Adams's well-illustrated promotional brochure featured futuristic streamlined trains that in an uncanny way anticipated the appearance of Amtrak's high-speed Acela trains that a century later zipped along tracks of the Northeast Corridor. After making numerous bold claims and promises, Adams slunk quietly out of sight and was seldom heard from again. Adams was ahead of his time both conceptually and technologically, but by 1907, the industry did at last possess the technology and vision needed to escape its local origins and implement long-distance travel involving the interchange of passengers and even a small but growing tonnage of freight among separate interurban companies.[34]

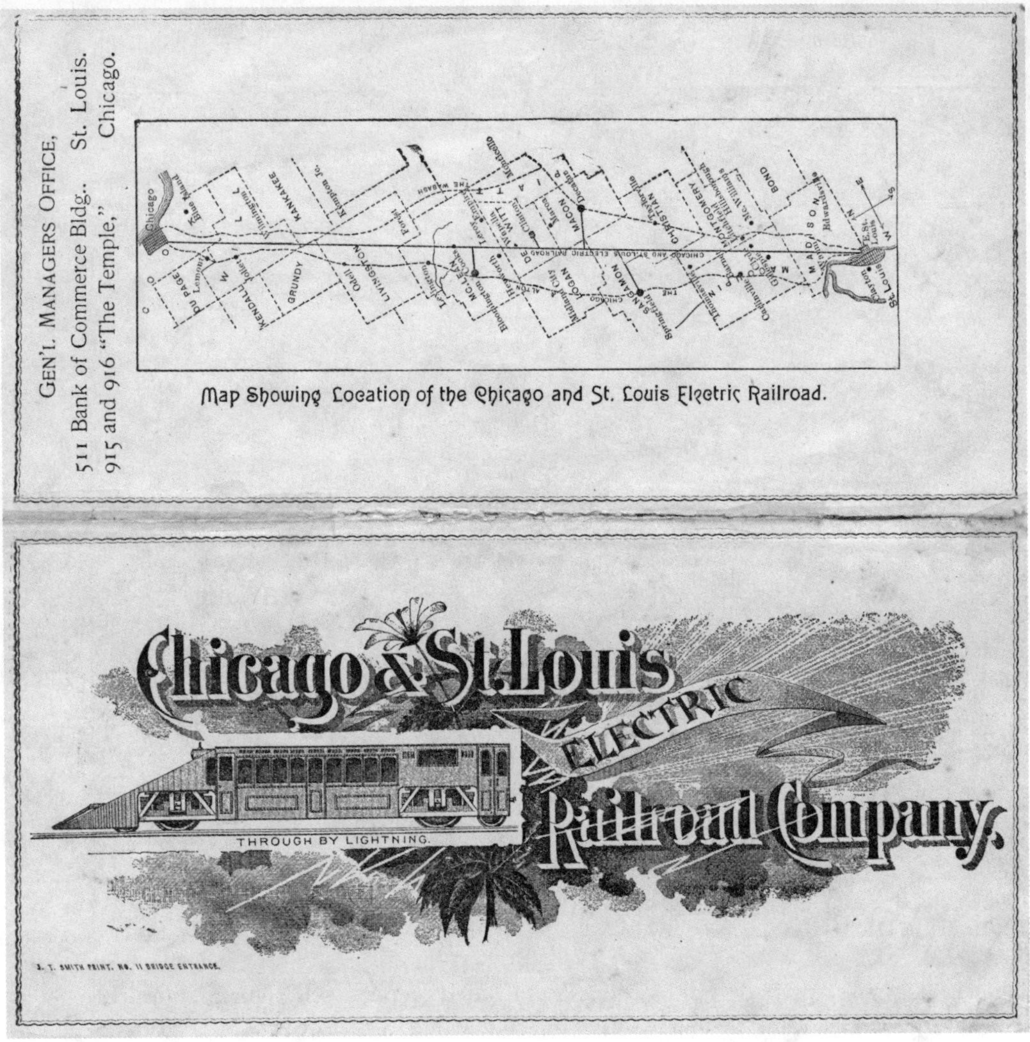

The 1890s prospectus for Wellington Adams's Chicago-Saint Louis interurban line promised far more than it ever delivered, which, according to its critics, was nothing but hot air. The depiction of its proposed locomotives was decidedly futuristic.

Hugh McGowan's Traction Terminal complex included a modest provision for interurban freight traffic, which was only tentatively embraced by Indiana's early electric railways. The crush of freight created by World War I changed minds and inspired construction of a massive new freight depot on the southwest side of Indianapolis.

8

Growing Traffic, Going the Distance

> The transportation of light freight and express matter promises to comprise an important portion of the traffic of the growing number of electric interurban freight systems. Those companies which have taken this up to any extent report themselves as more than satisfied with the results, and the possibilities in this line seem to be very large.
>
> —*Street Railway Journal* (February 1896): 114

The interurban industry was booming in early 1907, and the evolution of its trade journals that year serves as a useful measure of the intensity of interest in all facets of its growth. So much was happening all over North America that the *Electric Railway Review*, a monthly publication from 1891 to 1906, switched to a weekly schedule in 1907 to deal with the flood of information. At the time, it was not unusual for weekly issues of the *Electric Railway Review* or the *Electric Railway Journal* to require additional full pages to list all the new interurban incorporations, the latest construction projects, and the latest track extensions. Often, a single week's tally included several hundred individual news notes. Large and visually appealing advertisements by electric railway suppliers accounted for dozens more pages that further bulked up the special issues devoted to the industry's annual conferences. During the four or five days of meetings, the flood of information grew so overwhelming that both journals switched to a daily publication schedule that yielded a truly prodigious number of pages.[1]

Traditionally, the yearly fall conclave had barely ended before trade journals launched a discussion of the industry's next big conference to be held the following year. In October 1904, the convention-goers of the electric railway industry met in Saint Louis, together with the city's Louisiana Purchase Exposition. Only weeks later, the *Electric Railway Review* enthusiastically began to promote French Lick, Indiana, as its favored site for the 1905 gathering. Had the industry chosen the resort community to host its most important event of the year, Indiana would have gained additional recognition as the state fast coming to the fore nationally as a congenial site for interurban railways. Tucked away in the hills of southern Indiana, French Lick was geographically remote from Indianapolis and all other recognized hubs of electric railway activity.

Indiana, despite its newly achieved status as a world-class showplace for the interurban industry, had not yet hosted any of the industry's big annual conferences. Indianapolis would have been a logical place to hold a national meeting, but in contrast to the positive image of Indiana's numerous interurban lines and despite the appeal of an opportunity to visit the Traction Terminal showpiece, the street railways of turn-of-the-century Indianapolis had become famous for all the wrong reasons. Few, if any, large American cities offered a higher-profile saga of trolley mismanagement and financial ineptitude, bitter and sometimes violent labor strife, and endless litigation between company executives and city officials—at least until Hugh McGowan grabbed the troubled property by both ears in 1899, firmly turned the industry's most notorious problem child around and sent it in a promising new direction.[2]

There were other good reasons to skip meeting in Indiana in 1905, at least in French Lick. Two years earlier, the electric railway industry had held its annual convention in Saratoga Springs, a wealthy resort community in Upstate New York, but some exhibitors and attendees later complained that too many delegates had spent too much time savoring the many pleasures of Saratoga Springs instead of attending to the serious business of going to meetings or examining the latest wares displayed by the industry's many suppliers. French Lick might similarly tempt delegates. Finally, while French Lick could claim to have an interurban line in operation, it was barely one mile long. It connected French Lick and West Baden, the site of a gigantic hotel and architectural marvel that modestly billed itself as "the eighth wonder of the world" because of its domed atrium two hundred feet in diameter.[3]

If industry leaders had been interested in studying paper interurbans, then French Lick would have been the perfect venue. More than any other part of the state, the southwest quadrant of Indiana generated dozens of interurban projects that looked great on paper but never got built. No part of the state was less well served by railroads of all types, but the area's low population density and the marginal economic status of much of its rolling and heavily forested countryside made it a poor prospect for the interurbans proposed to connect French Lick with Louisville, Evansville, Vincennes, and several other centers of population, all of them on the periphery of the Indiana outback.

When French Lick was suggested as a meeting site, a rebellion took place among the ranks of the American Street and Interurban Railway Association. Though not one word of explanation ever appeared in any of the trade journals, French Lick was quietly forgotten after Philadelphia was announced as the site of the 1905 convention. If "serious" was the order of the day, then Philadelphia was an excellent choice. It not only showcased different types of electric railways; the Pennsylvania city that gave the

United States both its Declaration of Independence and its Constitution seemed the perfect venue for serious discussion of where the electric railway industry had been and where it might be headed in the coming years. No one ever mentioned in print that Philadelphia was also home to the investors who bankrolled several of Indiana's big interurban lines, nor was there any indication that electric railway financier Randal Morgan had ever attended the conference even as an interested observer.

Industry conferences, and especially the electric railway industry's international gathering each fall, offered managers from all over the United States and Canada the opportunity to meet together face-to-face to exchange ideas, view exhibits, listen to and afterward discuss special papers and other public presentations, or simply meet in hotel halls and bars to commiserate. Some presentations were highly technical, while others entertained historical reminiscences by industry pioneers like the now-famous electrical engineer Frank Sprague. Sprague's trolley installation in Richmond, Virginia, in 1888 had launched a thousand additional street railways across North America.

Perhaps because street and interurban railways had arisen in so many different places and were typically focused on local matters, the exchange of information and advice among the geographically scattered companies became more vital as the industry grew and matured. Management's desire to know more seemed insatiable.

A new publication introduced during the summer of 1912 was titled simply *AERA* (American Electric Railway Association). Its addition to the already-impressive roster of trade journals was no doubt encouraged by the organization's recent president, Arthur Brady, who wrote the salutary essay. What most distinguished *AERA* from *Electric Traction* or the *Electric Railway Journal* was that each monthly issue contained a lengthy question-and-answer section devoted to facilitating the exchange of highly detailed technical information among personnel connected in any way with electric railways. Participants might include everyone from company presidents to motormen or shop foremen. Job status made absolutely no difference; it was knowledge and hands-on experience that counted. Whether discussing matters in person or in print, the geographically scattered personnel of North America's electric railway industry were able to learn much of value from their industry peers.[4]

It might seem that the annual round of meetings would impose a heavy travel burden on busy interurban executives, but, at least for the men in the Midwest, the one- or two-day regional gatherings usually held every other month in Indianapolis, Toledo, Fort Wayne, Lima, Dayton, and elsewhere facilitated the exchange of useful information. Such meetings also offered management a pleasant opportunity to show off an interurban company's latest private railway car or at least to enjoy riding aboard someone else's car in comfort and style as a guest. The rapidly increasing interconnectivity of the heartland's electric railways made these regional journeys possible and so

The Pride of Union Traction: The Martha

As superintendent of Union Traction, Charles L. Henry wanted the St. Louis Car Company to create the most attractive interurban office car ever built. As readers of *Electric Indiana* had already realized, the dean of interurban executives loathed half measures. The Union Traction car was still under construction when Henry abruptly left the company in late February 1901. George McCulloch gladly agreed to complete what his predecessor had initiated. As Union Traction president, McCulloch valued the new office car not just for its stunning appearance but also because he intended to use it to transport himself and a small group of guests in luxury and style from central Indiana to the Pan-American Exposition in Buffalo, New York, in fall of 1901. When it rolled out the doors of the St. Louis Car Company shops, the Martha was so posh and represented such impressive craftsmanship that both the *Street Railway Journal* and the *Street Railway Review* described its appearance and interior furnishings in detail, as did many daily newspapers.

McCulloch was unable to take his planned trip to Buffalo. Given the disconnected pattern of the Midwest's interurban lines in 1901, he likely would have had to attach the Martha to steam passenger trains to bridge the gaps between the numerous and

Newspapers in some of the smaller communities served by Union Traction were delighted to report that the Martha was in town, an event that portended the arrival of one of the industry's big shots, or perhaps a visit by perennial presidential candidate William Jennings Bryan or Governor Thomas Riley Marshall, a future vice president of the United States.

still locally oriented electric railways. Within five years, however, the Union Traction's Martha would be able to transport company officials and their guests to conferences in almost any sizeable city in Indiana, Ohio, and Michigan—perhaps not yet in a straight line, but the necessary electric railway connections were now in place.

The Martha remained a company showpiece for years to come. Whenever it appeared in Hoosier communities, the locals all knew that bigwigs were aboard. When George McCulloch died in 1915 at his home in Summit, New Jersey, his final ride back to Muncie, Indiana, was aboard the Martha, which his brother-in-law, Arthur Brady, sent to Fort Wayne to meet the Pennsylvania Railroad train from New Jersey bearing McCulloch's remains. The luxurious car, incidentally, had been named for McCulloch's young daughter.

noteworthy that even general-interest newspapers commented on the gatherings and the array of finely appointed company cars displayed at the meeting sites.

Not to be outclassed by Union Traction and its Martha, William B. McKinley ordered a similarly luxurious office car for his Illinois Traction System. In 1911, his capable and long-serving vice president, H. E. Chubbuck, used the company showpiece to highlight the long-distance travel potential of the track network unfolding across the Midwest by making a round-trip journey of nearly fifteen hundred miles between Saint Louis and Cleveland to attend the August meeting of the Central Electric Railway Association in nearby Cedar Point. The Illinois Traction car still required an assist from the Big Four, which obligingly attached it to the rear of one of its steam trains to pull it across the most conspicuous gap that remained in the Midwest traction network. That was the forty-mile break between the ends of interurban tracks that paused (temporarily, most people believed) in Danville, Illinois, and Crawfordsville, Indiana, but otherwise the Illinois Traction car moved entirely under electric power. And move it did! On the well-constructed "Ben Hur Route" between Indianapolis and Crawfordsville, it zipped along at an impressive speed of seventy-two miles per hour on what was reputed to be the fastest interurban raceway in the United States.[5]

Chubbuck was no exception to the observation that managers favored with access to posh private cars invariably enjoyed showing them off.[6] During his nine-day tour of the Midwest in 1911, he invited fellow executives from at least a dozen different interurban lines along the route to join him on his cross-country jaunt. Among those who did so across Indiana was the president of the Indianapolis and Cincinnati Traction Company, Charles L. Henry, now rapidly gaining increased respect as the industry's "grand old man."

Photographs of Henry at this time show a diminutive and always dapper individual who typically wore a somber three-piece suit with a gold watch chain draped neatly across his vest, the entire dark ensemble contrasting vividly with his snow-white hair. His always-stylish public appearance may have resulted from his days in the political limelight or from his one-time ownership of The When, a chain of men's clothing stores based in central Indiana, one of several business ventures that occupied his time apart from interurbans. Standing on a speaker's platform to address a large gathering of fellow executives, Henry displayed the quiet confidence of a man well equipped by intellect and experience to enjoy the best years of his career. National recognition as an elder statesman was something to be savored.

Apart from the usual array of technical papers and presentations, two questions of a more general nature attracted increased attention from conference attendees during 1905 and for several years afterward. Both resulted from the growing interchange of traffic among the interurban railways of the Midwest. In other words, the industry was rapidly outgrowing its local origins, and managers had become increasingly interested in exploring long-distance possibilities offered by the regional matrix of interconnected lines. Newspapers and industry journals enthusiastically recorded each new distance record as the web of interurban tracks expanded. "All long-distance records for trolleys were broken the other day when two cars passed through here [Lima. Ohio] going from Wabash, Ind. to Canton, O., the journey being a distance of nearly 425 miles." Less than two weeks later, a group of traction magnates raised the bar yet again when they ran an interurban from Cleveland to Indianapolis to attend a meeting of the Central Electric Railway Association. Setting new long-distance records became a newsworthy event in the traction business because each one served as a milestone to mark the transition from street railway to interurban.[7]

Two developments stimulated interest in lengthening the scheduled runs of interurban cars across the Midwest. The first was the increasing desire among interurban executives to outgrow their trolley origins and model their companies on steam railroads. The second was that private automobiles nibbled away an ever-larger portion of electric railway revenue derived from passenger jaunts of twenty miles or less. Interstate travel between Indianapolis and Dayton or Louisville held a special appeal for interurban management, which hoped to close the remaining short gaps that prevented cars from running through from Indianapolis to Cincinnati, Saint Louis, and Chicago and might even make overnight sleeping car travel at last practical.[8]

Serious discussion of sleeping car travel highlighted the industry's rapidly evolving perception of the interurbans' purpose and its conviction that individual lines would soon coalesce into a service network extensive enough to justify long-distance overnight trains. Early interurban companies, even if they cooperated to offer through passenger service, were low-budget carriers that ran frequent trains between cities seldom more than a hundred miles apart. The concept of luxurious sleeping car service, while intriguing, made no sense unless the interurban companies outgrew their street railway origins, filled in the obvious gaps between states, and thus greatly expanded their web of tracks across the Midwest.[9]

In their quest to operate more like the steam railroads, interurban managers nonetheless convinced themselves that they should implement overnight sleeper service between Indianapolis and Columbus, Ohio. For years, George M. Pullman had operated sleeping cars on the steam railroad so successfully that his name became synonymous with the upscale class of overnight travel. In the early twentieth century, the Pullman Company operated the world's largest hotel chain, and its prestige was so great that it lured Abraham Lincoln's sole surviving son, Robert Todd Lincoln, to serve several years as president and chairman of the board of the Chicago-based company.[10]

The car manufacturing side of the Pullman enterprise built interurban cars in competition with the J. G. Brill Company, the St. Louis Car Company, and other big rollingstock manufacturers during the early years of the Interurban Era. It soon exited that line of business, however, and chose not to run overnight sleeping cars on interurban lines. Here was a golden opportunity handed to Harris F. Holland, an Indianapolis inventor, who eagerly embraced it with the expectation of making his fortune. He and half a dozen Hoosier investors founded the Holland Palace Car Company in 1903. The enterprise hired Harlan and Hollingsworth, a Delaware car builder, to construct an initial two-car "fleet" of luxury sleepers to Holland's patented specifications. In this way, he sought success by offering interurban travelers of the Midwest an elevated level of comfort aboard the parlor cars and sleepers that he planned to operate in much the same way as the Pullman Palace Car Company had for steam railroad passengers.[11]

The idea may have looked good on paper, but the proposed bistate sleeper between Indianapolis and Columbus soon proved a financial failure. The concept was simply premature, and the Holland firm went bankrupt in 1906. With additional track in place, the proposal for interurban sleepers resurfaced the following year with an even more ambitious reach. "That traction sleeping cars will soon be in demand is the opinion of a number of Indiana traction men who recently made a trip over the trolley lines between Indianapolis and Detroit. They say that it is now possible to travel from Indianapolis to the principal points in the neighboring states requiring from eight to twelve hours and, and if sleeping accommodations could be obtained, they would be patronized."[12]

Holland was ready to resurrect his concept and operate overnight cars on an even grander scale than he had attempted four years earlier. In fact, in 1907, he was "working on plans for an interurban combination sleeping and parlor car, which he claims will eclipse any sleeping car now in existence." The nagging question remained: If he built and operated his luxury cars, would anyone patronize them? He expected to have cars ready to roll in 1908, but the Panic of 1907 upset his plans and those of many others connected to the industry who failed to realize how the financial meltdown would permanently end the interurban's growth years and upset many grand proposals for all kinds of upgrades across the Midwestern network.[13]

Another question that animated interurban discussions before the 1907 Panic was how electric railways might best go about adding a successful freight and express business to their accustomed role of carrying passengers, originally the only reason for their existence. Here, as in so many things, Union Traction was an industry pioneer. As early as 1903, it had begun to haul packaged cargo in dedicated freight cars, and just a year later, in what was one of the industry's earliest interline traffic agreements, it exchanged freight cars with the Indianapolis and Northwestern, a line extending to Lafayette that later became one of the several building blocks of the Terre Haute, Indianapolis and Eastern.[14]

Other individuals had casually discussed this question for years, and by the pivotal year of 1907, some executives had firmly concluded that the "interurban freight business does not pay, and the quicker the traction lines get 'out of the habit' the better." Individuals more in favor of freight prevailed on most interurban lines, however, and by 1907, the time seemed right for carriers to get serious about handling freight and express and how best to facilitate interchange among different companies. A related question was how best to lengthen the runs of interurban passenger trains. Money was to be made by properly addressing both questions, and members of the newly formed Central Electric Railway Association implemented positive responses to both matters.[15]

Industry pioneers had given little thought to questions of distance other than running their interurban cars successfully over the short and locally oriented lines that originally typified the industry. The myopia of the early years was soon recognized to be a "very expensive mistake," as Charles L. Henry candidly admitted to members of Indiana's Board of Tax Commissioners in early 1907. When interurban railways were first projected, he and the other pioneer builders considered them to be "a mere means of transit between large cities and suburbs," and so with that limited horizon in mind they constructed them as cheaply as possible. The result, explained Henry, was that "the old construction is not fit for lines carrying long distance traffic, and companies are compelled to reconstruct their roadways." Improved infrastructure and better rollingstock, both of which would be very expensive, would enable them to handle through passengers and freight. Henry asked that annual tax assessments reflect the financial burden Indiana interurbans must shoulder during their industry-wide makeover.[16]

Increasing the amount of freight interurbans hauled became one of Henry's long-term goals. During his 1912 presidential address to members of the Central Electric Railway Association, he reiterated much of what he had explained to Indiana's tax commissioners five years earlier. Noting that while interurban companies received about 15 percent of their gross receipts from hauling freight, he advanced the radical notion that "75 to 85 per cent should come from this source." Despite Henry's elevated standing among his industry peers, most listeners took his advice with a grain of salt because in 1912, interurban passenger revenue was still climbing, and the rising number of private automobiles had not yet grown worrisome. No significant uptick in freight haulage occurred until traffic during World War I staggered the steam railroads and encouraged Indiana's electric carriers to add livestock, most noticeably, to their cargo mix. During the 1920s and 1930s, it was money derived from freight that kept many struggling interurban companies afloat, including Henry's Indianapolis and Cincinnati Traction Company.[17]

When interurban lines initially reached out from or into urban centers across the Midwest, their builders never expected to connect with one another to form a state or regional network such as they had in place by 1907. Individual companies discovered that while they worked independently from one another to grow their business in the vicinity of hub cities, their tracks increasingly intersected to create an interconnected network of lines. The resulting web was never nationwide, as was the case for the steam railroads, but it eventually came close to blanketing the most populated portions of the nation's heartland. With these often unintended connections came the new possibility that two intersecting lines could merge to form a single company. Or they could at least join to operate through trains, such as a chain of three interurban lines did between Indianapolis and Louisville before they united under the Interstate Public Service Company banner.[18]

Another pleasant surprise not anticipated by interurban pioneers was the growing importance of the freight and express business. Every interurban enterprise was supposed to make money for its investors. Some never did because they were the result of irrational enthusiasm for the new technology. The thinking seemed to be that after a line was opened, it would change people's travel habits and they would gladly climb aboard the interurban cars. In this way, a swelling volume of passenger traffic would pay the company's bills.

Originally, interurban companies were almost wholly dependent on passenger revenues. Further, their charters and franchises often limited them to accommodating only the "carry-on" items brought by passengers. Heavier and bulkier items such as suitcases and steamer trunks were forbidden. This was especially true for some of the small lines built in the New England states. In their quest to turn a profit, an increasing number of Midwest carriers devoted ever greater attention during the years after 1907 to hauling freight and express. Fortunately for them, the state of Indiana did not attempt to prevent interurbans from carrying any cargo except for livestock. "While most of the interurban roads handle freight, this business has heretofore been more of the nature of a small sideline with them than one of their chief sources of income," editorialized the *Street Railway Review*, which had asserted in 1901 "that the importance of the subject has not been fully appreciated."[19]

After World War I, when Indiana legislators voted to loosen restrictions on interurban livestock, the Terre Haute, Indianapolis and Eastern developed a prosperous freight business hauling cattle from farms along its tracks in rural Indiana to Kingan's huge meatpacking plant, which in the early 1920s was the largest single enterprise in Indianapolis. Other interurban companies hauled milk, and some shipped auto parts from General Motors suppliers in Indiana to assembly plants in Michigan. Any express items typically rode in a separate compartment aboard passenger cars, but the freight business on a number of interurban lines grew so large that they devoted entire trains to cargo. Some carriers developed specialized freight cars, such as the refrigerated ones needed to keep milk cool while in transit from rural dairy farms to urban processing plants or special cars intended to transport live cattle to the meat packers.[20]

The Traction Terminal in downtown Indianapolis was just one part of a huge assemblage of related buildings that occupied a block of real estate. It embodied McGowan's expectations for the future because he devoted at least a few of his newly constructed buildings to the shipment of interurban freight and express. In 1904, when it opened for business, the small freight depot seemed adequate to handle the amount of cargo Indianapolis permitted to travel along its city streets. With the loosening of such restrictions during World War I, freight tonnage grew so immense that Henry and three of his industry peers erected a huge new Indianapolis warehouse complex on the south side of the city near the stockyards. Like the city's Traction Terminal, it was the largest of its kind in the world.

Steam railroads did not welcome the interurban freight initiative. Most of them initially regarded their potential competitors as interlopers and refused to allow tracks of steam and electric carriers to interconnect or even to physically cross one another except by means of a bridge. During a legislative inquiry held in Indianapolis in 1901, a group of steam and electric railroad advocates, including Charles L. Henry and Elmer J. Binford of the Greenfield Line, engaged in a heated exchange about intersecting tracks. Urban settings like downtown Indianapolis, Fort Wayne, Muncie, and Hammond featured a dense network of steam railroads, so it was nearly unavoidable for steam and electric tracks to cross at ground level, with trolley cars required to wait for steam trains before proceeding across their tracks. That perceived injustice caused the vice president of the Indianapolis Street Railways to ask his steam railroad counterparts, "Why don't you stop your trains?"

An advocate for the Lake Erie and Western, a steam railroad, shot back, "Simply because your cars are insignificant affairs and our trains are great machines." To which the electric spokesman responded, "Yes, I found that out when one of your engines smashed a car for us in this city not long ago." The Lake Erie man snorted, "If your conductor had done his duty there wouldn't have been any accident." The state senator chairing the hearing interrupted their heated exchange to remind both men to stick to the merits of the bill.[21]

Charles Henry, who had been listening quietly to the arguments, suddenly complained about the many hours he had wasted attempting to persuade steam railroads to allow his interurban lines to cross their tracks.

Interurban tracks used an overhead bridge to cross steam railroad tracks in Monroeville, Indiana. Some steam lines so opposed the physical interchange of tracks with their electric cousins that they dispatched squads of railroad detectives to block interurban construction gangs.

> "I have spent more time in the last three years chewing the rag with railroad lawyers than in all the other details of road construction."
>
> "Oh, Mr. Henry," interjected the Lake Erie and Western spokesman, "you and I came to terms in about three minutes."
>
> "Yes," Henry responded, "after I had chewed it over with your engineer for about three months."

As if to highlight the intensity of the intermodal exchange, the chair used by the spokesman for the Lake Erie and Western Railroad "gave way, letting him fall to the floor, and he was somewhat pugilistic all the evening," observed the reporter from the *Indianapolis News.*[22]

One reason for the fierce rivalry was that steam railroads feared the heightened competition. Another and far more emotionally compelling reason was that a serious accident might result if a trolley or interurban car attempted to dash across the steam railroad tracks ahead of an onrushing locomotive but stalled because of its sudden loss of electric current. In the January 1901 legislative hearing, Charles Henry dismissed that concern as highly improbable. But that much-feared scenario took place in Muncie a couple of years later when, during a severe electrical storm, a Union Traction interurban car "went dead" while crossing the tracks ahead of an oncoming Lake Erie and Western excursion train. The resulting collision was not fatal, but thirty interurban passengers were shaken up by their brush with death. The Indianapolis motorman explained that the intensity of the storm prevented him from seeing the headlight of the approaching locomotive.[23]

Gradually, the relationship grew more cordial, and there was a limited interchange of freight cars between electric and steam railroads. Far more common, however, was the handoff of cars, both passenger and freight, among separate interurban lines. In the Midwest, no electric railway hauled freight with any greater commitment than William B. McKinley's Illinois Traction, which, more than most other electric railways, pushed the boundaries of money-making possibilities and thus served as an industry role model and a conspicuous success well past World War II after hundreds of its interurban peers had failed.[24]

Charles L. Henry and other industry pioneers freely admitted that they lacked suitable role models when they launched their separate enterprises in the late 1890s. Some of the early interurban builders thought mainly in terms of creating an electrified version of a steam railroad with a dedicated right-of-way, substantially built passenger cars capable of providing comfortable and rapid travel between cities, and commitment to a state-of-the-art infrastructure. Others regarded the interurban as little more than an extension of an urban trolley line into the nearby countryside. That meant obtaining a franchise from the appropriate government bodies to lay track in or alongside a public roadway and using lightweight cars and track on a par with the trolleys that bobbed along city streets. Speed was not a consideration, distances were not great, and some early franchises, particularly in the New England states, expressly prohibited electric railways from hauling freight.

A huge controversy arose over the matter of track. The debate lasted throughout the early years and centered on the question of the distance interurban cars might travel toward the center of a large city. Would they need to exchange passengers with trolley lines at the edge of the metropolis, or would interurbans enjoy the opportunity to whisk passengers through from one city center to another, a convenience that would greatly add to the appeal of the journey? Steam railroads by the late 1890s all used T-shaped rails, but the typical trolley company favored grooved or girder rails that could easily be embedded in city streets that their municipal franchises often required them to pave and maintain. Only gradually did street railways across the United States switch to T-rails, although Terre Haute, Indiana, proved early on that the T-rail design worked well in city streets and thus could be used anywhere in the United States or Canada—if city officials would permit them. The primary concern of city governments was that the installation of T-rails would open urban streets to steam railroad freight traffic as well as pose a serious hazard should the narrow wheels of horse-drawn wagons and carriages become wedged in the space needed for the wheel flanges of the electric cars. The other type of rail featured a shallow groove and was not considered a danger to street traffic. One additional concern was that lightweight trolley tracks were not meant to support the weight of heavy interurban cars.

Furthermore, in terms of developing long-distance interurban travel, the electric streetcar proved a poor model for interurbans to emulate, especially for the companies that carried passengers across the Midwest. In that region, their cars typically used a dedicated right-of-way and raced across level terrain conducive to speeds much higher than those of the typical rural trolley in New England that poked along the shoulder of the country lane it shared with horse-drawn carriages and assorted farm animals. The early electric trolleys, in addition, inherited some undesirable features from the horsecar era, such as hard bench seats, no heat on cold winter days except that provided by other human bodies, and floors covered with a filthy mixture of straw and tobacco juice spat by male passengers, a custom so typical at the time that foreign visitors often thought it was a defining feature of travel in the United States. If this sort of discomfort had typified long-distance travel by interurban, passengers would have found the journey unappealing or even repugnant instead of pleasant and inviting.[25]

Across North America, the same intense localism prevailed among pioneer interurban operators in terms of company rules and practices. Every company functioned more or less as an island unto itself with its mission narrowly defined by the limited area it served. The concept of interchanging passengers and goods with any other electric railway was initially beyond comprehension, as was the need to develop an industry-wide set of operating rules. Insular thinking is what made McGowan's idea of constructing a single large traction terminal in the heart of Indianapolis to accommodate all interurban lines entering the city so advanced. To ensure that his grand edifice enjoyed long-term success, he promoted the equally advanced idea that all of the big intercity cars should use his trolley tracks in Indianapolis. That was not the case in many urban areas. Some early interurban lines, for example, terminated passenger service at the outskirts of Cincinnati or Chicago and expected riders to switch to local trolley cars or commuter railways to reach the heart of the city. This was the case for Indiana's South Shore Line when its cars first reached the suburbs of Chicago but could not continue into its downtown.[26]

In many instances, the interurban companies in Indiana and other Midwestern states intentionally laid their track alongside existing steam railroads. During the initial years of the Interurban Era, these were expected to remain the main carriers of freight and express, while the interurban's primary purpose was to haul passengers at frequent intervals for low fares over relatively short distances. Likewise, long-distance travel aboard trains that featured luxuries such as dining and sleeping cars was originally expected to remain the exclusive domain of the steam railroads.

The early years of Union Traction provide a perfect picture of the industry's limited horizons. It constructed its tracks between Anderson and Indianapolis so close to the Big Four's right-of-way that on a hot summer day, a passing steam locomotive could easily blow clouds of coal smoke and soot onto interurban passengers sitting near the open windows. Some steam railroads complained that power for the nearby electric railways created static in the telegraph and telephone wires that paralleled their tracks. Nonetheless, most miles of interurban track across Indiana did parallel a steam railroad despite the opposition. Passengers were always thrilled whenever a race took place between one of the fast-running interurban cars and a steam train pounding along the adjacent tracks

Union Traction trains between Indianapolis and Fort Wayne could attain speeds easily the equivalent of Big Four or Pennsylvania Railroad expresses that crisscrossed Indiana. The ever-larger interurban cars that Union Traction purchased for its longer-distance runs featured an increasingly impressive array of luxuries, and the way things were evolving, Fort Wayne could well have become an intermediate stop for fast multicar interurban trains running between Indianapolis and Toledo. In 1907, only a small gap prevented the interurban lines extending northeast from Fort Wayne from linking with a line reaching west from Toledo. If these tracks could be connected, then Indiana interurban cars could run via Fort Wayne to Detroit and Cleveland—even to Buffalo and cities in Upstate New York. The first interstate connection for Indiana interurbans had been forged in 1903 at the Ohio border east of Richmond. It opened numerous interline possibilities with interurban companies already in operation, or likely to be built, in the Buckeye State. The industry took note of each additional gap as it was closed, sometimes with elaborate final spike ceremonies worthy of a transcontinental steam railroad.

For Arthur Brady "the most noteworthy changes in the interurban situation in Indiana in 1910 were the completion of the Indianapolis-Newcastle line and the Warsaw-Peru line." These two lines for the first time bridged the gap between the separate interurban networks in northern and central Indiana that had evolved independently of one another and in an almost random fashion. "The new line to Newcastle," noted Brady with a generous measure of Hoosier pride, added another spoke to the ten interurban lines already radiating from Indianapolis, "a development unexampled elsewhere in the world." As for the newly forged link between Warsaw and Peru, it is "only about 70 miles long, but it presents a fair example of the interurban situation throughout the middle West. The construction of a few links, each of no great mileage, would immensely enlarge the territory reached and benefited by the existing interurban railroads, from which they in turn would profit. For example, only a few additional miles are needed—none in Indiana—to make an all-interurban route between New York and St. Louis."[27]

Wherever interurban lines extended, passenger transportation was certain to be more affordable than aboard a steam train. In the early days of Indiana interurbans, it was customary for conductors to collect a nickel from all passengers each time the car crossed a zone boundary. On the short interurban line completed between Anderson and Alexandria, conductors initially collected nickels three separate times from through passengers, as would be the case on urban trolley lines. Even with the repeated deposit of nickels, the typical ride cost less than a dollar.

As distances traveled grew longer and as they developed an identity separate from their city railway ancestors, interurban companies gradually implemented paper tickets instead of repeatedly collecting nickels. Individual carriers, particularly the several dozen members of the Central Electric Railway Association, developed ways to sell interline tickets among their interconnected interurban lines to facilitate long-distance travel

From 1898 to 1907, the interurban railways of North America enjoyed one spectacular success after another, and the industry remained optimistic about its future. As a result, enthusiasts supported construction of one new line after another, especially those projects that bridged obvious gaps, such as the one between the potentially lucrative markets represented by the South Bend and Chicago hubs, but electric railway enthusiasm also began to outrun common sense. Every issue of the *Street Railway Journal* and the *Street Railway Review* contained news of dozens of fanciful schemes, all of which sounded very promising—on paper.

During that prosperous decade, moreover, there were no serious financial disruptions to test their belief in the money-making potential of every new interurban line. Until October 1907, not a cloud darkened the industry's bright blue sky. Year after year, the statistical yardsticks the industry used to measure its progress had recorded nothing but positive news as more and more Americans used electric railways to ship produce to markets or to enjoy a pleasant ride.

The industry's blue-sky thinking changed abruptly on October 9, 1907, when in a single day, the bottom dropped out of the American economy, sparking panic on Wall Street that rapidly spread all across the United States and within days witnessed runs on banks that collapsed like a row of toppling dominos. The worst of the financial crisis was over in about a month, but its impact on the interurban industry lasted for years by scaring investors and drying up money needed to fund new electric railway projects.[28]

The industry's rocket-like takeoff was finished. Gone was the unrealistic optimism that initially animated the interurban promoters, investors, and builders. Many interurban companies had trouble remaining solvent depending only on passenger traffic.

As never before, they required the added income that freight and express would generate. Moreover, they needed somehow to outgrow the locally oriented thinking of the industry's early years. Travel just between Indianapolis and Anderson or Muncie no longer sufficed. Union Traction and the Fort Wayne and Wabash Valley needed to combine forces to run interline passenger and freight trains between the big cities of Indianapolis and Fort Wayne. Fortunately, regional organizations like the Central Electric Railway Association were already in place to facilitate the type of cooperation that needed to occur. This was also the time that the Philadelphia financiers grew more publicly visible as they encouraged consolidation of the badly fragmented industry. The money moguls promoted the merger that created the Terre Haute, Indianapolis and Eastern, and even when two allied carriers like Union Traction and the Fort Wayne and Wabash Valley retained their separate identities, the same Philadelphians dominated the boards of what were effectively sister enterprises.

In early 1910, the Central Electric Railway Association published a large and attractive map of the interurban lines across the Midwest. It caught the eye of the *Electric Railway Journal*, and its editor praised the cartography for its clarity and detail. One thing the new map clearly illustrated was how close the interurban industry was to eliminating the remaining gaps to make its Midwest system truly comprehensive. Already, members of various trade organizations were traveling significant distances to promote their communities, as an Indianapolis business group did by journeying around Indiana by interurban. Another delegation of businessmen based in Utica, New York, chartered an interurban car and traveled the entire distance to Louisville, Kentucky, and back to promote their home city. They encountered no gaps during their two-thousand-mile loop trip from Upstate New York and across the Midwest, a newsworthy milestone in the eyes of interurban enthusiasts.[29]

An unusual "sport" that caught the eye of newspapers and electric railway publications in the early twentieth century was the quest by individuals determined to see just how far they could travel across the eastern half of the United States by using only the interconnected network of interurban lines. Albert Bigelow Paine, a writer best remembered as the literary executor of Mark Twain, completed one of the earliest such odysseys between New York City and Chicago in September 1902. His conclusion on completing the lengthy journey: "Steam for speed; trolley for a good time." Paine encountered many gaps in the electric network that he expected to see closed within the next two or three years—"but I am anticipating. It is a habit acquired from interurban promoters."[30]

It took Paine nine days, fifty-seven changes of cars, and fifty dollars in cash "to cover something like a thousand miles of electricity and steam, about one-half of each." Apart from time spent in interviews and fishing in country streams along the way, "it could have been done in a week, allowing ample time for sleep and meals." At the end of his trip, Paine still insisted that he thoroughly enjoyed riding across the eastern half of the United States by means of the electric railways.

> I like to stand out on the rear platform and talk to the conductor while we are speeding up hill and down, through daisied fields and over crystal brooks. I like to make the acquaintance of my own country in this pleasant way, often acquiring intimate knowledge of many goodly cities whose very existence has been unsuspected heretofore. I like to ride through the best parts of a town, and not go rumbling and jangling through the swampy and squalid environs that are peculiar to [steam] railroad right-of-ways. I like to pay my fare five cents at a time, with the privilege of getting off at any place I may select at a moment's notice.[31]

Indeed, electric railway builders soon eliminated nearly all the network gaps Paine noted in 1902. A determined rider could complete the same interurban odyssey in 1909 and encounter only two short gaps, one in Upstate New York and another along the Hudson River. Here was proof that interurban promotion of interline travel for passengers and freight had yielded positive results. An electric railway network at last spanned half the nation, although an interline journey between New York and Chicago remained exceedingly long and arduous, and the trip never grew any easier during the remainder of the Interurban Era.[32]

The intense localism of the early days was now history, and the industry's new emphasis was on executives using their numerous meetings throughout the year to hammer out a uniform set of rules, procedures, and documents that would further facilitate interline transportation. As always, officials from Union Traction and other Indiana interurban companies were prominent and influential at the gatherings of the Central Electric Railway Association and the American Electric Railway and Interurban Association. They often chaired one or more of each organization's numerous subcommittees and served as wordsmiths to craft the resulting reports.

Longevity was one key advantage enjoyed by the Hoosiers—not just personal longevity but also within their positions of regional and national leadership during the first three decades of the twentieth century. Charles L. Henry and Arthur W. Brady were pioneers who lived long enough to become industry elder statesmen, as was Brady's right-hand man at Union Traction, Harry A. Nichol. On the other hand, Robert I. Todd, the executive who helped Hugh McGowan run both the Traction Terminal and the Terre Haute, Indianapolis and Eastern, was a member of the next generation of leaders, but by 1910, he had already gained a wealth of hands-on experience to complement his first-rate engineering education at Johns Hopkins University. The frequent presence of all four Hoosiers at industry conferences made them easy men to buttonhole for advice in the hallways and at luncheons and banquets.

Recall that the interurban network in 1910 originated as an outgrowth of metropolitan streetcar lines, and its builders had originally focused on extending the reach of specific urban centers. Ohio's first-in-the-nation rank in terms of miles of interurban line completed was without doubt a reflection of how the state's five largest population centers—Cleveland, Columbus, Cincinnati, Dayton, and Toledo—all functioned as hubs for separate interurban lines that eventually coalesced to create a statewide network. Indiana ranked second to Ohio, but it originally had only three large hub cities, Indianapolis, Fort Wayne, and South Bend, plus a smaller interurban hub in Evansville. Still missing from electric railway maps published before 1907 were the big consolidations that gave rise to the Terre Haute, Indianapolis and Eastern and the Interstate Public Service between Indianapolis and Louisville. Conspicuously absent from the maps of that era were the lines that soon emerged in northwestern Indiana and extended the reach of the South Bend hub west to Chicago, east to Elkhart and Goshen, and north to St. Joseph, Michigan. Though Evansville remained a conspicuous outlier throughout the Interurban Era, interurban builders had by 1910 successfully connected many of the Midwest's largest urban dots to create a truly impressive regional network.

The process of forging interconnectivity took a giant stride forward with the completion in 1903 of the first interstate link of any type between the interurban networks emerging in Ohio and Indiana. Express trains soon offered through service between Indianapolis and Dayton. It seemed only a matter of months before separate carriers interchanged cars to whisk Indiana travelers to or from any of Ohio's five largest cities. It seemed only a matter of time before interurban lines running from Ohio, Indiana, and Michigan to Chicago or Saint Louis or Pittsburgh were completed, as only relatively short gaps remained to be bridged by interurban tracks already in place by 1907.

The greatest obstacle to Indiana interurbans interchanging through cars with Illinois electric railways as smoothly as they did with the Ohio, Michigan, and Kentucky was the short gap of forty miles that separated Crawfordsville, Indiana, from Danville, Illinois, or the even shorter gap separating track ends farther south at Ridge Farm and Paris, Illinois. During 1906 and 1907, interurbans companies with tracks on the ground as well as half a dozen paper enterprises promised to bridge the gap between Indiana and Illinois lines, which was easily among the most conspicuous in the expanding Midwestern network. Partly to blame for the delay was the Panic of 1907, which at least temporarily dried up both capital and enthusiasm for such projects. Just months before the Wall Street debacle, during the high tide of Indiana interurban enthusiasm, a newspaper could assert, and readers were likely to believe, that all the arrangements needed to complete a line of tracks between Terre Haute and Danville were "assured."

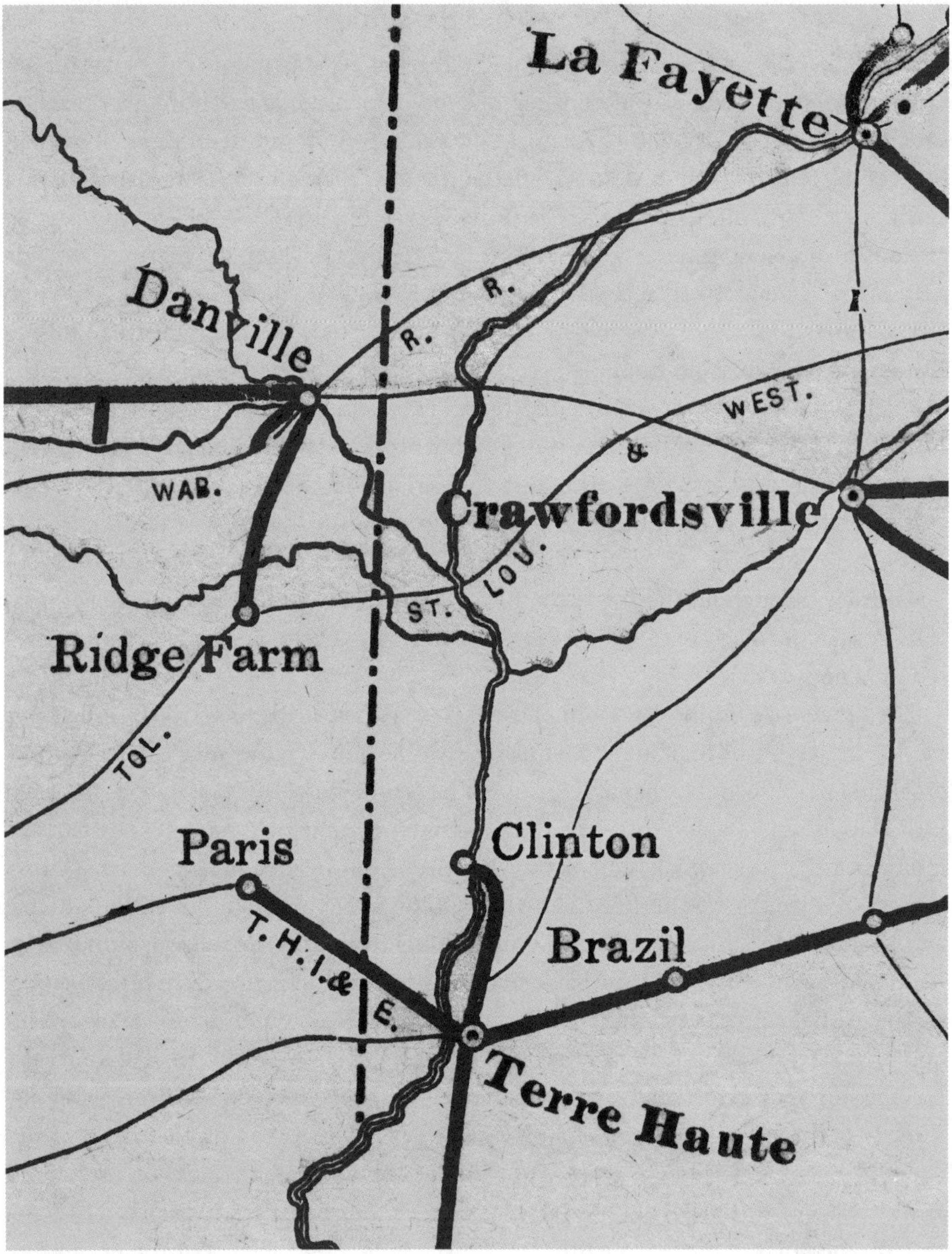

The Danville Connection could have been forged between Crawfordsville and Danville over scenic but rugged country that included today's Turkey Run State Park, or much more easily across a few miles of Illinois prairie between Paris and Ridge Farm.

The Panic of 1907 made a mockery of the commonly heard claim that an interurban project was *assured of success.*[33]

The primary reason that neither short gap was ever closed or that Indiana and Illinois interurban lines never forged the same close alliance as did Indiana and Ohio lines—a spirit of cooperation made visible in the Central Electric Railway Association and the extension of tracks across state boundaries in several different places—was mainly a matter of personality and philosophy, not topography. That is, the failure to bridge either of the short gaps separating Indiana and Illinois interurban networks was not a question of geography; rather, it highlights two different schools of thought that had emerged in the Midwestern interurban industry by 1907.

The expansive-minded business partners Hugh McGowan and Kesley Schoepf thought in broad and encompassing geographical terms as they pondered the growth of their interurban network then developing across the region. At one point, their Schoepf-McGowan Syndicate proposed to create a single huge company that would unite its Indiana and Ohio properties under one banner. More practical thinking gave rise to two state-oriented and thus more easily managed companies, the Terre Haute, Indianapolis and Eastern and the Indiana, Columbus and Eastern, separate Indiana and Ohio enterprises that worked closely with one another. Other executives, including William B. McKinley of Illinois Traction, adhered to a far more focused strategy limited to developing business opportunities close at hand instead of promoting an ever-larger network of tracks, which increasingly seemed like an expensive commitment to growth as end in itself.

Following a decade of construction across the Midwest, only a few more miles of track on the ground in eastern Illinois would complete a chain of interurban lines that stretched from Buffalo, New York, to Saint Louis, Missouri. The industry, which regarded completion of this long-distance route as confirmation of its transformation from a motley collection of country trolley lines into a bona fide railroad network, was poised in 1907 to celebrate this landmark achievement. Farmers in the rural corridor between Crawfordsville and Danville were eager to donate land for an interurban right-of-way and even to join the workforce poised to get tracks into place.[34]

It was not to be, and therein lies an intriguing tale of how money; topography; demography; and, most importantly, personality determined the location of interurban lines. It is a tale of three trolley titans, each of whom was dominant in one Midwestern state: Kesley Schoepf in Ohio, Hugh McGowan in Indiana, and William B. McKinley in Illinois. Schoepf and McGowan, as noted, had a history of friendly collaboration, but while McGowan and McKinley showed public respect for one another, each man jealously guarded his own turf.

On several occasions, newspapers published rumors that Illinois Traction was ready to extend its tracks east from Danville to Crawfordsville to close the gap, but

McKinley vigorously denied them. In 1906, he claimed that Illinois Traction did not wish to run tracks across state lines because it wanted to avoid the regulatory headaches that interstate operation would create. Moreover, he complained that it would be very expensive to bridge the Wabash River, which flowed near the state border.[35]

McKinley did backtrack a few years later when he claimed he had been ready to complete the connection, but the late Hugh McGowan had requested that his tracks remain outside Indiana. The Panic of 1907 then put all construction plans on hold. McKinley insisted that Illinois Traction was no longer interested in bridging the gap. If tracks ever united the Illinois and Indiana systems, McKinley expected his Hoosier counterparts to assume full responsibility for the construction and pay all the attendant costs.[36]

When the economy recovered following the 1907 meltdown, McKinley no longer desired to forge a connection with the central Indiana network that McGowan and his Philadelphia financiers dominated. He turned his gaze southwest instead, and after jettisoning his concerns about interstate regulation and the cost of bridge construction, he decided to link his growing regional network in downstate Illinois with Saint Louis, the nation's fourth-largest city and the metropolis destined to be the single-most important generator of Illinois Traction freight and passenger traffic. McKinley would, however, need to bridge the Mississippi River to forge the connection. Saint Louis was an especially tempting prize because in 1910, the city's population was 687,029—one-quarter of Indiana's population, which was 2,700,876.

As for Illinois Traction bridging the much shorter and far less topographically challenging gap between Ridge Farm and Paris, Illinois, to connect with the Terre Haute, Indianapolis and Eastern: "We, as you know, lack but a few miles of having a southern connection with the Indiana system," explained McKinley. "We would have completed the gap between our lines and the Terre Haute branch but became immersed in the larger affair of our Missouri extension and have not taken that up. When we decide to build a line we do not have to finance it. If the project is approved by our stockholders, we build it without further ado." Worth noting is that McGowan's traction empire had already bridged the Wabash River between Terre Haute and Paris. If McKinley had truly wanted to connect with the Indiana and Ohio networks, he would have spent few dollars to lay a mere twenty miles of track across a stretch of flat and featureless Illinois prairie.[37]

Neither gap was ever closed, and the passage of time proved McKinley's disciplined strategy very wise. When he declined to link with Indiana interurbans simply to enhance the Midwest's network of long-distance lines, the Pennsylvania and the Big Four already operated fast and frequent passenger service between Saint Louis and Indianapolis, and trains of another steam railroad, the Peoria and Eastern, linked another major Illinois Traction profit center, Peoria, with Indianapolis. In contrast to dreamers who promised to extend interurban tracks into every conceivable corner of the Midwest, McKinley's focused strategy stood the test of time, and Illinois Terminal continued to haul passengers and freight long after the Indiana and Ohio networks of McGowan and Schoepf had vanished.[38]

Congressman and US senator William B. McKinley was identified with interurban and utility properties in his home state of Illinois, but he also had investments in Indiana and other areas of the Midwest.

For years, electric railway trade journals measured industry progress by faithfully noting each time interurban tracks filled one of the gaps remaining in the Midwestern network. Another measure of the seemingly ever-upward trajectory, at least in Indiana, was the annual count of the number of travelers that passed through the Traction Terminal in Indianapolis. That figure continued to climb until it reached its apogee in 1916. Of course, no one at the time realized a statistical landmark had been attained. Even before that year, there were occasional troubling statistics that industry executives tended to dismiss as temporary pauses in the ever-upward trajectory of the interurban but that hindsight reveals were significant omens of troubled times ahead. Probably foremost among these harbingers was the noticeable decline in miles of new interurban line constructed across Indiana and many other states after 1907.

Fortunately, the network of tracks already in place did not shrink noticeably until the onset of the Great Depression in 1930. Here and there, a few weak companies were abandoned, but often these were outliers that should never have been built in the first place. Travel remained popular at least through World War I. In addition to regularly scheduled passenger trains, interurban companies took note of ways trolley companies boosted traffic and did likewise. That included a willingness to operate chartered cars for any interested group and promotion of special outings that allowed patrons to escape summer heat and humidity in the city and enjoy a refreshing ride into the countryside or visit one of the many special parks electric railways had created.

Interurban companies picked up the idea of park outings pioneered by the trolley companies and vigorously promoted the concept of relaxed journeys into the countryside, a leisure-time activity that was no doubt a forerunner of the Sunday afternoon automobile drive. In the 1950s, the Sunday outing was still a favorite activity in many parts of the United States, though it is unlikely most drivers were aware that this popular pastime originated years earlier with the street railway and interurban companies.

9

Travel by Interurban

> People ride on interurban railways for convenience, to avoid dirt and smoke, and to save money. These three factors are responsible for the present stupendous development of the interurban.
>
> —*Electric Traction Weekly* (January 1908): 13

"A railroad trip is a journey, and undertaking, a matter of care and consideration. A trip on the electric cars is simply a streetcar ride—no going to a station, no purchase of a ticket in advance, no waiting for a long and expected signal. It simply means swinging aboard in front of your own door and getting off wherever you please." Those words were true in 1895 and would continue to describe the contrasting travel experiences in Indiana and elsewhere until the opening years of the twentieth century. Nonetheless, during that period, the country trolley or "suburban street railway" evolved from the transportation model that dated back to the horse railways of the 1850s as it adapted many of the features of the steam railroads. Perhaps no one did more to push electric interurban railways into transforming themselves from a country trolley into a bona fide railroad than Hugh McGowan, who thought his Traction Terminal to be the equivalent of the Indianapolis Union Station down the street.[1]

Whether McGowan knew anything about Roman mythology, his use of the word "terminal" rather than "station" or "depot" was significant. Terminus was the god of boundaries, and his name in modern times signified the end of the line for a railroad. It was as if McGowan chose the name intentionally to signify that all interurban roads led to Indianapolis and none of their scheduled cars would pass through the capital city without ending or beginning their journeys there.

When the Traction Terminal opened in September 1904, interurban enthusiasm was unrestrained. If the dozens of interurban lines proposed to link Indianapolis with

The Traction Terminal featured a capacious waiting room beneath the nine-story office building.

Chicago, Cincinnati, Evansville, and even Vincennes and Madison had been completed, as McGowan no doubt expected they would be, the Traction Terminal would have been a hub for Indiana and a sizeable portion of the Midwest. The Indianapolis Union Station, by contrast, witnessed the daily arrival and departure of hundreds of steam-powered passenger trains, but most of them only paused in Indianapolis before hurrying on to terminal destinations such as New York, Saint Louis, Chicago, or some other city of consequence.

In the context of its times, McGowan's Traction Terminal was a courageous venture. The federal census of 1900 ranked Indianapolis as the twenty-first-largest city in the United States, with a population of 169,165. In the Midwest, Chicago, Saint Louis, Cleveland, Cincinnati, Detroit, Milwaukee, Louisville, and Minneapolis all had larger populations, but none of them had yet built an interurban terminus comparable to the one erected in Indianapolis, and some large cities like Chicago never benefited from a unified interurban station of any type.

McGowan's Traction Terminal truly represented the capstone of the nation's interurban landscape. Next door, when William B. McKinley extended the reach of his Illinois Traction system across the Mississippi River into Saint Louis in 1910, he built two noteworthy structures: the longest interurban bridge in the world (which he named for himself) and a beautiful new downtown terminus. Although the population of Saint Louis in 1910 was four times larger than that of Indianapolis, its interurban station was small by comparison.

The Traction Terminal opened to the public on September 12, 1904. A huge crowd turned out to see the Indianapolis architectural wonder for themselves and to watch the daylong parade as hundreds of interurban cars boarded or discharged their passengers in the adjacent train shed. One older gentleman seemed wholly transfixed by the spectacle. For nearly an hour, he stood motionless as he leaned on his umbrella and just absorbed the details of his surroundings. To the friends who had gathered around the most beloved figure in Indiana at the time, he pronounced the unfolding scene as "all very fine, indeed." One of them called out, "Going to write a poem about it?" "No, I believe not," responded James Whitcomb Riley, the Hoosier author of more than a thousand nationally esteemed poems. "Only I'm very much interested in this new station. All of us ought to be proud of it." Riley, who had immortalized "The Old Swimmin' Hole" and "Little Orphant Annie" in his native Greenfield, apparently found no poetic words eloquent enough to describe McGowan's contribution to the municipal landscape. Had Riley wished to, he could have boarded one of the big cars and been dropped off an hour later in front of his boyhood home in Greenfield.[2]

Another observer just as transfixed as Riley by the immense crowd steaming through the newly opened Traction Terminal was the visionary most responsible for its construction, Hugh J. McGowan. "I'm so tired I'm almost in a trance," he sighed, "but I just can't keep away from this place. I am fastened to it with ribs of steel." For the past week, he and gangs of workmen had toiled nearly around the clock to get the terminus open in time to accommodate the expected rush of state fair visitors. "Someone will have to pull me away from here," laughed McGowan.[3]

Unlike McGowan or Riley, few travelers cared to hang around the Traction Terminal for an hour or two just to study the crowd of passengers or to admire the unending parade of interurban cars arriving from and departing to locations all over central Indiana. The station was not a destination unless a person happened to work in the nine-story office building attached to the waiting room and train shed. Travelers alighted from inbound cars and passed quickly through the Traction Terminal to enjoy a day of shopping in one of the several commercial emporiums in downtown Indianapolis, to attend the theater, or to deal with the business of state government. The busiest time of

The Big Man Lends a Helping Hand

Late one night during the Traction Terminal's opening week, McGowan was once again admiring his million-dollar masterpiece before heading home. A group of travelers in obvious distress recognized the now-famous president of the Indianapolis Traction and Terminal Company and approached him with a question. Having just missed the last interurban to Greenfield, they asked McGowan if any other cars would be running that way during the night. There were none, and he could not help but note the weary and defeated expressions on the faces of the men and especially of the women. The big-hearted and always chivalrous McGowan immediately summoned one of his local streetcars, boarded the tardy group, and instructed the motorman and conductor to drive them twenty miles to their destination. "The city car started out on its strange journey into the country. The Greenfield citizens arrived home safely, but while the motorman and conductor were returning home, the power was turned off on that line and they waited in the country until 5 o'clock in the morning, letting the trolley feel the cool country breezes."[4]

Interurban companies typically shut off the power at night so that employees could complete routine maintenance in the powerhouse and around other support structures without fear of electrocution. The nocturnal shutdowns, however, provided an opportunity for sneak thieves to steal valuable copper trolley wire. A clever thief working in the dead of night when the power was shut off could steal several hundred feet of wire and make money selling it to an unscrupulous scrap dealer for cash. When a thief stole newly installed copper wire at Union Traction, general manager Harry A. Nichol was determined to foil future larceny. His innovative solution was to add a couple of bloodhounds to the interurban's payroll. It was a matter of debate whether the dogs earned their keep, as wire thieves were crafty and determined crooks.

Interurban cars from a variety of companies are lined up under the massive train shed of the Traction Terminal as they prepare to depart for local and interstate destinations.

the year was always in early autumn during the annual state fair in Indianapolis when interurban cars departed the Traction Terminal every fifteen seconds.[5]

While the capital city was a magnet for numerous residents of outlying communities who rode the inbound cars, the Traction Terminal also functioned as a portal for outbound city dwellers. Departing cars whisked many of these urban riders to suburban parks specially created by trolley and interurban lines to generate what the industry called "artificial" travel—that is, travel not normally done by anyone without a serious destination or purpose in mind. Because cars could stop anywhere, a day trip to a country stream to catch fish became a popular form of "artificial" travel.

An amusement park, itself an invention of the trolley industry, was a favorite way to stimulate "artificial travel." The leading cities of Indiana all featured one or more pleasure parks in the early twentieth century. Union Traction of Indiana once operated four separate parks, the largest ones being Mounds, a forty-acre retreat on the leafy banks of the White River near Anderson, and Broad Ripple, about the same size and also on the White River where it traced a lazy course along the northern outskirts of Indianapolis. A five-cent ride whisked Anderson residents to Mounds Park, the gates of which they entered at no cost to access an array of "high class amusement devices" scattered about the tree-shaded grounds that also featured a dance pavilion, a skating rink, and a bandstand offering vaudeville and motion picture entertainment. Movies were still quite a novelty in the early twentieth century.[6]

Broad Ripple Park, easily accessible from downtown Indianapolis, provided a similar range of attractions, plus a "bathing beach" in the form of a concrete swimming pool filled with purified and chlorinated water and big enough to accommodate as many as two thousand swimmers eager to escape the heat and humidity of the city. The name Broad Ripple was derived from a sweeping bend in the White River. The waterway was normally far too shallow to permit steamboat navigation except for recreational ones offering rides in a few restricted areas, but the scenic five-mile stretch of lazy current was a highlight of the park and provided an ideal environment for casual boaters. "This park has never had a losing season and furnishes the main outdoor attraction for the people of Indianapolis and surrounding territory."[7]

Among the thousands of travelers who crowded the Traction Terminal one morning during the summer of 1905 were three young men eager to use the interurban to get as far away as possible from their urban environment, including its amusement parks. They planned to ride one of the interurban cars operated by the Indianapolis and Martinsville Rapid Transit as far south as it could travel and then hike through the wooded hills of southern Indiana. One of the outdoor enthusiasts was named Kurt and his companions were Jake and Clemens, who kept a diary account of their adventurous trek through scenic Brown County. They had purchased an assortment of camping gear a day earlier at Vonnegut's Hardware, an Indianapolis store run by Kurt's family.

Evolution of an Interurban Landscape

One spring afternoon, I waited across the avenue from Broad Ripple High School for a city bus to take me home. I stood there every afternoon after school, but for the first time, I noticed some half-buried rails showing through the gravel at my feet. I did not fully connect the dots of history until many years later. I did realize that the city buses I rode to and from school went by the name Indianapolis Railways (though the company no longer operated any street railways), but only years later did I learn that the track buried alongside Broad Ripple Avenue had belonged to an eight-mile-long trolley line that linked downtown and what was once the city's northernmost suburb of Broad Ripple.

The line had been the earliest of the city's *long-distance* street railway lines to open. In some respects, the Indianapolis and Broad Ripple Transit Company was the first interurban line to serve Indianapolis, though the term was not yet in common use when its cars began running in 1894. Union Traction acquired both the trolley line and its Broad Ripple Park in 1911. The park had suffered a devastating fire in 1908, but the interurban company rebuilt a bigger and better facility that it operated until 1922. The former Union Traction trolley line was integrated into the trolley network that became Indianapolis Railways. The last streetcar that made the run north to Broad Ripple in 1953 was also the last for the Hoosier capital.[8]

The Broad Ripple Park I came to know in the late 1950s and early 1960s was municipally owned. The roller coaster and similar thrill rides had vanished years earlier, although the park still featured an enormous outdoor swimming pool reputed to be the largest in the world. The star attraction for me was the retired Nickel Plate Road steam locomotive preserved there. Perhaps "preserved" is not the right word,

White City was in Broad Ripple Park in the northern suburbs of Indianapolis.

as anyone was allowed to climb into its cab, and many a vandal must have done so because the glass had been broken out of its numerous gauges. Regardless, the cab was still a fun place to visit when my father took me there, even if it provided a poor substitute for the Pennsylvania Railroad's steam locomotives that once stormed past our Greenfield home. Never in my wildest dreams could I have imagined that one day in 1983, the weather-worn Nickel Plate hulk would be trucked out of Broad Ripple Park, restored to its original glory, and returned to active service as Locomotive 587 pulling trainloads of rail enthusiasts.[9]

Their trip began with a breakfast rendezvous at the Baltimore Dairy, one of the round-the-clock eateries in the Traction Terminal's waiting room. Kurt purchased their tickets at sixty cents each, and an electric car whisked them south as far as the end of the line in Martinsville. Along the way, Clemens noted in his diary, their interurban had to wait "pretty long" to cross the tracks of the Indianapolis Belt Railway because of the "freight trains that kept seesawing back and forth over the crossing at Kentucky Avenue, but from there we made good time arriving at Martinsville at 8:05."[10]

Before commencing their walk in the woods, Clemens paused briefly at the Martinsville Sanitarium to fortify himself with "a drink of sulphur water," while Kurt, who had forgotten to bring along some basic hardware, went off to buy himself a knife, fork, and spoon. For five cents apiece, he picked up three spoons for the entire group. Martinsville, as Clemens must have known, was famous for its mineral springs and the several sanitarium buildings intended to help patrons recover their failing health. This was where traction mogul William B. McKinley came after the Illinois voters failed to return him to the US Senate in 1926. He sought the out-of-state retreat not to forget his recent election loss but rather as a place of healing that somehow might relieve the suffering caused by incurable prostate cancer. He died in a Martinsville sanitarium in late December 1926.

Heading south from Martinsville, the three young men hiked through the rural countryside. They stopped to cook themselves a warm meal or to set up camp for the night. Had they continued to follow one of the dirt roads that led south, they would have reached Evansville, the second-largest city in Indiana at the turn of the century but separated from the center of the state by an overwhelmingly rural landscape. The area's two other primary centers of population were Bloomington and Vincennes. The bucolic setting made the trek through Brown County all the more appealing to the three young men from Indianapolis.

Near Beanblossom Creek, they encountered a crew grading the right-of-way for a rail line to Bloomington, a steam railroad building out from Indianapolis that, unlike the area's many paper interurban lines, actually was constructed. It would do much to open a portion of Indiana that Clemens considered so isolated that it retained the character of the Hoosier frontier a century earlier. The trio continued by foot to Columbus, where after a few refreshing days in the countryside, they boarded one of the Irwins' big interurban cars for the two-hour return ride to Indianapolis.[11]

In the Clemens diary account of the trio's weeklong adventure through darkest Indiana, Kurt says little but is an always helpful presence in obtaining food from local farmers and helping to prepare the meal at their nightly campsite. In 1905, at the age of twenty, he was on the cusp of his lifetime career as an architect. Still farther ahead was the recognition that came to Kurt Vonnegut's son, one of Indiana's most famous authors.[12]

For interurban travelers, the journey began in a waiting room such as McGowan constructed as a central feature of his Traction Terminal complex. Though no other city emulated the size of the Indianapolis structure, other large cities of the Midwest—with the conspicuous exception of Chicago—eventually witnessed the completion of some sort of interurban station worthy of the name—a true terminus in large hub cities, or a small depot or just a storefront waiting area in lesser locations.

Along the tracks in rural areas, the interurban companies typically built unmanned shelters for waiting passengers. Unlike the urban stations, these little structures typically had few redeeming features architecturally. Many were built of solid concrete and resembled an aboveground bomb shelter, as vandalism was a problem even in the early twentieth century. Mercifully, the disfiguring effects of graffiti were largely unknown during the Interurban Era. Boarding the big cars was usually a simple process, although the nine tracks and the constant stream of traffic through the Traction Terminal made the process in Indianapolis more complex and even a bit intimidating for inexperienced travelers.

Indiana's interurban companies originally justified their existence by providing riders with increased mobility and door-to-door convenience at a lower price than the steam railroads did. Luxury and comfort came later. The earliest interurban cars were not radically different from city streetcars, but by the early twentieth century, they had grown noticeably larger and more comfortable. By 1907, it could be truthfully claimed that the "interurban trolley car today on the best lines and the best trains is quite as luxurious in its way as any vehicles found on the best steam trains in the country."[13]

Gone were the hard bench seats of the typical trolley. Carmakers competed with one another to design the most beautiful and functional interurban cars. They proudly displayed some of the best examples of their craftsmanship at the Saint Louis World's Fair of 1904, and when electric railway executives held their annual conference in the Missouri metropolis that same year, they likely visited the fairgrounds to examine for themselves the latest handiwork of the St. Louis Car Company and other rollingstock manufacturers.

In contrast to a trolley, which elicited numerous complaints because they were mercilessly crowded during the morning and evening rush hours when most people rode them, interurban cars featured commodious seats for patrons and an absence of the hubbub typical of a rush-hour trolley. As time went on, they came to resemble the coach typical of a steam railroad. "Union Traction has some beautiful cars for its 'limited service.'" Even more impressive were its buffet dining cars, and, representing the very apex of luxury, "the Indianapolis & Eastern is about to put on sleeping cars, so it will not be long until interurbans here are as well-equipped as the big trains of the steam roads."[14]

The comfortable interior of one of the interurban cars operated by the Ben Hur Route between Indianapolis and Crawfordsville.

Interurban seats were soft and comfortable, unlike the rattan-covered frames or hard wooden benches of a typical trolley, and a few of the best intercity cars featured seats upholstered with fine Moroccan leather. Many newer interurban cars provided an onboard toilet, a smoking compartment for men, and an area behind the motorman to store baggage, areas all lacking aboard a trolley car. "On the limited trains of Indiana and Ohio one may find complete comfort, amounting to almost a luxury. When the habit of traveling by trolley is once firmly established one wonders that the nuisances of the steam roads were ever submitted to. The electric line is the perfection of traveling—at least for short distances."[15]

Perhaps the most controversial portion of an interurban car was its smoking compartment. "[It] cannot be abolished and it would not be politic to urge its abolition," complained one passenger who wished that conductors were more vigilant about keeping the door closed between smokers and passengers seated in the main section of the car. Opening a window often provided little relief from secondhand smoke because many rural residents had "a fear of fresh air and, if a poor unfortunate has the audacity to open it, he shortly finds himself accosted" by fellow travelers fearful of hay fever or a chilly breeze.[16]

One urban protest movement—unsuccessful but giving the public yet another opportunity to vent its frustration with the trolley companies—suggested that patrons need not pay any fare if no empty seats were available. For street railways, this would have resulted in a disastrous loss of revenue. Adequate seating was not usually a problem aboard an interurban, though patrons might crowd the cars to travel to special events like the annual Indiana State Fair.

The idea that interurban cars should carry any baggage at all was part of the big debate that marked the industry's transition in thinking from its street railway origins to its steam railroad aspirations. When Union Traction drew up a list of rules regarding baggage handling, it placed corpses in a special category and refused to handle the remains of any victims of smallpox or other loathsome diseases. Only gradually did interurban companies around the Midwest warm to the idea of carrying a passenger's baggage for free. Most member interurbans of the Central Electric Railway Association dropped the added charge in 1907 or 1908.

One important question during the informal public debate over the nature of interurban railway service was how much luxury, if any, to offer patrons of their cars. Illinois Traction became an early-day pioneer when it added parlor cars, buffet diners, and even sleeping cars to trains running between Saint Louis and Peoria, the second-largest city in Illinois after Chicago in 1910. This was a rare instance of an interurban company offering luxury and convenience that the steam railroads could not match.

Because interurbans were originally envisioned as locally oriented, low-budget carriers, running overnight sleeping cars was barely considered because it was of little practical value, at least initially. In many instances, the endpoints of an interurban line were spaced a mere two hours apart, a distance far too short to justify any type of sleeping car service. The concept quickly failed when first implemented on an interurban railroad linking Columbus with Zanesville in eastern Ohio. The distance was too limited to be practical and the market too thin. In the end, only three interurban companies made a long-term success out of overnight sleeping cars: Interstate Public Service between Indianapolis and Louisville, Illinois Traction between Saint Louis and Peoria, and the Oregon Electric between Portland and Eugene. A traveler who rode the overnight car between Indianapolis and Louisville in 1924 praised Interstate's new sleeping cars as "comfortable and luxurious" and noted that especially appreciated by tall people were oversized beds several inches longer than those aboard steam railroad Pullman cars.[17]

The longest of these overnight journeys, the one between Saint Louis and Peoria, was not even 150 miles in length. The full trip could have been completed in about four hours. Passengers thus spent half the night stationary in Springfield. At least a journey by sleeper saved the cost of a hotel room, and a traveler awoke refreshed and ready to conduct a day's business in a new destination.[18]

A good interurban trip, like one made aboard a commercial airliner today, operated as advertised in the timetable and experienced no unexpected delays. But delays occasionally happened. It was not common for a section of trolley wire to break, but because interurbans carried no onboard source of motive power, a break anywhere along the line between the powerhouse and the car meant a delay.

Lightning presented a special problem. It could wreak such havoc that most interurban companies simply shut down during violent thunderstorms because a single lightning strike could send two or three hundred million volts pulsing along wires to burn out costly powerhouse transformers and car motors alike. For powerhouse and substation operators, the spectacle of clouds of acrid smoke from a burning transformer and electric arcs flashing and darting around the building interior was as memorable as it was frightening. Interurban car riders inconvenienced by the temporary shutdown could not imagine "that men are standing amid flashes of flame that would terrify the uninitiated—we heard of a newly hired substation employee who leaped through a window, taking sash and all with him when lightning entered the station—their minds intent on only one thing, that service should be uninterrupted no matter what happened."[19]

Winter weather, while generally free of lightning, presented its own set of challenges. "The electric railway manager dreads a sleet storm even more than he does a snow storm." An ice-coated trolley wire could not make proper contact with the trolley wheel or shoe to transmit electricity to onboard motors. Some sort of sleet cutter had to be dragged along miles of overhead conduit to restore normal operations.[20]

The ultimate delay to an interurban car came with a derailment or wreck. As with commercial aviation today, interurban accidents were exceedingly rare. Over the years, they took many different forms and invariably generated newspaper headlines. Not only did head-on collisions occur, most disastrously at Kingsland (1910) and Alfont (1924); industry's journals also recorded stories of interurban and trolley cars hit broadside by fast-moving passenger trains as they sought to cross a set of steam railroad tracks or that plunged off the end of a bridge and drowned nearly everyone aboard.

Of all the natural events that disrupted interurban operations—from blizzards to summer thunderstorms—none was more disastrous than the great flood of March 1913, when heavy rains turned hitherto dry parts of Indiana and Ohio into lakes and raging rivers. The Interstate's interurban cars between Indianapolis and Louisville were out of service for at least six weeks because so many sections of track had been undermined by the floodwaters or entirely washed out.

As Indiana became known worldwide as the most important place to witness electric interurban railways in daily operation, out-of-state newspapers occasionally dispatched a reporter to Indianapolis to describe the latest developments. The *Chicago*

Deep water stranded this Indianapolis trolley during the great flood of 1913, the worst natural calamity ever experienced by the interurban lines of Indiana and Ohio.

Tribune in 1908 dispatched Elliott Flower to Indiana as an appropriate way to launch his "attempt to travel from Chicago to New York exclusively by trolley car." Following the obligatory visit to admire McGowan's Traction Terminal, Flower boarded one of the through cars for Dayton. After a slow exit from the crowded streets of Indianapolis, the car sped alongside the National Road at an average speed of thirty-two miles per hour, although the *Tribune* reporter did note an occasional mile-a-minute sprint along good stretches of track through rural portions of the route. As for the quality of the ride, "It was like life on the bounding wave when we went through an undulating countryside. It would be no trial at all to get seasick on a limited interurban trolley."[21]

Because interurban runs typically covered only a fraction of the distance of the best passenger trains linking New York and Chicago, and especially the two- or three-day journeys between the Midwest and Pacific coast, they failed to generate the same kind of romantic travel accounts that transcontinental train travel did. The finest trains of the Atchison, Topeka and Santa Fe or Union Pacific were posh hotels on wheels, and names like the Overland Limited or Santa Fe De-Luxe conveyed a cachet that the Union Traction's Muncie Meteor or Marion Flyer could never hope to match. Something about train travel from one side of the continent to the other was magical, an attraction that an interurban journey, even one aboard an express train between Indianapolis and Dayton or between Cincinnati and Toledo, could never match.[22]

New electric railway construction projects had become a rarity across Indiana by 1910, but improvements to the existing network of lines kept the state at the forefront of all things related to the interurban. That year, the Lee Syndicate of Iowa newspapers sent J. C. Carmichael, editor of the *Davenport Times,* to Indianapolis to write a series of reports titled "What Interurban Railroads Are Doing for Cities in the East." Carmichael began his fact-finding tour in Indianapolis where he noted that "in eleven different directions with Indianapolis as a center, extend interurban lines, connecting the capital with every important city in the state" as well as with every metropolitan center of Ohio and even as far east as Buffalo, New York. Even more amazing was that all eleven lines converged in the heart of Indianapolis in McGowan's million-dollar Traction Terminal. Carmichael found it "impossible to convey" to readers in Iowa "the impression which a visit to this big passenger station Sunday morning made on me. In the immense wide waiting room a block long, there were no less than a thousand people, coming and going, waiting for trains, hurrying, talking, and gesticulating, crowing around ticket windows and information bureaus, grabbing a hurried lunch in the restaurant, plying the guards with questions, soothing crying babies and creating a pandemonium, equal only to that of any other crowded passenger station on a convention day."[23]

The early months of 1910 were an exhilarating time for America's interurban industry. Passenger traffic increased at a healthy pace, as Carmichael observed during his July visit that year to the Traction Terminal. After a decade of frenzied growth, it seemed that the impact of the Panic of 1907 was not entirely negative. True, the resulting lack of investment capital had dramatically slowed the pace of new construction, but some projects of dubious merit needed to be paused. When viewed from the perspective of the summer of 1910, the financial storm three years earlier had a salutary effect. It reined in the runaway enthusiasm that was the hallmark of the industry's first decade and encouraged it to achieve a much-needed measure of maturity. This time around, its prosperity seemed more healthy and perhaps even more sustainable than during earlier times—at least until late September 1910 when a string of fatal accidents unexpectedly cast a dark shadow across the interurban's path going forward.

It was clearly time for some sober reflection on the interurban industry's safety shortcomings, a topic not seriously addressed during its frenzied years of geographical expansion and technological breakthroughs. One word frequently applied to the early years of the Interurban Era was "optimism," but perhaps a more expressive term in light of the catastrophic events of September and October 1910 is "hubris." This word accurately describes the industry's excessive confidence, even arrogance, that resulted in pride in its many accomplishments only to be followed by public humiliation when deep-seated operating flaws were unexpectedly exposed.

The Kingsland crash took place during daylight hours, unlike the fiery Alfont crash of 1924, and postcard photographers recorded many details of the grisly 1910 event.

10

A Time for Sober Reflection

> Serious collisions, accompanied by great loss of life, have recently occurred upon interurban electric lines. The rapid development of these lines during the past few years has emphasized the unsafe methods under which they are operated.
>
> —William Kilpatrick, secretary of the Illinois Railroad and Warehouse Commission (1910)[1]

Electric railway industry executives could view the decade before 1907 with understandable pride. The years between 1898 to 1907—from the year the word "interurban" first gained widespread traction until the high-water mark of the interurban excitement—truly deserve to be called the Interurban Era. That period offered seemingly boundless opportunities to electric railway promoters, investors, and inventors. Canny investors like Charles Yerkes grew so wealthy and powerful building mass transit systems in Chicago and London that Indiana-born author Theodore Dreiser composed a fiction classic called *The Titan*, which immortalized a malevolent Yerkes-like character. Long before *The Titan* was published in 1914, the American public was ready to believe the worst about its electric railways and the supposedly grasping individuals who managed them.

In Indiana and elsewhere across the Midwest, many of the early interurban lines passed from the hands of local people to distant owners "in the form of syndicates or so-called 'holding companies.' The reason for this at first was usually the lack of funds to replace worn-out apparatus or to purchase additional equipment necessary to serve a growing community." One of the foremost legal geniuses who made these financial schemes work to his advantage was Randal Morgan, who made millions from his clever utility investments. As a result of manipulation by Morgan and others, many investors regarded electric railway securities with growing suspicion, and the popular press found it easy to demonize traction magnates, even those who sought to run an honest enterprise.[2]

When Charles L. Henry finished his after-dinner reminiscence at the first (and last) annual banquet of the Indiana Electric Railway Association in 1906, Arthur Brady, the evening's toastmaster, introduced the next speaker with an interesting and revealing choice of words, reflecting that "there were two classes of unfortunates who served the great public," and that no matter how hard they tried, the public reviled them both. He referred to street railway managers and journalists. The next speakers were both Indiana newspapermen, one of whom, the editor of the *Indianapolis Star*, no doubt understood exactly what Brady was talking about. Criticism of the press was probably as old as the press itself, but why was the street railway industry so reviled, and why did it matter?[3]

Few if any business enterprises defined the daily lives of so many millions of Americans more than the street railway industry. Six days a week, the public rode the streetcars to and from work. If the cars were late, overcrowded, or overheated, or if a conductor was grumpy from a poor night of sleep, the riders felt they had a right to complain. They protested vigorously if a streetcar company dared to propose adding even a single cent to the time-honored fare of one nickel, and local politicians tasked with approval of the increase tended to side with the constituents who had elected them and against the trolley companies. When Theodore Dreiser wrote *The Titan* about a corrupt trolley magnate, he effectively tapped into the negative perception already held by many streetcar riders.

Interurban companies escaped most of the public hostility because their fares were typically determined by the length of the ride, and not nearly as many people rode them on a regular basis as they did the trolleys. Nonetheless, in 1919, both segments of the electric railway industry were tarred with the same brush when they were desperate to increase fares to cover rapidly rising expenses caused by raging inflation during and after World War I. The situation so imperiled the future of the industry that President Woodrow Wilson established a special commission to study the problem and make recommendations. Public hostility had surfaced earlier in 1914–15 in the form of the public's widespread support for the jitney, the unlicensed automobile alternative to the trolley, but even in 1906, when Brady took note of rising public animosity, a number of Americans had already purchased automobiles and used them instead of the streetcars. One visible result was that traffic jams clogged downtown streets, slowed street railway travel, and caused late-running commuters to grumble.

In 1907, the compass of investment opportunity began to point in a new direction favorable to the automobile industry. The problem was that when the compass needle started to swing, especially if it moved slowly, most investors could not easily perceive that the change was truly permanent except through hindsight. That was the case during 1907. Despite the Wall Street crash that October, the momentum created by ten good years caused observers of the electric railway industry to conclude that despite a momentary pause, the good times would again roll on and on. Thus, additional interurban projects continued to be proposed and bankrolled as if nothing had changed. In truth, the momentum created by the industry's best decade of growth enabled it to weather the Panic of 1907 in better shape than the steam railroads, which suffered greater pain than their electric little brothers when investment capital unexpectedly dried up.

Despite the incorporation of dozens of Indiana interurban lines that showed great promise on paper, after late 1907, it grew significantly harder to push the construction of a newcomer through to completion. Among the final big interurban projects launched in Indiana was the grandly titled Indianapolis, New Castle and Toledo Electric Railway. Its lengthy struggle to get tracks on the ground highlighted the permanent changes that overtook the industry between the unplanned downturn in late 1907 and the recovery of confidence in early 1910.

When a group of Indianapolis entrepreneurs launched the state's newest interurban project in 1905, they had no reason to doubt that its tracks would reach the Ohio metropolis as expected. Construction crews were busy grading a right-of-way and laying track when the Panic of 1907 struck. Just days later, the leaders of the electric railway industry convened in Atlantic City for their big annual gathering. The conference program took no notice of the financial storm, though delegates may have discussed the week's disquieting events among themselves, and no one could ignore the newspaper headlines that unveiled the woes unexpectedly besetting one of their most important suppliers, the gigantic Westinghouse enterprise, which abruptly entered receivership.

At almost the same time, the Indianapolis, New Castle and Toledo ran short of money to pay its construction costs and was among the first of Indiana's interurbans to enter receivership because of the Wall Street crash. Contractors had completed tracks about four-fifths of the way from Indianapolis to New Castle when they abruptly halted work in a rural part of Hancock County. The interurban's nickname, the "Honey Bee and Wild Flower Line," was an appropriate moniker given that its bucolic right-of-way remained idle for the following two years while lawyers waged a lengthy court battle in Indianapolis for its survival.

The interurban's fate rested with Vinson Carter, the circuit court judge tasked with deciding whether the railway should resume construction across Hancock County or tear up the forty miles of track already in place and sell it for scrap. Judge Carter, who at the time also oversaw the receivership of Charles L. Henry's Indianapolis and Cincinnati line and seemed supportive of interurban railways, pondered the matter before urging the company to press forward. With the court's blessing, the Honey Bee and Wild Flower Line did begin to creep once again toward New Castle, a Gas Belt community barely sixty miles from Indianapolis and two hundred miles short of the interurban's stated goal of Toledo.

New Castle was not a large city. Its population in 1910 was a modest 9,446, and interurban cars of the Terre Haute, Indianapolis and Eastern already connected it to the capital city via Dunreith and Greenfield. The single-largest population center that Honey Bee cars served between Indianapolis and New Castle was Shirley, a village of 1,519 residents in 1910.

Promoters of the Indianapolis, New Castle and Toledo had previously built a steam railroad, the Indianapolis Southern, and profited by selling the line to the Illinois Central, which thereby gained access to the vibrant Hoosier heartland. By sandwiching their interurban to New Castle between Union Traction and Terre Haute, Indianapolis and Eastern routes already in place, they may have intended their latest enterprise to serve mainly as an irritant, and so they could expect to reap their financial "honey" not from any actual interurban operations but from a buyout by one of the two rivals.

In any case, runaway enthusiasm as exemplified by the saga of the Indianapolis, New Castle and Toledo never could compensate for the fact that it was an interurban latecomer that closely paralleled tracks of the Big Four's Peoria and Eastern subsidiary and served mainly a string of rural villages like Shirley, Maxwell, and Mohawk, which if combined still numbered only a few thousand residents. The days of electric railway construction were rapidly nearing their end when the Honey Bee line finally limped into New Castle, a manufacturing center located northeast of Indianapolis but still a considerable distance from Toledo. Even attaining New Castle represented a triumph of sorts because, during its hesitant crawl, the line had prevailed over false starts, injunctions, receivership, and repeated visits to court.[4]

It required five years to get tracks on the ground and to launch regular service. The financially battered property operated under its own name for a few months and thereby allowed Indianapolis boosters to brag that twelve separate interurban companies now extended the city's reach across central Indiana. In addition, the Indianapolis, New Castle and Toledo provided a prime example of an interurban line that never should have been built but that somehow made sense to its backers during the height of industry enthusiasm.[5]

The lengthy struggle ended in October 1912 when Union Traction gained control of the hard-luck enterprise by means of a 999-year lease and provided it with a much-needed infusion of working capital. After laying a short stretch of connecting track between Muncie and New Castle, Indiana's largest interurban used the Honey Bee line to acquire a third entrance into Indianapolis. Ironically, despite its financial woes, the Honey Bee line did build a nearly arrow-straight line—one of the longest straight stretches of interurban track in the United States and one made for speed. Its cars, moreover, featured a sharply angled prow intended to split the wind as they sprinted across the farmlands. Union Traction thus gained an unusually fast entrance into the Hoosier capital.

The line might have remained marginal, serving mainly the rural residents of northern Hancock County, if the newly formed Indiana Railroad of the early 1930s had not unexpectedly abandoned a lengthy section of track alongside the National Road and transformed its unassuming Honey Bee into a new main line linking Indianapolis and Dayton via Richmond.[6]

The Honey Bee line was perhaps lucky. Many new companies announced during the boom years never got beyond surveying and then grading a few miles of their proposed line. In most cases, if and when industry leaders paused to take an in-depth look at what afflicted new electric railway projects, they blamed the increasing difficulty they faced in raising investment money after the Panic of 1907 or the noticeable increase of negative public opinion during the early twentieth-century era of the "muckrakers." Seldom, however, did they cite the ever-rising number of private autos—at least not until 1914 and 1915, when the "jitney plague" in a matter of mere weeks had visited fearsome financial destruction on the electric railway industry. Because the jitney remained an industry bugaboo for at least another decade, its role in awakening the electric railway management to the dangerous impact of the automobile deserves an in-depth look in the following chapter.

The years from 1908 until 1915 would, in fact, see continued growth among interurbans, though not at the blistering pace of the decade before 1907. Momentum built up during the good years encouraged interurban executives to expect a return to boom times despite the dwindling enthusiasm of investors, an unexpected turn of events that industry leaders considered only a temporary setback.

The year 1910 witnessed an unusual number of interurban accidents. The first smashup occurred on New Year's Day and might have been seen as an omen of the several far-worse accidents that occurred later in the year. The eastbound Dayton Limited and the westbound Newcastle Limited, two of the finer trains of the Terre Haute, Indianapolis and Eastern, met head-on at a siding just west of Greenfield. Shrouded in dense fog, the two trains telescoped into one another with an impact that demolished the head-end smoking compartments. The miracle of January 1 was that, apart from two gravely injured motormen, passengers escaped with nothing more serious than bruises and superficial cuts from shattered window glass.[7]

In the collisions that occurred during the fall of 1910, travelers were not nearly so fortunate. The rapid succession of tragedies, one of which resulted in the death of forty-one passengers near Bluffton, Indiana, shook the industry to its very foundation and forced its proponents to reflect as never before on the interurban's obvious

Who's On First?

Midwest interurban executives loved baseball both for the fun it provided them during their numerous gatherings and for the game's potential to boost ridership and revenues by encouraging fans to use the electric cars to attend out-of-town games. Electric railways of central and northern Indiana sought to encourage the formation of "Interurban Leagues" among the cities they served. Often the plan was to situate a baseball diamond and a set of bleachers close to an interurban stop for the convenience of fans expected to travel aboard the electric cars.

As to who played first base, it was Arthur W. Brady. At least, that was the case when members of the newly formed Central Electric Railway Association (CERA) gathered in Fort Wayne in September 1906. At the time, the interurban executives of Indiana and Ohio were still getting better acquainted after the merger of their respective trade organizations. A friendly game between teams dubbed the "Hoosiers" and the "Buckeyes" seemed like a good way to build collegiality among leaders of approximately two hundred separate interurban companies.[8] Thus, Brady of Union Traction manned first base for the Hoosiers, Charles Henry second base, Will Irwin third base, and Charles Emmons right field, with lesser-known interurban managers taking outfield positions. Harry Nichol, Brady's capable manager at Union Traction, pitched for the Hoosiers.[9]

The Hoosiers had the bases loaded and were poised to overtake the Buckeyes when somehow the only baseball available disappeared into the tall grass nearby and could not be found. At this point, the umpire summarily declared the game over and fled the confused scene aboard a departing streetcar. In his younger days, Henry had played baseball as a member of a team fielded by his hometown of Pendleton, Indiana.

Try as they might, the interurban companies of Indiana had no better success in launching successful baseball leagues, despite repeated attempts, than the Hoosiers and Buckeyes had in determining who won their 1906 game in Fort Wayne. In one typical case, a 1904 attempt to form an interurban league with paid players from Anderson, Muncie, Alexandria, Tipton, Kokomo, Logansport, and Peru failed because of a lack of financial agreement—or, in the words of an Elwood newspaper, it vanished "up the flue" like a puff of smoke.[10]

shortcomings. One of the best opportunities for interurban managers to confer, or commiserate, came just days later.

Ever since the dawn of the Interurban Era, the geographically scattered industry leaders had considered conferences of all types to be vitally important. Every year, they held many such gatherings, and 1910 was no different. Their most important yearly conclave took place that October in Atlantic City, New Jersey. Industry experts presented papers on an array of topics, but as was typical for such gatherings, some papers were interesting while others proved so boring that most delegates preferred to remain in the exhibit hall to "kick the wheels" of the latest rollingstock on display. Others escaped outdoors to stroll along Atlantic City's famous boardwalk.

Prominent among the hundreds of delegates who attended the Atlantic City gathering in 1910 was Arthur W. Brady, Union Traction president and president-elect that year of the American Electric Railway Association. That office, typically a one-year appointment, was the highest honor the industry could confer on one of its members. One evening, the ever-gracious Brady hosted a special banquet that included several of the organization's past presidents and other guests. Ordinarily, an occasion like this would have offered Brady's guests an abundance of delicious food and time for some good-natured banter. This evening, one topic above all others may have been quietly discussed among the tablemates, but certainly not within the hearing of their genial host and president-elect. Some guests were no doubt surprised that Brady even showed up, given the recent interurban crashes and the resulting avalanche of public criticism that threatened Union Traction back home in Indiana.

Atlantic City lent itself well to the sociable side of the annual electric railway gathering. A friendly game of baseball would encourage camaraderie among players and spectators alike, and delegates could always enjoy the bracing air from the Atlantic Ocean as they ambled along the city's boardwalk.

Everyone attending the 1910 conclave in Atlantic City could use the diversion offered by a friendly baseball game or the tonic of a boardwalk stroll because of the oppressive atmosphere that unexpectedly had threatened their industry's well-being. As usual, the *Electric Railway Journal* published its daily editions detailing the previous day's happenings, but none of its four special issues dared mention the brewing crisis, though informal discussions of the recent string of horrific interurban crashes almost certainly took place in hallways and along the boardwalk. The next week, however, the *Electric Railway Journal* finally broached the topic that most troubled interurban delegates meeting in Atlantic City and especially the organization's incoming president, Arthur Brady. That he showed up at all is testimony to his personal courage. Neither of his two closest lieutenants accompanied him because they needed to deal with urgent matters back in Indiana.

The names of the closely allied Fort Wayne and Wabash Valley and Union Traction Company are clearly visible on the sides of the two wrecked cars, as is a swastika, an ancient symbol commonly used in Asian countries and among Native Americans.

Under the headline "The Interurban at Bay" the industry's leading journal took note of the recent fatal crashes in Indiana and Illinois. All involved multiple fatalities as two fast-running interurban cars rounded a curve and dramatically smashed headlong into one another. The unthinkable events had occurred only days apart, and so they collectively contributed to an industry-wide crisis of confidence: "Several unfortunate accidents which have occurred on interurban roads recently have led to the hasty suggestion that if happenings like these cannot be prevented it is best to discontinue operation of the roads. But the destruction of the properties would benefit no one and would remove an excellent and much desired public service."[11]

The most serious of these "happenings" took place in northern Indiana on September 21, 1910, only days before the Atlantic City convention. At Kingsland, a village several miles north of Bluffton—where the Union Traction intersected with the Fort Wayne and Wabash Valley Traction Company to form a through route between Indianapolis and Fort Wayne, two of the state's most important interurban hubs—two fast-running cars met head-on. The resulting crash killed forty-one passengers. The death toll must have weighed heavily on president-elect Arthur Brady; the Fort Wayne and Wabash Valley was a sister company to his own Union Traction. To make matters even worse, just three days after the Kingsland crash, on September 24, 1910, Brady's own Union Traction suffered a head-on smashup as two interurban trains rounded a curve near Tipton. The wreck killed six Kokomo-bound passengers and injured twelve others. At about the same time, two other Union Traction cars met head-on in a fatal crash near Union City.[12]

As if to confirm the superstition that bad luck comes in threes (or maybe fours), just days after the three fatal Indiana crashes, on October 4, two Illinois Traction cars rounded a sharp curve two miles north of Staunton. Thirty-seven passengers died in the head-on crash. Illinois Traction president William B. McKinley described the latest wreck as "inexcusable."

That three of the largest and best-run interurban companies in the United States should suffer such "inexcusable" crashes in close succession loosed the furies. In Greek mythology, the furies were a fearsome trio, goddesses of vengeance and retribution who punished humans for crimes against the natural order. In 1910, the furies were well represented by the popular press, and not just by newspapers that specialized in the muckraking articles so popular at this time. "When a wreck occurs," observed the *Electric Railway Journal*, "there is a loud public outcry." That classic understatement appeared in October 1910.[13]

The year 1910 was thus both exhilarating and very sobering—exhilarating because the growth of the interurban's Midwest network far exceeded the humble expectations of its pioneers, and sobering because the industry had suffered so many accidents in quick succession. The head-on crash near Bluffton, Indiana, was a public relations nightmare as well as the worst-ever disaster to befall the young industry.

Photos of the Bluffton crash were crystal clear when published in newspapers and magazines across the nation, and their details conveyed to readers the full horror of what happened when two wooden and rapidly running interurban cars ran headlong into one another. One photo showed a line of sheet-covered bodies arranged alongside the pair of smashed cars. Americans were far more sensitive to such human tragedies in 1910 than they would be at the time of Union Traction's Alfont crash in 1924 because the public had not yet experienced the emotionally numbing effects of World War I trench warfare, the unleashing across the battlefield of poison gas, and the influenza pandemic that killed millions of people during the war's waning weeks and immediate aftermath.[14]

Two industry pioneers expected to serve as public spokesmen during this time of crisis were Arthur W. Brady and Charles L. Henry, both well-educated lawyers trained at two of the Midwest's finest universities, Michigan and Indiana, respectively. Both men had honed their public speaking skills as elected public officials before they joined the interurban industry—or, more accurately, before they helped create it a decade earlier. Many of their colleagues, by contrast, were technically oriented.

Thomas Riley Marshall, governor of Indiana at the time of the Kingsland Crash, convened a series of meetings in the state capitol to identify ways to prevent future interurban crashes.

A few were university-trained engineers, while others had learned their skills through hands-on education. It is unlikely that any of them would relish entering the public arena to confront a hostile public to defend their industry.

In December 1910, the public arena was the office of Governor Thomas Riley Marshall and nearby committee rooms in the Indiana capitol. Marshall had summoned Henry, Brady, and other interurban executives from around the state to explain to him and state railroad regulators the status of their industry and suggest ways it might improve its suddenly dismal safety record. Their conversations were no doubt punctuated by the screech of wheel flanges as a succession of interurban cars departed the nearby train shed, made the sharp right turn onto Market Street, and then made another sharp turn onto Capitol Avenue at the east entrance to the statehouse as they threaded their way along the main streets of Indianapolis to Terre Haute, Martinsville, Crawfordsville, Fort Wayne, and other destinations across Indiana. Conference attendees had already heard the shrill denunciations voiced by industry critics.

Given the personalities of Henry and Brady, the gathering in the governor's office was no doubt cordial. Marshall was anything but an intimidating figure. In fact, he was the embodiment of a humble man of the people—something of a Hoosier rustic, a character type known and appreciated in Indiana. No doubt it had helped him win the election to the governor's office. Later, as vice president of the United States, he no doubt used his Midwest rusticity to political advantage, much as Abraham Lincoln had done half a century earlier when East Coast sophisticates had tended to underestimate their president.

Amid a chorus of critics claiming that interurban travel was no longer free from danger and that the entire industry ought to be shut down, Henry and Brady found themselves in Indianapolis called on the carpet, literally. They had to explain to

Governor Marshall and the railroad commissioners what remedial steps the industry might now take to make interurban travel safer and restore public confidence.[15]

A month later, in early 1911, the Indiana governor served as spokesman for the interurban executives when he announced a series of safety measures that the industry would soon implement or had already implemented. These ranged from simple fixes like removing trees and brush obscuring the blind curves that were partly responsible for two of the Indiana crashes in 1910 to significantly stepping up the training of interurban motormen and the installation of block signals along heavily used portions of track. New laws to govern interurban safety animated legislators who met in the state capitol that January and February. The resulting safety legislation could well have inspired Booth Tarkington to pen the following acerbic words three years later in *The Turmoil*: "The politicians let the people make all the laws they liked; it did not matter much, and the taxes went up, which is good for politicians. Law-making was a pastime of the people; nothing pleased them more." One such law banned smoke. "They forbade chimneys to smoke and they forbade cigarettes to smoke. They made laws for all things and forgot them immediately; though sometimes they would remember after a while, and hurry to make new laws that the old laws should be enforced—and then forget both new and old."[16]

For the big 1911 conference of the CERA, Illinois Traction executives may have sought to divert public attention from the recent Staunton crash by staging a newsworthy event that reflected positively on their company. The general superintendent seemed in a celebratory mood as Illinois Traction's luxurious office car rumbled slowly east across the company's new Mississippi River bridge to commence a long-distance journey from Saint Louis via Indianapolis to Cleveland. The lengthy journey across the Midwest was an achievement that Arthur Brady considered worthy of mentioning at length in his presidential address in Atlantic City in October 1911. Not surprisingly, the one thing he did not care to mention was the crashes that had stunned the industry just a year earlier.

Looking ahead, implementation of the suggested improvements that resulted from special meetings held in the Indiana governor's office and another in Illinois in 1910 should have made interurban travel nearly immune to crashes. Union Traction's Alfont crash fourteen years later suggests otherwise. Perhaps because of its noticeably improved safety record during the intervening years, the industry had grown lax and complacent once again, an all too human tendency. That was a charge that government investigators leveled at President Brady and Union Traction management in their assessment of the causes of the 1924 crash.

The tragic autumn of 1910 gave interurban operators a scare, but after a season of soul searching and implementation of new safety measures, life returned to normal, more or less. Gone were the years of frenzied construction of new lines. Noticeably less common were the alluring proposals that enriched unscrupulous promoters. At the 1912 conference of the CERA held in Columbus, Ohio, one of the public presentations was titled "Interurbans: Retrospective and Prospective." During the fifteen years since its takeoff in 1897, the industry had learned valuable lessons from its successes and failures, and some of its leading spokesmen were now ready to pause for reflection. As for its shortcomings, none were viewed as cause for alarm as the industry headed into the future. Failures were simply youthful growing pains. In the industry's initial "rush of exploitation," observed the chief engineer of the Ohio Electric Railway at the CERA's Columbus conference, "hundreds of companies were chartered and franchises greedily sought for and in most cases exploited without much appreciation of the obligations incurred." Moreover, during those first fifteen years, even those interurban companies that got tracks on the ground and cars in motion were run by leaders who were unfamiliar with the financial and operational terrain ahead.[17]

In his annual presentation to the Indiana Board of Tax Commissioners in 1911, Arthur Brady candidly enumerated some of his company's early mistakes. Several of Union Traction's lines serving the Gas Belt, the source of the interurban's original good fortune, would never have been constructed if executives had realized early on that the supposedly huge underground natural gas reservoir would be exhausted so soon. Trains that served the city of Elwood, for example, operated at a loss because nearly all the city's gas-dependent factories, except for one tinplate mill, had closed. The Gas Belt malaise was only one example of the disruptive changes that could unexpectedly upend the young and financially vulnerable interurban industry. Brady also commented on the downturn afflicting the automakers who had located factories in the Gas Belt cities, asserting that their payrolls were only about 50 percent of what they had been just a year earlier.[18]

A related question that transcended Indiana's Gas Belt and was important to interurban executives across the United States was whether the market for automobiles was now saturated, as many of them hoped it was. Had history proved the vehicles to be nothing more than a passing fad, yet another example of conspicuous consumption by America's idle rich? President William Howard Taft weighed in on the subject in a 1911 speech to seven hundred affluent listeners at New York's posh Waldorf-Astoria Hotel for the annual banquet of the Automobile Club of America. Although Taft spoke of "the automobile class," a term that implied he still considered motor cars to be a machine identified with wealthy Americans, he hastened to add that the auto now ranked alongside the telephone and the trolley car in its usefulness for all classes. "It had begun a revolution in country life which might have most momentous results, and it was no longer a mere plaything for the wealthy." Here was yet another reason for interurban executives to pause for reflection.[19]

The years from 1911 through 1914 could best be described as the interurban industry's time of renewing, rebuilding, and refurbishing. Investors continued to make money from well-conceived enterprises like Union Traction of Indiana, and Hoosiers continued to hope for a return on investment from a highly promising project that did not yet have any tracks on the ground. The Indiana Northwestern Traction Company, which promised to bridge one of the most obvious gaps remaining in the Indiana interurban network, was widely regarded as a certain moneymaker if and when it ever got tracks on the ground between Lafayette and Chicago. Or so it seemed in 1909 when the railway was originally incorporated. The terrain separating the two networks radiating from Indianapolis and Chicago was flat, thus requiring no major feats of engineering to cross, and its numerous farms promised to furnish valuable carloads of corn, wheat, and soybeans.[20]

Despite its glowing prospects, the Indiana Northwestern Traction Company proved a thoroughgoing disappointment, and the name of its promoter and president, Eugene Purtelle, became synonymous with fraud and deception across the Midwest. He was without doubt the absolute worst of a bad lot of interurban promoters, the era's equivalent to the internet fraudsters today. The young man's Chicago Board of Trade credentials when combined with his sartorial splendor and ever-confident manner of speaking always greatly impressed his Hoosier investors, whom he cleverly managed to bilk with three separate interurban projects he proposed to launch in various parts of Indiana. Besides his Lafayette-to-Hammond "hot-air line," he also promoted two other interurban projects. He claimed that one would link Frankfort and Tipton, and another would connect Richmond and Hamilton, Ohio. In the end, Purtelle's "accomplishments" could best be summed up as five miles of graded right-of-way and a lengthy trail of accusations, lawsuits, bankruptcy, and, even weeks in jail in Frankfort and Chicago thanks to passing bad checks and bilking hotels out of their room rent. By early 1911, his most ardent supporters, and there were a few, grew convinced that the Chicago shyster had become "mentally unbalanced because of hard work and worry over his projected road." The *Times* of Munster, Indiana, which had been following Purtelle's shenanigans closely, summed up the outlook for his investors in a headline that minced no words as it took note of the promoter's rapidly dwindling assets: "Might as well kiss yours goodbye." Purtelle, like many of his brand, simply disappeared and left no paper trail.[21]

Two words seldom appended to the interurban industry from 1911 through 1914 were receivership and retrenchment. During that span of peace and plenty, interurban companies worked hard to improve infrastructure and operating procedures.

They modernized power plants by replacing old-fashioned belt drives with much more efficient direct connections to drive the dynamos, they added new cars to the fleet of rollingstock, and they built beautiful new passenger stations. Commitment to numerous betterment projects between 1911 and 1915 confirmed that confidence had returned to the industry, and its leaders expected their electric interurban railways to enjoy prosperity for many more years. Shortly before he boarded a train for Atlantic City to preside over the October 1911 convention of the American Electric Railway Association, Arthur Brady predicted in his hometown newspaper that the industry could soon expect to carry twenty billion riders annually, a number double their current passenger load. That meant a coming financial bonanza for interurban companies, the manufacturers of rollingstock, and investors. "President Brady and his associates are confident that men of capital and of large business will not dispute the statement that electric traction is the largest and possibly the most amazing of all the new industries."[22]

Charles D. Emmons, a Lafayette native, emerged from the Kingsland crash with his reputation and ascending career intact. He left Indiana to head the huge transit system in Baltimore and later became president of New York's Hudson and Manhattan Railway. He was one of the Hoosiers conspicuous in the leadership of the American Electric Railway Association between 1910 and 1925.

Brady's optimistic projection failed to note the betterment of another sort taking place along the roads and highways of the United States and the automakers' steady and noticeably successful improvement of the mechanical reliability of their vehicles, especially models that used the once-balky gasoline engines. Interurban executives appeared to remain oblivious to the competitive threat these advances would soon pose, at least until the jitney phenomenon of 1915 dealt electric railways the financial equivalent of a baseball bat's blow to the head.

11

Jitney, The Emergence of a Disruptive Technology

> The rapid growth of the automobile industry and particularly the development of cheap reliable cars selling for under $1,000 naturally had made some inroads on mass transportation, but it was only with the appearance of the so-called jitney between 1915 and 1920 that the industry first realized just how serious automobile competition could be.
>
> —John H. Hanna, president, American Electric Railway Association (1931)

"There has recently been an enormous increase in the number of privately-owned automobiles that solicit 'fares' at five cents each on the streets of Los Angeles. The automobiles are operated chiefly during the rush hours and have so considerably affected the earnings of the street railways that there has been much discussion on the question of passing some ordinance to regulate their operation." When this comment appeared in the *Electric Railway Journal* in 1914, the phenomenon did not yet have a name. Soon, however, the designation "jitney" became the industry's equivalent of a six-letter swear word.[1]

The rapid rise of the jitney in 1914 and 1915, the electric railway industry's first serious introduction to how disruptive the automobile might be, highlights a question that is easier to ponder than to answer definitively: What year witnessed the high-water mark of the Interurban Era? My personal choice is 1913, but much depends on what feature of the electric interurban railway's rapid evolution an observer measures. Two years earlier, Dr. Thomas Conway Jr., one of the industry's most respected analysts, used an academic essay to note the decreasing financial returns of electric railways. In terms of annual miles of new track construction, a slowdown first grew noticeable even earlier, in 1908 and 1909. The *Electric Railway Journal* observed that interurban mileage across the Midwest "showed comparatively little growth during 1910. The largest additions to the interurban network of these states were made by roads that were well under way toward completion before the year began."[2]

While electric railways fumed and fretted about the jitney's negative impact on their earnings, the American public found a great deal of humor in the automobile's cheeky underdog role in humbling the trolley and then the interurban companies.

Because of the financial momentum created during the industry's growth decade, interurban mileage across the United States maintained a slow upward climb for a few more years, as did ridership, until the jitney forced executives and investors to rethink their fundamental assumptions of the assured future growth and prosperity of electric railways. Passenger traffic nationwide peaked in 1916 but declined each year thereafter. A corresponding increase in freight traffic enabled the industry to mask its steady loss of passenger revenue and thus remain atop a plateau in terms of its mileage, with the wholesale abandonment of track commencing only with the onset of the Great Depression. In the opening years of the 1920s, the interurban's short-lived rebound from its near-death experience in 1919 only masked the underlying sickness, the first symptoms of which the jitney exposed. Regardless of any statistic recording an industry decline, optimists always insisted that the downturn was only temporary and that interurban companies would soon bounce back from adversity—at least that was the prevailing conviction until the late 1920s.

The following "joke" appeared in an Indiana newspaper in 1911, and if it happened to catch the eye of interurban executives, they no doubt smiled in agreement:

> Did you enjoy a cross-country trolley ride?
>
> Oh, yes.
>
> And what was the most enjoyable feature?
>
> The number of automoblists one sees all along the road, fuming over their disabled machines.

The humor this quip was supposed to convey may have been recycled from an earlier era because "automobilists" and "cross-country trolley" were popular terms at the turn of the century. By 1911, both words sounded archaic. Moreover, by that year there were fewer reasons to joke about the steady mechanical improvement of the automobile, a fact that became both frightening and obvious to electric railway executives in 1914.[3]

Electric railway executives considered automobile competition inconsequential until one day, in mid-1914, a giant-killer soon to be known as the jitney appeared on the streets of downtown Los Angeles. The unassuming jitney attracted scant attention outside Southern California until January 1915 when, during just a few weeks, or even in a single day in some locations, a motley assortment of jitneys numbering in the hundreds and soon in the thousands crowded downtown streets of cities across the United States and Canada. "Street railway and other traction interests are thoroughly frightened by the astonishing growth of the jitney bus movement. Operating under franchise from the cities, and paying large sums into the city treasuries, traction firms feel themselves unable to compete with the little vehicles."[4]

The typical jitney was neither impressive nor glamorous. Many jitneys were secondhand Ford automobiles, but some were nothing more than delivery trucks fitted with improvised bodies that made them resemble washtubs on wheels. According to *Jitney Bus*, the official journal of the new "industry": "Anything that runs on four wheels and gasoline and 5 cents" qualified as a jitney. Usually driven by its owner, a jitney followed no fixed route; when it carried passengers, it typically ran along the same streets as the trolley lines. In many cases, these were the streets that franchises had required the trolley companies to maintain in good condition at their expense! The jitney was, in a word, an outlaw.[5]

Incidentally, the origin of the word "jitney" remains uncertain, but the best explanation is that it derived from the name of a small French coin called a "jeton," the value of which was approximately one nickel, the common price of a jitney ride. In the United States, however, the word "jitney" was street slang for a nickel and was commonly associated with cheap merchandise, lowbrow entertainment, and sometimes even criminal activity.[6]

Like a swarm of angry hornets, the sheer number of jitneys made them a danger to trolley profits—their numbers, ubiquity, and instant popularity among the commuters who gladly abandoned the familiar streetcars in droves to enjoy the thrill of a jitney ride. No vehicle had ever won the hearts of urban dwellers more quickly.

That the jitney posed a threat to the financial well-being of a long-established and supposedly robust industry was remarkable. It was a disruptive technology like no other. The jitney threat resulted from the rising number of private automobiles on city streets and long-standing public resentment of the power of the street railway industry and its supposedly enormous profits. This criticism was repeated so frequently in the early twentieth century by journalism's muckrakers that many Americans swore the charge had to be true. The jitney seldom impacted interurban and steam railroads, but how a swarm of automobiles threatened to ruin trolley companies should have alarmed all railway executives. Anyone with eyes to see must have watched with shock at how private automobiles could upend an industry's best financial calculations. Electric traction officials believed their profits had been "burglarized" by jitney drivers, a group of interlopers they uniformly denounced as unlicensed, untaxed, unregulated, and probably uncouth. The little prefix "un" conveyed a great deal of anger.[7]

Following the initial shock of unregulated competition, the electric railway industry recovered its equilibrium and was even able to sound a somewhat optimistic note going into its annual fall 1915 convention: "After playing the part of a seven-year locust the jitney seems doomed to a grave unmourned, unhonored, and unsung save by the trader in used automobiles. Yet the jitney will leave more than a scar on electric railway finance and operation. Above all it has shown that all public transportation, car and bus together, should be under one control."[8]

Other words like "locust," "pest," and "plague" came easily to the lips of electric railway executives trying to describe the financial upheaval the jitney had caused them. The pressing question no industry leader could answer with confidence during the initial days of the disruption was "whether this competition will be permanent or whether it will practically disappear, as in the case of the bicycle," the fad vehicle of the 1890s.[9]

As it turned out, industry leaders who in 1915 believed the jitney would soon vanish were far too optimistic, as even a decade later, they and their legions of lawyers still battled the jitney menace. An additional "un" word used to convey a growing sense of frustration was "unstoppable." From 1884 (the date of its first issue) until 1915 or 1916, the *Electric Railway Journal* had discussed many technical problems encountered by the young industry and how best they could be overcome, but few topics consumed more ink or seemed so intractable as the jitney. Weekly issues of electric railway trade journals published during the height of the craze might include a dozen or more articles devoted to the industry's most irksome foe. Again, nothing before the jitney had more forcefully demonstrated the power of automobile competition.

Like the jitney itself, it was amazing the damage a few nickels—a few million nickels spent on jitney rides—could do almost overnight to the street railway industry across the United States. Utility executives practically foamed at the mouth when describing their nemesis: "The jitney was conceived in iniquity and brought forth in sin," opined the editor of *Public Utility* in 1918. "It was based on injustice, it flourished in the grossest of wrong. It was a parasite."[10]

According to the terms of many municipal franchises granted to the construction of street railways in the 1880s or earlier, the trolley, cable car, and even horse railway companies were required to maintain the streets along which their tracks ran. This no doubt represented a good bargain for city dwellers familiar with streets defined by dirt, mud, and potholes. City railroads did what their franchises required them to do, using cobblestones, bricks, and even large wooden blocks to maintain a hard surface surrounding their tracks, and sometimes that meant paving the entire street from curb to curb. The injustice arose when interlopers like the many jitney drivers of 1914 and 1915 took advantage of the streets that trolley companies were required to pave and maintain and stole their customers. Among the complaints from electric railway executives during their desperate year 1919 was that many trolley companies were still required to shoulder the expense of maintaining city streets, and, as a consequence, they were unfairly forced to subsidize their rubber-tired competitors.

The years 1914 and 1915, as has been mentioned in earlier chapters, formed a tipping point in many ways. But why these two years? Because, if the Panic of 1907 had provided the electric railway industry a sobering wake-up call, then the pivotal events of 1914 and 1915 delivered a surprise blow to the head that left its victim, the North American electric railway industry, dazed, uncomprehending, and bleeding financially. Corporations, intoned the Reverend Sydney Strong of Seattle, are "bound to 'walk more humbly' and 'do righteousness' more spontaneously when they reflect that in a day their income may be cut by 50 per cent or almost annihilated." The left-leaning Strong insisted to readers of his article, published by a reform-minded journal called *Survey*, that the jitney represented a return to the "old social democracy of the country store when manager and customer shook hands and swapped stories over the counter."[11]

Again, the mugging came neither from the Panama Canal that opened in 1914 nor from the recently implemented moving assembly line that produced unprecedented numbers of Model T Fords at an equally unheard-of price that dipped to a low of $360. Ford sold more than one-third of a million Model Ts in 1914 alone. The popularity of owning a new Ford, however, created a used car glut until the jitney boom emptied the dealers' lots.

Nor did electric railways suffer noticeably as a result of the brief but severe recession of 1914 that bankrupted one-quarter of their steam-railroad big brothers. Industry publications scarcely took notice of these landmark events: the interoceanic canal had no impact on electric railway traffic, the ever-growing number of private automobiles was annoying mainly because they clogged city streets and caused traffic jams that slowed trolleys, and the recession of 1914 seemed to confirm the belief that electric transportation rested on a more solid financial foundation than did America's steam railroads. Collectively, all of these developments could be dismissed as minor annoyances.

No, the industry-humbling blow of 1914–15 was delivered by a creative *application* of automobile technology. The first jitney is supposed to have originated when an unknown motorist acted on a whim and pulled his automobile to the curb alongside a crowd of commuters waiting for a streetcar. He invited any interested riders to join him for a quick trip downtown at five cents each, the same fare a trolley typically charged for a ride aboard a car that during rush hours was often crowded beyond capacity and made frequent stops along the way. Streetcar patrons who had complained for years about slow and overcrowded trolleys did not hesitate to squeeze into an overloaded and unregulated vehicle driven by a stranger who may not even have possessed a valid driver's license.

The jitney fad spread like wildfire to all the big cities of the United States and Canada. Even now, no one can say for certain how many jitneys ran along urban streets at their peak in 1915 given that everything about their operation was irregular and illegal. During the recession of late 1914 and early 1915, many men were out of work, and with time on their hands, they could easily turn an idle automobile into a jitney that might at least pay for gasoline as well as offer a diversion from unemployment. Many motorists had no intention of being full-time jitney drivers (or "jitneurs," as some people styled the cheeky interlopers). They simply saw an opportunity to treat the family car as a temporary jitney to pick up some nickels on their way to and from work, if employed. In terms of numbers, only this much was certain: streetcar revenues plummeted alarmingly.

Street railway accountants convincingly demonstrated that the jitney was a financial loser when depreciation, maintenance, and other expenses were added to the cost of operation. What the corporate bean counters did not seem to understand was that, with so many people out of work, an automobile was useful to drive around and look for new employment, and the nickels earned as a jitney driver helped to pay for gas and oil. If he collected enough nickels during the week, a jitney driver might also buy a few gallons of gasoline needed to take family members on a Sunday drive. None of these simple personal pleasures, or necessities, seemed to enter into the accounting done by the street railway industry.

Since the dawn of the twentieth century, it had been easy for Americans to think of electric railways in terms of corporate power and control, a perception aided and abetted by muckraking journalists in search of something to criticize and equally quick to perceive bicycles and automobiles as personal mobility vehicles that greatly enhanced individual freedom. In a word: they were liberating. Never mind that autos, most of them, were assembled by large corporations, were fueled by energy produced by another set of large corporations, and were dependent on governments to construct the national network of all-weather highways that emerged after passage of the federal highway acts of 1916 and 1921. The jitney fit nicely into the popular narrative of personal freedom versus corporate control. Americans tended to cheer for the underdog as well as to fear large-scale combinations such as those represented by the numerous trusts that rose during the 1890s. These included trolley trusts and syndicates, which worked behind the scenes to exercise financial control over many of the electric railways. In Indiana and Ohio, the Schoepf-McGowan Syndicate controlled a network of trolley and interurban lines across the central portions of both states, and the word "syndicate" suggested to many Americans something sinister, the same menacing aggregation of power as one of the outlawed "trusts."

It tickled many Americans to see the trolley trust howling in pain. The jitney thus became an instant hit in terms of popular culture. Among the numerous examples of sheet music devoted to the jitney were "I Didn't Raise My Ford to Be a Jitney," "Mr. Whitney's Little Jitney Bus," and "Father Is Driving a Jitney Bus." The many examples of jitney sheet music testify to popular interest in the topic—and popular support for the common man (and a few women) who became jitney drivers.[12]

Also worth mentioning is the jitney's stimulation of the American love affair with the automobile. Until the jitney came along, many urban dwellers had never

This is one example of the many hastily composed and easily forgotten musical ditties that found humor in the meteoric rise of the jitney. More sheet music was composed about the jitney in a span of a year or two than was composed about the interurban during its entire life span.

experienced the sensation of riding on "rubber and air." Popular magazine *Collier's* claimed (erroneously) that "most folks helped pay for our paved city streets; they'd like to ride thereupon in autos, and the jitney gives them a chance as nothing else ever did." Another contemporary observer remarked that "one blessed feature of the jitney is that wherever introduced it gave poor women a chance to ride in an auto for a nickel, thus affording to thousands the first opportunity for an auto ride." Once experienced, the auto ride apparently became addictive.[13]

At a personal level, streetcar companies impacted the daily lives of millions of Americans. "There is no industry in which the public exhibit a livelier or keener interest," insisted Dr. Thomas Conway, one of the electric railway's most astute observers, in 1911. "The intimate contact into which everyone is brought with these properties and the comparative simplicity of the business is probably responsible for this widespread interest and for the growth of the general belief that the public knows all about this business."[14]

If a trolley were overly crowded or too hot or improperly cleaned or late, it was the company's fault. One popular movement that ultimately failed could best be described by the slogan "No Seat, No Fare." That is, if no seat were available, a patron need not pay for the trolley ride. Alarmed, the street railways battled this threat with all the resources at their command. Another popular movement called for fares to be reduced to three cents from the customary nickel a ride, but this time the street railways were less successful in beating back this revenue threat.

At a time when the average American worker earned approximately $500 a year, every penny mattered. Apart from food, few expenses impacted a personal budget more than the cost of getting to and from work by streetcar. Given that the popular perception was that a few individuals (or those shadowy "syndicates") were making millions from street railways, politicians were reluctant to permit fares to rise even to six or seven cents a ride. Better yet, any politician in search of votes could demand that fares be reduced to three cents. This kind of populism also saw state legislators, such as in Indiana, legally mandate that interurban companies charge passengers no more than two cents per mile.

Because city officials had already forced Indianapolis trolley fares down to three cents a ride, jitney operators were a rarity in the Hoosier capital because they could not compete by charging the same low price. They preferred Terre Haute, for example, where, during the height of the 1915 craze, at least two hundred jitneys prowled city streets in search of nickel fares. When banned there, they simply reappeared on the downtown streets of Evansville, Muncie, and other communities in which a streetcar ride cost the time-honored five cents.[15]

Although the jitney craze did not immediately impact interurban lines in the same way it did street railways, it served as an important precursor to the intercity bus and truck competition that grew ever more worrisome to interurban executives during the 1920s. After the trolley companies recovered from their initial shock, the largest operators marshaled battalions of lawyers to beat back the jitney threat. The battle proved to be exceedingly difficult to win. In response to legal measures intended to eliminate jitneys in Seattle and Portland, for example, the cheeky drivers announced that henceforth all rides would be free (and thus supposedly not constrained by any new ordinance), but they would gladly accept donations from their passengers. Local traction companies returned to court yet again to outlaw the "free" jitneys. As if

The Great Three-Cent Coin Scam

In early 1912, Democratic congressman Robert Johns Bulkley from Cleveland, Ohio, introduced a bill to add a three-cent coin to fill the gap between a penny and a nickel. Several decades earlier, a variety of three-cent coins had been minted, but they had never proved popular. Why would Bulkley want to reintroduce the coin in 1912? On the surface, this seemingly innocent, if quirky measure was actually a mean-spirited and politically motivated attack on trolley operators across the United States. Cleveland, Toledo, and Detroit were three major cities that had sought for years to force local street railways to reduce the time-honored trolley fare from a nickel to three cents, and Bulkley cleverly surmised that the convenience of a three-cent coin would aid their populist cause.

The coinage bill sailed through the House of Representatives with scarcely a dissenting vote. It seemed certain to pass the Senate as well. Newton D. Baker, the mayor of Cleveland and a politician at odds with the local streetcar company, endorsed the measure, as did both Theodore Roosevelt and Woodrow Wilson. Suddenly, banks realized the extra burden the odd coin would impose on them, and they joined with the street railways to keep the three-cent coin bill bottled up in the Senate Finance Committee.

The bizarre episode illustrates the depths politicians would plumb to satisfy voters even if it meant hobbling local transportation by imposing a financially half-baked three-cent fare. The interurban operators were not directly impacted by the three-cent coin scam of 1912, but their time was coming in the 1920s, when politicians voted to spend millions of tax dollars to pay for improved roads and highways that paralleled thousands of miles of interurban lines already in place. In this way, they steadily diminished the value of interurban securities held by thousands of investors, few of which fit the profile of the grasping street railway magnate that was a staple of the Progressive Era's antibusiness narrative.[16]

to underscore the perverse localism that afflicted the electric railways of the United States and Canada, jitneys continued to plague the industry for years to come, popping up in a thousand different communities on both sides of the international border, being banned by municipal councils and courts, and finally disappearing from the streets of one city only to reappear a short time later in a new location or in a new guise.[17]

When faced with injunctions and other legal threats, some jitney drivers banded together to hire lawyers of their own. Others chose to avoid legal expenses and quietly moved on down the road, literally, to launch an intercity jitney business. Called "super jitneys" and "fast-flying super stages," the high-powered, elongated touring cars grew especially popular in California, a state that pioneered the development of a network of paved highways and that was blessed by a mild climate conducive to the year-round operation of automobiles. These illegal operations, which proliferated during the interwar years, were popularly titled "wildcat" bus lines. They took business away from not only California's interurban companies but also the mighty Southern Pacific and Santa Fe, two steam railroads that complained bitterly to state regulators during the 1920s and 1930s. Such complaints fell on deaf ears until the exigencies of World War II imposed gasoline rationing and a thirty-five-mile-per-hour national speed limit, a combination that finally drove the extralegal carriers off the highways of California. In 1940, Hollywood even produced a movie melodrama called "Wildcat Bus," in which a penniless playboy helped a "young beauty" save her financially struggling outlaw enterprise.[18]

In Indiana, the problem of outlaw intercity jitneys was less acute. Nonetheless, by the early 1920s, the state recorded nearly two hundred bus companies in operation, all of them using streets and highways funded by tax dollars. Indiana legislators had created a highway commission in 1917, but the state supreme court had declared it unconstitutional. Two years later, a second measure survived the legal challenges and began the process of creating a network of all-weather highways intended to crisscross the Hoosier State. By the end of the 1920s, long-distance trucking companies emerged to use public highways to further erode the interurban freight and express business, which operated over a right-of-way paid for by private investors.

In terms of injustice, just as jitneys took advantage of streets paved by money paid by street railways, intercity bus and truck competitors operated free of federal government regulations until 1935. Meanwhile, steam railroads and any interurbans that crossed state lines shouldered the increasingly heavy burden imposed by literally millions of Interstate Commerce Commission (ICC) regulations. That number kept growing toward one billion regulations until federal officials finally dissolved the ICC and its mountains of red tape in 1996.

Bristol, Indiana, on the electrified portion of the St. Joseph Valley line. By agreement, the Chicago, South Bend and Northern Indiana ran its cars here, too.

The Medicine Man and the Doodlebug

Probably the strangest interurban built in Indiana, and certainly one of the shortest-lived, was the St. Joseph Valley Traction Company that Herbert E. Bucklen launched in 1903 to serve the far northeastern corner of the state. In a neighborly gesture, he offered to sell securities in his "Valley Line" to any interested purchaser, although in the end, Bucklen tapped into his own considerable fortune for the money required to build and equip the railway. Thus, more than most Indiana interurban companies, the Valley Line was a one-man, low-budget enterprise cobbled together using proceeds derived largely from "Bucklen's Arnica Salve," a patent medicine that newspapers across the Midwest advertised as a cure-all for bodily afflictions ranging from pimples to lockjaw.

To save money, Bucklen relied heavily on "interurbans without wires." That is, to avoid the expense of trolley wires and other components of an electric infrastructure, he purchased an assortment of gasoline-powered railcars to carry passengers. To haul freight, he used light-duty steam locomotives, and, finally, almost as an afterthought, he electrified a portion of his hybrid railway that at its peak extended fifty-nine miles from Elkhart to Angola via Bristol and LaGrange. Bucklen died in early 1917, and the Valley Line only barely outlived its patron. The following April 1918, his son and executor ran a final train and sold for junk a motley collection of equipment that included

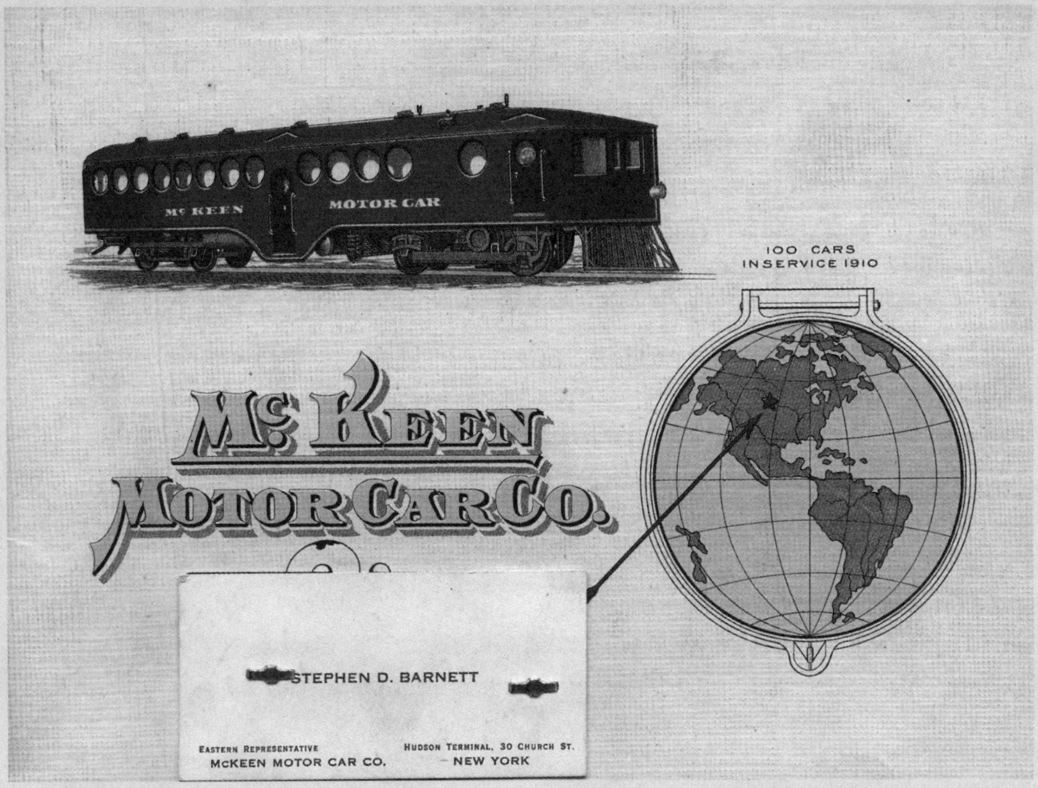

William Riley McKeen Jr. was a Terre Haute native and a member of a prominent Indiana railroad family. He is best known for engineering the railroad motor cars commissioned by Union Pacific and manufactured in the railroad's headquarters city of Omaha, Nebraska.

a gasoline-powered rail car. If the chain of interurban lines Bucklen expected to see forged across northern Indiana between Toledo and Chicago had ever been completed, his Valley Line would have formed a vital but exceedingly weak link, one that, metaphorically speaking, was cast from the cheapest and weakest pot metal.[19]

Bucklen's beggarly railway represented a partial accommodation to the once-feared explosive power of gasoline because it used internal combustion engines in several of its low-budget rail cars. The most famous of all gasoline-powered rail cars ("doodlebugs") were constructed in Omaha, Nebraska, by William Riley McKeen Jr., a native of Terre Haute.[20] Most McKeen cars featured a distinctive wedge-shaped front that was widely thought to make them more efficient by "splitting the wind." It did not, but that arcane bit of physics was proved only years later. A McKeen car resembled the typical interurban car and could serve much the same purpose, except that instead of needing a distant power plant to supply its energy, it carried its own onboard source of power, a gasoline engine linked by a mechanical transmission to the wheels. Other manufacturers joined the competition, and when the imperious Pennsylvania

Railroad finally took notice of the interurban interlopers alongside its tracks in Indiana, it turned to General Electric in 1909 to construct a rail motor car as an experimental replacement for its half-empty steam-powered local trains.[21]

A few Hoosier interurbans apart from the Valley Line pondered whether to purchase one of the doodlebugs to trim their infrastructure costs. One of the most novel proposals among the state's many paper interurbans was to encircle the capital city with tracks that interconnected the surrounding county-seat towns and thereby facilitate interline movement of freight among the spokes of the electric railway wheel without having cars crowd downtown streets of Indianapolis. The plan entailed the familiar application of electric propulsion, but as investment capital grew increasingly scarce after 1907, promoters of the Capital Circuit Traction Company announced that they would trim costs by using gasoline rail cars instead, an option that grew increasingly appealing as inventors and hands-on tinkerers steadily improved the formerly shunned motive power. As the miles of paved streets and highways increased and gasoline engines grew safer and more reliable, a question naturally arose: Why spend money to install overhead wires and rails when a motor bus that used taxpayer-financed roadways could satisfy demand for public transportation?[22]

The year 1916—the jitney menace notwithstanding—proved to be a good year for Charles L. Henry. He stood at the apogee of his career, simultaneously heading both the regional Central Electric Railway Association and the national American Electric Railway Association and enjoying the accolades of his many industry colleagues. It was purely coincidental that 1916 also represented the pinnacle of the Interurban Era if measured by the number of travelers using the Traction Terminal in Indianapolis. No one understood this as they anticipated the future, certainly not Charles L. Henry, who "permits neither the depression of the past few years nor the advent of the jitney bus to dim the glow of the electric railway's future. He is confident that further extensive development is assured and that we shall soon see a revival of electric railway building exceeding even the rush that in a few brief years placed the interurban line among the big factors in American transportation."[23]

Even as Henry insisted on a bright future for the interurban, the tide was turning. Never again would industry statistics be as positive as they were in 1916, the year Henry shared his rosy vision for the future with colleagues at the Central Electric Railway Association's spring gathering in Dayton. Miles of new track construction had fallen dramatically since the Panic of 1907, but in most parts of the United States and Canada, interurban ridership had continued to increase. Statistics reflected the positive results of the industry's multifaceted commitment to safety following the disastrous series of fatal accidents during the fall of 1910. "Safety First" became the watchword, and weekly issues of the *Electric Railway Journal* invariably featured accounts of how best to promote safety. Union Traction of Indiana did everything conceivable to implement safe operations on its sprawling system, and as a result, in 1915, it won the industry's top award for safety.

One word seldom heard in 1916 was "abandonment." Interurban companies might suffer financial shortfalls that ended in receiverships. Few Indiana interurbans, in fact, escaped a humbling bout of receivership, but they invariably recovered without having to pull up track. There were odd cases across the United States and Canada of companies that abandoned an unremunerative branch line, usually one that amounted to a short segment of the system as a whole. Even rarer were interurban companies that ceased all operations—at least until 1918 when Great War stringencies turned the industry's familiar world upside down and conferred the aura of patriotism on acts of abandonment and their contribution of scrap metal to the fight. Copper trolley wire transformed into the alloy brass was used to make casings for the bullets and artillery shells that turned the Western Front in France into the world's largest killing field.

On the home front, small and ugly motorized vehicles dignified by the term "bus" appeared in cities here and there across the United States and Canada, but they were mainly a trolley company's cheap and ineffective response to jitney competition. There was not yet an industry-wide movement to implement buses on street railways, and intercity buses, the few that existed before World War I, posed no threat to the interurban lines.

Also, on the positive side, a growing number of interurban railways marketed surplus electricity generated by their powerhouses to the communities and industries located along their tracks. The Terre Haute, Indianapolis and Eastern, for example, sold surplus power to coal mine operators in western Indiana. The added stream of income was welcome, though few industry observers in 1916 expected that a decade later some interurban companies would cease running trains altogether and transform themselves into electric utilities. Throughout the history of electric railways up to 1917, by far the least glamorous part of interurban operations was the boiler room in the powerhouse, and the men who tended the banks of furnaces required to produce steam to run the electric generators toiled unsung and largely out of sight. Their dusky lair was not the portion of the powerhouse that interested visitors. The Great War changed that. Now boiler tenders became frontline workers in the national struggle to conserve precious coal, and the more coal this group of interurban employees saved, the greater their demonstration of patriotism during the Great War.

Generating electric power and operating interurban cars had always appeared to be two distinct enterprises connected by an overhead infrastructure of feeder wires and cables, but seldom before the mid-1920s had interurban executives considered severing that vital connection to prune their money-losing rail operations from the profitable sale of surplus electric power. Wartime inflation, the near death of the industry in 1919, and the steady rise of highway competition during the 1920s made scenarios unthinkable in 1916 or 1917 a grim reality a decade later.[24]

In addition to the several landmark events that impacted electric railways across the United States and Canada during 1914, the summer months that year witnessed the nations of Europe stumbling blindly into a monumental conflict. The Guns of August commenced the bloodletting known then as the Great War, which lasted until November 1918. Originally, hardly anyone expected the conflict to continue longer than a few months, and few Americans in 1914 could have imagined that the United States would be drawn into the fight in April 1917. "With the die cast and the entrance of the United States in the war against Germany the electric railways of the country stand shoulder to shoulder with every other industry to co-operate with and help in every way possible the federal authorities."[25]

During the first months following the declaration of war, it was business as usual for America's electric railways, but with the addition of various public proclamations of patriotism. The industry's desire to hold its usual series of meetings and conferences in 1917 conflicted with self-imposed restraint intended to underscore its total commitment to winning the war. For the first time, the American Electric Railway

Association "annulled" its big fall conference. The Central Electric Railway Association announced that its now-traditional midsummer cruise of the Great Lakes would continue as usual, but a few weeks later, it adjusted to the new stringencies the conflict encouraged, and it, too, "annulled" its popular outing.

For a time, it appeared that electric railways might also close their more than five hundred parks, both their bucolic lakeside retreats and sites devoted mainly to thrill rides. It was important to save coal and other resources vital to the nation's war effort, to spend money on war bonds instead of pleasure cruises and park outings, and to upgrade infrastructure to better accommodate the swelling volume of traffic that military bases and war industries generated. For example, the street railways of Indianapolis and Union Traction both hastened to add new track to better serve Fort Benjamin Harrison, a major army base at the end of a spur line near the suburb of Lawrence.[26]

The question of operating amusement parks during the grim times brought by the war caused hand-wringing within the electric railway industry. Many wondered if it was patriotic for trolley and interurban companies to encourage frivolity at home when young Americans were suffering on the battlefields of Europe. Some public officials argued that despite the wartime stringencies, "the working people must have proper recreation—it is the desire of the [Wilson] administration—and the park is the workers place for healthful recreation during the summer months." Electric railway executives in Canada, which had been at war since August 1914 and thus had already addressed many of the issues that now troubled their American colleagues, advised them to run their trolley and interurban parks as usual because war workers needed a place of relief from the stress of their jobs. Trolley and interurban parks functioned as easily accessible resorts for people of modest means and limited leisure time and were much-needed retreats from the cares and stresses created by World War I. After much debate, the American consensus was that it was their patriotic duty to operate trolley and interurban parks as usual.[27]

Although American involvement in World War I lasted only a year and a half, it left a permanent imprint on the nation's steam and electric railroads. In an especially dramatic wartime move, the US government nationalized the nation's steam railroads in December 1917, and only after much debate did Uncle Sam relinquish them to their private owners on March 1, 1920. The stated pretext for creating the United States Railroad Administration was that the investor-owned steam railroads had failed to deliver the goods, literally, that were needed to win the war. Most obviously, a monumental railroad traffic jam resulted in gridlock at East Coast ports. Loaded freight cars could not reach the docks, and empty ones could not return west for new cargoes. The so-called progressives seemed not to realize that the burden of regulations that federal, state, and municipal governments had heaped on the steam railroads since 1901 might

This postcard image of Union Traction's Kokomo station illustrates one of the unexpected flaws in interurban transportation that automobiles exposed. Interurban tracks in Indiana cities were expected to run along the middle of streets—local laws often mandated it—but increased automobile traffic heightened the risk of an accident when handling passengers and freight from cars stopped in the center of a roadway rather than at the curb.

have contributed in large measure to the troubles they experienced in 1917. It required money for railroads to modernize, and the rush to regulate them had created a hostile climate that discouraged investors in steam railroad securities. It was the same for the electric railways.

War and nationalization forever changed the steam railroads and the world in which they operated. Wartime conditions offered the nation's electric railways the perfect opportunity to demonstrate their patriotism, which they did in every possible way. William G. McAdoo, the director general overseeing the United States Railroad Administration, repeatedly urged the nation's interurban lines to haul more freight to relieve the glut that staggered the steam railroads. Adding urgency to McAdoo's request was the recent federal legislation that empowered him to assume control of the electric railways, if need be. "A golden opportunity now exists for the electric interurban lines to display their improved facilities and prove their ability to handle a large amount of the passenger traffic of the country and thus relieve the strain on the steam railroads." Although interurbans gave little serious thought to hauling freight during their early years, the unprecedented wartime burden that staggered the steam railroads opened

Table 11.1. Indiana's interurbans in 1915

	Miles of track	Capitalization per mile
Bluffton, Geneva & Celina Traction Company	18.5	$36,863
Chicago, Lake Shore & South Bend Railway	77.8	$34,451
Chicago, South Bend & Northern Indiana Railway	120.4	$99,317
Cincinnati, Lawrenceburg & Aurora Electric Street Railroad	[ ]	$82,767
Evansville Railways	68.3	$46,568
Evansville, Suburban & Newburgh Railway	24.7	$32,221
Fort Wayne & Northern Indiana Traction Company	192.5	$103,463
Fort Wayne & Northwestern Railway	42.9	$39,289
Fort Wayne & Springfield Railway	21.7	$32,198
Gary & Interurban Railroad	74.8	$97,186
Gary & Southern Traction Company	14.5	$38,950
Hammond, Whiting & East Chicago Railway	19.9	$118,874
Indiana Utilities Company	3.7	$29,600
Indiana Railways & Light Company	59.5	$71,262
Indianapolis & Cincinnati Traction Company	104.4	$59,083
Indianapolis & Louisville Traction Company	40.9	$49,820
Interstate Public Service Company	58.5	$163,236
Lebanon & Thorntown Traction Company	9.3	$32,416
Louisville & Northern Railway & Lighting Company	19.4	$276,131
Louisville & Southern Indiana Traction Company	22.7	$179,728
Marion & Bluffton Traction Company	31.8	$23,051
Muncie & Portland Traction Company	31.7	$31,698
Ohio Electric Railway	600.7	$42,256
Public Utilities Company	54.1	$172,724
Southern Michigan Railway	32.9	$98,168
Terre Haute, Indianapolis & Eastern Traction Company	428.9	$84,080
Union Traction Company	403.2	$65,594
Winona Interurban Railway	72.4	$19,813

Source: Second Annual Report of the Indiana Public Service Commission for the Fiscal Year Ended September 30, 1915, as reprinted in *Electric Railway Journal* (March 1917): 518. Bucklen's St. Joseph Valley Traction was such an odd hybrid that it did not make the list.

new doors for interurbans. The *Electric Railway Journal* published information on how to convert passenger rollingstock into interurban freight cars. Although most executives may not have recognized it in 1917 and 1918, Uncle Sam's wartime emphasis on interurban freight proved a godsend to interurbans in Indiana and elsewhere in the Midwest during the 1920s as growing competition caused their income from passenger traffic to dwindle. Many carriers would have gone bankrupt much earlier than they did were it not for their income from freight.[28]

Not only was the industry motivated by genuine patriotism, but an unspoken reality was that by doing all it could to support the war effort, it might thereby gain greater favor with the American public at large, a need the recent jitney craze had made uppermost in the thinking of industry executives. Interurban lines that served military bases worked especially hard to shoulder the extra-heavy load of passengers and freight.

Peace returned with the armistice of November 11, 1918, and Americans were giddy with joy as they pondered the prospect of a quick return to normal life. It was not to be. Although the electric railways avoided nationalization, they suffered nonetheless as a result of the crippling wartime inflation that caused an ever-increasing number of executives to wonder aloud in 1919 whether their industry could survive. During the war years, worrisome words seldom used before—"retrenchment," "suspension," and "abandonment"—along with ominous references to the "suspension of dividends" and the closure of electric railways and their cars and infrastructure sold for scrap, appeared with growing frequency on the pages of the *Electric Railway Journal* and *Electric Traction*. But no word or phrase, except perhaps "jitney," inspired more intense hand-wringing by interurban executives than "high cost of living" as they faced the cruel new economic realities of the postwar world.

In 1918, in a first for Indiana, two interurban companies, the Bluffton, Geneva and Celina and H. E. Bucklen's idiosyncratic St. Joseph Valley line, had ceased all operations and their property been sold for scrap. Soon after, a new business, the interurban liquidators who disposed of a growing number of idle cars and miles of infrastructure, advertised for customers in the trade journals. According to nationwide statistics compiled for 1917, the first year of the Great War, scrappers claimed the bones of thirteen electric railways and 127 miles of abandoned track nationwide. Another seven companies totaling eighty miles of track suspended operations. On the plus side, in the United States 1,029 electric railway companies, both trolley and interurban, continued to operate 48,175 miles of line at the year's end. However, by lumping together street railways and interurbans, these aggregate figures tended to gloss over the precarious condition of many interurban companies, and the industry's financial situation only grew darker after the end of the Great War on November 11, 1918.[29]

12

Losing Traction, Rising Highway Competition

> For the last several years the interurbans have been on the downgrade, as far as making money has been concerned, and they have frequently asked the state tax board for relief from high taxation. There is no question but that there is some merit in their claims of poverty, and it is true, too, that in many instances the present owners are "holding the bag" for some of the investors and speculators who built interurbans and street railroads some years ago and then got out from under, leaving the properties heavily overcapitalized and full of water.
>
> —*Fort Wayne Sentinel*, April 26, 1918, p. 7

The year 1919 was chaotic. The bloodletting on the battlefields of Europe ceased with the armistice of November 11, 1918. It was a day worth celebrating, but the United States was not ready to sign any formal peace treaty to end World War I, nor did it anticipate the time of trouble at home that lay just ahead.

The world stage was nothing like it had been when the fighting began in August 1914. Three formerly imposing world empires—Austria-Hungary, Germany, and Russia—had collapsed like a house of cards because of the prolonged conflict, and their former rulers had fled into exile or been shot by revolutionaries. The name "Soviet Union" replaced "Russia" on world maps, and observers feared the Communists might soon triumph elsewhere. Germany was in chaos as a result of its defeat, and it seemed particularly vulnerable to Communist agitators.[1]

None of the global disorder had a direct impact on North America's electric railway industry, except that the end of World War I coincided with a global pandemic that claimed millions of lives, including some electric railway executives and up-and-coming leaders. When the Central Electric Railway Association met in Indianapolis in late November 1918, every member donned a gauze mask as a precaution against the Spanish influenza. Two weeks later, Lewis W. Henry, Charles L. Henry's dutiful son and heir apparent, who was shouldering more and more management responsibility at the Indianapolis and Cincinnati Traction Company, died of influenza at his home

Union Traction cars have paused in the center of a downtown Anderson street to load a crowd of passengers. A special occasion such as the Indiana State Fair, always a time of heavy interurban travel, may account for the large number of waiting cars and travelers.

in Rushville. Financially, the pandemic sliced the earnings of the nation's electric railways nearly in half in late 1918.[2]

Another debilitating consequence of World War I was inflation, which electric railway executives first considered worrisome in 1914, a year of multiple concerns for the industry. Operating costs spiraled relentlessly upward after the United States joined the conflict in April 1917, posing a serious economic challenge. Interurban executives did not complain about the high cost of living during America's twenty months of active engagement on the battlefield. Their vigorous support for the nation's war effort was all but obligatory, and any criticism or complaint would have been viewed as unpatriotic. Nonetheless, during the chaotic two years that followed the November 1918 armistice, the electric railway industry—not just its interurban sector—was in such serious financial trouble because of wartime inflation that it could easily have collapsed like the three great European empires.

The rapidly rising cost of everything, including everyday foods fundamental to the diets of millions of Americans, grew so worrisome and was so often discussed that newspapers resorted to using the abbreviation HCL, meaning "High Cost of Living," in the numerous news and feature stories they devoted to the rapidly eroding value of the dollar. There was, however, one notable exception to the HCL, and that was the price of a streetcar ride. For as long as most living Americans could recall, it had been five cents or less, and elected officials responsible for granting fare increases were unwilling to risk the voters' wrath by allowing street railway fares to climb even as much as one or two cents so that traction operators could cover their rapidly rising operating costs. Once again, political myopia trumped economic common sense.

Only with a great deal of effort were trolley companies able to pry the much-needed fare increases from local regulators, who reluctantly permitted them to charge riders six or seven cents. As for raising their time-hallowed nickel fares to ten cents during the war, an amount widely considered to be the industry's new break-even point, only a handful of carriers succeeded in wrangling the necessary concession from most officials whether elected or appointed. Interurbans faced a similar uphill struggle as they sought the approval of state regulators to raise their fares from two cents per mile to three, and sometimes it took a last-ditch appeal to federal authorities to win the needed increase.

Washington agencies proliferated during the war, and it often seemed that bureaucrats worked at cross-purposes. The War Labor Board might grant workers a wage increase, while another agency might (or might not) permit an electric railway to raise fares to cover its increased labor costs. A popular analogy showed a barrel filled from the top with the added income from hard-won fare increases but simultaneously draining from the bottom through the wide-open spigot of added costs. When more money was drained away than added, even if only temporarily and justified in the name of wartime patriotism, it created an unsustainable economic squeeze during the critical months that followed the armistice.

The local orientation of the electric railway industry was never a greater curse than in 1919. One company, the Chicago North Shore and Milwaukee, earned an impressive wartime income because its trains were loaded with military personnel from the many bases it served. The same was true for the Chicago, Lake Shore and South Bend because of the heavy industry located along its tracks in the Gary, Indiana, area. It greatly benefited from the war workers who surged aboard its trains twice daily to commute to and from their jobs. But for each prosperous interurban company like these two, a dozen others struggled to survive because passenger traffic that had formerly served as their bread and butter had shrunk noticeably because of highway competition.

In addition, harried executives battled not only the rising cost of every commodity from coal for their power plants to copper cable and wire required to rejuvenate aging infrastructures; they also dealt with widespread labor unrest as wages failed to keep pace with inflation or were cut by interurban executives desperate to keep their enterprises afloat. One interurban company in Upstate New York trimmed employee wages three times in rapid succession, but the desperate action failed to avert its shutdown and abandonment. Workers with family budgets squeezed unmercifully by rising costs demanded higher wages and staged frequent strikes to dramatize their economic plight. The obvious solution was to raise fares across the board to cover the increased cost of labor, but regulators remained reluctant to sanction any increase.

A crazy-quilt pattern emerged across the United States. Officials in one community might grudgingly permit the local street railway to charge riders one cent more to cover its rising expenses, while city fathers in a nearby community generously agreed to a dime fare, a sum double the nickel ride that had prevailed for decades and an amount many industry executives in 1919 thought essential to remain in business. In Indianapolis, for example, a battle royal erupted when the street railway sought a one-cent increase.

If interurbans could not persuade regulators to grant them the fare increases to cover their rapidly rising costs, they would have to trim those costs or go out of business—if the regulators permitted, which, during the troubled postwar times, they generally did not. Trimming wages would likely result in a bitter strike, but some trolley companies had learned during the prewar years how to operate their streetcars with just a motorman and a farebox, thereby eliminating the wages paid to a conductor. Single-operator cars rapidly gained popularity in response to postwar inflation. A one-person crew was not an option for Hoosier interurban operators: Indiana law mandated that the companies employ at least two crew members per train. Safety concerns required a motorman to focus his full attention on the track ahead, while the conductor collected passenger fares, dealt with baggage, and tried to keep the train running on time. Indiana law also mandated a second train conductor if a trailer was attached behind the power car.

The railway infrastructure, most notably the power plants, was under close scrutiny as interurbans left no stone unexamined in their quest to save money. The typical power plant and the manned substations were both *models of inefficiency*. The development of automatic substations saved labor costs, as did improvements to powerhouses, even if that meant installing something so basic as better lighting. Older powerhouses were nearly always dingy and dangerous places that required "extreme care in movement," even in daylight, because of inadequate illumination. "The old dirty, dark boiler room can never be made to operate efficiently" simply by adding more stokers and gauges, insisted the *Electric Railway Journal*, because to "see the instruments and control the levers and to produce the proper psychological and physiological condition in power plant operators" good interior lighting was required.[3]

One of the grand old men of the interurban industry, Arthur W. Brady of Union Traction, used various public forums to analyze the industry's postwar troubles by sharing his insights from nearly two decades of observation and active participation in

In typical fashion, Cambridge City required interurban tracks to occupy the center of the old National Road as they passed through town. Along rural stretches of the highway, however, the tracks followed the edge of the road and were separated from wagon and subsequent automobile traffic by nothing more than a slightly raised right-of-way.

the industry's evolution. One cause of the current malaise, noted Brady, dated from the early years of the Interurban Era when investors almost literally threw money at any proposal that looked promising. The industry greatly overbuilt its network by adding miles of track that would never earn a profit, and as a result, many interurban companies failed to earn enough money to pay their bills in the face of rising costs and were forced into receivership. Some never reemerged. In more recent times, and especially as a result of wartime inflation, meddlesome government officials refused to allow electric railway fares to rise rapidly enough to cover the industry's mounting expenses.

In a written presentation to fellow members of the American Electric Railway Association titled "The Needs of the Interurban Electric Railway Companies," Brady commenced his analysis of the industry's troubles by emphasizing that it had no ills "money would not cure." The organization's former president continued by noting that the situation was far more complex than his introductory quip suggested and that even an immediate infusion of money could not address its systemic ills. The situation was far worse for interurbans than for street railways, especially in his home region, the Midwest.

Brady, it might be noted, was a keen student of history, a busy executive who nonetheless found spare time to read about the history of the law—one of his passions—and to write a book about Moravian missionary activity among the Indians of his home state. So it was natural for him to analyze the electric railway industry's current set of problems by methodically reviewing the evolution of the Midwest's interurban lines during the past two decades, a history he knew from firsthand experience. During the industry's early years, when "only a few enthusiasts" thought the automobile "would ever become anything more than a rich man's toy," the region eagerly embraced the interurban with the expectation that any tracks on the ground would attract enough business to turn a profit. For many marginal lines, that was never possible. Meanwhile, as Brady reminded readers, Elwood Haynes, his fellow Hoosier, had launched an alternative mode of transportation that had the effect of "depriving" the interurban companies of the "year to year increase in their earnings, which they had a right to expect."[4]

Brady noted that in Indiana, "the automobile furnished a means of locomotion between the same points that are served by the interurban railways, and that, of course, has contributed very largely to the money lack of the interurbans." Franchise terms and various regulatory restrictions imposed during the industry's vigorous youth prevented interurban companies from addressing rising highway competition. Making this injustice even worse in Brady's estimation was "the failure of public officials of various classes to realize the situation in which the interurbans are placed and to act courageously and broadmindedly in view of that situation."[5]

The ever-diplomatic gentleman from Indiana wisely refrained from calling the populist politicians responsible for this mess the obtuse, duplicitous, and vote-grubbing hacks that many truly were. As one of Brady's colleagues phrased it, the electric railway industry needed to be "kept off the rocks of complete financial disaster" despite the "aim of some politicians and newspapers to put it there." With the rise of the regulatory state during World War I, it was convenient and at least partially accurate for industry spokesmen to blame politicians for the ills besetting electric railways.[6]

Regardless of the cause, the interurban industry's three "Rs" of 1919 were "retrenchment," "receivership," and "removal," all referring to financial belt-tightening measures and even to the once-unthinkable final resort of abandoning and removing track in what had clearly become a struggle for survival. Words that conveyed a negative message appeared with distressing frequency on the pages of the industry's trade publications during the dark days of 1919 and 1920. "Getting Near the End of the Rope" was how the editor of *Electric Traction* headlined a news report that fully 13 percent of the electric railway mileage in the United States was in the hands of receivers. "It is the nature of the American people to await a calamity instead of realizing a danger in time to avoid the calamity."[7]

The electric railway industry in 1919 still reeled from the recent pummeling by the jitney interlopers, and wartime inflation made an already difficult financial squeeze wholly intolerable. If during 1915 or 1916 the industry believed it was beginning to slip downhill; in 1919, it feared it hovered at the very edge of a financial cliff. When a formerly prosperous interurban company like the Fort Wayne and Northern Indiana—a cash cow in past years for its Philadelphia financiers—entered receivership, it was as if a pillar of Hoosier enterprise had unexpectedly crumbled. The spectacle left industry observers fearful that the entire electric railway edifice might collapse into bankruptcy. So many street railway and interurban executives voiced public alarm that their once-robust industry was on the brink of total disintegration that President Woodrow Wilson hastily convened a special panel. The Federal Electric Railways Commission's purpose was to compile a report based on the oral and written testimony it obtained from a variety of experts.[8]

The commission held a series of hearings during the summer and fall of 1919. Any summer spent on Capitol Hill in the days before air-conditioning was a form of torture because of the oppressive heat and humidity that blanketed Washington, DC. Nonetheless, the panel of commissioners dutifully listened to and frequently questioned a parade of ninety-five witnesses representing the electric railway industry, organized labor, the general public, and government regulators. When former congressman Charles L. Henry returned to the halls of power in Washington, DC, he exuded his usual confidence as he addressed matters specific to interurban railways. The ever-genial Hoosier even added a needed note of levity to the generally downbeat tone of the hearings. Bentley W. Warren, the counsel for the commission, began in a perfunctory manner by asking Henry to state his full name and address. Warren then quickly added, "And you have sometimes, I think, been referred to as 'the father of the interurban railway.'"

Henry considered how best to respond: "That is when they do not have respect for my old age." Warren's line of questioning then took a serious turn that resulted in thirty-three pages of published testimony about Indiana interurbans from the individual who more than anyone else had witnessed and also participated in their ups and downs during the past quarter century.[9]

Not all witnesses who dutifully journeyed to Capitol Hill during the summer of 1919 were certain what the outcome of the commission's inquiry was supposed to be, but if nothing else, the hearings afforded long-suffering street railway executives and a variety of supporters a high-profile opportunity to vent their frustrations. Witnesses occasionally lashed out with bitter words, and perhaps no one expressed the industry's frustration with the current intolerable situation more forcefully than Dean Mortimer E. Cooley of the University of Michigan's School of Engineering. Cooley was an oracle who, apart from Dr. Thomas Conway of the University of Pennsylvania, was perhaps the most highly regarded academic in electric railway circles. For Dean Cooley, the nation's current regulatory mess was nothing less than a "stench in the nostrils."

After members of the Federal Electric Railways Commission wrapped up weeks of collecting testimony, they submitted their findings to President Woodrow Wilson in mid-1920 in the form of a massive three-volume report. The weighty document, which represented a distillation of a mountain of information compiled by the commissioners, encapsulated the frustration experienced by nearly everyone connected with the electric railway industry in 1919, but apart from providing a discussion forum, little of lasting improvement came from the yearlong inquiry.[10]

A streetcar conductor in his resplendent navy-blue uniform. Because many of Indiana's interurban companies operated city trolley lines as well as intercity trains, it was not uncommon for them to advance seasoned streetcar conductors to interurban service.

The president's attention was focused on the Paris Peace Conference held in Versailles, France, throughout 1919 to shape a new postwar world order—his topmost priority—and on convincing the US Senate to commit the nation to full membership in the recently formed League of Nations. This was a task so difficult and ultimately so impossible that Wilson suffered a massive stroke in October 1919 that incapacitated him for the remainder of his presidency. It is highly doubtful that he had the mental capacity to read the copy of the lengthy report that reached the Oval Office. Mercifully, the ailing president was spared the typescript version that totaled an impossibly long 6,195 pages! The president (or, more likely, a secretary) dutifully sent a letter of thanks to commission members, and that was the White House response. In the end, the main benefit of the document was to provide electric railway executives leverage in the form of quotable material when they or their lawyers petitioned state and local regulators for higher rates.[11]

For all its bulk, the report sent to President Wilson addressed mainly the woes of street railways. Of the 174 questions the special commission included in a survey it sent to the mayors, chambers of commerce, boards of trade, central labor unions, and electric railway executives of every community in the United States that had a trolley or interurban line, only fifteen dealt specifically with interurban matters. In addition, most of the questions addressed to the commission's in-person witnesses and the numerous statistical tables and graphs it presented to President Wilson yielded few remedies for the ills afflicting interurbans. This was likewise true for the many statistics published during the 1920s, which, by focusing mainly on the health of the entire electric railway industry, tended to gloss over the ever-worsening financial health of the interurban lines.[12]

As might be expected, low morale prevailed throughout the electric railway industry during 1919 and into the early 1920s. The war had ended, but conditions for trolley and interurban operators did not improve. It was wrenching to see familiar faces—long-time industry colleagues in many cases—disappear from professional meetings because the interurban line they formerly managed had ceased to run and been sold for scrap. These time-hallowed gatherings educated and informed geographically scattered individuals, but some people in the industry also likened them to alumni reunions. But as was the case for high school and college reunions, sickness or death occasionally claimed a valued friend. Some colleagues died during the influenza pandemic of 1918 and 1919 or were felled by heart attacks and strokes as a result of the increased physical and mental stress of the Great War. More frequently, however, from 1919 through the early 1920s, it was the death of a company that thinned the ranks of interurban management at professional meetings.

News of abandonments grew noticeably more frequent on the pages of the *Electric Railway Journal* in 1919. Mostly these represented small segments of larger systems, typically a money-losing branch line, or, if a company shut down completely, it was one of the industry's many marginal operators. After all, industry luminaries like Arthur Brady had publicly stated that the rush to build interurban lines during the first decade had resulted in a number of poor prospects for long-term survival. The attrition process might be compared to the removal of isolated bricks here or there, the result being minor and geographically scattered losses that seldom alarmed anyone because in the 1920s few observers believed the entire interurban edifice might crumble. Until the Great Depression in the early 1930s, in fact, the network of interurban lines across the Midwest remained almost entirely intact. In many ways, it functioned better than ever because with the steady loss of passenger traffic and the increased operating expenses that resulted from World War I, interurban companies learned to tighten their financial belts and turn an ever-greater profit by carrying freight, and especially livestock, cargo forbidden on the streets of Indianapolis until the wartime emergency.

With the wartime freight traffic of the steam railroads tied into knots, Indiana farmers clamored for interurban freight cars to haul their hogs to the stockyards in Indianapolis, but without success. They then turned to the state's governor, James P. Goodrich, who lent them a sympathetic ear.

"He picked up his telephone and called Robert I. Todd, president of the Terre Haute, Indianapolis & Eastern Traction Company. Briefly and concisely, he stated the facts. The steam roads could not carry the livestock offered them, so the traction lines must carry it."

Todd explained that franchise provisions governing the Indianapolis Street Railway and the several interurban lines that rented use of its tracks expressly forbade the transport of livestock through city streets. His traction company and others would gladly add this business, but the franchise blocked their way.

"'You carry those hogs,' the governor insisted. 'We're at war, and this is no time to let anything stand in the way of winning the war."

Thus, with orders from the governor, the state's interurbans began transporting livestock to Indianapolis markets. The 1920 session of the Indiana legislature altered the law to affirm the governor's wartime action, and in this way, Indiana interurbans gained long-term access to a profitable market that had previously been the exclusive domain of steam railroads.[13]

Electric railways hastened to rebuild old and unused passenger cars into livestock haulers, or they purchased new ones designed for that purpose. "Interurban cars loaded with bleating calves, bellowing and grunting pigs, will soon be a common sight on the streets of Greenfield by reason of the special session of the legislature having passed a law permitting traction lines to haul livestock." The newspaper was not complaining, however, because it expected the new law to be of "great benefit to farmers." The million-dollar, twelve-acre freight complex that the combination of central Indiana interurban lines opened on Kentucky Avenue in 1924 was located conveniently close to the massive stockyards of Indianapolis and to the city's single-largest enterprise in the early 1920s, which continued to be Kingan's meatpacking plant.[14]

In retrospect, it seems clear that most electric railways failed to capitalize on the unprecedented growth opportunity that the federal government handed them on a silver platter. In December 1917, at the behest of President Wilson, Congress in an unprecedented power grab authorized the federal government to nationalize the major steam

The Dixie Flyer made a daily sprint from Indianapolis to Louisville.

railroads, but not the electric interurban lines unless absolutely necessary. Freight congestion offered interurban lines a perfect opportunity to demonstrate their cargo-carrying ability, but as industry officials later admitted, they dropped the ball, and nothing much happened during the war emergency to alter their status as marginal freight haulers. Nonetheless, and going largely unnoticed during the industry's public hand-wringing of 1919, seeds of change were being planted and would bear fruit with the sudden and unexpected flowering of the interurban freight business during the early 1920s.

Interurbans now rushed trainloads of fresh fruit from Michigan orchards to central Indiana dining tables, and auto parts from Hoosier factories to assembly lines in Detroit, to cite just two examples of the industry's growing interline cooperation to move cargoes expeditiously. Some Indiana carriers also demonstrated faith in the future by borrowing money to purchase passenger cars and inaugurate luxury services, such as the Interstate Public Service did during the 1920s when it added dining cars to its express trains between Indianapolis and Louisville.

In the year following World War I, the electric railway industry's precarious finances prompted much public soul-searching. The year 1919 was notable for its many meetings and conferences in which executives commiserated about the woes that overregulation and inflation had inflicted on trolley and interurban operators, the industry that one public speaker described as the "sick man" of American business.[15]

The frequent meetings held during 1919 seemed to provide electric railway executives a measure of catharsis as they commiserated together. At one such meeting, held in New York City, Charles L. Henry and Philadelphia financier Randal Morgan, the two individuals instrumental in launching the Union Traction Company of Indiana, shared the same public stage for possibly the first time since early 1901, when Henry abruptly departed the railway for reasons neither man ever stated publicly. If there had been bad blood between them back then, the postwar economic turbulence encouraged them to work together again for the greater good of the industry.

13

Deadly Delusion

The Comeback That Never Was

> In the recent past we have had our back to the wall, making a desperate fight for existence. Not the least of our trouble was the fear of what the bus business was going to do to our electric railway transportation systems. Now, I believe, this bugaboo has been exploded and, instead of being a bugaboo, the bus can be used to great advantage for the development of electric railway transportation systems as a co-ordinated adjunct to them.
>
> —Ray P. Stevens, Penn Ohio Edison Company, as quoted in the *Electric Railway Journal* (September 1927): 466

"Boston may be the center of the universe," quipped Robert I. Todd in his February 1922 address to members of the New England Street Railway Club, "but we believe that Indianapolis is the center of the electric railway systems." Todd, a New Jersey native, current president of the American Electric Railway Association, and the university-educated successor to Hugh McGowan as the "big man" of central Indiana tractions, was the club's guest of honor and banquet speaker. His talk underscored the industry's abrupt abandonment of the gloom-and-doom thinking that hung over it like a black cloud after World War I: Todd now predicted a bright future for America's electric railways of all types. "Those who have studied the electric situation are unanimous in their opinion that we have passed through the darkest days and that electric railways will in the not far distant future occupy a most important place in the business of the country."[1]

One year later, Charles D. Emmons, the Hoosier who headed the United Railways and Electric Company of Baltimore and who was Todd's elected successor as president of the American Electric Railway Association, detailed the "darkest days" of the recent past for listeners at the organization's annual midwinter dinner. Emmons recalled 1919 as a terrible time during which conditions "continued to grow darker and darker for the industry and toward the end approximately one-sixth of the electric railway properties were bankrupt, abandoned or junked, and the future of many of the rest was in doubt."[2]

The station agent and onboard crew members handle baggage at the Delphi interurban depot.

After its near-death experience, any evidence of the electric railway industry's improved health could be interpreted as a miraculous recovery. "Interurban Lines Are 'Coming Back' After Long Fight," insisted the headlines of an *Indianapolis Star* article on the revival of Indiana's electric railways. This upbeat financial assessment from 1925 was typical of the steady drumbeat of news of the industry's comeback during the first half of the 1920s. There had been little public realization, or so the *Star*'s observer now claimed, of the "desperate straits" to which the electric railway system of Indiana had been reduced during the war years. Some observers familiar with the industry had feared their "complete collapse." Even during the industry's darkest days, there had been some persistent optimists, men "now engaged in surveying the damages to once prosperous interurban lines and determining what can be done toward rehabilitating them." The hard-core optimists convinced themselves that "the improving conditions of the electric railways is reflected in the larger financial markets of the country, where there now exists a disposition to treat interurbans as inherently sound investments."[3]

In January 1920, with a new decade's promise of better times ahead, the industry's main trade publication in its lead editorial mandated that everyone connected with electric railways had better be an optimist or else. "There is no room in the industry for pessimists," thundered the *Electric Railway Journal*. "It seems almost imperative that all electric railway executive positions be occupied by men whose visions are not handicapped and beclouded with pessimistic prejudice." Thus, optimism became the industry's new watchword. So infectious was the upbeat spirit that it became impossible to believe that the future would not be as rosy as everyone claimed. Like a strange contagious disease, optimism would run its course by 1925, but it left some notable casualties in its wake.[4]

Portrait of Harry Reid, who, as head of Interstate Public Service during the 1920s, prodded fellow interurban executives to add bus and truck operations to the electric interurban railway to provide a more comprehensive network of rail and highway lines.

One optimist asserted that "every serious illness, unless death intervenes, is followed by convalescence." He continued: "So it is with the electric railway industry. It passed through its serious illness and recovery set in after 1918." In fact, 1919 easily ranked as the darkest year in the industry's history, when the number of electric railways forced into receivership "exceed in number, miles, and capitalization those of any year since statistics have been compiled." An analogy that used human recovery from serious illness to bolster claims of an interurban comeback was absurd, but it was typical of the industry's desperate need to believe that better times were at hand.[5]

Among Indiana's most outspoken interurban optimists was Harry Reid, head of the Interstate Public Service Company. During the Great War's time of rapid and often disconcerting change, however, even Reid had to admit that the future of the interurban was "a mystery" and "predictions are largely based upon what has transpired in the past. In our business we have no precedent to follow as the first interurban was put into operation in 1885 and this business is, therefore, a comparatively modern development."[6]

With the end of wartime uncertainty and the return of prosperity during the Warren G. Harding presidency, Reid recovered his customary good cheer. By 1923, he could confidently assure the holders of traction securities that they "need have no fear of the safety of their investment," and they could look to the future with "assurance and optimism." Their money was safe because the infant industry had survived the grim war years and was evolving into a mature and prosperous long-distance hauler of freight in addition to its traditional role as a passenger carrier. Shareholders had no reason to fear "the developments of the so-called 'rubber age.'" Reid's upbeat prediction of a prosperous future for electric railways formed part of a veritable chorus of industry prophets who from 1921 through 1924 claimed to see only boom times in the coming years that ensured "a fair, just, and safe return" to investors. Charles L. Henry was foremost among the true believers in the industry's miraculous comeback, and when he borrowed millions of dollars to completely rehabilitate the Indianapolis and Cincinnati Traction Company, he made the costliest mistake of his lengthy business career.[7]

Just months after the November 1918 armistice, a beautiful new interurban station opened in downtown Akron, Ohio. It featured seven tracks sufficient to handle current traffic as well as the growth expected during the coming years. For observers in search of rays of hope during the dark days of 1919, the Akron station was viewed as a positive sign. Industry optimists, and some individuals did manage to maintain their faith in the interurban's future, spoke anew of the benefits to be derived once the several obvious gaps in the still-disjointed network of tracks across the Midwest were closed.

Most often mentioned was the short gap that continued to defy attempts to link Indiana and Illinois lines so that fast and frequent interurban trains could connect Indianapolis and Saint Louis. When the writer of an anonymous letter to the *Electric Railway Journal* dared to ask whether the electric railway industry was "tottering" (citing census statistics confirming that during the previous five years, US trolley and interurban companies had abandoned nine hundred miles of track, or about 2 percent of their total), the publication responded with a front-page editorial and a thunderous headline affirming in no uncertain terms that "The Electric Railways are Coming Back."[8]

Not surprisingly, among the first industry spokesmen to assert a comeback of any type was Charles L. Henry, who after the Central Electric Railway Association's (CERA) 1919 gathering in Cleveland used that soon-to-be familiar phrase to describe what he perceived as the renewed vigor of the Midwest organization. The editor of the *Electric Railway Journal* picked up on what he described as a "happy phrase" and amplified its meaning: "We agree with Mr. Henry in this conclusion and will go him one better by saying that the industry as a whole is 'coming back,' or we mistake greatly the signs that are about." Belief in an industrywide comeback encouraged electric railways across the Midwest to invest in a variety of improvements, some of them exceedingly expensive but financed by willing lenders equally intoxicated by repeated claims of the interurban's return to long-term prosperity.[9]

At the dawn of the new decade, the editor of the *Electric Railway Journal* dared to imagine what might lay ten years down the road for the electric railway industry in 1930: "Prophecy is risky unless the prophet has accurate and ample knowledge in the field of his proposed prognostications. At the same time some kind of vision of the future is necessary in any line of endeavor if effort in that line is to be more than mere drudgery." His prediction for the traction business was that it "appears certain that the industry will be here and that it will be prosperous." This kind of giddy optimism lasted for three or four years, but well before the onset of the Great Depression in 1930, events five years earlier had already exposed the claim as wholly delusional, and no one suffered greater personal loss as a result than Charles L. Henry, who spent his remaining years ensnared in litigation stemming from the multimillion-dollar improvements he made to the Indianapolis and Cincinnati Traction Company in the belief that prosperity during the coming decades would reward his willingness to shoulder an enormous financial burden.[10]

The United States slowly and sometimes painfully adjusted to the peacetime conditions that President Warren G. Harding labeled "normalcy," a term the former Ohio newspaper publisher and wordsmith coined and that was an apt description of the early 1920s. The return of calm in late 1921 was reassuring despite several brutal postwar labor disputes and yet another bout of hard times at the dawn of the decade that Union Traction described as a "violent economic readjustment."[11]

From 1922 through 1924, America's daily newspapers, electric railway journals, and numerous industry luminaries contributed to a steady stream of good news that collectively amplified the claim that the interurban was poised to enter a new era of prosperity. "Electric Railways Prospering" read a late 1924 headline in the *Indianapolis News*. The article noted that just "five years ago one-sixth of all the electric railways of this country were in bankruptcy. All were destined for the scrap heap according to the views of most people." By way of contrast, the interurbans were destined in 1924 to play a "big part in solving the freight transportation problem of the country." That was especially true in Indianapolis and the Midwest, and the region's interurbans could be expected to prosper. Harry Reid, head of the Interstate Public Service Company, claimed that 1922 was the best year his company had ever experienced. This development "augurs well for the future," especially in terms of the emergence of interurban railways as freight haulers of significance.[12]

For many carriers, any serious effort to build freight traffic happened only in slow motion, and the reluctance of executives like Will Irwin to embrace anything but human cargo could probably be traced back to the days when the "country trolley" was exclusively a passenger hauler. During the interurban's early 1920s comeback, illusory though it proved to be, the industry was leaning heavily on freight revenues to stay afloat.[13]

A prime example of the transformation was Reid's own Interstate Public Service. During the post–Great War years, it dramatically increased its gross revenue derived from freight from a measly 6 percent to 42 percent. Reid boldly predicted that Interstate

Interurban First-Class Indianapolis to Louisville

In late 1924, *Electric Traction* published a firsthand account of a journey from Chicago to Louisville made entirely aboard interurban cars. The writer, styling himself as "Traction Traveler," reported his overnight ride in one of Harry Reid's new sleeping cars, themselves a statement of confidence in the industry comeback that never was. The traction sleeper left Indianapolis nightly at 11:30, although passengers could board it and bed down as early as 9:00 p.m. Because the run to Louisville was so short, the sleeper paused in Scottsburg for two and a half hours before continuing south to the Kentucky metropolis, which it reached at 7:05 a.m.

The berths were longer than those on a standard Pullman car and provided a touch of opulence that prompted the lanky "Traction Traveler" to claim the Interstate sleepers were "the most comfortable and luxurious I have ridden upon in many a day, and that goes for the steam roads too." A lower berth cost $2.50, and an upper was $1.75, and neither required a surcharge as Pullman cars did.

On the return day trip to Indianapolis, "Traction Traveler" took note of the main frustration experienced by the electric railways of the Midwest: "The Interstate, like most interurbans, is handicapped in the matter of speed by having to run through the city streets of several towns between terminals and at the two terminal cities. At that, however, they pass the trains of the Pennsylvania railroad [between Indianapolis and Louisville] as if the latter were standing still."[15]

freight traffic would at least double in size after the huge new cargo-handling complex opened in southwest Indianapolis. Newspapers cited other improvements that to Reid and his industry peers signified the return of confidence and a bright future for the interurban railways in Indiana, though hindsight suggests that the foundation supporting the industry's presumed comeback was composed of wishful thinking, self-serving puffery, and the misleading use of statistics.[14]

An industry that had slogged through seven demoralizing years that followed the unexpected appearance of a pesky swarm of jitneys on Los Angeles streets in 1914 continued with the high-cost-of-living crisis during the Great War, which worsened with unprecedented labor unrest during postwar 1919 and 1920, was desperate to hear good news. During the seven troubled years, every weekly issue of the *Electric Railway Journal* contained downbeat news of the industry's seemingly eternal struggle with the cheeky jitney drivers. Neither jail time nor laws deterred jitney drivers. Only lawyers profited from the seesaw battle. The same dynamic had applied in a thousand different communities as electric railways and their attorneys sought to persuade the regulators to raise fares enough to cover their increased costs. Once again, the *Electric Railway Journal* spilled barrels of printers' ink to list even briefly the battles won and lost. The industry's lengthy struggle to drive jitneys from city streets and to contain the high cost of living made for depressing reading.

The industry had placed a great deal of faith in the Federal Electric Railways Commission hearings of 1919 and in the massive report presented afterward to President Woodrow Wilson. However, as the months went by, it grew painfully obvious that the reams of testimony the commission collected amounted to little more than a feel-good exercise in which talk had become an end in itself. Likewise, the industry welcomed the incoming president, Warren G. Harding, as its advocate and even savior. Harding had taken time in 1920 to address a major electric railway conference held in Ohio, and his listeners came away with the conviction that he was a great friend of the trolley and interurban lines. Finally, they placed hope in Charles L. Henry, selected by members of the American Electric Railway Association to represent their interests on Capitol Hill (to be the industry's lobbyist, in today's terms) and to exercise leverage with Congress and the Interstate Commerce Commission. Even though none of these expectations panned out quite as hoped, industry spokesmen told one another repeatedly in their public presentations and again in print that a comeback was at hand. Indeed, in 1921 and 1922, it did seem as if the worst was finally over.

The steady drumbeat of upbeat news and various statistical indicators that seemed to promise better times ahead encouraged interurban executives to launch a series of expensive betterment projects with giddy abandon. First, all four of central Indiana's largest interurban companies pooled their resources to open a massive new freight complex on Kentucky Avenue in southwestern Indianapolis in 1924, which the American Electric Railway Association praised as the "nation's great electric freight center." Interurban executives were convinced that even if the decline in passenger traffic could not be reversed, their rapidly growing freight business would more than make up the difference. "The carrying of livestock in car loads has been a great source of income in Indiana for several years past. This business, which originated during the time of the World War and which was actually forced on the interurban companies, has grown to such a volume that during the year 1923 some ten thousand carloads of livestock were brought into Indianapolis and delivered directly to the stockyards."[16]

Second, Arthur W. Brady of Union Traction and Harry Reid of Interstate Public Service invested in modern, all-steel rollingstock and added amenities such as café service to woo passengers back to the rails. However, all such projects combined could not begin to equal the leap of faith Charles L. Henry made when he confidently reinvented the Indianapolis and Cincinnati Traction Company from the ballast up, believing that traffic would rebound to justify his optimism and would retire the enormous load of debt his interurban shouldered in the decades ahead.

In a 1948 interview, James A. VanOsdol, the last survivor among the Union Traction founders of fifty years earlier,[17] reminisced that when his law partner, Henry, returned home to Anderson, Indiana, in 1897 during his second term in Congress, he was convinced that electric interurban railways were the transportation of the future. VanOsdol caught Henry's "interurban fever," and for the next three decades, until Indiana Railroad acquired Union Traction in 1930, he served as its general counsel. "From the day he first became interested until his death in 1927 [Henry] lived and thought the traction business," recalled the now octogenarian VanOsdol. "[He] interested me. He interested others and we all felt there was not only a definite need for the service such lines could give but they would be well received."[18]

Henry's enthusiastic embrace of the interurban was as strong as ever in 1923, and in midyear, he persuaded members of his board of directors to support a bold plan he had conceived to modernize the railway. So contagious was Henry's belief in an industry comeback that otherwise levelheaded bankers and investors willingly provided the millions he needed to make the improvements, even though the company's financial record to date was dismal. One company executive revealed in 1913 that the Indianapolis and Cincinnati had not paid a single cent in dividends to stockholders since its founding eleven years earlier.[19]

Henry charmed one of his longtime Indiana backers, J. F. Wild and Company, an Indianapolis state bank, into loaning Indianapolis and Cincinnati Traction much of the $4 million to purchase new rollingstock and, even more amazing, to scrap its former state-of-the-art single-phase alternating current system and replace it with a new direct current one. The revamped infrastructure required the company to add no fewer than twelve substations and various other kinds of expensive electrical equipment. A rumor surfaced, as might be expected in Indiana, that Randal Morgan and his Philadelphia money were behind the interurban's sweeping makeover, but Henry vigorously denied it and emphasized that the company's loan represented a Hoosier investment.[20]

Finally, Henry insisted (for the umpteenth time) that he still intended to link Indianapolis and Cincinnati and that the interurban's expensive upgrade would make that long-deferred dream possible. It was more than a dream, in fact, because as Henry had publicly admitted back in 1907, "I will be very frank in saying that this line will never pay until we get it through." Henry had constructed what he described as "perhaps the best and most expensively built line in the state" with traffic all the way to Cincinnati in mind. "Such a cost is too high for local business, and our hopes are centered in a through business. When our line is completed I believe that we will have a splendid property."[21]

After countless false starts and numerous disappointments, the realization of Henry's twenty-year quest to extend tracks into the Ohio River metropolis would serve as the capstone of his personal Interurban Era. In reality, his obsession was responsible for the darkest years of his life.

Henry's eye-catching leap of faith left the editor of the *Electric Railway Journal* scratching his head in amazement. The gambit was financially dangerous and made little sense given the mainly rural area Henry's Indianapolis and Cincinnati Traction Company served across southeastern Indiana. Besides, by 1923, private automobiles had drained away much of the interurban's passenger traffic and left it dependent on revenue from freight. Henry had only one viable move left if he were to avoid financial checkmate: unless his interurban tracks could somehow access downtown Cincinnati, its cargoes of crops and cattle from southern Indiana could not possibly generate enough money to cover the railway's outstanding bills, especially its huge new loan obligation, which, if calculated in terms of inflation, represented a sum equal to $70 million in 2023 dollars.

Consultants hired by Henry convinced him that a line from Rushville to Cincinnati would run through prosperous farm country poorly served by existing steam railroads. That was exactly what Henry wanted to hear. Getting tracks into Cincinnati had been his goal since the beginning of the interurban company. There had always been some obstacle, an unexpected downturn on Wall Street or the Great War's disruptive impact. Even if he did somehow manage to bridge the gap across the hills of southeastern Indiana, he still had to find a way for his cars to access the vibrant heart of Cincinnati. The single-most promising event to date was voter approval in 1917 of a subway along an abandoned canal bed into the city center, but it remained unbuilt in the early 1920s and, in fact, would never be completed.[22]

Perhaps Henry was inspired by the rollingstock and infrastructure modernization projects launched by his peers, Reid and Brady, but there simply was no meaningful

Greensburg was the end of the line for Charles L. Henry's big red cars from Indianapolis. From this point or from Connersville, he sought to continue his interurban tracks all the way to Cincinnati.

comparison among their three Indiana interurban companies. When Reid upgraded Interstate Public Service by purchasing several impressive dining and sleeping cars[23] and reworked its infrastructure to use a single standard of voltage, his company's finances profited from existing traffic between two of the Midwest's largest population centers, not to mention several prosperous Indiana cities along the way. The federal census of 1920 recorded that Louisville had attained a population of 234,891, a total that grew by a whopping 31 percent during the Prosperity Decade of the 1920s. Indianapolis residents numbered 314,194 in 1920, and Cincinnati's population increased to 401,247. By contrast, neither of Henry's two endpoint communities, Greensburg and Connersville, could in 1920 count as many as ten thousand residents. In fact, apart from Indianapolis, only two other communities along the entire interurban line in place when Henry launched his latest Cincinnati gambit in 1923 had more than five thousand residents. These were Rushville (5,498) and Shelbyville (9,701). These numbers simply did not bode well.[24]

The *Rushville Republican* was always one of Henry's most loyal boosters, and its May 1924 salute of his "milestone" overhaul of the Indianapolis and Cincinnati Traction Company was brimming with praise: "With his usual vigor and fighting spirit, Mr. Henry has accomplished" what seemed to be "impossible" given the financial and economic challenges he faced. "Complete re-equipment, including twelve new all steel passenger cars with change in current cycle, in power distribution and change in trolley voltage—putting into what was known as a bankrupt road nearly a million dollars of new money in a way practically certain to protect the original investment in the property." In reality, just the opposite occurred: Henry's Cincinnati obsession soon sank his company, as the editor of the *Electric Railway Journal* had feared it might and cost the "father of the interurban" nearly all of his personal fortune.[25]

In a replay of Henry's 1906 financial debacle, in 1925, his company was unable once again to repay the loan used to purchase the Westinghouse electrical infrastructure it needed to modernize, and the Indianapolis and Cincinnati Traction Company entered receivership. Henry was once again tapped as its court-appointed receiver. It was a humiliating outcome.[26]

Henry's conviction that the interurban industry had made a comeback resulted in a series of flawed decisions that haunted him for the remainder of his life. It was as if the "father of the interurban" had grown so fixated on his Cincinnati quest that he was blind to the steadily rising tide of competition, private automobiles and intercity trucks most noticeably but also opportunistic and largely unregulated intercity bus operators, individuals whose parasitic vehicles competed head-on with interurban cars along both of Henry's routes. Encouraging the motor competition was the state of Indiana itself. On the final day of 1925, at the same time as interurban optimists loudly touted their industry comeback, another group took pride in Indiana's fast-expanding network of all-weather highways. "Roads Big Factor in Indiana's Prosperity," proclaimed the headlines of an *Indianapolis News* retrospective assessment that took note of the state's record year of highway construction activity.[27]

One ominous event that believers in the interurban's comeback completely ignored was the near abandonment in mid-1920 of a key portion of the Buffalo and Lake Erie Traction Company in Upstate New York and across Pennsylvania to the city of Erie. For the first time, the web of interconnected electric railways so painstakingly stitched together across the Midwest from Wisconsin to Upstate New York during the early years threatened to unravel. If that happened, it would no longer be possible for enthusiasts to boast of riding electric cars all the way from Chicago to New York City, except for a twenty-mile gap never completed across Upstate New York. Traffic between Buffalo and Erie that failed to justify the optimism of the line's promoters certainly offered a compelling reason to remove the money-losing tracks, but here the symbolism was of utmost importance. It was one thing never to complete a network of interurban lines across half the United States, but to rip up rails already in place and sell them for scrap portended serious trouble ahead.[28]

For more than two decades, the expanding interurban network across the Midwest had been heralded as a sign of the industry's unstoppable growth. Only a few short gaps remained to be bridged to make the electric railway's coming of age a reality. Any backtracking as represented by the creation of a gap between Buffalo and Cleveland would dash an expectation that had become a bedrock article of faith for the industry. The *Electric Railway Review* recognized that "an electric railway property cannot be kept in operation out of sentiment if there is not enough business to justify its existence." Nonetheless, its editor lamented, "We regret exceedingly to see the abandonment of an important connecting link in the greater electric railway system." No one grieved the loss of long-distance passenger traffic between the Midwest and Upstate New York, of which there was next to none, but abandonment's impact on the interurban industry's rapidly expanding business of long-distance freight haulage was huge because of the reversal it signified.[29]

Morale among interurban executives had already dropped to rock bottom in 1919 because their industry had clearly stagnated. Every January, the *Electric Railway Journal* published several pages of vital statistics that served to measure the health of the electric railway industry. In most years, the numbers had recorded growth and prosperity, but lately, they suggested serious trouble ahead. Although few new miles had been added to the Midwestern network since 1910, carriers had steadily improved their infrastructure and grown their passenger business. Now, for the first time, a major loss of miles and passenger traffic seemed imminent. Short segments of interurban lines and some small and marginal carriers had disappeared since 1916, but nothing like the wholesale abandonment threatened along the shore of Lake Erie had happened before.

Fortunately for believers in an industry comeback, a last-minute rescue kept the Buffalo and Lake Erie Traction Company's vital link intact until 1932, when, because of the belt-tightening required by the Great Depression, a miraculous deliverance was no longer possible. With the abandonment of tracks along Lake Erie came the destruction of the nation's single-largest network of interurban tracks.

Meanwhile, Charles L. Henry doggedly continued his quest to link Indianapolis and Cincinnati as if nothing about the Interurban Era had changed. Curiously, he took little, if any, notice of statistics showing that passenger traffic across Indiana had fallen steadily since its peak in 1916. Furthermore, the formerly energetic CERA that Henry had helped to found in 1906 and guide through the years had grown noticeably listless. It seemed to have lost its reason to exist. The organization's frequent meetings had once been well attended. Its numerous formal presentations and papers had provided hundreds of conference attendees with a wealth of useful information, and its banquets and baseball games pitting the Hoosiers against the Buckeyes had fostered camaraderie among the Midwest's geographically scattered traction executives, as had their opportunity to travel together to meeting sites aboard luxurious business cars such as Union Traction's Martha.

In the early 1920s, the CERA's former vitality seemed to be gone. Elected leaders occasionally failed to show up at meetings, and members made excuses for public presentations they had promised to give but somehow never completed. When leaders voted to abandon their formerly robust cycle of meetings in favor of just two perfunctory gatherings a year, the *Electric Railway Journal* had reason to lament yet another example of negative symbolism. The editor of *Electric Traction* even dared to question in print whether the CERA presentations were of benefit any longer to the electric railways that paid precious dollars for executives to attend. "Of what use are two dozen excellent suggestions made to one officer of the company unless these suggestions are communicated to other officers and the usable ones put into effect." Its editor further claimed the CERA's frequent meetings had devolved into little more than social gatherings: "What railway can show benefits in excess of actual expenditures?"[30]

A different type of malaise stunned the industry's national organization in the early 1920s. Much to their chagrin, the leadership of the American Electric Railway Association discovered that a bookkeeper in its New York headquarters had quietly embezzled more than $40,000. The malefactor was arrested, and the organization's secretary-treasurer resigned in disgrace. The loss did not bankrupt the venerable association, but it did contribute further to the industry's confusion about its future direction.

Providing Henry additional proof that the Midwest's ardor for electric railways in the early 1920s had cooled noticeably since the boom times fifteen or twenty years earlier was the dramatic rise of Ward Hiner, the would-be bus king of Indiana. Hiner, a freewheeling entrepreneur and Republican gadfly who ran unsuccessfully for every major political office Indiana had to offer, emerged for a brief time in the mid-1920s as the state's self-styled bus mogul. Hiner added new bus routes almost on a weekly basis until his Red Ball Lines network radiated outward from Indianapolis to every corner of the state. Best of all, from Hiner's perspective, his modern highway coaches traveled along the state's lengthening network of all-weather highways unencumbered by any of the regulations Indiana imposed on other common carriers, including the interurbans and steam railroads. Hiner could truly boast of the largest statewide bus operation, but several hundred other bus operators also emerged across Indiana in the early 1920s to take advantage of the same lack of regulation and the growing miles of all-weather highways.

Several local newspapers took note of the injustice suffered by the interurban railways: "No sooner was the paving finished to Knightstown than the bus line came into existence between there and Indianapolis." The bus company used the National Road, and its coaches ran parallel to the Terre Haute, Indianapolis and Eastern tracks the entire distance. "These bus lines get their right of way and road maintenance free and have no responsibility to the public. The traction line between Knightstown and

Indianapolis pays $40,000 a year to communities along the line and maintains its own roadway. The bus lines pay nothing and the public maintains the roadway for them."[31]

It might be expected that many other newspapers would voice similar alarms, but this was not the case. In fact, on May 19, 1925, when Hiner opened a huge new Indianapolis bus station just two blocks south of the capitol, some fifty thousand enthusiastic onlookers jammed downtown sidewalks and streets from early afternoon until late into the night to enjoy the public extravaganza the "bus baron" had orchestrated. The festivities included a mix of circus and vaudeville performers, strolling musicians, street dancers, a lengthy parade of a hundred motor buses of all vintages and even a horse-drawn stagecoach. Several Indianapolis industries set up outdoor booths to display their latest wares. The event was not entirely harmonious, however. Off to the side, a small crowd of African Americans protested that Hiner's coaches were not "accepting colored persons as passengers."[32]

The *Indianapolis Star* devoted a full page to Hiner's bus palace, a two-story brick structure that cost an estimated $2.5 million. It used the occasion to brag that the city that had given the world its first union railway station and its first union interurban station now also offered the world's first and grandest union bus station. In an editorial brimming with hometown pride, the newspaper proclaimed that the "bus is the next step in the evolution that is producing the Hoosierdom of the future."[33]

Hiner's hoopla was quite a contrast to Hugh McGowan's subdued and businesslike opening twenty-one years earlier of the Traction Terminal, the building often referred to as "Indianapolis's Front Door." Indeed, "hoopla" was a word used during the 1920s to describe Hiner's type of sensationalism, and it applied equally well to flagpole sitting, marathon dancing, and other frothy fads of the decade.[34]

Actually, the word "union" greatly stretched the truth. An earlier bus depot was located nearby on Kentucky Avenue, and operators based there were reluctant to move to a facility that Hiner dominated. In addition, less than a month after Hiner's hoopla, a group of interurban executives met in Indianapolis to plan a new bus station of their own. The irony is that instead of one union bus station, it appeared that Indianapolis would now have three!

Thanks to their growing freight business and its relocation from the Traction Terminal area to the recently opened warehouse complex on Kentucky Avenue, the executives had the perfect passenger facility in mind. In mid-1925, only days after Hiner's "union" bus station opened its doors, interurban executives agreed to remodel an unused freight terminal on Capitol Avenue into a Traction Terminal annex to accommodate the rapidly growing bus business. In terms of the seamless interchange of passengers between their buses and interurban cars, the location adjacent to the Traction Terminal was ideal.[35]

Indiana's network of bus lines operated by interurban companies grew significantly larger in 1926 after Hiner's statewide bus empire collapsed on December 21, 1925, only seven months after his Indianapolis station opened its doors. The sudden reversal of fortune, the result of the latest round of Indiana politics, was as dramatic as if all of the tires of Hiner's Red Ball buses had suffered simultaneous blowouts. Electric railway executives picked up his choicest bus routes at fire-sale prices, but they did not need his Indianapolis station. Originally, five thousand travelers a day had been predicted to pass through Hiner's much-ballyhooed facility used for a brief time by twenty-eight separate bus lines, all of them competing vigorously for interurban passenger traffic, but now the "overambitious project" stood empty. A few months earlier, a Fort Wayne newspaper had greeted its opening with a generous measure of skepticism: "Indianapolis, the largest inland railway center and the world's most extensive interurban plexus, has just opened the greatest motor bus terminal in the known universe. Somehow it doesn't seem to fit."[36]

It did not, and the rapid undoing of Indiana's bus tycoon could be traced a few blocks north of his idle bus station to the state capitol where a majority of lawmakers drained the financial fuel from Hiner's nonregulated enterprise. Indiana interurbans in recent years had steadily lost passengers to private automobiles and intercity buses, but in the mid-1920s, they still could muster the political clout needed to stop Hiner and other freebooters from taking advantage of Indiana's growing network of all-weather highways. Interurban lobbyists persuaded Indiana legislators in early 1925 that in the name of fairness, they needed to enact a law that defined the state's bus companies as common carriers and thus make them subject to the same regulations that governed the steam railroads and interurbans. Hiner, it turned out, had a flawed understanding of basic economic principles, because he operated his bus empire essentially out of his hip pocket and simply could not turn a profit under the state's newly imposed accounting standards. Numerous other bus operators met the same fate, and their receivers all agreed that the "only hope of making these lines pay is to allow the traction companies to buy and to run them."[37]

The Indiana Motor Transit Company, a subsidiary of Terre Haute, Indianapolis and Eastern, acquired several of Hiner's bus routes that paralleled its interurban tracks. Arthur Brady and Union Traction did the same thing, and included in the deal were operating rights that enabled its buses to reach far beyond the limits of the interurban's traditional service area in the former Gas Belt, such as when its newly acquired motor coaches made special runs to transport outdoors enthusiasts and trail hikers from downtown Indianapolis west to Turkey Run State Park for a day's outing.

Union Traction's bus operation was a money-loser from day one, but that was of no real concern to Arthur W. Brady or to general manager Harry A. Nichol. By acquiring Hiner's operating rights along Indiana highways running parallel to its tracks, the interurban company cleverly beat back the threat of bus competitors. "The tide against the interurbans was stemmed for a while with the enactment of a law through which it was possible to discourage the fast-growing bus industry, but no utility lawyers have as yet been able to legislate against the increase in the number of privately owned automobiles." In other words, Union Traction and other Indiana interurban operators had won an empty victory, and their war with motorbus operators did nothing to slow the exponentially expanding number of private automobiles that also enjoyed use of Indiana's network of all-weather highways. That proved fatal.[38]

In 1914, there was one "pleasure car," as the electric railway industry labeled private autos, for every sixty-two Americans. Only four years later, the ratio was one per nineteen, and the balance continued to tip in favor of the highway competitors until, by 1925, there was one automobile for every six Americans. One way that interurban operators sought to respond to the rising tide of motor competition was by joining it. That meant an ever-larger fleet of local and intercity buses to supplement their electric railway operations. In many cases, the concept of "supplementing" soon gave way to "supplanting" trolley and interurban cars completely.[39]

How the once lowly motor bus dethroned the interurban was a saga many years in the making. Most of the companies that operated municipal trolley lines recovered from the jitney crisis and survived the 1919 high-cost-of-living crisis by trimming expenses and prying fare increases from reluctant politicians. They subsequently pushed forward to maintain streetcar service, though not all years were particularly profitable. Interurban lines, on the other hand, found themselves locked in a losing battle after 1919 with private automobiles and a growing number of other highway competitors.

Despite the brave claims of a 1920s comeback, many interurban lines never regained a sound financial footing. Some were the electric railway equivalent of the walking dead, just one modest accident away from bankruptcy. Company after company sought to stay afloat by closing lightly patronized lines, cutting wages and discharging employees, and deferring maintenance until weeds choked the right-of-way. Finally, there was no option left but to shut down.

One graphic way to envision the slow-motion devolution of the interurban industry is to revisit the Indianapolis-Anderson transportation corridor, the most heavily used stretch of electric railway track in central Indiana. Although the specifics of this brief case study may differ from those pertaining to other interurban lines across the Midwest, the pattern of events leading to a final shutdown was much the same.

Forming the first modern transportation corridor between Indianapolis and Anderson was a steam railroad originally known as the "Bee Line" and later as the "Big Four," a highly prosperous component of the Vanderbilts' New York Central empire, the largest steam railroad system in the United States at the time Union Traction

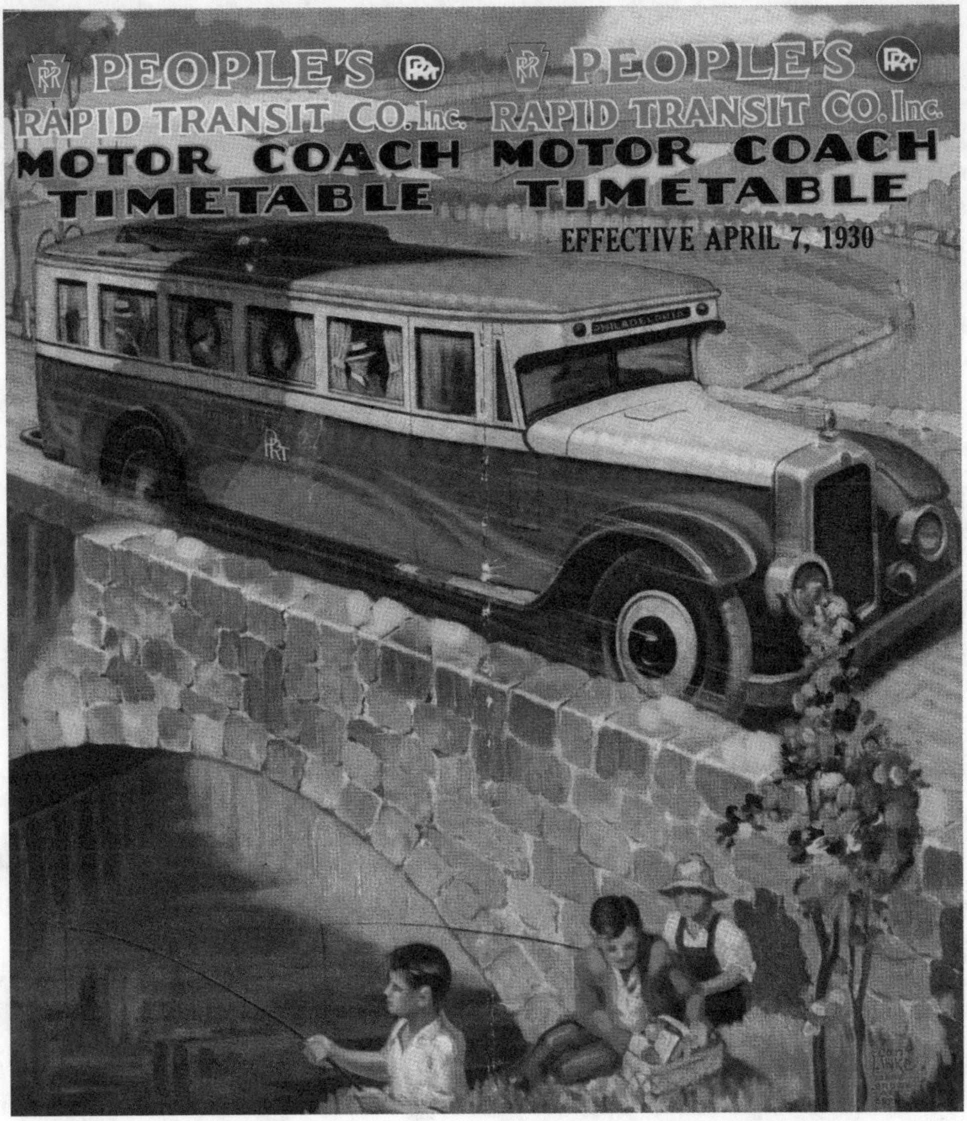

In terms of its use of stunning graphics, this Pennsylvania Railroad highway subsidiary continued the tradition of visually appealing promotional brochures and timetables issued frequently by other modes of transportation.

completed its initial interurban line between Anderson and Indianapolis in January 1901. The steam and electric tracks paralleled one another much of the way, with the main deviations occurring where interurban tracks followed local roads and streets into the heart of town, such as they did in Pendleton and Ingalls. It would be fair to say that after the Big Four's initial resistance to the interurban newcomer, the two rail carriers settled their differences and became friendly competitors after it became clear that their trains served two very different groups of travelers.[40]

The Alfont Crash, February 2, 1924

When two wooden interurban cars collided head-on as they rounded a slight curve in the village of Alfont in early 1924, the impact would likely have been serious and perhaps resulted in some fatalities, but it was the resulting fire that made it truly horrific. One of the cars carried several boxes of motion picture film, and when the impact knocked over a coal-burning stove, the resulting shower of sparks ignited the highly combustible cargo. Splintered wood burst into flame and immolated passengers trapped and unable to escape the conflagration.

Twenty-one people perished, and readers of Indiana newspapers must have shuddered as they read the gory details. Four victims were burned beyond recognition and never identified. Their remains were buried together in Anderson's Maplewood Cemetery, which Charles L. Henry had helped to create. Investigators from the Interstate Commerce Commission and Indiana's Public Service Commission, along with the Madison County coroner, all blamed the motorman and conductor of the eastbound car speeding toward Anderson. Both men were indicted for manslaughter, but a judge later dismissed the charges.

The accident reflected poorly on Union Traction management, which had shut down trackside block signals for extensive repairs, but the device intended to ensure safe operations had been out of service for more than a month. The system was scheduled to be reenergized during the following day or two. A further irony is that the company magazine was titled *Safety,* and a few years earlier, Union Traction and its general manager Harry A. Nichol had won national safety awards. The Alfont crash and the money it drained from the Union Traction treasury was a primary reason the carrier chose the protection of receivership on the final day of 1924 and Arthur Brady became its court-appointed receiver. The once-proud Union Traction remained a ward of the court until the Indiana Railroad acquired it in 1930, when both Brady and Nichol retired.[41]

Each monthly issue of Union Traction's *Safety* was packed with information to encourage companywide safe operating practices.

The disruptive technology that did most to upend the fortunes of the interurban line was, of course, the automobile, and with it, the rapidly unspooling miles of an all-weather state and federal highways system that greatly enhanced the appeal of owning a personal car. Union Traction was already struggling financially in the early 1920s, and the rising tide of competition along the improved highways that paralleled its tracks coupled with the financial burden resulting from the Alfont crash of 1924 only hastened its receivership on the final day of that year.

In 1919, better roads and highways first began to impact numerous interurban carriers across the United States, but the intercity competition they fostered, while irritating, was hardly debilitating. Ten years later, intercity bus and truck lines were well-established modes of transportation. As was true for the pioneer interurban lines after the turn of the century, newly formed bus lines extended ever farther from urban centers until they formed regional and then truly national networks like those of Greyhound. By the late 1920s, it was possible for the first time to cross the United States from coast to coast entirely by bus. Long-distance trucking companies were slower to develop extensive interstate networks, but by 1929, long-distance truck lines were a well-established presence, too.[42]

Union Traction trains were forced to compete head-to-head with the motor bus lines that covered virtually all the same routes as its interurban cars, but they enjoyed the additional boost of parallel highways paved and straightened with taxpayer dollars. The story was much the same across much of Indiana and the Midwest. To make a bad situation even worse, its numerous bus and truck competitors came and went wholly unregulated by the federal government until 1935. It was not the first time the electric railway industry had confronted a blatant injustice—and lost.

Very few trolley and interurban companies operated bus lines at the start of the 1920s. Successive issues of the *Electric Railway Journal* recorded the industry's dramatic transformation. All through the decade, the pages of the *Electric Railway Journal* noted the growing importance of highway transportation in its news and feature stories, but even more dramatic was the rising number of motorbus advertisements it published each week.

At the beginning of the 1920s, the journal devoted relatively little advertising copy to highway transportation, but that changed by middecade, and its numerous advertisements for buses, trucks, and rubber tires were often larger, more colorful, and more creative than comparable ones for trolley and interurban cars. With innovative and financially robust newcomers like General Motors and Mack pitted against old-line streetcar manufacturers like Brill and the St. Louis Car Company, the enterprise with the deepest pockets and the most contagious optimism about a prosperous future invariably featured the largest and most visually impressive displays. By 1925 or 1926, the deepest pockets and the greatest confidence belonged to the bus makers and their many powerful allies such as rubber tire manufacturers Goodyear and Michelin and suppliers of gasoline and lubricants like Standard Oil and Texaco.

So great was interest in the new mode of motorized travel that the *Electric Railway Journal*'s parent company, McGraw Hill, in a controversial move spun off a sister publication called *Bus Transportation* in early 1922. Even so, advertisements for highway vehicles and their accessories continued to crowd the pages of the McGraw Hill journal, which since 1884 had devoted itself to the electric railway industry. The times truly were changing!

Likewise, in its news and feature stories the *Electric Railway Journal* devoted more ink to buses and less to trolleys and interurbans. Electric railways became of secondary importance, a fact the venerable trade journal acknowledged in January 1932 when it renamed itself yet again. This time, it became the *Transit Journal*. It limped along under that title until it ceased publication entirely in 1941.

The number of interurbans using the Traction Terminal dropped steadily during the 1920s and 1930s from a high of approximately six hundred cars a day at the time Ward Hiner opened his Indianapolis bus station in 1925. To accommodate the rising number of buses calling at the terminal annex, management in 1931 paved over three of nine interurban tracks and gradually moved more and more bus traffic into the massive train shed.[43]

If the 1920s witnessed a two- or three-year period during which the gathering clouds parted and the future of Indiana interurbans seemed to brighten once again, the clouds returned in the late 1920s and never again lifted despite the heroic efforts of the Indiana Railroad, a last-ditch effort to save a once vital industry. The crisis-filled saga of the Indiana Railroad opened on an optimistic note in the late 1920s—just before the onset of the Great Depression that blighted the global economic landscape throughout the 1930s—and ended when a final interurban car completed its run between Anderson and Indianapolis in January 1941.

A final set of tracks disappeared beneath the asphalt paving, and intercity buses reigned unchallenged in the massive train shed of the Traction Terminal, a name Hugh McGowan's one-time landmark continued to use for several more years. At a sensory level, acrid diesel and gasoline engine fumes completely replaced the energizing ozone formerly created by dozens of electric interurban cars.

For a few months longer, a lone high-speed car completed a daily round trip between Indianapolis and Seymour under the auspices of the Public Service Company of Indiana as mandated in its franchise. Its place of departure from a freight warehouse near the Traction Terminal was unmarked and unwelcoming. Indiana's last interurban passenger car, apart from the South Shore Line, completed its daily schedule without incident for eight months until, on September 8, 1941, a freak and fatal accident put

The postcard photographer employed an unusual angle to record the interurban landscape at the Bunker Hill station south of Peru.

that stumpy remnant out of business, too. In an editorial published only weeks before the unexpectedly dramatic finale, the *Franklin Star* lamented that the line's impending abandonment would end the "golden age" of interurban travel in Indiana. "Not so many years ago Indiana boasted the greatest system of electric lines in the United States. One by one, however, the lines fell victim to increased automobile travel, and buses as a convenient transportation method."[44]

Conclusion

Remnants

> Six thousand millions of dollars, invested in street and interurban railways, might as well be charged off the books. The automobile has put them in the discard as the steam railroads put the stage coach in the discard.
>
> —Leonor F. Loree, president, Delaware and Hudson Railroad (1926)

While interurban industry optimists marched in lockstep in the early to mid-1920s, Leonor F. Loree was a notable dissenter. On April 9, 1926, Loree, one of the best-known luminaries of North America's steam railroads, delivered what might aptly be described as the "funeral oration for the electric railway industry" when he warned that it faced total extinction. His luncheon audience consisted of members of the Saint Louis Chamber of Commerce, some of whom were bankers closely connected with the electric railway industry. Perhaps some casual listeners thought that Loree's lifetime association with steam railroads disqualified him from speaking on interurban matters, but in 1926, he was thoroughly acquainted with the industry's recent troubles because he still presided over two electric railways in Upstate New York and a major steam railroad.

Despite the interurban industry's presumptive comeback in 1922 and 1923, Loree's presentation reminded listeners that at least a few naysayers could add a discordant note to the chorus of optimism. In the years that followed the financial crisis of 1919, interurban railways had occasionally been the subject of gloom and doom assessments, but never had a prophecy of their total demise been stated so bluntly by someone who knew so much about American railroads, both steam and electric, as Loree.[1]

Loree was one of the railroad industry's most colorful characters, and his heavily bearded face gave him a passing resemblance to Britain's King George V. In 1926, he was most often identified as president of the Delaware and Hudson, a steam railroad with tracks in Upstate New York and extending as far south as Scranton in Pennsylvania. Loree was also very smart. He was one of the most highly educated American

In the early twentieth century, trains of both the Indianapolis and Northwestern and the New York Central provided Lebanon residents a choice of electric or steam transportation to Indianapolis, Lafayette, and other Indiana destinations.

railroad executives of his time. He was a university graduate—from Rutgers in engineering—which made him a rarity among American rail executives, most of whom could claim to have earned a degree from the school of hard knocks, as valuable as that was when combined with a lifetime of work and accumulated experience.

In the mid-1920s, one of America's magazine newcomers was *Time,* a publication renowned for its snappy writing style that made it a favorite with general readers. One of *Time*'s early articles had this to say about Loree: "So ferocious in appearance is Leonor Fresnel Loree, the shaggiest of high railroad executives, that when he makes his rare appearance, hair, mustache and beard awry, thick bushy brows slanting up from his heavy-lidded eyes at the New Jersey College for Women or at Rutgers, the young people are always startled." He also had a "ferocious" way of stating his opinions. In 1923, at the celebration of the hundredth anniversary of the Delaware and Hudson, a pioneer among American railroads, Loree used the occasion to blast the ever-more meddlesome government regulators of the steam and electric lines: "Railroading is no longer a business; it has become a calamity."[2]

In addition to sounding and looking "ferocious" (and perhaps deliberately cultivating an intimidating public image), Loree was no stranger to electric railways. In 1907, the same year he was elected the eighth president of the Delaware and Hudson, he was simultaneously elected president of its two interurban subsidiaries, the United Traction Company of Albany and the Hudson Valley Railway of Glens Falls. Loree, the ambidextrous railroader, was likewise no stranger to the many large steam railroads based in Saint Louis and Kansas City. Early in the twentieth century, Loree had been invited to run a newly completed Missouri-based railroad, the Kansas City Southern. After a personal inspection, Loree was horrified by the railroad's woebegone condition, but in just three years, he had completely turned around the former streak of rust. Loree was thus well known and much respected by the Missouri listeners he shocked with his blunt claim that the interurban faced a bleak future. His use of the term "six thousand millions of dollars" instead of "six billion dollars" was probably carefully chosen to dramatize the size of the impending loss, an amount equal to $90 billion in 2023 dollars.

It was likely no coincidence that Loree chose Saint Louis to deliver his obituary for the interurban industry. The Missouri metropolis was one of North America's principal sites for the manufacture of trolley and interurban cars, and Loree surely understood from earlier visits to Saint Louis that no city provided a better epicenter for the shockwave equivalent to a 9.0 earthquake that he clearly sought to send through the interurban industry. Of course, Loree's pessimism sparked an intense debate that was recorded in successive issues of the *Electric Railway Journal*, with most responses taking the form of reasoned rhetorical pushback. Loree was never cowed by any pushback from fellow executives. In the end, his dire 1926 assessment proved to be uncannily accurate. He died in September 1940 at age eighty-two, but he lived long enough to see his 1926 prophecy almost wholly fulfilled. A mere five months after Loree's death, a final interurban train completed the journey from Anderson to Indianapolis along tracks that Charles L. Henry had opened with great fanfare in January 1901. Only the South Shore Line and the odd remnant linking Indianapolis and Seymour continued as passenger carriers, and the fatal collision north of Seymour eight months later left the South Shore Line as Indiana's sole surviving interurban.

Charles L. Henry died in Indianapolis on May 2, 1927. Arthur Brady not only served as a pallbearer but also arranged for one of Union Traction's deluxe cars to give the "father of the interurban" a final and entirely appropriate ride home to Anderson where he was interred in the city's Maplewood Cemetery, a civic project that he had helped to launch a quarter century earlier.[3]

In a sense, then, the story of Indiana's Interurban Era had come full circle in Anderson and in nearby Alexandria, the first two cities connected by Henry's pioneer interurban line in 1898. On a street corner in downtown Alexandria stands a prominent historical marker that commemorates "Indiana's First Interurban." I somehow

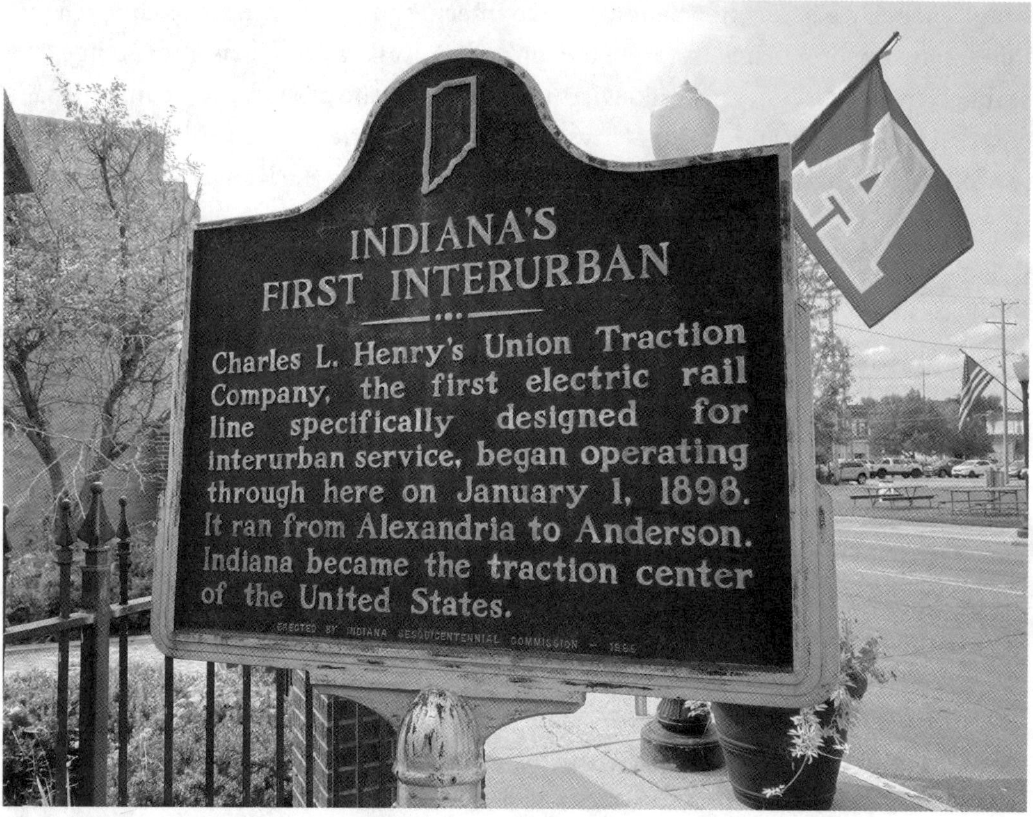

I made one of my "history-on-the-hoof" pilgrimages in September 2020 to Alexandria to see for myself the history marker commemorating Indiana's first interurban railway.

expected the tribute to add that Henry was the "father of the interurban" or that he had coined the word "interurban." It did not, and perhaps the author of the commemorative text realized that these often-repeated claims stretched the truth.[4]

About the time that Henry served a term as president of the American Electric Railway Association (1915–16), industry journals began referring to him as the "father of the interurban," and it was virtually obligatory for colleagues to use that title when introducing him at professional meetings. The man and his legend had become inseparable. Even if his honorific title did contain an element of poetic license, it nonetheless demonstrated well-deserved respect to someone who even in his seventies remained fully committed to the industry he had helped to pioneer. His peers helped him celebrate his seventieth birthday during the Central Electric Railway Association's 1920 summer cruise of the Great Lakes. Their special recognition took the form of a gift of luggage, which seemed to portend the considerable travel that lay just ahead as he regularly shuttled between offices in Indianapolis and Washington, DC.

Fountain Square, as depicted in this early twentieth-century postcard, defined the heart of Cincinnati and was the destination of Charles L. Henry's unending and ultimately ruinous quest to extend his interurban tracks into the Ohio metropolis.

At an age well past retirement for most people, the industry's elder statesman appeared to enjoy renewed energy when he willingly took on a new job title in Indiana and another in the nation's capital. Because Henry had served two terms as a member of Congress, he was the industry's natural choice in 1920 to head its legislative office in Washington, DC, and in that way serve as its government liaison with the Interstate Commerce Commission, which seemed determined to insert itself ever more forcefully into interurban matters. At the same time, back home in Indiana, Henry worked ever harder to keep his interurban company afloat in the face of rising highway competition. He also served dutifully as a trustee of Indiana University, and he agreed to become the first president of the Indiana Public Utility Association, an advocacy group he and his peers organized in 1920. In the pictures the *Electric Railway Journal* published of him at the time, Henry stands among his dark-suited colleagues, invariably the shortest member of the group but always with the erect bearing and the clear-eyed sense of purpose of a man at least twenty years younger.

When a Hancock County newspaper published an unusually long obituary for Henry, it honored a hometown boy who had achieved national recognition. Its essay dwelled at length on Henry's determination during the previous two years to keep the Indianapolis and Cincinnati Traction Company in business. The enterprise that he had served in various capacities since 1902—as general manager, president, and twice as receiver—ran across a southern corner of Hancock County, and so Henry had never really strayed too far from his roots. Little else in his long life remained so consistent. Especially after 1910 and the noticeable slowdown in new miles of track constructed across the United States, the bright promise of the interurban dimmed considerably. It dimmed further in 1919, only to be followed by a deceptive uptick in the early 1920s.

Henry's decision in 1923 to borrow millions of dollars to purchase new rolling-stock and modernize the infrastructure of the Indianapolis and Cincinnati Traction Company came back to haunt him two years later when the interurban again went into receivership. The intense legal wrangling continued through the spring of 1927 when, perhaps for the first time, Henry felt the heavy weight of old age. In his seventy-seventh year and burdened by his company's financial and legal woes, Henry as its court-appointed receiver was forced to summon all his remaining physical and mental energy and his lawyerly skills to dodge and outmaneuver the interurban's creditors in the Rush County courts during the final two months of his life. In the words of the *Greenfield Daily Reporter*: "At the time of his last illness Mr. Henry was fighting a courageous battle to save the dwindling finances of the traction company which he headed and steadfastly refused to give up hope of someday succeeding in his great ambition of a through electric line between Indianapolis and Cincinnati."[5]

The last months of Henry's life must have been worrisome to the point of keeping him awake many nights, because it grew increasingly clear that the cause to which he had dedicated much of his working life was in a desperate struggle to survive. Hoosiers who had known and respected him over the years could not help but admire his tenacity: "He gave the latter years of his life in trying to build a traction line from Indianapolis, and had a severe struggle; but he never gave up. He was unconquerable except by death."[6]

There would be no more comebacks, real or imagined, either for the interurban industry or for Henry. At a personal level, he had reason to feel depressed. Looking back to 1916, his term as president of the American Electric Railway Association had represented in many ways a last hurrah for Henry because repeatedly punctuating his final decade were numerous disappointments, both professional and personal. One of his two sons and obvious successor, Lewis W. Henry, had served as his father's most trusted aide ever since his days as a member of Congress. A few years later, and with his father's blessing, he steadily climbed the ranks at the Indianapolis and Cincinnati Traction Company. His brother George, a promising manager, had in 1911 bailed out of what was essentially a family enterprise and joined the Chicago and Milwaukee

Electric Railroad, a predecessor to the North Shore Line. No reason for his abrupt departure ever appeared in print.[7]

The big promotion for Lewis came in 1917 when he became the interurban's superintendent. He would likely have become its general manager and then succeeded his father as president had not the Spanish influenza pandemic cut his life short in late 1918 at age thirty-nine. Henry's youngest daughter, Leah, an Indianapolis librarian, succumbed a few years later to a prolonged illness, and then his wife and lifelong companion, Eva, died, too.

Finally, the grand old man of Indiana interurbans had to endure a humbling legal ordeal as his company's receiver. On one occasion, the lawyers representing the interurban's many creditors forced him to spend nearly a full day on the witness stand as they peppered him with complex questions about the Indianapolis and Cincinnati Traction Company's finances. More than two dozen lawyers had crowded into the Rushville courtroom that day. Among them was the one individual who had become Henry's closest friend and unfailing supporter, Arthur W. Brady. He took no part in the formal legal proceedings, yet the Union Traction president (and now its receiver) had over the years become like a younger brother to Henry. Brady sat silently, but his presence in the Rushville courtroom demonstrated much-needed support for his beleaguered senior colleague. Brady understood well the pain of loss and loneliness because death had claimed his wife, Jennie, a mere four months into their marriage in 1892. The young and popular mayor of Muncie remained a widower until he married Caroline, sister of Indiana interurban mogul George McCulloch, in 1901.[8]

Although newspaper accounts of the courtroom drama provide few details, Brady likely used a private automobile to travel the forty miles across rural Indiana between Anderson and Rushville instead of taking a roundabout interurban journey via Indianapolis and the Traction Terminal. That is what an ever-increasing number of Hoosiers would have done in the mid-1920s, and it was the primary reason Indiana's interurbans were struggling to retain their ridership.[9]

Significantly, when the Indiana Railroad took shape at the end of the decade, its organizers sought to unite several ailing interurban companies across the state into one large and efficient enterprise that they hoped would be successful. Thus, they folded Union Traction; Terre Haute, Indianapolis and Eastern; Indiana Service Corporation (successor to the Ft. Wayne and Wabash Valley); and the Interstate Public Service into their new statewide enterprise, but they conspicuously omitted the Indianapolis and Cincinnati Traction Company.

Henry never admitted defeat, but when new managers of the Indianapolis and Southeastern Railroad (created in 1928) finally closed the gap to Cincinnati, they did so on rubber tires with a fleet of intercity buses. It must have been difficult for Henry to accept the Motor Age, which he finally (and reluctantly) did in 1925 with his purchase of secondhand buses to augment his beloved interurban cars.[10]

The journey for through travelers between Indianapolis and Cincinnati initially entailed the inconvenience of switching from interurban cars to motor coaches partway through the trip. The company replaced its interurban trains with through buses in January 1932 when it abandoned the electric railway. Six years later, the one-time interurban line became Indianapolis and Southeastern Trailways.[11]

The interurban and its creator were gone, but memories lingered on. Charles Gordon, a Hoosier by birth in Indianapolis, served as editor of the prestigious *Electric Railway Journal* during the mid- to late-1920s. In 1929, when he left the publication to supervise the American Electric Railway Association's headquarters in New York City, Gordon took time to reminisce in print about how Henry's interurban had forever impacted his life. Though his parents had moved away from Indiana while he was still a small boy, he retained warm memories of his "native state." Gordon insisted that his lifelong fondness for Indiana guided him to Rush County during the summer of 1903 to sell books to earn tuition money to complete his engineering education at the University of Illinois. "Plodding up and down the late Charles L. Henry's interurban line, I aspired to work on such a road, and as quickly as possible I got into the local transportation business." The Chicago Surface Lines provided Gordon on-the-ground training before he joined the editorial staff of the *Electric Railway Journal* in 1923. His Midwestern pragmatism served him well when later, as editor, he ran stories about how electric railways might profit from the use of motor buses, but he thereby incurred the wrath of some of his readers, who promptly canceled their subscriptions.[12]

Arthur W. Brady died in Anderson on March 24, 1933, and was buried in Muncie, the Indiana community that formed the fixed star around which his life as a lawyer, politician, and business executive had revolved. If anything, the six years separating Henry's death in 1927 and Brady's in 1933 had seen prospects for the interurban industry grow ever more dismal. The shock of the Alfont crash in 1924 and the investigators' subsequent harsh criticism of Union Traction management seemed to take the zest out of Brady's step. The interurban company that in better times had served as an industry role model entered receivership on the final day of 1924 because earnings had declined so severely during the past twelve months that Union Traction had little money on hand to pay fixed charges that totaled approximately $300,000. Brady blamed the shortfall on unregulated bus competition and the rising tide of private automobiles. For the first time in its history, the interurban railway petitioned the Indiana Public Service Commission for permission to abandon service on one segment of its more than four hundred miles of line (Anderson to Middletown) and to substitute buses for trains.[13]

In the annual tabulation of bankruptcies that the *Electric Railway Journal* published every January, no other company in North America came close to matching the mileage of the Union Traction's receivership. A giant had been brought low, and if that could happen to an enterprise once ranked among the largest and most successful interurban companies in North America, how could the future be any brighter for the many weaker members of the industry in the years ahead?[14]

Interurban companies headed by Brady and Henry both added buses to their lineup of regularly scheduled trains in the mid-1920s. It was the way of the future. Union Traction started with a single bus connecting downtown Indianapolis with Fort Benjamin Harrison, but soon it added more buses until it seemed that the interurban railway was of secondary importance to its highway operation. It was no doubt a sign of a rapidly changing world that at the 1927 annual meeting of the American Electric Railway Association, the number of buses on display actually outnumbered trolley and interurban cars for the first time.

Union Traction became part of Indiana Railroad—serving as its cornerstone, in fact—when on July 2, 1930, Samuel Insull's Midland Utilities purchased the company and transferred ownership to its newly formed Indiana Railroad. With that transition, Arthur Brady retired from the interurban company he had headed for a quarter of a century.

The Indiana Railroad grew significantly larger during the coming months with the rapid-fire acquisition of several other large interurban properties that crisscrossed large portions of the Hoosier State. On a map, the new company looked impressive, but no map could reveal the soon-gathering storm called the Great Depression. During the "dirty thirties," the Indiana Railroad lopped off one unprofitable line after another, sometimes abandoning dozens of miles of money-losing track in a single day. Before the severity of the financial downturn became fully evident, it raised the money needed to purchase a fleet of high-speed cars and to modernize its infrastructure, but nothing worked to stave off its receivership on July 28, 1933.

Though insolvent, the Indiana Railroad continued to operate about six hundred miles of track for another four years, though with each passing year, it depended less on revenue from a steadily dwindling number of passengers and more on income earned from hauling freight, a business it actually managed to grow until 1937. That year, the abandonment of the Dayton and Western severed a vital link forged in 1903 between the Indiana and Ohio interurban networks, both now steadily withering during the late 1930s.

Despite its promising beginnings, the Indiana Railroad during the lean years of the 1930s jettisoned one money-losing line after another, including major links like the formerly important tracks connecting Indianapolis and Terre Haute, to preserve a financially viable core network until there was nothing viable left. With the exception of the South Shore Line, the Interurban Era ended for Indiana in mid-September 1941. All that remained of a once-vital enterprise were odd artifacts and largely forgotten remnants scattered here and there across the Hoosier landscape—abandoned bridge abutments; the Fort Harrison station that is now a coffee shop; an electric substation in Ingalls that is now its town hall; and the former interurban shops in Anderson and Greenfield that remain in place after more than a century, but both buildings have been converted to other uses. Several scattered interurban segments continued for a few more years to haul freight, but then they, too, shut down.

There were other remnants, but it took a trained eye and a determined seeker to identify them. Some remained in plain sight for years after the last interurban ran but lay ignored as the carpet of weeds grew thicker and caused them to gradually fade into the natural landscape. Near our family home on the northeast side of Indianapolis in the early 1960s, a low cinder-covered embankment ran along the north side of 38th Street. A discerning eye could have recognized it as the former right-of-way for Union Traction interurban cars that linked Indianapolis and Anderson on their way to Muncie and Fort Wayne. Charles L. Henry had required a train of four interconnected cars to carry 125 dignitaries he had invited to the line's festive grand opening in January 1901. Forty years later, a final interurban car passed this way. Then the electric power was shut off and scrappers reclaimed rails, wires, and anything else of value, but they left the weeds to grow unchallenged.

So, why did the automobile vanquish the interurban? While an answer may seem obvious, there are many reasons for the decline and fall of a once-promising mode of transportation. The automobile by itself was no giant-killer. Apart from some sort of highway support structure, it would have remained an interesting piece of machinery that lent itself mainly to automobile racing and to outings into the nearby countryside by the urban rich and their fellow upscale club members. During the first decade of the Interurban Era, the nation's roads and highways were not at all conducive to automobile travel beyond the city limits. In fact, their wretched condition before 1917 made nearly every auto outing an adventure worth writing about. Automobiles and an expanding network of all-weather highways certainly contributed to the interurban's demise, but industry leaders early on made some bad financial decisions that left several marginal companies especially vulnerable to highway competition.

In an essay he composed for the *Electric Railway Journal* to welcome the year 1914, Arthur Brady drew on decades of firsthand experience to dissect the industry's mounting problems, and his analysis, it should be noted, was published before the emergence of the jitney a few months later, which made the woes of the electric railway industry infinitely worse. "Many of the operators and managers of the early interurban lines," Brady noted, "were men of little, if any, railroad experience." Some of the more competent executives "had gained their experience in street railway operation, others in steam railroad operation. Here, again, methods varied almost in proportion to the number of lines." Brady reminded his industry readers that "interurban lines were built under varying conditions and according the varying standards." Some builders "adopted urban street railroad standards as the standards for interurban railroad construction," while others "adopted steam railroad standards. Between these extremes practices varied greatly."[15]

Brady considered that "the lack of system and standardization which thus characterized interurban lines in the earlier development was largely due to the exceedingly rapid rate at which that development had proceeded. The resulting condition was serious. Several thousand miles of interurban railway existed in the Middle West, connected together at many points, but, because of diverse practices and standards and lack of harmonious co-operation, the lines were incapable of accomplishing for public or owners all that both could rightly demand of them."[16]

One problem not mentioned by Brady in his 1914 essay, though he had often expressed his concern in earlier presentations, was the public's low opinion of the electric railway industry. Over time, the prevailing negativity among voters no doubt encouraged elected and appointed government officials to impose increasingly heavy-handed regulations on the industry, even as many of these same officials promoted the populist dream of good roads and highways funded by taxpayer dollars. Given the lack of any meaningful public transportation policy at the federal or state levels that might have encouraged *both* modes of transportation, it became increasingly difficult for investors in interurban securities to earn an attractive rate of return, and so many people simply diverted their money to more promising prospects—like the automobile industry.

Every year brought noticeable technological improvements to the latest auto models and widened the circle of owners, each one being a likely convert to the gospel of good roads. With the rapid advance of improved highways after 1921, it was at last possible for motorists to live in one community and commute to work in another without giving a moment's thought to motor breakdowns and blown tires along the way. It was the same for any auto trips to visit distant relatives or to enjoy a vacation in the mountains or at the seashore. In other words, when improved roads and highways made a trip by car so routine that it was no longer newsworthy, a tipping point had been reached. That occurred in the mid-1920s when automobiles at last sealed their victory over interurban railways. Despite a few encouraging upticks, the final fifteen years of the Indiana lines witnessed a slow-motion unraveling of a once-vital industry.

Improved vehicles and a nationwide network of all-weather highways created and continually improved by taxpayer dollars delivered a relentless stream of bad news to the interurban industry. So, when everything is properly weighed, it makes less sense to blame the automobile and its inventors for the slow-motion demise of electric interurban railways than to blame a generation of shortsighted politicians who ignored an existing and highly functional mode of transportation, the interurban, to lavish tax dollars on infrastructure to support its competitors. For nearly two decades (from 1900 at least through 1918), elected politicians—mayors and city councilmen; governors and state legislators; and, yes, even presidents and members of Congress; plus bureaucrats at government agencies like the Interstate Commerce Commission (created in 1887)—heaped one regulation after another on the steam railroads, the city streetcar lines, and finally on the interurbans until the burden became crippling. Left hamstrung, steam railroads became unattractive prospects to investors, who increasingly found the booming auto industry a much more appealing prospect. Lacking investor dollars, railroads struggled to modernize their facilities.

As for electric railways, one need only recall that 1919 was a year of tumult. Runaway wartime inflation combined with the shortsightedness of politicians and bureaucrats reluctant to permit them to raise fares enough to cover their rapidly rising costs put the entire industry at risk of collapse. It survived, thanks in large measure to fare increases pried from reluctant regulators, but interurbans faced another challenge during the 1920s as additional miles of hard-surfaced roadways unspooled without ceasing across the United States, and this challenge they simply could not overcome.[17]

I conclude by noting several of the happenstance juxtapositions that have made history as fascinating to me as the plot of a good novel. Indiana interurbans and Franklin D. Roosevelt's New Deal program launched in March 1933 ostensibly have nothing in common. Yet when Summitville, Indiana, sought to remove tracks recently abandoned by the Indiana Railroad from its streets, it used laborers provided by the New Deal's Civil Works Administration.[18]

Also on March 24, 1933, during the same month that the newly elected president launched his New Deal program to combat the Great Depression, Arthur Brady died at his home in Muncie. The Interurban Era had clearly entered its twilight years by that late date, and my interest in following the historical saga to its bitter end was rapidly fading. As I prepared to rewind a final reel of newspaper microfilm to conclude my research at the Indiana State Library, I happened to glance at headlines that recorded a significant event just one day before Brady's death. Across the Atlantic and seemingly light-years removed from Muncie, Indiana, members of the Reichstag had passed an Enabling Bill that conveyed unchecked authority to Germany's newly elected chancellor and dictator, Adolf Hitler. Like the Interurban Era, the bright hope of a peaceful postwar world had entered its twilight years and would soon be extinguished.

In September 2020, the manager of Riley Park Tire in Greenfield kindly permitted me to venture into the inner recesses of the sprawling automotive complex where rails of the former shops of the Terre Haute, Indianapolis and Eastern are still visible. The building fronts US 40 and the location of the former National Road.

What's in a name? Whether the nation's newest mode of transportation was to be called a "country trolley" or hyphenated as "inter-urban" or simply called an "electric railway" seemed to make a great deal of difference, and the honor of having coined the preferred term "interurban" seemed something worth treasuring.

Appendix

Who Really Coined the Word "Interurban"?

> I invented the word "Interurban" for this class of railroads, and though it is not perhaps well selected, it has come into general use, although not yet found in any of our dictionaries.
>
> —Charles L. Henry to the First Annual Meeting of the Indiana Electric Railway Association, *Street Railway Review* (January 1906): 48

Charles L. Henry claimed he coined the word "interurban" in the late 1890s to describe the twelve-mile-long electric railway he had completed between the Gas Belt communities of Anderson and Alexandria. His claim is undisputed in Indiana, but research reveals it to be an "interurban legend." When I kept encountering the word in industry trade publications well before 1897 or 1898, I decided to use a modern search engine to ferret out how often "interurban" appeared in electric railway journals in the years before Henry supposedly coined it.

This research technique revealed that it had appeared in print as early as 1890 alongside a variety of similar terms like "suburban" and "country railways" to describe the new type of electrically powered carrier that reached from a central city hub ever farther into the immediate outskirts and then extended deeper into the surrounding countryside. A computerized word search just of the 1895 volume of the *Street Railway Review* turned up nearly eighty instances of the word's use in news stories. The term was especially hard to miss when it appeared in bold type as the headline for a news story. The lead article in the February 1896 issue of the *Street Railway Review* was titled "Recent Interurban Electric Railways," and the publication spent fully nine pages (pp.

85–93) introducing readers to interurban railways across the United States. On the other hand, the *Street Railway Gazette* appears never to have used the word "interurban" but instead preferred the term "long-distance trolley."

I then expanded my word search to include journals devoted to the electric industry in general, classic texts, and general-interest newspapers. The same pattern of early usage emerged. In fact, one classic text published in 1892 featured a chapter titled "High Speed Interurban Railroads."[1]

Research using Newspapers.com, a modern, fully searchable database of America's popular press, made it crystal clear that the word "interurban" originated in Minnesota in the early 1880s and was used locally and frequently to describe the belt of open land that then separated Minneapolis and Saint Paul.[2] The Minnesota press also applied the word (both with and without a hyphen) to describe the portion of the Mississippi River that flowed between the Twin Cities.[3]

Likewise, research in Minnesota daily newspapers and in the journals devoted to the electric railway industry confirm that the world's first interurban was the Twin City Rapid Transit Company, which opened in late 1890 to link Minneapolis and Saint Paul. Rail moguls James J. Hill and Henry Villard both took notice of the new interurban line and probably invested in it to supplement their already vast holdings of traditional steam-powered railroads. When Villard of the Northern Pacific visited the area in December 1890, the *Minneapolis Tribune* headlined its story with these words: "Henry Villard calls the interurban line the best in the United States" and quoted him as saying, "There is no visible reason why this interurban line should not be a great success."[4]

The Kansas Newspaper Union broadcast the new word among several dozen small newspapers around the state in 1889 with the following quotation: "Interurban is a word coming into use in the west as to railroad rates between cities. It is an odd piece of word-making."[5]

The word "interurban" also appeared in Indiana several years before Henry supposedly invented it. Initially, it was used most frequently in the northern part of the state, not in the Gas Belt. A writer for the *Chicago Record* was recorded as saying in early 1896: "It is plain that the north end of Indiana will soon be able to boast of a complete system of interurban roads. Not only to passenger traffic to be looked after but the lines are all arranging to put freight cars into service that will haul everything from wheat to a basket of eggs."[6]

A few weeks later, the *Muncie Morning News* spread the word to its Gas Belt readers that "a syndicate of New York and Cleveland capitalists are behind a project to build a system of interurban electric car lines in northern Indiana, connecting various cities and towns." Within the Gas Belt itself, the word "interurban" first appeared in the name of the Indiana Interurban Railway that Noah J. Clodfelter incorporated in January 1896 to "run from Anderson to Marion, touching a number of the smaller towns in the gas belt." The fact that Clodfelter was the manic promoter of several electric railway projects that never got tracks on the ground has tended to diminish public perception of him as a serious contributor to Indiana's interurban history.[7]

In the end, I must conclude from an abundance of evidence that Henry did not coin the word "interurban," but his ever-growing stature within the industry allowed him to popularize it. Arthur W. Brady, the toastmaster at the first annual banquet of the Indiana Electric Railway Association in 1906, used the occasion to introduce Henry to the guests as the "father of the interurban." In his after-dinner reminiscence, Henry narrated his version of the origin of the interurban in Indiana and apparently for the first time publicly claimed to have coined the word.

As for the familiar accolade "father of the interurban," it seems certain that Arthur W. Brady invented it to express his great admiration for his senior colleague. The term never appeared in print before the 1905 formation of the Indiana Electric Railway Association, but that changed after Brady introduced Henry as the after-dinner speaker at its early 1906 banquet.

Brady, elected to a term as the mayor of Muncie in 1891, remained primarily a local attorney with an interest in municipal reform during the remainder of the decade. He did not get involved with the interurban industry until the early twentieth century, when his brother-in-law, George McCulloch, hired him as Union Traction's general counsel in 1902, a position that provided a convenient steppingstone to president of the company two years later. Before that time, he had never attended the big annual conferences of the American Street Railway Association. Henry attended at least one of the national conferences before 1898, but he remained an observer only. In the same way, neither man was actively involved with any state or regional associations before the formation of the Indiana Electric Railway Association in 1905, which was actually a latecomer among the several state groups. Finally, neither Henry nor Brady likely had access to back copies of the *Street Railway Journal* or *Street Railway Review* to learn just how frequently "interurban" had appeared in print before 1898. In an age innocent of newspaper databases and computer search engines, it would have been nearly impossible for either man to access back issues of Minnesota or Kansas newspapers or even those published in more recent years in cities around Indiana.

I feel certain that Henry, a man scrupulously honest in his business dealings, would not lie simply to satisfy the demands of an inflated ego. When running for Congress during the 1890s, he was at ease speaking to crowds of five hundred or more listeners, and in his public discourse, he was never given to exaggeration, theatrical gestures, or rhetorical flights of fancy. I cannot read literally thousands of newspaper and journal articles dating from the 1870s through the 1920s and conclude that he was an ego-driven man. The process of teasing meaning from the published record did help to

The Union Traction main line near Fort Benjamin Harrison was engineered for speed and not aesthetics. Henry completed the line between Anderson and Indianapolis in January 1901.

satisfy my curiosity about how Charles L. Henry came to emerge as the "father of the interurban." When virtually every newspaper in Indiana also repeated the assertion that he had coined the word "interurban," the legend became the truth. It is impossible at this late date to know what Henry thought in private about his legendary status. Incidentally, Frank J. Sprague, whose pioneering trolley system in Richmond, Virginia, launched similar systems in cities and villages across the United States, was called the "father of electric traction."[8]

Alas, the human side of interurban leadership was seldom, if ever, discussed in print. Three generations of leaders rose through the electric railway ranks, and industry journals printed brief notices of promotions and an occasional obituary. Introspection, however, was not common among men whose most obvious personality trait was a shared dedication to hard work.

Notes

Acknowledgments

1. Robin Winks, *The Historian as Detective: Essays on Evidence* (New York: Harper & Row, 1969).

Introduction

1. *Fort Wayne Sentinel*, as quoted in the *Indianapolis Journal*, October 31, 1901.
2. *Indianapolis News*, August 6, 1930.
3. *Republic* (Columbus, IN), November 21, 1933, and *Indianapolis News*, November 22, 1933. Not even the introduction of state-of-the-art dining and sleeping cars during the 1920s, a level of luxury rare among the hundreds of interurban companies of the United States, could generate the profits needed for Indianapolis-Louisville trains to turn a profit. President Harry Truman, who had served with Minton in the US Senate, appointed him to the US Supreme Court in 1949. Minton remained on the high court until 1956.
4. Indiana is widely known as the "Hoosier State," and though the origin of the term is much disputed, I have used it throughout this book in preference to the strange and unwieldy alternative appellation for the state's residents: "Indianians."
5. *Connersville News*, as quoted in the *Rushville Republican*, January 6, 1905.
6. *Tri-County Banner* (Knightstown), July 24, 1903, 1. Completely swept away by interurban ecstasy, the Knightstown newspaper proclaimed that with the arrival of luxurious sleeping cars "Indianapolis will then not only be the terminus of the longest system of interurban connections in the world but also of the most progressive and up-to-date."
7. *Journal and Courier* (Lafayette, IN), May 25, 1932, 6.

8. *Christian Science Monitor*, as quoted in the *Indianapolis Star*, January 3, 1913. This article provides an excellent summary of how interurban railways encouraged the growth of Indianapolis despite its lack of the navigable water highways considered essential to the fortunes of all great cities.

9. Statistics for the length of Indiana's interurban network at its peak depend on whether the mileage figures include city trolley lines. Sometimes there was no clear-cut distinction between the two. The line between downtown Indianapolis and the northern suburb of Broad Ripple was often described as an interurban during the 1890s, but in later years it formed just another segment of the Indianapolis street railway network. George W. Hilton and John F. Due in their authoritative *The Electric Interurban Railways in America* (Stanford, CA: Stanford University Press, 1964), 275, write that the Indiana interurban network peaked at 1,825 miles.

10. Charles D. Emmons, a native of Lafayette, served as the head of several large interurban systems in Indiana before being chosen to run Baltimore's sprawling transit system and later the Hudson and Manhattan Railway (now PATH) in New York City. Harry Reid, a New York native, relocated to Indiana to run the important interurban line that linked Indianapolis and Louisville. He later headed a New York utility company but returned to run the Indianapolis Railways. See also Robert I. Todd, "What Is a Hoosier?" *Electric Railway Journal* (March 1922): 347. Todd's unadulterated statement of pride in Indiana's commitment to electric railways was published when he headed the American Electric Railway Association *and* the Indianapolis Street Railway.

11. Joseph A. McGowan, "Interurbans Rendering Service of Incalculable Value," *AERA* (August 1924): 56. At the time of McGowan's presentation, electric railways were an industry worth approximately ninety billion dollars in 2023 inflated currency.

12. *Lafayette Journal and Courier*, June 15, 1929.

13. H. Roger Grant, *Electric Interurbans and the American People* (Bloomington: Indiana University Press, 2016), 23.

14. History also offers some interesting examples of technological false starts. An Indiana newspaper in early 1902 noted that a "Michigan man claims to have devised a telephone system whereby it is possible to call up one's friends and talk with them while riding on an electric car." The editor's rather bemused response was: "Who wants to talk with his friends from an electric car?" A little more than a century later, the answer would be obvious: every teenager who owns a cell phone! *Bristol Banner*, January 24, 1902.

15. I make no pretense of providing a comprehensive history of Indiana interurbans, which would require several large volumes. I seek to engage instead in what might be called "responsible reductionism" by concentrating on the central portion dominated by Indianapolis, the hub of a dense network of interurban lines that accounted for roughly two-thirds of the state's approximately eighteen hundred miles. Readers thirsting for greater detail should consult the following two-part nuts-and-bolts account of *every* Indiana interurban and a list of the most prominent people associated with each one. Glen A. Blackburn, "Interurban Railroads of Indiana," *Indiana Magazine of History* 20 (September 1924): 221–79 and (December 1924): 400–64. Another highly useful summary is Jerry Marlette, *Electric Railroads of Indiana* (Indianapolis: Council for Local History, 1959).

16. *Indianapolis Star*, June 30, 1907.

17. *Indianapolis News,* January 17, 1900. Transportation firsts are always noteworthy; however, attempting to assign a proper date to the event can be tricky. The date of the first regularly scheduled interurban car to depart Indianapolis, according to this contemporary newspaper account, was January 16 and not New Year's Day 1900, as is often claimed. Test runs of the first cars between Indianapolis and Greenwood took place in late 1899. Because there was no downtown Traction Terminal until 1904, the intersection of Washington and Illinois Streets served as the city's first interurban "station." Start-up pains afflicted both the Greenwood and Greenfield lines. One of the first large interurban cars outbound for Greenwood experienced trouble rounding a sharp curve on city streetcar tracks and tied up a line of twenty trolleys before help arrived. The first cars inbound from Greenfield in 1901 proved too wide to pass the light poles planted in the middle of Washington Street through the east-side suburb of Irvington.

18. *Indianapolis Star,* November 4, 1912.

19. H. Roger Grant, *Electric Interurbans and the American People* (Bloomington: Indiana University Press, 2016); William D. Middleton, *The Interurban Era* (Milwaukee, WI: Kalmbach, 1961); and Hilton and Due, *Electric Interurban Railways in America.*

20. Charles L. Henry made this optimistic claim during a conference of the Central Electric Railway Association in Dayton, Ohio, in late February 1916. See *Electric Railway Journal* (February 1916): 402–403.

21. Technology played a major role in the history of the interurban, and that facet of the industry has been explored thoroughly in numerous books devoted to the subject. The biographical side of the industry has received far less attention. Nonetheless, influential individuals in the electric railway industry are the subject of several biographies that I have listed in the Suggested Further Reading section.

22. James A. Ward, *Railroads and the Character of America, 1820–1887* (Knoxville: University of Tennessee Press, 1986). The Ward book is a thoughtful, interpretive look at the *meaning* of steam railroads within the context of American history, and it inspired me to ponder on these pages the meaning of North America's interurban railways during their era, brief though it was.

23. One highly visual reminder of the ways the nation fell short in the past is Otto L. Bettmann, *The Good Old Days—They Were Terrible!* (New York: Random House, 1974). Nonetheless, my immigrant father from Brazil instilled in me an appreciation for the many things that the United States got right.

24. *Weekly Tribune* (Tampa, FL), May 17, 1906.

25. *Indianapolis Star,* July 12, 1906, and *Brown County World* (Hiawatha, KS), July 6, 1906. The search engine Newspapers.com revealed that the nationwide press occasionally repeated the claim that Indiana was the "world's greatest interurban center" until the phrase quietly disappeared from use in the early 1930s because it was no longer meaningful.

26. *Ottumwa Tri-Weekly Courier,* June 21, 1906. Lee Enterprises, which dates to Joseph Wilson Lee's first Iowa acquisition in 1890, today publishes seventy-five daily newspapers in twenty-six states, including Joseph Pulitzer's historic *St. Louis Post-Dispatch.* In the early twentieth century, the newspapers of the United States often featured lengthy accounts of the latest interurban projects, both those that got tracks on the ground and their electric cars in operation as well as the "hot air" lines that amounted to nothing more than glib promises intended to impress gullible investors. In its 1899 tally of Indiana interurban projects, the *Logansport Pharos-Tribune* complained that of the state's fifteen hundred miles of projected electric

railways, only sixty-five miles had been completed. The remainder were "dead or sleeping." *Logansport Pharos-Tribune*, October 31, 1899.

27. *Sacramento Star*, July 19, 1906. Many books have been written on the Pacific Electric Railway and the crucial role it played in the creation of greater Los Angeles. Two scholarly studies of the railway and its creator are William B. Friedricks, *Henry E. Huntington and the Creation of Southern California* (Columbus: Ohio State University Press, 1992) and James Thorpe, *Henry Edwards Huntington, A Biography* (Berkeley: University of California Press, 1994). Also of note on this general topic is Robert M. Fogelson, *The Fragmented Metropolis: Los Angeles, 1850–1930* (Berkeley: University of California Press, 1993).

1. Memories and the Personal Discovery of Indiana's Interurban Era

1. Yi-Fu Tuan, *Landscapes of Fear* (New York: Pantheon, 1979).

2. Popularly known as the "Greenfield Line," the interurban originated as the Indianapolis and Greenfield Rapid Transit and commenced service between the two cities on June 13, 1900.

3. The American railroad industry was once separated into two broad categories: steam and electric. The term "steam railroad" persisted into the diesel era, and the designation even encompassed steam roads that electrified portions of their main lines, such as the Chicago, Milwaukee, St. Paul and Pacific. Not without reason did the nationwide mileage of *both* steam and interurban railroads peak in 1916, the same year the federal government resumed funding improved highways.

4. By providing an abundance of detail about the rise and fall of the industry, the standard reference is George W. Hilton and John F. Due, *The Electric Interurban Railways in America* (Stanford, CA: Stanford University Press, 1960). For an in-depth look at America's final interurban, see William D. Middleton, *South Shore: The Last Interurban*, 2d rev. ed. (Bloomington: Indiana University Press, 1999).

5. In a speech he gave in Saint Louis in 1926, railroad magnate Leonor F. Loree estimated the value of the interurban industry at that time to be $6 billion. In terms of 2023 inflationary currency, Loree's sum translates into approximately $90 billion.

6. *Indianapolis News*, January 18, 1941.

7. Greenfield was a community of fewer than five thousand residents in the early 1930s when Robert F. Reeves spearheaded the lengthy court challenge to the imperious Samuel Insull and his corporate bigwigs. *Greenfield Daily Reporter*, April 27, 1931.

8. Offering an illustrated summary history are James A. Glass and David Kohrman, *The Gas Boom of East Central Indiana* (Charleston, SC: Arcadia, 2005).

9. George J. Richman, *History of Hancock County, Indiana; Its People, Industries and Institutions* (Indianapolis: Federal, 1916) and J. H. Binford, *History of Hancock County, Indiana: From Its Earliest Settlement by the "Pale Face" in 1818, Down to 1882* (Greenfield, IN: King & Binford, 1882).

10. Indiana is blessed with several good histories of its interurban lines, which I cite throughout this book. Likewise, its steam railroads have been the subject of several histories: Graydon M. Meints, *Indiana Railroad Lines* (Bloomington: Indiana University Press, 2011); Craig Sanders, *Limiteds, Locals, and Expresses in Indiana, 1938–1871* (Bloomington: Indiana University Press, 2003); Richard S. Simons and Francis H. Parker, *Railroads of Indiana*

(Bloomington: Indiana University Press, 1997); and William J. Watt, *The Pennsylvania Railroad in Indiana* (Bloomington: Indiana University Press, 1999).

11. J. A. McGowan, "How the Interurban Serves," *Electric Railway Journal* (July 1924): 133. See also Robert Reed, *Central Indiana Interurban* (Charleston, SC: Arcadia, 2004).

12. Guy Morrison Walker, *The Why and How of Interurban Railways* (n.p.: G. M. Walker, 1904), 3.

13. *Street Railway Review* (December 1901): 922. On the same page is a report that the Detroit United and Rapid Railways facilitated urban outreach by publishing a special "hunter's guide" to encourage Detroit sportsmen to get out of the city and into the countryside served by its interurban trains. "The suburban lines of the Detroit United Ry. reach some of the best shooting grounds in Michigan."

14. On the geographical impact of the interurban, see Mildred M. Walmsley, "The Bygone Electric Interurban Railway System," *Professional Geographer* 17 (May 1965).

15. In the mid-twentieth century, the railroads serving Indianapolis were the Pennsylvania, New York Central (encompassing both the Big Four and Peoria and Eastern), Baltimore and Ohio, Monon (Chicago, Indianapolis, and Louisville), Nickel Plate (New York, Chicago, and St. Louis), and Illinois Central. In my boyhood calculations, I fully expected that trains would continue to use the Pennsylvania tracks between Indianapolis and Greenfield forever and that the far less impressive Nickel Plate and Illinois Central branches into Indianapolis would eventually become history's also-rans. In fact, the once-busy main line of the Pennsylvania is now a jogging trail, as is the Monon's former right-of-way into Indianapolis, while the Illinois Central's former streak-of-rust linking Indianapolis with the railroad's main line in Effingham, Illinois, was transformed in recent years by my friend Tom Hoback into The Indiana Rail Road, an innovative and prosperous five-hundred-mile Midwestern carrier headquartered in Indianapolis. See Christopher Rund, Fred W. Frailey, and Eric Powell, *The Indiana Rail Road Company*, rev. and expanded ed. (Bloomington: Indiana University Press, 2012).

16. For the historical context of the city's Union Station, see Jeffrey Darbee, *Indianapolis Union and Belt Railroads* (Bloomington: Indiana University Press, 2017).

17. Tracks of the Big Four crossed the northern portion of Hancock County, those of the Baltimore and Ohio crossed its southern portion, the Peoria and Eastern (a Big Four subsidiary) followed a more central route, and the Pennsylvania Railroad neatly bisected the county by way of Greenfield. Four separate interurban lines closely paralleled the tracks of each of these four steam railroads.

18. Hancock County in those days was a Democratic Party stronghold. One of its longest-published newspapers was the *Hancock Democrat*. William Jennings Bryan was the Democratic Party's presidential standard-bearer in 1896, 1900, and 1908, but American voters never elected him to the White House.

19. Interurban promoters proposed to close the gap between Greenfield and Fortville, but like the many hundreds of similar proposals across the Midwest, tracks never materialized. One of the most extreme examples of interurban inconvenience could be found in eastern Indiana. The communities of Milton and Connersville were a mere ten miles apart. There was talk of building an electric railway to close the short gap. None ever materialized, and anyone foolish enough to attempt the journey by interurban had to travel west from Milton to

Indianapolis, then turn around and head southeast to Connersville, an odyssey that required the better part of a day.

20. J. A. McGowan, "How the Interurban Serves," *Electric Railway Journal* (July 1924): 133. At this time, Joseph McGowan served as secretary and treasurer of the Terre Haute, Indianapolis and Eastern Traction Company, second only to Union Traction in terms of interurban mileage in Indiana. His late cousin, Hugh McGowan, was the mastermind behind the March 1907 creation of the Terre Haute, Indianapolis and Eastern and the Indianapolis Traction Terminal.

2. The Promise of Electricity, The Peril of Gasoline

1. For an illustrated overview of the important Chicago and Saint Louis World's Fairs of 1893 and 1904, respectively, and many other similar expositions, see Thornton Waite, *Fairs and Railroads: Railroads at World's Fairs, Expositions and Railroad Fairs* (Missoula, MT: Pictorial Histories, 2010).

2. Peter J. Ling, *America and the Automobile: Technology, Reform and Social Change, 1893–1923* (Manchester, England: Manchester University Press, 1990). Especially useful is his chapter on the automobile at the Chicago World's Fair of 1893.

3. A horse railway operated in New York City as early as the 1830s, but the concept did not "gain traction" there or in any other American city until the mid-1850s. See William D. Middleton, *The Time of the Trolley* (Milwaukee, WI: Kalmbach, 1967) and John Anderson Miller, *Fares Please! A Popular History of Trolleys, Horsecars, Streetcars, Buses, Elevateds, and Subways* (1941; repr., New York: Dover, 1960).

4. Clay McShane and Joel A. Tarr, *The Horse in the City: Living Machines in the Nineteenth Century* (Baltimore: Johns Hopkins University Press, 2007) and Ann Norton Greene, *Horses at Work: Harnessing Power in Industrial America* (Cambridge, MA: Harvard University Press, 2008).

5. *Indianapolis Journal* (May 20, 1894).

6. *Indianapolis Journal* (August 4, 1889).

7. Charles Smallwood, Warren Edward Miller, and Don DeNevi, *The Cable Car Book* (1980; repr., New York: Bonanza, 1983).

8. George W. Hilton, *The Cable Car in America*, rev. ed. (Stanford, CA: Stanford University Press, 1997).

9. *New York Sun*, March 20, 1893. Although the electrical industry first boomed during the 1880s with the application of electricity to light and power, the first commercial application of electricity was the telegraph, which dates from the 1840s. See Benjamin Sidney Michael Schwantes, *The Train and the Telegraph, A Revisionist History* (Baltimore: Johns Hopkins University Press, 2019).

10. *Indianapolis Journal* (March 28, 1899).

11. *Street Railway Journal* (February 1896): 113. One of the most insistent claims is that the first interurban opened in Oregon on February 16, 1893, when the Portland, Sellwood and Milwaukie Railroad (East Side Railway Company) began operating electrically powered cars along tracks connecting Portland and Oregon City, a distance of sixteen miles. The problem

with this claim is that an equally good, if not better, case can be made for the electric railway built to connect Minneapolis and Saint Paul, which opened in 1890.

12. Andrew D. Young, *St. Louis Car Company Album: A Photographic Record* (Glendale, CA: Interurban, 1984); Debra Brill, *History of the J. G. Brill Company* (Bloomington: Indiana University Press, 2001); Lawrence A. Brough and James H. Graebner, *From Small Town to Downtown: A History of the Jewett Car Company, 1893–1919* (Bloomington: Indiana University Press, 2004); Craig R. Semsel, *Built to Move Millions: Streetcar Building in Ohio* (Bloomington: Indiana University Press, 2008); Lawrence A. Brough, *The Electric Pullman: A History of the Niles Car & Manufacturing Company* (Bloomington: Indiana University Press, 2013). For an in-depth study of interurban cars, see William D. Middleton, *Traction Classics, Volume 1: The Interurbans, The Great Wood and Steel Cars* (San Marino, CA: Golden West, 1983).

13. Andrew D. Young and Eugene F. Provenzo Jr., *The History of the St. Louis Car Company* (San Diego: Howell-North, 1978); Andrew D. Young, *The St. Louis Streetcar Story* (Glendale, CA: Interurban, 1988); and Andrew D. Young, *When Missouri Took the Trolley* (St. Louis: Archway, 2007).

14. The fender of a trolley or interurban car corresponded to the cowcatcher of a steam locomotive. In Indiana, many interurban companies favored slatted wooded fenders that hung below the front of passenger cars and somewhat resembled an old man's chin whiskers. A frog is the crossing point of two rails, and one of the largest manufacturers of these specialized sections of track during the Interurban Era was the Indianapolis Switch and Frog Company based in Springfield, Ohio.

15. *Street Railway Review* (January 1895): 57. October was certainly a favored month for the industry's big annual conference, but on a few occasions, it took place in September and even in late August. The initial meeting of the American Street Railway Association took place in Boston in 1882, but in 1895, in a tip of the hat to its Canadian colleagues, the organization held its yearly conference in Montreal. After 1910, and as membership grew significantly larger and convention exhibits more numerous, the association often met for the sake of convenience (and sufficient meeting space) in Atlantic City, New Jersey.

16. Other manufacturers of streetcars in Saint Louis were the Laclede Car Company, founded in 1883; the Brownell Car Company, founded in 1875 as the Brownell and Wight Car Company; and the Missouri Car & Foundry Company, established in 1876 and which at the turn of the century evolved into the American Car and Foundry Company.

17. The number of books devoted to the electrical revolution is truly mind-boggling. Here is a sample of the many titles: David Bodanis, *Electric Universe: The Shocking True Story of Electricity* (New York: Crown, 2005); John A. Jakle, *City Lights: Illuminating the American Night* (Baltimore: Johns Hopkins University Press, 2001); Jill Jonnes, *Empires of Light: Edison, Tesla, Westinghouse, and the Race to Electrify the World* (New York: Random House, 2004); Tom McNichol, *AC/DC: The Savage Tale of the First Standards War* (San Francisco: Jossey-Bass, 2006); David E. Nye, *Electrifying America: Social Meanings of a New Technology* (Cambridge, MA: MIT Press, 1990). Offering convenient overviews are Wolfgang Schivelbusch, *Disenchanted Night: The Industrialization of Light in the Nineteenth Century* (Berkeley: University of California Press, 1988) and Michael E. Webber, *Power Trip: The Story of Energy* (New York: Basic Books, 2019). Likewise, numerous books are devoted to Thomas Edison and his

contemporaries. Again, I will list only a sample of them: Neil Baldwin, *Edison: Inventing the Century* (New York: Hyperion, 1995); L. J. Davis, *Fleet Fire: Thomas Edison and the Pioneers of the Electric Revolution* (New York: Arcade, 2003); Matthew Josephson, *Edison* (New York: McGraw-Hill, 1959); William D. Middleton and William D. Middleton III, *Frank Julian Sprague: Electrical Inventor & Engineer* (Bloomington: Indiana University Press, 2009); Randall Stross, *The Wizard of Menlo Park: How Thomas Alva Edison Invented the Modern World* (New York: Crown, 2007); and Wyn Wachhorst, *Thomas Alva Edison: An American Myth* (Cambridge, MA: MIT Press, 1981).

18. John F. Wasik, *The Merchant of Power: Samuel Insull, Thomas Edison, and the Creation of the Modern Metropolis* (New York: Palgrave Macmillan, 2006) and John Franch, *Robber Baron: The Life of Charles Tyson Yerkes* (Urbana: University of Illinois Press, 2006).

19. Especially during its boom years, the industry supported many weekly and monthly journals. These include *Street Railway Journal* (1884–1908), *Street Railway Review* (1891–1906), and *Electric Railway Review* (1906–1908). These merged to form the *Electric Railway Journal* (1908–32). Other publications include *Electric Traction* (1905–32) and the *Street Railway Gazette* (1886–95). In addition to the trade journals devoted to electric railways of the United States and Canada, numerous other publications explored all things electric. Among these were *Electrical World; Electricity, the Popular Journal*; and *Elektron.*

20. Thomas A. Kinney, *The Carriage Trade: Making Horse-Drawn Vehicles in America* (Baltimore: Johns Hopkins University Press, 2004).

21. As quoted in Ralph D. Gray, *Alloys and Automobiles: The Life of Elwood Haynes* (Indianapolis: Indiana Historical Society, 1979), 222.

22. John B. Rae, *The American Automobile: A Brief History* (Chicago: University of Chicago Press, 1965) and James J. Flink, *America Adopts the Automobile, 1895–1910* (Cambridge, MA: MIT Press, 1970).

23. *Street Railway Review* (February 1900): 61. *The Horseless Age* (1895–1918) is a remarkable historical resource not just for the wealth of technical information it contains but also for the human interest accounts it regularly published about the application of automotive technology during the industry's formative years.

24. *Indianapolis Journal* (July 18 and 19, 1899).

3. Investor's Dilemma: Interurban or Automobile?

1. Booth Tarkington, *The Turmoil, A Novel* (New York: Grosset & Dunlap, 1915), 38. The second novel in his "Growth Trilogy" was *The Magnificent Ambersons* published in 1918. It won a Pulitzer Prize for fiction and was transformed into a 1941 movie by legendary director and actor, Orson Welles. The third book in the series, *The Midlander*, was published in 1923. Tarkington became the best-known author in Indiana and perhaps in the United States also—but only for a few years. His unusual career trajectory is discussed in Robert Gottlieb, "The Rise and Fall of Booth Tarkington," *New Yorker*, November 4, 2019.

2. James J. Flink, *America Adopts the Automobile, 1895–1910* (Cambridge: MIT Press, 1970).

3. *Street Railway Journal* (April 1899): 224–25, and *Muncie Star Press*, May 2, 1901. The Muncie paper described Moore as "a resident of the county all her life."

4. Dennis E. Horvath and Terri Horvath, *Indiana Cars: A History of the Automobile in Indiana* (Indianapolis: Hoosier Auto Show and Swap Meet, 2002). Thomas E. Bonsall, *More Than They Promised: The Studebaker Story* (Stanford: Stanford University Press, 2000).

5. Guy Morrison Walker, "The Interurban Railway as an Investment," *Street Railway Review* (September 1901): 561–63.

6. *Indianapolis Star*, October 1, 1932, and St. Louis *Republic*, as quoted in the *Electric Railway Journal* (August 28, 1915): 380.

7. *Indianapolis News*, February 8, 1906, *Noblesville Ledger*, June 7, 1935, and *Lafayette Journal and Courier*, May 25, 1932.

8. J. F. Wild & Company, a state-chartered bank, was perhaps the largest dealer in interurban securities in Indiana. In addition, Wild not only served as the first president of the Indianapolis Stock Exchange but also numbered among the directors of Charles L. Henry's second interurban enterprise, the Indianapolis and Cincinnati Traction Company, and loaned him the money to advance the interurban's tracks toward Cincinnati. *Hamilton County Ledger*, October 31, 1902, and *Indianapolis Journal*, November 7, 1902. When interviewed in Cincinnati in 1905, Morgan discounted the idea that he and his associates were manipulating Midwest interurban securities for personal gain: "We are interested in the interurban business as permanent operators and owners of properties, not as sellers of properties. We believe that if the roads are well constructed and economically operated, and are managed with an intelligent perception of the requirements of the public and an intelligent purpose to accommodate the public, they will be profitable permanent investments." *Richmond Item*, December 8, 1905.

9. Booth Tarkington, *The Turmoil, A Novel* (New York: Grosset & Dunlap, 1915), 38.

10. *Hartford Courant*, as quoted in the *Muncie Evening Press*, June 28, 1897. In this era, newspapers across the United States quoted freely from one another, and thus warnings like this one enunciated in Connecticut could reach a broad spectrum of readers in Indiana and many other states. Even in Indiana, an occasional newspaper critic warned unwary investors: "An electric railway scheme is a good speculation for speculators—that's all." *Garrett Clipper*, February 13, 1902.

11. The roller-coaster metaphor offers an apt description of the trajectory of the Interurban Era because the popular thrill ride was closely identified with the several hundred turn-of-the-century amusement parks operated by trolley and interurban companies. See Stephen M. Silverman, *The Amusement Park: 900 Years of Thrills and Spills, and the Dreamers and Schemers Who Built Them* (New York: Black Dog & Leventhal, 2019). Likewise, my use of the word "romance" is an apt description of the close relationship that once existed between Hoosiers and their electric railways. The term was used by contemporaries as well: "Story of Interurban Reads Like Romance," insisted the headline of a feature story published in the *Muncie Evening Press*, January 31, 1911. "Indiana is now the most highly developed interurban railway center in the country and Muncie, which with Anderson and Marion made the beginning on the development of the Hoosier trolley network, is today the second interurban center in the state, being surpassed in this respect only by Indianapolis."

12. George S. Davis, "The Interurban Electric Railways of Ohio," *Street Railway Journal* (August 1, 1901): 145–49. Davis quotes here from an unnamed newspaper in northern Ohio.

13. Any serious investor was wise to consult the "Red Book," a financial guide that the *Street Railway Journal* published "for the Use of Bankers, Brokers, Capitalists, Investors and Street

Railway Companies." Its official title was *American Street Railway Investments* (New York: McGraw, 1904). The annual compendium, which provided maps and a wealth of statistical data and other information on individual street railway and interurban companies, was first published in 1894.

14. Louis C. Hunter, *Steam Power: A History of Industrial Power in the United States, 1780–1930* (Charlottesville: University Press of Virginia, 1985) and William Rosen, *The Most Powerful Idea in the World: A Story of Steam, Industry, and Invention* (New York: Random House, 2010).

15. Although wood ties supported the rails on most electric and steam railroads, a few trolley companies used steel ties. Likewise, although copper and copper alloys prevailed on overhead trolley wires, a few companies experimented with less expensive steel wires, but steel was also a less efficient conduit of electricity than copper.

16. *Indianapolis Star*, June 30, 1907.

17. George Krambles, "Lebanon-Thorntown Traction Company: The Biography of an Anomaly in 'Interurbanland,'" *Railroad History* (Spring 1996): 51–67. Krambles notes that the interurban line was not quite ten miles long, and that Lebanon had a population of 4,465 in 1900, while Thorntown's population was less than one-third that number. The electric railway was launched in 1904, one of the years of intense enthusiasm for interurbans, and shut down in 1926 after the loss of business to highway competitors had become clearly irreversible.

18. Pennsylvania's Widener University traces its roots back to 1821, but it adopted its present name in 1972 to honor the memory of Eleanor Elkins Widener. Harvard University's Widener Library, which also traces its origins to the Philadelphia Widener and Elkins families, is a campus landmark and an incredible resource for scholars.

19. J. H. Pardee, "The Tendency of the Times," *Electric Railway Journal* (December 1912): 1194–95.

20. Dr. Thomas Conway Jr., "The Decreasing Financial Returns upon Urban Street Railway Properties," *Annals of the American Academy of Political and Social Science* (January 1911): 14–30.

21. Earl Swift, *The Big Roads: The Untold Story of the Engineers, Visionaries, and Trailblazers Who Created the American Superhighways* (Boston: Houghton Mifflin Harcourt, 2011); Phil Patton, *Open Road, A Celebration of the American Highway* (New York: Simon & Schuster, 1986).

4. Hoosier Hysteria; or, The Interurban Boom Years

1. *Indianapolis Journal*, June 29, 1901.

2. Robert F. Bruner and Sean D. Carr, *The Panic of 1907: Lessons Learned from the Market's Perfect Storm* (Hoboken, NJ: John Wiley & Sons, 2007).

3. *Palladium-Item* (Richmond, IN), March 20, 1937, and *Cambridge City Tribune*, November 20, 1902.

4. Guy Morrison Walker, *The Why and How of Interurban Railways* (n. p.: G. M. Walker, 1904), 5; *Greensburg Daily News*, April 23, 1966; *Brookville Democrat*, April 24, 1902; and *Marion New-Tribune*, as quoted in *Interurban Railway Journal* (November 1905).

5. Today, that dubious distinction probably belongs to Phoenix, Arizona, a city of nearly 1,700,000 residents landlocked in the Sonoran Desert.

6. Paul Fatout, *Indiana Canals* (West Lafayette, IN: Purdue University Press, 1972). Indiana's earliest railroads built north from ports along the Ohio River to enlarge existing patterns of trade based on the Ohio River and Lake Michigan. The state's first railroad, for instance, linked Madison on the Ohio River with landlocked Indianapolis. Another early railroad, a predecessor to the Monon, completed a line of tracks from the Ohio River opposite Louisville to Michigan City, from where ships used Lake Michigan to connect to Chicago.

7. The population of Saint Louis remained greater than that of Chicago through the 1870 census, and both were exceeded in size only by Philadelphia and New York until Chicago emerged as the nation's second-largest city after New York in the 1890 census. At the dawn of the Interurban Era in 1900, Saint Louis ranked fourth with a population of 575,238 residents compared with Chicago's 1,698,575. New York at that time had a population of 3,437,202. Indianapolis ranked a distant twenty-first, with 169,164 residents.

8. The five most prominent railroads that operated through trains across northern Indiana between New York City and Chicago in the early twentieth century were the New York Central, the Pennsylvania, the Baltimore and Ohio, the Erie, and the Nickel Plate. Those with through trains between New York and Saint Louis were the New York Central, the Pennsylvania, and the Baltimore and Ohio. Across hilly and less prosperous southern Indiana, the Baltimore and Ohio operated the only through line, a historic route that connected Cincinnati and Saint Louis by rail for the first time in the late 1850s.

9. In mid-1916, for example, the Big Four ran three daily accommodation trains through Warsaw in each direction: three continued south to main line connections at Anderson, and two ran north as far as Benton Harbor, Michigan. In either direction, they made numerous stops.

10. Baseball fans may wonder if "home base" is an appropriate term to use here instead of the sport's modern preference for "home plate." For an answer, this Saint Louis Cardinals fan willingly turned to an ardent Chicago Cubs fan, Tom Hoback, for an answer. Tom's knowledge of baseball is phenomenal, as is his knowledge of railroads, and his research convinced me that "home base" was entirely appropriate for the Billy Sunday era.

11. From 1905 until its demise as a freight-only railroad in 1952, the Winona Interurban Railway went by several different names. For the sake of convenience, I use the name applied between 1905 and its receiver's sale in 1924. For an account by an enthusiast who endured the long journey via the only through interurban route between Chicago and Louisville in the mid-1920s, see *Electric Traction* (December 1924): 580.

12. The topic of railways and proper Sunday observance was once a hot-button topic. William E. Dodge, a wealthy New York dealer in imported metals, so vehemently opposed Sunday trains that he resigned from the board of directors of the Central Railroad of New Jersey in protest. When the railroad later went bankrupt, he considered it a sign of divine intervention and punishment. The best book on the history of Sunday observance was written by my former University of Idaho colleague Craig Harline, *Sunday: A History of the First Day from Babylonia to the Super Bowl* (New York: Doubleday, 2007).

13. William B. Friedricks, *Henry E. Huntington and the Creation of Southern California* (Columbus: Ohio State University Press, 1992).

14. J. C. Shade, "Little Things That Count," *Electric Railway Journal* (August 1911): 353–54.

15. *Electric Railway Journal* (December 1909): 1154, and Schade, "Little Things That Count," *Electric Railway Journal*.

16. *Electric Traction Weekly* (September 1907): 909.

17. *Electric Railway Journal* (October 1909): 619. The Indianapolis and Louisville also opted to supply its trains from one large powerhouse and a higher-than-normal voltage that avoided the use of maintenance-intensive substations along its line.

18. *Electric Traction Weekly* (April 1912): 423.

19. *Electric Traction Weekly* (April 1912): 423, and (June 1912): 637–38. The Chicagoans who organized the Interstate Public Service holding company in September 1912 negotiated a 999-year lease of the Indianapolis, Columbus and Southern that required payment of $92,000 a year. See Jerry Marlette, *Interstate: A History of Interstate Public Service Rail Operations* (Polo, IL: Transportation Trails, 1990), 49.

20. Interurban passenger statistics for 1903 do not include the approximately forty electric railway freight trains serving Indianapolis each day. *Indianapolis News*, January 1, 1904.

21. *Indianapolis Journal*, December 3, 1902, and *Indianapolis News*, July 25, 1903. The site of the Cyclorama Building, once described as the most "pretentious" structure in downtown Indianapolis, was among the locations Edward Fay Claypool considered for his luxury hotel. The Claypool Hotel opened in 1903 and was a block away from the Cyclorama at the busy corner of Washington and Illinois Streets, within easy walking distance of the state capitol. Indiana interurban companies made frequent use of the hotel's capacious ballroom and other meeting facilities for their regional and national conferences. *Indianapolis Journal*, June 9, 1899.

22. Burnham's station in Washington, DC, opened in 1907.

23. *Street Railway Journal* (December 1902): 867.

24. *Indianapolis News*, March 10, 1905. Everett's delegation included traction executives from Detroit, Toledo, Cleveland, Dayton, and Akron. In addition to inspecting the Traction Terminal, they toured Anderson and other cities of the still-famous Gas Belt. Raymond [W. Patterson], "Trolley a Boon to Indianapolis," *Chicago Tribune*, September 10, 1907. His *Tribune* feature story also noted that the Traction Terminal was "something entirely foreign to the commercial life of Chicago. It is in the heart of the city and represents a direct connection with the smaller cities of the state such as is not enjoyed by Chicago, Milwaukee, or Saint Louis."

25. Bion J. Arnold, *Report on an Interurban Electric Railway Terminal System for the City of Cincinnati Submitted to the Cincinnati Interurban Rapid Transit Commission*, 1912. The Arnold report is remarkable for the wealth of comparative data it provided. On page 160, he ranked six hubs according to their 1911 "earnings per mile of road of interurban electric railroads operating out of various cities on a per capita basis." Among the major cities of Ohio and Indiana, Cincinnati ranked last at 100 percent, while Indianapolis ranked first at 177 percent, with Toledo, Cleveland, Columbus, and Fort Wayne placing between these two extremes.

26. *Indianapolis News*, November 9, 1905, and *Indianapolis Star*, March 27, 1912.

5. Gas Belt Prosperity and Indiana's Interurban Pioneers

1. The electric railway industry's main professional association was originally called the American Street Railway Association, but over the years, it was renamed to reflect new

realities. From 1905 through 1910, it was the American Street and Interurban Railway Association, and from 1911 through 1931, it was the American Electric Railway Association.

2. *Electric Railway Journal* (March 1914): 533–35.

3. *Scientific American* (October 1905): 314, and *Daily Republican* (Rushville), October 25, 1905.

4. Henry initially installed the state-of-the-art power-delivery system on his interurban line between Indianapolis and Rushville. The results were so favorable that he soon added it to the line between Indianapolis and Greensburg, with a high-voltage link from the Rushville powerhouse to the trolley wire in Shelbyville. Among the relevant details of Henry's single-phase alternating current system: 25 cycle power, 3,300 volts on the trolley wire, and high-tension distribution from the Rushville power plant at 33,000 volts. Steady improvements to the direct current system that used 600 volts on the trolley wire to power heavy interurban cars eventually nullified the advantages claimed for alternating current. *Rushville Republican*, May 22, 1924.

5. What the railroad station meant in the life of a young man leaving his small hometown to make his way in the larger world is beautifully captured in the final lines of the Sherwood Anderson classic, *Winesburg, Ohio* (1919; repr., New York: Penguin, 1976). As the train departed, George Willard looked out the window as "the town of Winesburg had disappeared and his life there had become but a background on which to paint the dreams of his manhood," 247.

6. Henry composed his brief memoir well after his 1892 trip to Missouri, and some of its details border on poetic license. The electric railway that greatly impressed him was not yet in operation that year. Its incorporation, in fact, took place only in late August 1892. The line opened for business in mid-1893, just about the time of the Wall Street crash that blighted the American economy until 1897 or 1898. Hard times forced Henry to wait four years before he launched his Indiana interurban between Anderson and Alexandria. The Southwest Missouri Electric Railway that served as Henry's inspiration is discussed at length in the *Electric Railway Review* (September 1906): 543–48.

7. *Street Railway Review* (January 1906): 47. Henry delivered the banquet address in which he shared basic details of his career with industry colleagues who attended the first annual meeting of the Indiana Electric Railway Association, which also proved to be its last meeting. In the words of Arthur Brady, who in typical fashion had introduced his senior colleague, the banquet was the "wake" of the Indiana association because it soon merged with its Ohio equal to form the Central Electric Railway Association.

8. *Champaign Daily Gazette* (IL), November 10, 1903.

9. *Indianapolis Star*, February 19, 1911.

10. A lengthy account of Union Traction's inaugural run to Indianapolis is provided by Muncie's *Star Press*, January 4, 1901.

11. When Henry's family donated a portion of his typescript memoir to the Indiana Historical Society, they included only the first twelve pages, which ended with his creation of Union Traction. The remaining pages, which included details of the Henry family's sojourn to Europe aboard the steamship *St. Louis*, were of interest only to family members, or so they claimed. Thus, the real reason for Henry's abrupt departure from Union Traction, if he ever stated it, is lost to history.

12. *The Fourth Estate*, June 11, 1904, 2. McCulloch's flirtation with journalism ended badly. He soon sold his three-newspaper chain to a somewhat sketchy Chicago publisher with Indiana roots. Charles Warren Fairbanks served as a US senator from Indiana (1897–1905) and as vice president of the United States (1905–1909). He was the Republican vice-presidential nominee again in the 1916 election in which Charles Evans Hughes was defeated by incumbent Democrat Woodrow Wilson, with Fairbanks's fellow Hoosier, Thomas R. Marshall, reelected vice president. Oddly, Fairbanks' name is immortalized in the Alaska city named for him.

13. *Street Railway Journal* (September 1902): 431. One other interurban, still a paper enterprise in 1902, was the Indiana and Ohio Traction Company. This line had surveyed a route through Brookville that at a length of 103 miles between Indianapolis and Cincinnati was claimed to be shorter than any of the steam railroads connecting those two cities. *Street Railway Journal* (March 1902): 317.

14. Henry had earlier equipped the Union Traction with rollingstock purchased from the St. Louis Car Company. Among these was the office car later named "Martha," widely admired in 1901 as the most elegant interurban car yet created in the United States and arguably the most elegant ever created.

15. Randal Morgan's first name was often misspelled as "Randall," an error that likely will throw a search engine off track. When I first checked the Philadelphia newspapers for his obituary in 1926, I found nothing for "Randall Morgan," so I wrongly concluded that the money mogul wished to remain as anonymous as possible. The use of the computer in historical research brings problems I never could have imagined in my graduate school days as well as exciting new possibilities, such as facilitating my search for the true origin of the word "interurban," as discussed in the appendix.

16. The *Indianapolis News* claimed in 1906 that Henry's Indianapolis and Cincinnati line was probably the state's only interurban to be built entirely with Indiana money, a claim the *Rushville Republican* proudly republished under the headline "Built Entirely of Hoosier Capital." *Rushville Republican*, July 12, 1906. Perhaps the *News* forgot about the Columbus-based line built by Joseph and Will Irwin, which was also supposed to have been built entirely with local dollars.

17. *Indianapolis Journal*, February 7, 1901.

18. Both men appear to have inherited their interest in politics. Brady's grandfather served as Muncie's first mayor, and Henry's father, an immigrant from Ireland at age twelve, served a term in the Indiana House of Representatives. Arthur Brady's hometown of Muncie, Indiana, was the subject of one of the best sociological studies of American life in the 1920s and 1930s: Robert S. Lynd and Helen Merrill Lynd, *Middletown: A Study in American Culture* (New York: Harcourt, Brace, 1929); see also the 1930s sequel: Robert S. Lynd and Helen Merrill Lynd, *Middletown in Transition: A Study in Cultural Conflicts* (New York: Harcourt, Brace, 1937).

19. William Gibbs McAdoo Jr. (1863–1941) completed the Hudson and Manhattan Railroad in 1907. Later, as the son-in-law of President Woodrow Wilson, he was tapped to serve as the first director general of the US Railroad Administration during World War I.

20. *Indianapolis News*, October 17, 1911. Henry not only headed the interurban industry's political office on Capitol Hill for fifteen years; from 1920 until his death seven years later, he also presided over the Indiana Public Utility Association. "He was held in high esteem by railroad and interurban men and respected especially for his knowledge of interurban law, obtained

when he was a pioneer in the field, working out successfully interurban practice in days when there were no laws to govern their operation." *Greenfield Daily Reporter*, May 3, 1927.

21. Thomas R. Marshall, *Recollections of Thomas R. Marshall, A Hoosier Salad* (Indianapolis: Bobbs-Merrill, 1925).

22. *Indianapolis News*, March 22, 1907. The Irwin company made a trial run into the capital city on January 1, 1900—a first car entering Indianapolis on the first day of the new century was thought to be historically memorable—but regular service did not begin until the following January 16.

23. In a few places in Indiana, competing interurban companies did offer patrons the choice of alternate routes, but their respective tracks followed widely divergent corridors, such as between Crawfordsville and Indianapolis and also between New Castle and Indianapolis. The interurban lines that combined in 1912 under the Interstate Public Service Company banner were the Irwins' original Indianapolis, Columbus and Southern Traction Company plus the Indianapolis and Louisville Traction Company and the Louisville and Northern Railway and Lighting Company. Jerry Marlette, *Interstate A History of Interstate Public Service Rail Operations* (Polo, IL: Transportation Trails, 1990).

24. *Journal and Courier* (Lafayette), March 2, 1980.

25. George K. Bradley, *Northern Indiana Railway* (Chicago: Central Electric Railfans' Association, 1998).

6. Hugh McGowan, Interurban Empire Builder

1. *Richmond Palladium-Item*, August 3, 1907.

2. *Indianapolis Journal*, June 13, 1901.

3. *Fort Wayne Journal-Gazette*, October 18, 1901; *Indianapolis Star*, June 30, 1907.

4. *Street Railway Journal* (September 1902): 343.

5. *Richmond Palladium-Item*, January 24, 1922. See also Margaret Wynn, "Natural Gas in Indiana: An Exploited Resource," *Indiana Quarterly Magazine of History* (March 1908): 31–45; James A. Glass, "The Gas Boom in East Central Indiana," *Indiana Magazine of History* (December 2000): 313–35; and James A. Glass and David Kohrman, *The Gas Boom of East Central Indiana* (Charleston, SC: Arcadia, 2005).

6. *Indianapolis Star*, June 30, 1907.

7. *Indianapolis Sun*, as quoted in the *Indianapolis Journal*, January 10, 1903.

8. *Indianapolis Star*, July 22, 1906. McGowan's younger brother, James, who had followed in his footsteps to become head of the Kansas City Gas Company, died of sudden heart failure at forty-five only months before Hugh succumbed at age fifty-four to the same malady, one that also cursed his mother and other family members. Curiously, in the *Star*'s 1906 interview, McGowan seemed more concerned about his height than about his heart. At one point he interjected, "Another question which has been asked me is this, whether men short of stature have been extraordinarily successful." He quickly answered his own question by referring to a recent US president from Indianapolis. "Benjamin Harrison was short, and others who have been successful have been short." Looking down at "his own not overtowering form," he smiled as he insisted to his interviewer, "The height makes no difference." At this point, McGowan realized that he had strayed far from the primary purpose of the interview, to share

with newspaper readers the secret of his remarkable road to personal success, a popular topic in turn-of-the-century United States. One is left to wonder if his obsession with hard work was a way to compensate for a perceived physical impediment. Though short in stature, he was an imposing man nonetheless.

9. *Richmond Item*, June 17, 1908. Early in his career, McGowan drove himself so mercilessly that his health failed, and he returned to the family farm near Liberty, Missouri, to recuperate. In 1903, he traveled to his brother James's home in Saint Louis for a mysterious operation. The *Kansas City Star* (September 11, 1903) reported that McGowan "is pronounced to be entirely out of danger and will be able to leave his bed shortly." In later years, he would periodically go to Hot Springs, Arkansas, or to the spas of Europe in his unending quest for improved health. Incidentally, Martinsville, Indiana, located at the end of one branch of the McGowan-created Terre Haute, Indianapolis and Eastern line, was home to sanitariums famous for mineral waters that were supposed to cure a variety of ailments. Sanitariums and mineral spas figured prominently in the health history of the nineteenth century, and it should not be surprising that McGowan and other heavily stressed business tycoons, including William B. McKinley of Illinois Traction, were among their clients.

10. *Kansas City Times*, December 20, 1911. For additional details of the remarkable rise of Hugh McGowan, see the lengthy biography in Jacob Piatt Dunn, *Memorial and Genealogical Record of Representative Citizens of Indiana* (Indianapolis: B. F. Bowen, 1912).

11. *Kansas City Star*, September 17, 1898.

12. *Indianapolis Star*, October 31, 1904. A few days earlier on a nearby stretch of Missouri Pacific track at Warrensburg, an eastbound special train packed with world's fair passengers had smashed head-on into a westbound freight in a wreck that killed thirty and injured at least fifty more fairgoers. The press in McGowan's day had a curious way of reporting such grim news. For example, it seldom discussed sexual matters except in highly circumspect language but seemed to revel in printing accounts of death and dying that were personally invasive in their lurid details. An alliance of Kansas newspapers, for example, ran its story of a fatal steam railroad accident under a two-word headline "Engineer Roasted" (*Abilene Weekly Chronicle*, September 28, 1904). Gory headlines such as this are unthinkable today except in the tabloids. For more on this odd bit of turn-of-the-century popular culture, see Michael Lesy, *Wisconsin Death Trip* (New York: Pantheon, 1973). McGowan's premonition of his own sudden death was the kind of spooky story that newspapers of the day loved. For details, see the lengthy account published in the *Kansas City Star*, December 20, 1911.

13. Curiously, two massive biographies of J. P. Morgan do not mention Randal Morgan. See Ron Chernow, *The House of Morgan: An American Banking Dynasty and the Rise of Modern Finance* (New York: Simon & Schuster, 1990) and Jean Strouse, *Morgan, American Financier* (New York: Random House, 1999). The financial storm known as the Panic of 1907 should interest any serious student of the rise and fall of America's electric interurban railways. See Robert F. Bruner and Sean D. Carr, *The Panic of 1907: Lessons Learned from the Market's Perfect Storm* (Hoboken, NJ: John Wiley & Sons, 2007).

14. Morgan's grand tour of Europe is recorded in John F. Cushman, *Cruise of Steam Yacht "Waturus"* (Philadelphia: Allen, 1906). The captain of Morgan's maritime palace was his daughter, Anne, one of a handful of women formally licensed in the United States to command such

large vessels. As might be predicted given her passion for all things nautical, Anne married the son of Admiral John Arbuthnot Fisher, recently First Sea Lord of the British Navy and close associate of Winston Churchill. She relocated to England to live the life of a real royal. At the start of the Great War in Europe in 1914, First Lord of the Admiralty Churchill wisely coaxed "Jackie" Fisher out of retirement. He was widely regarded then as now as the greatest British admiral since Horatio Nelson.

15. *Indianapolis News*, February 11, 1913.

16. Randal Morgan, despite his many successes, could not escape the pain that comes with being part of the human race. He sent his son Marshall to Cincinnati to serve as an understudy to Kesley Schoepf. The father was obviously grooming the young man to be his successor. A few years later, while enjoying a cruise along the Delaware River near Philadelphia aboard his steam yacht with his daughter Anne in command, Morgan was surprised to see a small boat pull alongside. One of his trusted assistants brought news that a younger son, Randal Morgan Jr., was near death in a New York hospital as the result of a ruptured appendix. The father and daughter rushed to his bedside in New York, but they arrived too late. The young man died of peritonitis.

17. *Street Railway Review* (January 1906): 47.

18. McCulloch was involved in Muncie-area natural gas enterprises, which may have been how he met Randal Morgan and other Philadelphia venture capitalists who provided much of the financing that sustained Union Traction's rapid growth. McCulloch, briefly a rising eminence among Indiana newspaper publishers in the early twentieth century, owned the *Indianapolis Star*, the *Muncie Star*, and the *Terre Haute Star*. Apparently, journalism was not nearly as profitable as he had hoped because he soon sold his "Star League of Indiana." McCulloch left Muncie and moved to Summit, New Jersey, where he lived until his death in 1915. In Muncie today is McCulloch Park, land the interurban entrepreneur donated to the city, and within the park stands a large statue of McCulloch, which may represent the only such public memorial to an Indiana interurban pioneer. *The Fourth Estate*, May 9, 1908, 2.

19. The fantastical interurban line Adams envisioned never did get built. Its chief promoter died in Saint Louis in 1898.

20. *Muncie Evening Press*, April 30, 1901. Clodfelter is listed today among notable Indiana authors. Out of curiosity, I acquired an online copy of Clodfelter's final book called *The Gotham of Yasmar: A Satire* (Buffalo: Peter Paul, 1897). Some critics suggest it shows evidence of the author's increasing mental instability. I found it virtually unreadable. In one place, for example, Clodfelter writes in an unintelligible language entirely of his own creation. The words seemed to me like pure gibberish, but in a bizarre way, they may help to explain why Clodfelter's scattershot approach to his interurban projects left observers uncomprehending and then openly derisive.

21. From 1896 to 1901, the firm produced cars under the Haynes-Apperson label. The Apperson brothers, Elmer and Edgar, left in 1901 to form a separate company under their own family name. Ralph D. Gray, *Alloys and Automobiles: The Life of Elwood Haynes* (Indianapolis: Indiana Historical Society, 1979).

7. The Expansive Dozen Years

1. *Electrical Review* (New York) (February 1905): 291.

2. Henry was widely regarded in 1905 as a type of interurban miracle worker. When it was rumored that he planned to extend Indianapolis and Cincinnati tracks from Shelbyville east to Greensburg and then to the historic Ohio River community of Madison, the *Review* of Greensburg, Indiana, wrote: "With Hon. Charles L. Henry and his I. C. Traction line directors backing the enterprise, there can be no doubt of its success." *Greensburg Review,* as quoted in the *Columbus Republican,* June 29, 1905. In fact, no interurban line ever accessed Madison despite years of rumored plans to do so. Likewise, the *Brookville Democrat,* which expected Indianapolis and Cincinnati tracks soon to pass through town on their way to the Ohio metropolis, described Henry as "always" known as a "man who could be relied upon in any statement that he would emphatically make. His word in the business world in Indiana is as good as his bond." Despite that extravagant claim, Henry's interurban line did not make it to Brookville either. *Brookville Democrat,* March 19, 1913.

3. "Charles L. Henry," *Brill Magazine* (November 15, 1915): 321.

4. "Charles L. Henry," *Brill Magazine* (November 15, 1915): 321.

5. *Electrical Review* (New York) (February 1905): 291–96. The New York designation is needed to distinguish one of the oldest American journals devoted to all things electric from an equally venerable journal by the same name published in London.

6. *Electrical Review* (New York): 291.

7. *Richmond Item,* May 3, 1902.

8. Railroads typically reduced the frequency of their passenger trains on Sunday, and thus this tally records only scheduled weekday service. It does not include any special or extra passenger trains or freight trains that may have steamed along these two long-established routes between Cincinnati and Indianapolis. *Official Guide of the Railways* (New York: National Railway, September 1905).

9. *Cincinnati Inquirer,* April 16, 1909. Brady noted that completion of the two Indianapolis and Cincinnati Traction Company lines to Greensburg and Connersville had reoriented the local pattern of trade away from Cincinnati and toward Indianapolis.

10. "Cincinnati's Rapid-Transit Ordinance," *Electric Railway Journal* (April 7, 1917): 633.

11. "Cincinnati's Rapid-Transit Ordinance": 633–37. The plan called for an interurban "loop" that linked together lines confined to the city's perimeter and brought their cars downtown via a portion of the unused Miami-Erie Canal. A highly detailed 163-page analysis of Cincinnati's traction dilemma, with useful comparisons to Indianapolis and other major cities of the Midwest, appears in Bion J. Arnold, *Report on an Interurban Electric Railway Terminal System for the City of Cincinnati Submitted to the Cincinnati Interurban Rapid Transit Commission* (Chicago: Bion J. Arnold, 1912). A summary history of how Cincinnati struggled but failed to resolve its traction muddle is Allen J. Singer, *The Cincinnati Subway: History of Rapid Transit* (Charleston, SC: Arcadia, 2003).

12. *Indianapolis News,* November 9, 1905.

13. *Daily Republican* (Rushville), April 23, 1907.

14. *Street Railway Journal* (September 1903): 593.

15. I speak from personal observation. My government teacher at Broad Ripple High School took his students to the 1962 Democratic Party's state convention in the Coliseum at the Indiana State Fair grounds. US senator Vance Hartke introduced himself to our class and kindly provided his personal overview of the proceedings. What he chose not to mention (or did not notice) were the open-top voting booths on the floor below and the tough-looking guys in the balcony who used binoculars apparently to monitor how delegates voted. They were probably connected to the Lake County political machine run by Metro M. Holovachka, a tough-minded boss who tolerated no dissent among his northwest Indiana operatives.

16. During a remarkable career trajectory, Emmons oversaw the Fort Wayne and Wabash Valley and then the Chicago, South Bend and Northern Indiana. He left Indiana in 1919 for Baltimore, then headed the Hudson and Manhattan Railroad, William G. McAdoo's triumph of engineering that ran beneath the Hudson River to connect New York City with Newark and Hoboken, New Jersey.

17. Jerry Marlette, *Interstate: A History of Interstate Public Service Rail Operations* (Polo, IL: Transportation Trails, 1990).

18. *Electric Railway Journal* (November 1912): 1054–56.

19. If interurban tracks had followed a less direct route between Evansville and Indianapolis, the trains might have served Vincennes, which had a population of 14,895 in 1910.

20. *Electric Railway Journal* (November 1913): 1120. While compiling a 1924 list of paper interurbans, Glen A. Blackburn received a letter informing him that the New Albany and French Lick Valley Interurban Railroad Company still possessed a valid charter and hoped to complete its line. See Glen A. Blackburn, "Interurban Railroads of Indiana," *Indiana Magazine of History* 20 (December 1924): 457.

21. George K. Bradley, *Northern Indiana Railway* (Chicago: Central Electric Railfans' Association, 1998) and William D. Middleton, *South Shore: The Last Interurban*, rev. 2d ed. (Bloomington: Indiana University Press, 1999).

22. *Chicago Tribune*, as quoted in the *Indianapolis Star*, April 9, 1908.

23. In 1909, a newly incorporated enterprise, the Indiana Northwestern Traction Company, promised to extend tracks from Lafayette to Hammond in Lake County and thus bridge the most obvious gap remaining in the state's interurban network. As was typical for most projects proposed at this late date, nothing more substantial than a paper trail resulted from this projected line to the Chicago area. *Times* (Munster, IN), September 4, 1909. Providing a convenient and heavily illustrated overview of the interurbans of northern Indiana is *Electric Railways of Indiana, Part II, Bulletin 102* (Chicago: Central Electric Railfans' Association, 1959).

24. Jerry Marlette, *Terre Haute, Indianapolis and Eastern Traction Company* (Indianapolis: Dog Ear, 2011).

25. See Marlette, *Interstate*.

26. *Street Railway Journal* (April 1903): 609.

27. See Glen A. Blackburn, "Interurban Railroads of Indiana," *Indiana Magazine of History* 20 (September 1924): 221–79, and Glen A. Blackburn, "Interurban Railroads of Indiana," *Indiana Magazine of History* 20 (December 1924): 400–64. The list of companies that Blackburn labels "failures" includes more than one hundred and twenty individual paper interurbans.

28. *Street Railway Journal* (July 1903): 81; *Electric Traction* (June 1917): 418–19.

29. Muncie *Star Press*, October 29, 1906. This interurban rumor featured added speculation about the attempt of McCulloch, Brady, and Ball (all three men related by marriage) to persuade the Maxwell Motor Company to build an automobile plant in Muncie. Even in the rumor mill, the interurban and automobile were often linked and news of either one could produce a frisson of excitement among Hoosiers.

30. Charles N. Wilson, "Why Forty-Nine Projected Electric Roads Fail and the Fiftieth Succeeds," *Interurban Railway Journal* (October 1906): 228–29.

31. *Crawfordsville Journal*, as quoted in the *South Bend Tribune*, April 29, 1907.

32. *South Bend Tribune*, May 13, 1905.

33. Thomas R. Bullard and William M. Shapotkin, *Faster Than the Limiteds: The Story of the Chicago–New York Electric Air Line Railroad and Its Transformation into Gary Railways* (Chicago: Central Electric Railfans' Association, 2004). The Murdock Syndicate in 1908 apparently considered extending the tracks of its Chicago, South Bend and Northern Indiana Railway into Chicago by acquiring the troubled Chicago–New York Electric Air Line Railroad, which to date had completed its line only from LaPorte to Gary, a distance of twenty-one miles. From Gary, the Murdocks could have continued west into the Windy City, but nothing resulted from this rumored idea. *Electric Traction Weekly* (November 1908): 1222.

34. Adams died in 1898, and nothing ever resulted from his idea of a Chicago-Saint Louis interurban line. What made the sleek 1892 train designs of Wellington Adams so unusual is that streamlining as a concept had not yet been popularized. See Robert C. Reed, *The Streamline Era* (San Marino, CA: Golden West, 1975).

8. Growing Traffic, Going the Distance

1. Joining the ranks of electric railway publications during this time of boundless enthusiasm was the *Interurban Railway Journal*, an Indianapolis-based weekly that first appeared in November 1905. Perhaps its range of interests was too narrow or its geographical orientation too confining, because a year later, new owners acquired the publication and renamed it *Electric Traction Weekly*. With the industry's waning interest in new projects, the journal adopted a monthly format in 1911. Nonetheless, *Electric Traction* remained a lively source of industry news for another two decades.

2. Jerry Marlette, *Indianapolis Railways, A Complete History of the Company and Its Predecessors from 1864 to 1957* (Terra Alta, WV: Pioneer Press of West Virginia, 2002).

3. The historic West Baden Springs Hotel was renovated in 2007 after years of neglect, and its atrium is once again a wonder to behold.

4. *AERA* launched publication with its August 1912 issue. A primary purpose of the publication, stated Brady, was to promote "friendly relations" with the public in order to overcome its "hostility" to electric railways, which was having an increasingly negative impact on the industry's finances. Another purpose was to foster the exchange of information among electric railway personnel by means of its monthly "Question Box." The first issue posed no fewer than fourteen questions for members to discuss in subsequent issues. One of these questions was: "Are motor propelled vehicles for emergency and construction wagons better than horse-drawn vehicles? Give reasons." Only recently, for the first time, the association had set

up a permanent office in New York City. Monthly publication of the *AERA* continued at least through early 1933, the same year, coincidentally, that Brady died.

5. *Electric Railway Journal* (September 1911): 395–96. The formal name of the Ben Hur Route was the Indianapolis, Crawfordsville and Western, a ninety-mile-long interurban that became part of the Terre Haute, Indianapolis and Eastern. The nickname honored General Lewis Wallace of Crawfordsville, the author of a bestselling novel published in 1880 and titled "Ben Hur: A Tale of the Christ."

6. *Electric Railway Journal* published a detailed description of Illinois Traction's general manager's car: (January 1910): 188–89. Constructed by the American Car and Foundry Company, it served as a mobile office for Chubbuck, who in addition to running the interurban system oversaw the thirty public utilities that William B. McKinley had acquired in cities along his 225 miles of electric railway track as well as in more distant locations outside Illinois. The office car included an office, kitchen, and sleeping quarters.

7. *Lima Times-Democrat*, February 22, 1906, and *Richmond Item*, March 3, 1906.

8. George H. Gibson, *High-Speed Electric Interurban Railways* (Washington, DC: Government Printing Office, 1904).

9. *Bradstreet's* (February 1906): 78: "There are farsighted electric railway men who believe the day is not far distant when there will be [a] continuous trolley connection between Portland, Me., and Portland, Ore., perhaps not by a direct route, but continuous."

10. Jason Emerson, *Giant in the Shadows: The Life of Robert T. Lincoln* (Carbondale: Southern Illinois University Press, 2012). On Pullman cars and operations, see Peter T. Maiken, *Night Trains: The Pullman System in the Golden Years of American Rail Travel* (Chicago: Lakme, 1989); August Mencken, *The Railroad Passenger Car: An Illustrated History of the First Hundred Years with Accounts by Contemporary Passengers* (Baltimore: Johns Hopkins University Press, 1957); and John H. White Jr., *The American Railroad Passenger Car* (Baltimore: Johns Hopkins University Press, 1978).

11. *Indianapolis News*, January 26, 1903. Holland built two cars named "Theodore" and "Francis." A low bridge in Richmond thwarted Holland's plans for Indiana service.

12. *Electric Traction Weekly* (September 1907): 909.

13. *Electric Traction Weekly*. When Holland died in the late 1930s, he was employed as a traveling salesman. Illinois Traction acquired one of the original Holland sleeping cars.

14. *Electric Traction* (February 1922): 110–11. This issue of *Electric Traction* also contains an excellent overview of Union Traction's "profitable freight traffic" on 109–12. One interurban pioneer much opposed to carrying freight was Will Irwin, who in 1912 did not wish to haul through cargo between Louisville and Indianapolis on his segment of the newly formed Interstate Public Service line. When asked, "You love the passenger business more than the freight, Mr. Irwin?" His curt response was, "That's where our profits come from." *Republic* (Columbus, IN), December 4, 1912.

15. *Palladium-Item* (Richmond), February 27, 1907.

16. *Indianapolis Star*, April 23, 1907. When Henry spoke to the tax commissioners in 1907, he addressed a mistake made by the industry as a whole. He quickly added that his Rushville line was "probably the first" of Indiana's many interurban lines to be constructed on a more substantial basis than was typical for the state's electric railways. He seems to have forgotten that seven years earlier, when he was general manager of Union Traction, he had constructed a

substantial line between Anderson and Indianapolis that used a dedicated right-of-way typical of a steam railroad.

17. *Daily Republican* (Rushville), November 22, 1912.

18. While many interurban companies originated as rural trolley lines that reached ever farther into the surrounding countryside from a city hub, that was not always the case. Turn-of-the-century Indianapolis was *the* destination for three separate interurban lines that in 1900 and 1901 extended their tracks *into* the capital city from Greenwood, Greenfield, and Anderson.

19. *Street Railway Review* (August 1901): 464.

20. Indianapolis Chamber of Commerce, *Activities*, June 1925, p 7.

21. *Indianapolis News*, January 29, 1901.

22. Among those present at the 1901 face-off was a representative of the almighty Pennsylvania Railroad, an extremely powerful presence in Indiana at that time, but he observed the vigorous exchange in silence. *Indianapolis News*, January 29, 1901.

23. *Indianapolis News*, May 25, 1903.

24. *Street Railway Review* (January 1899): 1. William D. Middleton provides an in-depth look at interurban freight in *Traction Classics, Volume 3: The Interurbans, Interurban Freight* (San Marino, CA: Golden West, 1985).

25. Robert G. Athearn, *Westward the Briton* (1953; repr., 1962, Lincoln: University of Nebraska Press), 95–96.

26. *Electric Railway Journal* (January 1914): 8–9. In fact, the industry never escaped the "curse" imposed by its origins as the outgrowth of hundreds of scattered street railways. As late as 1923 and well past the industry's peak years, the trade journal *Electric Traction* still urged individual companies to consolidate and fill the remaining short gaps to reinvent the industry as a freight hauler of significance. When it listed obstacles to overcome, they were essentially the same ones that had existed twenty years earlier; namely, "lack of standardization in rolling stock and track. Some interurban systems have heavy rolling stock with suitable roadbed and bridges, but unfortunately may have a logical connection with other systems which have sharp curves, heavy grades, lighter roadbed, and bridges not strong enough to support safely heavy equipment." *Electric Traction* (May 1922): 409.

27. To be precise, through cars between Indianapolis and Fort Wayne used the tracks of Union Traction as far north as Bluffton, where they switched to those of a sister company, the Fort Wayne and Northern Indiana, for the remainder of their journey. Brady composed a retrospective essay on Indiana interurban developments during 1910 that was published in the *Indianapolis Star*, January 2, 1911, and soon disseminated to an industry-wide audience when republished by the *Electric Railway Journal*.

28. Robert F. Bruner and Sean D. Carr, *The Panic of 1907: Lessons Learned from the Market's Perfect Storm* (Hoboken, NJ: John Wiley & Sons, 1907).

29. *Electric Railway Journal* (January 1910): 40–41 and (May 1910): 908; *Electric Traction Weekly* (February 1910): 196. Offering a detailed account of Utica's promotional meander along the electric lines of the Midwest is Larry Plachno, *The Longest Interurban Charter* (Polo, IL: Transportation Trails, 1988).

30. Albert Bigelow Paine, "By Trolley from New York to Chicago," *World's Work* (September 1902): 2553–61.

31. Paine, "By Trolley from New York to Chicago," 2560.

32. J. S. Moulton, "New York to Chicago by Electric Railway," *Electric Railway Journal* (August 1909): 321.

33. *Herald* (Jasper, IN), March 1, 1907.

34. *Electric Railway Review* (November 1907): 838.

35. *Champaign Daily Gazette* (IL), May 3, 1906.

36. *Electric Railway Review* (October 26, 1907): 714.

37. *Electric Railway Review* (October 26, 1907): 714; *Champaign Daily Gazette* (IL), June 28, 1912.

38. The two steam railroads and the number of trains they operated both ways between Saint Louis and Indianapolis in late 1905 are as follows: Big Four (fourteen) and Pennsylvania (fourteen). The Big Four's Peoria and Eastern subsidiary operated a total of six trains between Peoria and Indianapolis each day.

9. Travel by Interurban

1. Charles M. Swift, "Suburban Railways and Their Possibilities," *Street Railway Review* (January 1895): 46.

2. *Indianapolis Star*, September 13, 1904. A portrait of Riley by John Singer Sargent had been on public display in Indianapolis the previous spring before being sent to the Saint Louis World's Fair to form part of an educational exhibit. *Palladium-Item* (Richmond), April 25, 1904. The bestselling author would have been fifty-four when the Traction Terminal opened. Though born in Greenfield in 1849 (the same year as Charles L. Henry was born on a nearby farm), he moved to Indiana's largest city in 1879 to become a writer for the *Indianapolis Journal*, and he lived there until his death in 1916. When Riley first wrote for the *Journal*, it enjoyed a large readership, but it had many competitors and had grown old and weary by the time Henry purchased it in 1903.

3. *Indianapolis Star*, September 15, 1904. The first inbound car arrived from Plainfield the night of September 11 and brought thirty passengers to the capital city. *Indianapolis Star*, September 12, 1904.

4. *Indianapolis Star*, September 18, 1904.

5. *Electric Traction Weekly* (September 1907): 909.

6. F. D. Norviel, "Parks That Pay," *Electric Traction* (April 1920): 241–42. Other noteworthy trolley and interurban parks in Indiana included Springbrook, operated by the Chicago, South Bend and Northern Indiana Railway, and Blue River Park on the Indianapolis and Cincinnati line near Morristown.

7. *Electric Railway Journal* (April 1920): 243–46. The Winona Interurban Railroad generated considerable income from trolley traffic to and from Winona Lake two miles east of Warsaw. The lakeside resort was the site of four enormous hotels and hundreds of boarding and rooming houses and lakeside cottages. Summer visitors to Winona Lake might number as many as twenty-five thousand per day. Some people made the journey simply for the pleasure it afforded, while others attended one of Billy Sunday's Christian camp meeting revivals or sought mental stimulus from the Chautauqua lectures held in an auditorium that seated eight thousand people.

8. Some Hoosiers contend that Dr. R. C. Light, originator of the Broad Ripple line, deserves to be called the "father of the interurban." They thus proposed a third claimant to that title in addition to Charles L. Henry and Noah J. Clodfelter.

9. Jerry Marlette, *Indianapolis Railways: A Complete History of the Company and Its Predecessors from 1864 to 1957* (Terra Alta: Pioneer Press of West Virginia, 2002).

10. The Belt Railway functioned as an important common link among the several steam railroads serving Indianapolis. See Jeffrey Darbee, *Indianapolis Union and Belt Railroads* (Bloomington: Indiana University Press, 2017). During the summer of 1966, when I followed Kentucky Avenue south on my way to work at the Eli Lilly warehouse, the passing trains never made me late because during the second decade of the twentieth century, the tracks, including those that still passed through nearby Union Station, had all been elevated well above ground level.

11. Christopher Rund, Fred W. Frailey, and Eric Powell, *The Indiana Rail Road Company* (Bloomington: Indiana University Press, 2012, rev. and expanded ed.). The line under construction would have been the Indiana Southern Railway, later part of the Illinois Central branch into Indianapolis, and still later the main line of The Indiana Rail Road founded in 1986 by Thomas G. Hoback.

12. I am indebted to Kathy Mulder of the Indiana Historical Society for calling the Clemens Mueller diary to my attention. The full text of this remarkable document is easily accessible online at the IHS website. Its author seems to have had a special interest in railroads and trains. Kurt Vonnegut Jr., the acclaimed author of *Slaughterhouse-Five*, fourteen novels, and numerous other literary works, was born in 1922 and died eight-four years later as the result of a fall on the steps of his Manhattan brownstone.

13. *Coffeyville Weekly Journal* (KS), September 13, 1907.

14. *Richmond Item*, October 8, 1903.

15. Raymond [W. Patterson], "Comfort Rules Trolley Travel," *Chicago Tribune*, September 11, 1907; *Indianapolis Sun*, September 10, 1907.

16. *Electric Traction Weekly* (October 1910): 1293.

17. *Electric Traction* (December 1924): 581.

18. A fine account of the best in interurban passenger service is William D. Middleton, *Traction Classics, Volume 2: The Interurbans, Extra Fast and Extra Fare* (San Marino, CA: Golden West, 1985). See chapter 8 for his account of "The Holland Interurban Sleeping Car."

19. *AERA* (August 1923): 37.

20. *Electric Traction Weekly* (December 1907): 1400.

21. Elliott Flower, "Indianapolis Hub in Trolley World," *Chicago Tribune*, March 31, 1908.

22. A transcontinental journey by air evoked the same kind of magic in early travelers. See Daniel L. Rust, *Flying Across America: The Airline Passenger Experience* (Norman: University of Oklahoma Press, 2009).

23. J. C. Carmichael, "What Interurban Railroads Are Doing for Cities in the East," *Tri-Weekly Courier* (Ottumwa, IA), July 9, 1910. Carmichael was one of several investigators regularly dispatched by newspapers around the United States to report on Indiana's always newsworthy interurban railways.

10. A Time for Sober Reflection

1. As quoted in *Electric Railway Journal* (November 1910): 1061.

2. J. H. Pardee, "The Tendency of the Times," *Electric Traction* (December 1912): 1173–74, and *Progressive Age* (August 1908): 484.

3. *Street Railway Review* (January 1906): 49. The banquet closed with a toast to "the peaceful rest of the Indiana Electric Railway Association and to the future success of the Central Electric Railway Association." Leaders of the CERA confidently expected to add neighboring states to their ranks, which soon included both Kentucky and Michigan, but Illinois traction interests hung back for several years.

4. The nickname "Honey Bee Line" is supposed to have derived from the interurban's arrow-straight right-of-way between Indianapolis and New Castle, but it may also have represented a clever play on words and geographical proximity. Between Indianapolis and New Castle, its tracks ran alongside the Big Four's Peoria and Eastern subsidiary, while a few miles farther north ran the Big Four's main line between Cleveland and Indianapolis, a stretch of track nicknamed in earlier years the "Bee Line." See Arthur Andrew Olson III, *Forging the Bee Line Railroad, 1848–1889: The Rise and Fall of the Hoosier Partisans and Cleveland Clique* (Kent, OH: Kent State University, 2017).

5. The intent of promoters of the Honey Bee line was mainly to make money. They were not captivated by interurbans in the same way as Charles L. Henry. Foremost among the project's backers was David Maclean Parry, who made his name as an Indianapolis automobile manufacturer, and Charles S. Hernley of New Castle, who was also a promoter and builder of the local auto industry. Milton Rubincam, "David M. Parry," *Indiana Magazine of History* (June 1938): 165–74.

6. *Indianapolis Star*, January 6, 1932.

7. *Indianapolis Star*, January 2, 1910. Both motormen remained at their controls and thus experienced the full impact of the collision. Over the years, the name of today's community of New Castle, Indiana, was occasionally spelled as a single word.

8. It is difficult, if not impossible, to cite precise statistics for Indiana interurbans. Some "official" tallies of mileage lumped together the state's street railways and interurban lines. Individual companies underwent frequent changes of name. The Greenfield Line, for example, originated as the Indianapolis and Greenfield Rapid Transit and ended its days as a segment of the Indiana Railroad. Along the way it had become the Indianapolis and Eastern and then the Terre Haute, Indianapolis and Eastern.

9. *Fort Wayne Journal-Gazette*, September 27, 1906. Representatives from Michigan interurban lines also attended the Fort Wayne gathering, but they only watched as Hoosiers battled Buckeyes on the baseball diamond in a game that ended inconclusively.

10. *Elwood Daily Record*, April 29, 1904.

11. *Electric Railway Journal* (October 1910): 866–67.

12. Larry W. Owen, *The Kingsland Wreck, A Memorial* ([Bluffton?]: Larry Owen, 2011).

13. *Electric Railway Journal* (October 1910): 867.

14. One victim of the Kingsland tragedy was motorman Benjamin Corkwell, whose carelessness caused the accident. Though apparently unhurt, the enormity of the loss of life caused him

to lose his sanity and be committed to a state mental hospital in Richmond. Even after his later release, the remainder of his life was marked by one personal disappointment after another.

15. After Vice President Marshall returned home to Indiana following eight years in Washington, DC, he composed an autobiography that is informative and sprinkled with numerous examples of his homespun humor. Thomas R. Marshall, *A Hoosier Salad: Recollections of Thomas R. Marshall, Vice President and Hoosier Philosopher* (Indianapolis: Bobbs-Merrill, 1925).

16. Booth Tarkington, *The Turmoil, A Novel* (New York: Grosset & Dunlap, 1915), 4-5. Young Tarkington won election to the Indiana House of Representatives in 1902, and his comments were no doubt based on personal observations. *Indianapolis News*, February 21, 1903.

17. Gaylord Thompson, "Interurbans—Retrospective and Prospective," *Electric Traction* (December 1912): 1168–69.

18. *Star Press* (Muncie), April 29, 1911; *Indianapolis Star*, April 29, 1911.

19. *New York Times*, December 20 and 21, 1911; *New York Globe*, as quoted in the *Sioux City Journal*, December 25, 1911.

20. *Times* (Munster, IN), September 4, 1909.

21. *Times* (Munster, IN), January 17 and 24, 1911. At various times, Purtelle claimed he would add Crawfordsville and Logansport to his proposed interurban line to Chicago, a ploy that no doubt enlarged his pool of bond and stock purchasers. The two best sources for ongoing news of Purtelle's investment frauds are the *Times* of Munster and the *Item* of Richmond.

22. *Muncie Evening Press*, October 3, 1911. During the week before the industry's October 1911 convention in Atlantic City, Arthur Brady spent several days in Muncie to prepare his presidential address. The *Muncie Evening Press* exuded hometown pride when it headlined its news account: "I. U. T. Man Will Preside Over Important National Convention of Trolley Men."

11. Jitney, The Emergence of a Disruptive Technology

1. *Electric Railway Journal* (November 1914): 1222.

2. Thomas Conway Jr., "The Decreasing Financial Returns upon Urban Street Railway Properties," *Annals of the American Academy of Political and Social Science* 37 (January 1911): 14–30, and *Electric Railway Journal* (January 1911): 20. My personal selection of the year 1913 as the apogee of the Interurban Era is reinforced by the assessments of those who witnessed the decline firsthand. "Electric interurban lines have been 'on the slide' in Indiana since about 1913 and are generally doomed sooner or later with the possible exception of the Chicago South Shore, which now serves the populous lake shore area of Northern Indiana." *Tri-County Banner* (Knightstown), July 3, 1931.

3. *Angola Herald* (IN), September 20, 1911.

4. *Commercial Vehicle*, March 1, 1915, 12. For detailed accounts of the jitney phenomenon and its impact on electric railways, see Ross D. Eckert and George W. Hilton, "The Jitneys," *Journal of Law and Economics* (October 1972): 293–325, and Carlos A. Schwantes, "The West Adapts the Automobile: Technology, Unemployment, and the Jitney Phenomenon of 1914–1917, *Western Historical Quarterly* (July 1985): 307–26.

5. Jane Dixon, "Jitneys Rise in Popularity." *Jitney Bus* (April 1915): 19. This was the first issue of a Kansas City publication that served as the authoritative voice of jitney operators.

6. The word "jitney" as slang for a nickel appeared in a hobo glossary that the *Indianapolis News* featured on October 7, 1913, after an interview with Jeff Davis, the self-styled international president of the "Hobos' Union," as he was passing through town. When an Oakland, California, savings bank sponsored a contest to discover the word's origin, it received scores of suggestions, all of which were discounted by language experts at the University of California, Berkeley. Its origin remains an etymological riddle, but its widespread use as street slang before the first jitney in 1914 is undisputed.

7. *Alexandria Times-Tribune* (IN), October 4, 1915. Members of the Central Electric Railway Association addressed the topic of automobile competition at their conference in November 1915: "This is not the first time such a subject has come before transportation interests, but the fact that the 150 members of the central association, representing Indiana, Illinois, Kentucky, Ohio, Michigan and western Pennsylvania, undertook to solve some of the problems indicates how far the competition has developed. One need only consult the license statistics to discover the cause traction men have for alarm. The automobile industry is flourishing as never before." *Indianapolis News*, November 19, 1915.

8. *Electric Railway Journal (Annual Convention Issue)* (September 1915): 473.

9. *Electric Railway Journal* (December 1914): 1243.

10. *Public Utility* (July 1918): 132.

11. Sydney Strong, "A Nickel a Ride—When the Jitney Comes to Town," *Survey* (March 13, 1915): 647.

12. Some other titles of this sort of sheet music include "Gasoline Gus and His Jitney Bus" and "All Aboard for That Old Jitney Ride." One piece of music simply titled "The Jitney Bus" featured a picture of actor Charlie Chaplin on its cover. He was the star of a 1917 silent film called "A Jitney Elopement."

13. F. W. Doolittle, "The Economics of Jitney Bus Operation," *Journal of Political Economy* (July 1915): 668, and *Oregon Voter* (May 1915): 98. Despite a title that suggests a local orientation, the *Oregon Voter* compiled popular assessments of the jitney from all over North America.

14. Conway, "Decreasing Financial Returns," 14–30. Conway's doctoral dissertation was on electric railways, and following its completion, he taught at the University of Pennsylvania's Wharton School of Finance and Commerce until he left academia to run several different interurban properties. He was undoubtedly the industry's most highly educated leader. Worth noting, perhaps, is that among the Philadelphia university's wealthiest trustees during Conway's academic years was electric railway mogul Randal Morgan.

15. *Rushville Republican*, July 13, 1915. Some Indianapolis merchandisers advertised "Jitney Sales," forerunners, perhaps, of the once-popular five-and-ten-cent stores. One of the city's venues that featured inexpensive mass entertainment called itself a "jitney theater."

16. *Washington Herald*, May 13, 1912; *Electric Railway Journal* (May 1912): 719.

17. *Electric Railway Journal* (October 1921): 571.

18. Mark Wilcox, "California Capitalizes on the Jitney," *Illustrated World* (July 1918): 733–34, 736.

19. Jerry Marlette, *Electric Railroads of Indiana* (Indianapolis: Council for Local History, 1959), 105–106; Elmer G. Sulzer, *Ghost Railroads of Indiana* (1970; repr., Bloomington: Indiana University Press, 1998), 127–44. Sulzer provides a profusely illustrated summary of the

complex history of the Valley Line, which at various times called itself a "Traction Company" and a "Railway."

20. One thing that never ceased to amaze me as I researched this book was the web of connections that bound Indiana entrepreneurs together. William Riley McKeen Jr. was the Hoosier son of the longtime head of the Vandalia Railroad, the Pennsylvania subsidiary that linked Indianapolis with Saint Louis. Young McKeen married Elizabeth Marie New, daughter of John Chalfant New (1831–1906), publisher for twenty-three years of the *Indianapolis Journal*, the staunchly Republican newspaper that Charles L. Henry purchased from the New family in 1903. New served as chairman of the Republican Party in Indiana and had played a major role in getting Indianapolis resident Benjamin Harrison elected president of the United States. New's son, Harry, served as chairman of the Republican National Committee and also as a US senator from Indiana.

21. *Electric Traction Weekly* (July 1909): 703. A beautiful example of McKeen's car-building skills is preserved at the Nevada State Railroad Museum. See George A. Forero Jr., "Virginia & Truckee McKeen Motor Car No. 22," *Railroad History* (Fall–Winter 1921): 78–87.

22. *Hancock Democrat*, April 6, 1911, described the project as a "modern Phoenix" because after a long pause it seemed to reappear from the state's well-populated graveyard of paper interurbans, but the "phoenix" had no substance to it. The idea was clever, nonetheless, because interurbans would in this way have avoided downtown congestion as well as the restrictions Indianapolis imposed on freight traffic using city streets.

23. *Fort Wayne Weekly Sentinel*, March 1, 1916.

24. Conway, "Decreasing Financial Returns," 14–30.

25. *Electric Traction* (April 1917): 288.

26. Canada had joined the Great War along with Great Britain in August 1914, and so the wartime experience of its electric railways offered some guidance to those of the United States as they faced all kinds of unfamiliar and unprecedented demands after the nation declared war in April 1917.

27. Carl I. Palm, "Observations on the Park Situation," *Electric Traction* (April 1918): 185–86; Arthur C. Carty, "Summer Parks and Patriotism in Canada," *Electric Traction* (May 1918): 237–42; John A. Murkin, "Parks and Duties They Can Perform," *Electric Traction* (April 1918): 187. "All things considered this season should be one of the most important in the history of our park," insisted the editor of *Electric Traction* (April 1918): 204.

28. *Electric Traction* (August 1918): 484.

29. *Railway Review* (January 1918): 102.

12. Losing Traction, Rising Highway Competition

1. Edmond Taylor, *The Fall of the Dynasties: The Collapse of the Old Order, 1905–1922* (Garden City, NY: Doubleday, 1963).

2. *Electric Railway Journal* (February 1919): 251.

3. *Electric Railway Journal* (September 1920): 487.

4. Arthur W. Brady, "The Needs of the Interurban," *AERA* (November 1918): 333–35. Brady once said that among his great loves was reading the history of the law. His embrace of history was more than an idle pastime. After he retired from Union Traction in 1930, he served as

president of the Delaware County Historical Society in Muncie. Fascinated by Native American history, he compiled a huge cache of documents regarding the work of Moravian missionaries among the Indians of Indiana and paid for their translation into English. Lawrence Henry Gipson edited the volume of nearly seven hundred pages, which he dedicated to "the late Arthur W. Brady." Gipson had been a professor of history and political science at Wabash College from 1911 to 1924 and was familiar with the subject. Lawrence Henry Gipson, ed., *The Moravian Indian Mission on White River* (Indianapolis: Indiana Historical Bureau, 1938). Brady's interest in the prehistory of Indiana also led him to preserve Indian mounds along the banks of the White River, an area that later became a state park.

5. Brady, "Needs of the Interurban": 334.

6. *Electric Traction* (July 1919): 418.

7. *Electric Traction* (July 1919): 438.

8. *Electric Traction* (July 1919): 416–18.

9. *Proceedings of the Federal Electric Railways Commission*, 3 vols. (Washington, DC, Government Printing Office 1920): 696–729.

10. To leave no possibility unexamined, the commission compiled three lengthy questionnaires that it sent to public officials and others involved with electric railways around the United States. It must have been a nearly impossible challenge for busy recipients to provide meaningful responses, which were at best summarized in the polished report of 2,349 pages forwarded to President Wilson in mid-1920.

11. Margaret MacMillan, *Paris 1919: Six Months That Changed the World* (New York: Random House, 2001) and Gene Smith, *When the Cheering Stopped: The Last Years of Woodrow Wilson* (New York: William Morrow, 1964).

12. Here are two examples of the fifteen interurban-specific questions published on p. 2,257 of the report sent to the White House: "120. Compare the service of interurban lines with the service rendered by automobiles and auto trucks. 121. Does such an interurban line have to meet automobile competition and if so to what extent, both in passenger and freight?" Either of these two open-ended questions was worthy of a multipage essay, a task many busy recipients found impossible because of the time required to provide a detailed answer.

13. John W. Colton, "Indianapolis, the Nation's Great Electric Freight Center," *AERA* (November 1924): 581–95.

14. *Daily Reporter* (Greenfield), July 31, 1920. The same story appeared in newspapers around Indiana, but with the location changed as appropriate to the place of publication.

15. *Electric Traction* (August 1919): 483.

13. Deadly Delusion: The Comeback That Never Was

1. *Indianapolis Star*, February 2, 1922.

2. C. D. Emmons, "Electric Railways Keep Faith," *AERA* (March 1923): 891–97.

3. Robert A. Butler, "Interurban Lines Are 'Coming Back' After Long Fight," *Indianapolis Star*, December 31, 1925. Butler insisted that "it is now the commonly expressed opinion that within a short time the electric railway lines [of Indiana] will be 'out of the woods.'" Despite his optimism, the author did note that between 1923 and 1924, the number of passengers using the Indianapolis Traction Terminal fell by almost 13 percent, and just during the first ten months

of 1925, the decline over 1924 was nearly 25 percent. "These figures indicate that interurban traffic was not only slipping, but slipping twice as fast each year." Butler ascribed this loss to the rising popularity of automobile and bus travel. Nonetheless, the increase in freight traffic moved by interurban lines supported the belief that the industry had at last turned a financial corner.

4. *Electric Railway Journal* (January 1920): 57.

5. *Electric Railway Journal* (March 1924): 385.

6. Harry Reid, "The Interurban After the War," *Electric Railway Journal* (November 1918): 956.

7. Harry Reid, "The Future of the Traction," *AERA* (February 1923): 747–48.

8. *Electric Traction* (January 1919): 58, and *Electric Railway Journal* (November 1923): 779. One writer asserted that the loss of miles was not particularly worrisome because the industry was overbuilt, but he nonetheless believed it was "certainly dead from its ears up" because out of some 850 electric railways operating in the United States and Canada, only seventeen companies had cared enough to apply for the prestigious Coffin Award intended to recognize outstanding achievement. The Chicago North Shore and Milwaukee was the first recipient.

9. *Electric Railway Journal* (March 1919): 497. The concept of a comeback was repeated so often by industry leaders and disseminated so widely by trade publications and daily newspapers from 1919 through 1924 that to cite all examples would result in one huge and unwieldy footnote. I have sought to capture the essence of the deadly delusion in the text of this chapter. An excellent summary of the buoyant thinking of the times is John T. Flynn, "Electric Railways Prospering," a syndicated essay that appeared in newspapers across the United States, including the *Indianapolis News*, November 29, 1924.

10. *Electric Railway Journal* (March 1920): 461.

11. James Grant, *The Forgotten Depression: 1921, The Crash That Cured Itself* (New York: Simon & Schuster, 2014). On wartime life in the United States and the postwar labor unrest, see David M. Kennedy, *Over Here: The First World War and American Society* (New York: Oxford University Press, 1980) and William E. Leuchtenburg, *The Perils of Prosperity, 1914–32* (Chicago: University of Chicago Press, 1958).

12. Reid, "Future of the Traction": 747–48; *Electric Traction* (August 1923): 436; Edmund J. Murphy, "Electric Railways Made Good Gains in 1922," *AERA* (April 1923): 1078–80; and John T. Flynn, "Electric Railways Prospering," *Indianapolis News*, November 29, 1924.

13. *Rushville Daily Republican*, November 22, 1912.

14. Bert Henley, "Traction Executive Sees Freight Traffic Increase," *Indianapolis Star*, July 27, 1923.

15. Traction Traveler, "Via Electric Traction," *Electric Traction* (December 1924): 580–81.

16. John W. Colton, "Indianapolis, the Nation's Great Electric Freight Center," *AERA* (November 1924): 581–95, and Joseph A. McGowan, "Interurbans Rendering Service of Incalculable Value," *AERA* (August 1924): 57.

17. The group that incorporated Union Traction on September 1, 1897, was composed of Charles L. Henry, James A. VanOsdol, Philip Matter, John L. Forkner, and Ellis C. Carpenter. Muncie's George McCulloch and his brother-in-law Arthur W. Brady would be part of the company's early history a few years later.

18. Dick Greene, "Our Neighborhood," *Star Press* (Muncie), January 19, 1948.

19. *Rushville Republican*, August 10, 1913.

20. It is worth noting that John F. Wild was a longtime member of Henry's board of directors, and so the prominent Indianapolis banker did not make the loan without firsthand knowledge of the considerable risk involved. Investments are always about perceptions of future prospects, and Wild seems to have believed that the interurban comeback was truly happening. In the end, the Indianapolis and Cincinnati Traction Company's failure to repay the loan may have helped to bankrupt Wild's bank, which Indiana regulators closed in mid-1927 and subsequently liquidated. The ostensible reason given for the abrupt closure of J. F. Wild and Company was the mysterious disappearance in 1926 of more than $100,000 worth of Liberty Bonds it had supposedly held.

21. *Indianapolis News*, April 22, 1907.

22. For details of how the industry's early localism impacted Cincinnati, see Bion J. Arnold, *Report on an Interurban Electric Railway Terminal System for the City of Cincinnati Submitted to the Cincinnati Interurban Rapid Transit Commission*, 1912. Arnold identified the city's hilly topography as a major contributor to the snarled web that defied repeated efforts to rationalize the city's electric railway lines.

23. How the times had changed! Back in 1907, Will Irwin wanted no part of dining car service on the soon-to-be-completed interurban connection between Indianapolis and Louisville—at least, none was welcome on his Indianapolis, Columbus and Southern portion of the three-company joint venture. He did not think it would become a paying investment. *Republic* (Columbus, IN), April 15, 1907.

24. Communities along the Interstate Public Service line between Indianapolis and Louisville with more than five thousand residents in 1920 are as follows: Columbus (8,990), Seymour (7,348), and New Albany (22,992).

25. *Rushville Republican*, May 22, 1924. The news account cited the changeover from the 3,300 volts alternating current system that once had been "the last word in efficient electric railway operation" to a 600 volts direct current one as being responsible for the noticeable improvement in the technology of the latter system during the intervening nineteen years. The numerous substations originally required to maintain the voltage along a direct-current railway were expensive to maintain as well as labor-intensive, but improvements that resulted in efficient and wholly automatic substations helped tip the scales in favor of direct current. In the obituary it published on May 3, 1927, the *Cincinnati Enquirer* reported that "Mr. Henry is said to have lost his fortune in his effort to build the proposed Indianapolis-Cincinnati line."

26. Apart from technical or financial considerations, Henry may have felt a personal but never publicly stated reason to switch to a lower-voltage system because his nephew, Ernest Shanklin, an employee in the Indianapolis and Cincinnati Traction Company shops in Rushville, was electrocuted in 1906 while working atop an interurban car. He accidentally brushed against one of the unforgiving high-voltage conduits that he had forgotten to shut off. *Rushville Republican*, August 13, 1906.

27. *Indianapolis News*, December 31, 1925. "New roads and bridges are transforming the state," the story continued. A quarter-century earlier, the same claim had been made for the electric interurban railways.

28. The Buffalo and Lake Erie Traction Company was ninety-two miles long and connected Erie, Pennsylvania, with Buffalo, New York. The company entered receivership in 1915. After

its near-death experience in 1920, it survived intact and continued running cars until late 1932 when it fell victim to the Great Depression.

29. *Electric Railway Journal* (July 1920): 160.

30. *Electric Traction* (December 1920): 949. Disagreements voiced in CERA meetings were rare, but when Charles L. Henry proposed that it hold only two gatherings a year, Harry A. Nichol of Union Traction pushed back and asserted that it needed more and not fewer meetings per annum. Henry's suggestion prevailed. At their 1921 meeting in Toledo, members engaged in an extended discussion of the future of the organization. At that time, the big question was whether it had any future. True to form, the widely acknowledged dean of the fifteen-year-old organization, the ever-optimistic Charles L. Henry, insisted that a bright future awaited the CERA because of the "splendid development" he anticipated in coming years that was certain to boost interurban freight, express, and passenger traffic. *Electric Railway Journal* (March 1921): 431–32, 446; *Electric Traction* (March 1921): 17.

31. *New Castle Daily Times*, as quoted in the *Tri-County Banner* (Knightstown), December 22, 1922.

32. *Indianapolis Star*, May 20, 1925. Mayor Samuel Lewis Shank used a floral three-foot-long key to formally open the building. Hiner's bus station was located at the intersection of Maryland and Senate Avenues on the site of the city's historic Haymarket.

33. Given the *Star*'s effusive praise of intercity buses, it might be well to remember that the newspaper had been founded two decades earlier by George McCulloch, the president of Union Traction. History is full of ironies.

34. *Indianapolis Star*, May 19, 1925, and December 31, 1925. Ward B. Hiner (1880–1948), a self-made entrepreneur, conceived the novel idea of a long-distance moving company in 1919. Based in Indianapolis, his Red Ball Transit was successful enough to lure him into the intercity bus business as well. He unsuccessfully sought to win Republican nominations for state legislator, governor, US senator, and mayor of Indianapolis. Always a colorful candidate, Hiner traveled about Indiana in a bus fitted with a portable organ to attract a crowd of listeners. Because of his personal experience with intercity buses, it is not surprising that one of his main proposals when running for public office was to abolish government regulation of business. *Indianapolis News*, December 24, 1924. The classic portrait of the decade and its abundance of wonderful nonsense is Frederick Lewis Allen, *Only Yesterday, An Informal History of the 1920s* (New York: Harper & Brothers, 1931).

35. *Indianapolis News*, July 7, 1925. The Big Four interurban presidents involved with the bus annex were Robert I. Todd of the Terre Haute, Indianapolis and Eastern, Arthur W. Brady of Union Traction, Charles L. Henry of the Indianapolis and Cincinnati Traction Company, and Harry Reid of the Interstate Public Service Company.

36. *Fort Wayne Journal Gazette*, as quoted in the *Indianapolis Star*, May 26, 1925; *Electric Railway Journal* (April 3, 1926): 566.

37. *Richmond Item*, February 12, 1926. Hiner's unbounded enthusiasm for bus transportation seems to mirror that of Noah Clodfelter, the peripatetic promoter of new interurban projects in the Gas Belt during the late 1890s.

38. *Times-Mail* (Bedford), July 26, 1927. Just in 1925, Union Traction lost nearly $36,000 on its bus venture, which nonetheless left the big interurban company with a gross annual income of $289,000. *Muncie Star-Press*, April 15, 1926.

39. For statistics on the growing number of automobiles ("pleasure cars"), see *Electric Traction* (October 1919): 694.

40. Arthur Andrew Olson III, *Forging the Bee Line Railroad, 1848–1889: The Rise and Fall of the Hoosier Partisans and Cleveland Clique* (Kent, OH: Kent State University Press, 2017).

41. During the days following the crash, every newspaper in Indiana followed the unfolding drama. The best ongoing coverage appeared in the *Indianapolis News*.

42. John A. Jakle and Keith A. Sculle, *Supplanting America's Railroads: The Early Auto Age, 1900–1940* (Knoxville: University of Tennessee Press, 2017).

43. *Indianapolis Star*, August 1, 1931.

44. *Franklin Evening Star*, as quoted in the *Republic* (Columbus, IN), May 8, 1940. One passenger who completed the "franchise run" only days before its dramatic end was Richard George, whose photos of the sunset days of central Indiana's interurbans appear in *First & Fastest* (Spring 2022): 24–33.

Conclusion

1. No verbatim copy of Loree's speech apparently exists, but the *St. Louis Post-Dispatch* (April 10, 1926) and electric railway publications quoted key portions of it. At the time, Loree was actively involved with three different Missouri-based railroads. He was chairman of the board of the Kansas City Southern and had become "a controlling influence" in the Missouri-Kansas-Texas and the Cotton Belt. The *Electric Railway Journal* pushed back mightily with a bold front-page headline on April 24, 1926, that read: "The $6,000,000,000 Won't Be Wiped Off the Books." The passage of time proved the *Journal* wrong and Loree right.

2. *Time*, May 3, 1926. The Delaware and Hudson Canal Company was chartered in 1823 as a canal company, but by the end of the decade, it had evolved into one of America's earliest railroads as well. Its Stourbridge Lion imported from England made an initial run on August 8, 1829, and thus became the first steam locomotive ever to burnish America's rails. Loree's quote comes from the *Electric Railway Journal* (April 1923): 710.

3. The historical record does not tell whether Henry's posthumous last ride was aboard the Union Traction's famous Martha, the deluxe office car delivered to the property in 1901 shortly after he had abruptly "retired."

4. After reading and then rereading all of the industry's trade journals, I came to a firm conclusion about the "father of the interurban" that I share with readers in the appendix.

5. *Greenfield Daily Reporter*, May 3, 1927, 1, 4.

6. *Noblesville Ledger*, May 3, 1927. The paper concluded its editorial with this sentence: "Indiana can not have too many men like Charlie Henry."

7. There is good reason to believe that George S. Henry was a far more dogmatic and less genial man than his popular father. In 1914, he was promoted to general manager of the Chicago and Milwaukee Electric Railroad (later renamed the Chicago North Shore and Milwaukee). After only a few months on the job, the company abruptly forced George to resign. It claimed that his heavy-handed management style had alienated the interurban's wealthy Gold Coast clientele as well as railway motormen and conductors, who threatened to walk off their jobs to protest the highly unpopular rule changes he imposed. Finally, it was claimed that Memorial Day receipts usually averaged $25,000, but with the interurban's new general manager

they had dropped to a mere $8,000 in 1915. The latter charge was probably unfair because at that time, jitney competition caused electric railway earnings to decline across the United States. *Chicago Tribune*, July 1, 1915.

8. Brady's first wife, Jane Ninde, was the musically talented daughter of an eminent Fort Wayne judge. She died after a long bout of typhoid fever. Following the Brady-McCulloch wedding in late 1901, the newlyweds departed Muncie aboard the Martha, the Union Traction's recently acquired showpiece car, for a then-secret destination. The honeymoon journey to the US South and the Caribbean launched aboard the Martha was McCulloch's appropriate send-off for his new brother-in-law, now a rising star among interurban luminaries of Indiana.

9. Both of the industry's leading trade journals published obituaries for Lewis W. Henry, but they only hint at the close relationship between father and son. *Electric Railway Journal* (December 1918): 1031, and *Electric Traction* (December 1918). Young Lewis, like his father, was educated at DePauw University, but he pursued additional studies at Swarthmore College and abroad in Germany. George, on the other hand, must have felt like the odd man out, because he quit the Indianapolis and Cincinnati Traction Company many years before death claimed his brother and father, and following his mismanagement debacle at the Chicago and Milwaukee Electric Railroad, he seems to have disappeared completely.

10. *Electric Railway Journal* (February 1925): 275.

11. The Trailways network, a brand licensing agreement among several dozen independent bus lines across the United States, originated in 1936 with the merger of bus subsidiaries created by three major railroads (Atchison, Topeka and Santa Fe; Chicago, Burlington and Quincy; and Missouri Pacific) and two nonrail companies. The Santa Fe had earlier created a bus subsidiary called Santa Fe Trails Transportation Company, and that enterprise became the basis for the Trailways name.

12. *Indianapolis Star*, July 17, 1929. In a story the *Star* proudly headlined "Hoosier Managing Director of Electric Railway Group," the newspaper wrote, "Walks up and down an interurban right of way while paying passengers whiz by on the cars do not often breed a love for railroads in the luckless pedestrian, but an exception has been found." Gordon, incidentally, was an active member of the Presidents' Conference Committee (PCC) that developed the famous eponymous streetcar in the 1930s, refurbished models of which are still plying the streets of San Francisco in 2023. See Stephen P. Carlson and Fred W. Schneider III, *PCC, The Car That Fought Back* (Glendale, CA, Interurban, 1980).

13. *Electric Railway Journal* (January 1925): 79.

14. Although interurban industry publications reveal little of Brady's personal life, he appears to have had a keen interest in history and literature, something strongly suggested by his involvement with his fellow lawyers in Indiana. For years, the Indiana State Bar Association published an annual volume containing the proceedings of that year's meeting along with special presentations and papers. The 1905 publication contained three special papers, including one by Brady titled "Some Phases of Historical Jurisprudence." Incidentally, appearing in the same scholarly volume was a paper titled "The Lawyer's Conscience" by future Indiana governor and vice president of the United States, Thomas R. Marshall. Obviously, the two attorneys knew one another long before Marshall summoned Brady and his peers to the Indiana capitol in late 1910 to discuss the recent spate of fatal interurban accidents. Leander J. Monks, ed.,

Courts and Lawyers of Indiana, vol. 2 (Indianapolis: Federal Publishing, 1916), 468. Six years earlier, Brady had offered a toast at an Indiana Bar gathering titled "Lawyers and Literature."

15. Arthur W. Brady, "The Central Electric Railway Association and the Interurbans," *Electric Railway Journal* (January 1914): 8–9. Having served a term earlier as president of the American Electric Railway Association, Brady was president of the Central Electric Railway Association for a second time in 1914.

16. Brady, "Central Electric Railway Association."

17. Two books that document government mishandling of America's steam railroads during the so-called Progressive Era are Albro Martin, *Enterprise Denied: Origins of the Decline of American Railroads, 1897–1917* (New York: Columbia University Press, 1971) and Robert E. Gallamore and John R. Meyer, *American Railroads: Decline and Renaissance in the Twentieth Century* (Cambridge, MA: Harvard University Press, 2014). Placing the interurban's losing battle with the automobile in a broad historical context is Stephen B. Goddard, *Getting There: The Epic Struggle between Road and Rail in the American Century* (1994; repr., Chicago: University of Chicago Press, 1996). See also Mark S. Foster, *From Streetcar to Superhighway: American City Planners and Urban Transportation, 1900–1940* (Philadelphia: Temple University Press, 1981).

18. *Muncie Star Press*, January 6, 1934.

Appendix

1. Carl Hering, *Electric Railroads* (New York: W. J. Johnston, 1892), 247ff.

2. A real estate advertisement for a development called St. Anthony Park North described a "magnificent tract of land" as occupying "the interurban territory between St. Paul and Minneapolis." *Saint Paul Globe*, May 16, 1886.

3. Examples abound in the *Minneapolis Tribune* and the *St. Paul Globe*.

4. *Minneapolis Tribune*, December 12, 1890. Early on, the word "interurban" was also used to describe intercity telephone lines.

5. Kansas Newspaper Union, as quoted in the *Abilene Weekly Chronicle*, March 14, 1889.

6. *Chicago Record*, as quoted in the *Bremen Enquirer*, February 7, 1896, and numerous other newspapers across northern Indiana. News of Clodfelter's "Indiana Interurban Railway" comes from the *Indianapolis Journal* (January 28, 1896).

7. *Muncie Morning News*, March 18, 1896.

8. *Kokomo Tribune*, July 25, 1946.

Interurban versus automobile. From the motorman's perspective, the most dangerous part of the interurban landscape was a highway crossing where fast-running interurban cars occasionally encountered egotistical automobile drivers determined to outrun the oncoming train. In rural Indiana, the tall corn of late summer could obscure the view of intersecting interurban and motor cars and increase the danger of a collision.

Suggested Further Reading

Weedgrown interurban roadbeds stretching hither and yon over Indiana are a vivid commentary on the changing habits and tastes of Indiana people. Thousands of people are yet living who were here when the electric traction lines were born. They saw them leap into such popularity that for many years they afforded far and away the chief method of transportation in the state. Now these same people, many of them, are witnessing the passing of the electric lines, which were once the state's pride and joy, and which furnished a means of transportation for the public far more economical and satisfactory than anything which had previously been devised.

—Editorial Comment, *Alexandria Times-Tribune*, September 22, 1933

Susan Berfield, *The Hour of Fate: Theodore Roosevelt, J. P. Morgan, and the Battle to Transform American Capitalism* (New York: Bloomsbury, 2020).

Michael L. Berger, *The Devil Wagon in God's Country: The Automobile and Social Change in Rural America, 1893–1929* (Hamden, CT: Archon, 1979).

David Bodanis, *Electric Universe: The Shocking True Story of Electricity* (New York: Crown, 2005).

George K. Bradley, *Indiana Railroad: The Magic Interurban* (Chicago: Central Electric Railfans' Association, 1991).

Robert F. Bruner and Sean D. Carr, *The Panic of 1907: Lessons Learned from the Market's Perfect Storm* (Hoboken, NJ: John Wiley, 2007).

Thomas R. Bullard and William M. Shapotkin, *Faster Than the Limiteds: The Story of the Chicago-New York Air Line Railroad and Its Transformation into Gary Railways* (Chicago: Central Electric Railfans' Association, 2004).

Stephen P. Carlson and Fred W. Schneider III, *PCC: The Car That Fought Back* (Glendale, CA: Interurban, 1980).
Ronald D. Cohen and Stephen G. McShane, *Moonlight in Duneland: The Illustrated Story of the Chicago South Shore and South Bend Railroad* (Bloomington: Indiana University Press, 1998).
Thomas Crump, *A Brief History of the Age of Steam: The Power That Drove the Industrial Revolution* (New York: Carroll & Graf, 2007).
Brian J. Cudahy, *Cash, Tokens, and Transfers: A History of Urban Mass Transit in North America* (New York: Fordham University Press, 1982).
L. J. Davis, *Fleet Fire: Thomas Edison and the Pioneers of the Electric Revolution* (New York: Arcade, 2003).
John Franch, *Robber Baron: The Life of Charles Tyson Yerkes* (Urbana: University of Illinois Press, 2006).
William B. Friedricks, *Henry E. Huntington and the Creation of Southern California* (Columbus: Ohio State University Press, 1992).
Stephen B. Goddard, *Getting There: The Epic Struggle between Road and Rail in the American Century* (1994; repr., Chicago: University of Chicago Press, 1996).
H. Roger Grant, *Electric Interurbans and the American People* (Bloomington: Indiana University Press, 2016).
———, *Ohio on the Move: Transportation in the Buckeye State* (Athens: Ohio University Press, 2000).
———, *Railroads and the American People* (Bloomington: Indiana University Press, 2012).
———, *Transportation and the American People* (Bloomington: Indiana University Press, 2019).
Ralph D. Gray, *Alloys and Automobiles: The Life of Elwood Haynes* (Indianapolis: Indiana Historical Society, 1979).
George W. Hilton, *The Cable Car in America*, 2d ed. (Stanford: Stanford University Press, 1997).
George W. Hilton and John F. Due, *The Electric Interurban Railways in America* (Stanford, CA: Stanford University Press, 1960).
James R. Hetherington, *Indianapolis Union Station: Trains, Travelers, and Changing Times* (Carmel: Guild Press of Indiana, 2000).
Thomas P. Hughes, *American Genesis: A Century of Invention and Technological Enthusiasm, 1870–1970* (New York: Viking, 1989).
Louis C. Hunter, *Steam Power: A History of Industrial Power in the United States, 1780–1930*, vol. 2 (Charlottesville: University Press of Virginia, 1985).
John A. Jakle, *City Lights: Illuminating the Night* (Baltimore: Johns Hopkins University Press, 2001).
———, *The Tourist: Travel in Twentieth-Century North America* (Lincoln: University of Nebraska Press, 1985).
John A. Jakle and Keith A. Sculle, *Supplanting America's Railroads: The Early Auto Age, 1900–1940* (Knoxville: University of Tennessee Press, 2017).
Jill Jonnes, *Empire of Light: Edison, Tesla, Westinghouse, and the Race to Electrify the World* (New York: Random House, 2003).
Edmund Keilty, *Doodlebug Country: The Rail Motorcar on the Class I Railroads of the United States* (Glendale, CA: Interurban, 1982).

———, *Interurbans without Wires: The Rail Motorcar in the United States* (Glendale, CA: Interurban, 1979).
Maury Klein, *The Power Makers: Steam, Electricity, and the Men Who Invented Modern America* (New York: Bloomsbury, 2008).
James H. Madison, *The Indiana Way, A State History* (Bloomington: Indiana University Press, 1986).
Jerry Marlette, *Electric Railroads of Indiana* (Indianapolis: Council for Local History, 1959). Though spiral-bound and inexpensively printed, this publication is encyclopedic in its coverage. Thus, it serves as an indispensable reference tool for anyone interested in Indiana interurban and street railway companies.
———, *Indianapolis Railways: A Complete History of the Company and Its Predecessors, 1864–1957* (Terra Alta: Pioneer Press of West Virginia, 2002).
———, *Terre Haute, Indianapolis and Eastern Traction Company* (Indianapolis: Dog Ear, 2011).
John Bartlow Martin, *Indiana, An Interpretation* (1947; repr., Bloomington: Indiana University Press, 1992).
Albert E. Meier and John P. Hoschek, *Over the Road: A History of Intercity Bus Transportation in the United States* (Upper Montclair, NJ: Motor Bus Society, 1975).
William D. Middleton, *The Interurban Era* (Milwaukee, WI: Kalmbach, 1961).
———, *South Shore: The Last Interurban*, rev. 2d ed. (Bloomington: Indiana University Press, 1999).
———, *The Time of the Trolley* (Milwaukee, WI: Kalmbach, 1967).
William D. Middleton and William D. Middleton III, *Frank Julian Sprague: Electrical Inventor & Engineer* (Bloomington: Indiana University Press, 2009).
John Anderson Miller, *Fares Please! A Popular History of Trolleys, Horsecars, Streetcars, Buses, Elevateds, and Subways* (1941; repr., New York: Dover, 1941).
David E. Nye, *Electrifying America: Social Meanings of a New Technology* (Cambridge, MA: MIT Press, 1990).
Clifton H. Phillips, *Indiana in Transition: The Emergence of an Industrial Commonwealth* (Indianapolis: Indiana Historical Bureau & Indiana Historical Society, 1968).
Larry Plachno, *The Longest Interurban Charter* (Polo, IL: Transportation Trails, 1988).
Mark H. Rose, *Cities of Light and Heat: Domesticating Gas and Electricity in Urban America* (University Park: Pennsylvania State University Press, 1995).
William Rosen, *The Most Powerful Idea in the World: A Story of Steam, Industry, and Invention* (New York: Random House, 2010).
Wolfgang Schivelbusch, *Disenchanted Night: The Industrialization of Light in the Nineteenth Century* (1983; repr., Berkeley: University of California Press, 1995).
———, *The Railway Journey: Trains and Travel in the 19th Century* (New York: Urizen, 1979, transl. from German ed., 1977).
Carlos A. Schwantes, *Going Places: Transportation Redefines the Twentieth-Century West* (Bloomington: Indiana University Press, 2003).
———, *Just One Restless Rider: Reflections on Trains and Travel* (Columbia: University of Missouri Press, 2009).
John R. Stilgoe, *Metropolitan Corridor: Railroads and the American Scene* (New Haven, CT: Yale University Press, 1983).

Paul H. Stringham, *Illinois Terminal: The Electric Years* (Glendale, CA: Interurban, 1989).
Elmer G. Sulzer, *Ghost Railroads of Indiana* (1970; repr., Bloomington: Indiana University Press).
Jon C. Teaford, *Cities of the Heartland: The Rise and Fall of the Industrial Midwest* (Bloomington: Indiana University Press, 1994).
James Thorpe, *Henry Edwards Huntington, A Biography* (Berkeley: University of California Press, 1994).
Margaret Walsh, *Making Connections: The Long-Distance Bus Industry in the USA* (New York: Routledge, 2016).
Sam B. Warner Jr., *Streetcar Suburbs: The Process of Growth in Boston, 1870–1900* (Cambridge, MA: Harvard University Press and MIT Press, 1962).
John H. White Jr., *Wet Britches and Muddy Boots: A History of Travel in Victorian America* (Bloomington: Indiana University Press, 2013).
Andrew D. Young and Eugene F. Provenzo Jr., *The History of the St. Louis Car Company* (San Diego: Howell-North, 1978).

Index

Electric interurban railways had a history of frequent, and often minor, name changes as a result of mergers or receiverships. I have italicized the names of all interurban railways mentioned in the text, but I have not attempted to distinguish between minor name changes over the years or whether a carrier preferred to define itself as a "traction company" or "railway" or something else in its official title.

abandonment of Indiana interurbans: post–World War I, 213, 218, 227–228, 242; result of years of decline, 255, 260, 264; mentioned, 4, 7, 10, 19, 22, 26, 213. *See also* Loree, Leonor, F.

accidents, 128, 156–157, 181, 183, 184, 189, 191, 192–193, 251. *See also* Alfont crash (1924); and Kingsland crash (1910)

Adams, Wellington, 115, 142, 143, 287, 290

AERA (Journal of the American Electric Railway Association), 147, 290. *See also* trade journals (electric railways)

Akron, Ohio, 81, 234

Alexandria, Indiana: first interurban connection to Anderson, 256, 267; interurban baseball, 190; mentioned, 22, 31, 83, 92, 113, 124, 160

Alfont crash (1924): details, 248–249; mentioned, 181, 184, 193, 195, 250, 260

American Electric Railway Association: annual conferences, 187, 191, 214, 261; federal lobbying, 237; presidents from Indiana, 231, 256, 296; victimized by embezzlement, 243; mentioned, 14, 74, 98–99, 121, 128, 147, 223, 282–283

American Street and Interurban Railway Association, 146, 282–283

American Street Railway Association, 13, 43, 87, 94, 122, 282–283

Amtrak, 27, 79, 142

amusement parks, 168, 174, 175, 215, 279, 293

Anderson, Indiana: early interurbans, 83, 91, 92, 160, 267; horse railway, 36; photographs, 86, 220; Union Traction headquarters, 86, 93, 123, 136; urban growth, 94–95; mentioned, 14, 22, 24, 27, 31, 67, 71, 88

Angola, Indiana, 210

Aurora, Indiana, 9, 125

automobile: disruptive technology, 8, 196–197, 252, 263; history, 10, 45, 46, 50–51, 58, 196, 246; Indiana manufacturers, 10, 51–52, 289–290
automobile inroads and interurban competition, vii, 7, 13, 34, 105, 151, 186–187, 204, 259, 297. *See also* jitney competition with electric railways
automobile trade journals. See trade journals (automotive)

Ball brothers, 25, 92, 114, 138, 28–290
Ball State University, 117
Baltimore & Ohio Railroad, 120, 281
Baltimore, Maryland, 7, 128, 198, 231, 272
baseball and interurban railways, 69, 75, 133, 190, 191, 281
Batesville, Indiana, 121, 125
Ben Hur Route. See *Indianapolis, Crawfordsville & Western*
bicycle fad (1880s and 1890s), 33, 61, 77
Big Four Route (Cleveland, Cincinnati, Chicago & St. Louis Railway), 69, 70, 88, 120, 125, 135, 246, 281, 295
Binford, Elmer J., 155
Bloomington, Indiana, 132, 140, 177
Bluffton, Geneva & Celina, 21
Bluffton, Indiana, 189, 192, 193, 292
Bookwalter, Charles, 92
Brady, Arthur Wolfe: biography, 86–87, 97–98, 223–224, 248, 259, 284, 303–304; death in 1933, 260; friendship with Charles L. Henry, 97–98, 127–128, 259; industry leadership roles, 147, 162, 191, 193, 198; interest in history, 298, 304; portrait, 98; mentioned, xiv, 23, 29, 90, 114, 125, 186, 269
Brazil, Indiana, 132
Brill, J. G., Company, 18, 41, 42, 152, 250
Bristol, Indiana, 210
Broad Ripple (suburb of Indianapolis), 174–175, 272
Broad Ripple Park, 174, 175, 176
Brown County, 174, 177
Brownstown, Indiana, 36
Bucklen, Herbert E., 210–211, 218
Buffalo & Lake Erie Traction, 241–242
Buffalo, New York, 159, 165, 241, 242
Burnham, Daniel (Chicago architect), 79, 80. *See also* Traction Terminal (Indianapolis)
bus, intercity: competition with interurban lines, 243–244, 250, 261; jitney origins, 209; Pennsylvania Railroad's bus subsidiary, 247; Trailways, 259, 304; mentioned, 26, 212, 213, 259–260

cable railways, 35, 37, 52
California interurban history, 17, 85, 132
Cambridge City, Indiana: interurban photograph, 223; mentioned, 65, 66
canals of the Midwest, 68, 281
Capital Circuit Traction, 212
Capone, Al, 133
Carmichael, J. C., 183
Carter, Vinson, 187
Central Electric Railway Association: baseball game, 190, 295; decline (1920s), 243; meetings and conferences, 213, 219, 234, 242, 256, 301–302; origin, 283, 294–295; mentioned, 90, 99, 150, 151, 153, 161, 165
Chesapeake & Ohio of Indiana, 70
Chicago & St. Louis Electric Railroad, 142, 143
Chicago, Illinois: interurbans, 170, 178, 282; Indiana hinterland, 135, 160; population, 281; rivalry with Saint Louis, 68; mentioned, 33, 72, 73, 76, 81, 132, 133, 134, 236
Chicago–New York Electric Air Line, 141–142, 290
Chicago North Shore & Milwaukee, 221, 258–259, 300, 303, 304
Chicago, South Bend & Northern Indiana, 73, 101–102, 132, 210, 289, 290, 293
Chicago South Shore & South Bend (formerly *Chicago Lake Shore & South Bend*), iv, 22, 70, 123, 132, 221, 251, 255, 262, 296
Chubbuck, H. E., 150, 291
Cincinnati, Hamilton & Dayton Railway, 120, 125
Cincinnati, Lawrenceburg & Aurora, 9, 125

Cincinnati, Ohio: destination for Indiana interurbans, 121, 124, 126, 239, 257; interurban access to central city, 288; street railways of, 82, 125; mentioned, 67, 68, 73, 75, 79, 119, 170
Claypool Hotel, Indianapolis, 17, 50, 282
Cleveland, Ohio, 68, 79, 81, 120, 151, 159, 170
Clodfelter, Noah Jasper: biography, 115–116, 268–269; portrait, 116; mentioned, 287, 293
Columbus, Indiana: photograph, 120; population, 301; mentioned, 57, 100, 101, 136, 177
Columbus, Ohio, 151, 180
Connersville, Indiana, 26, 97, 124, 125, 240, 275–276
Conway, Thomas, Jr., 60, 199, 206–207; 226, 297
Corydon, Indiana (second state capital), 67, 133
Crawfordsville, Indiana: interurban history, 140, 150, 163; interurban link to Danville, Illinois, 164–165; mentioned, 2, 26, 134, 137, 296
Cummins, Inc., 100

Danville, Illinois: interurban link to Crawfordsville, Indiana, 164–165; mentioned, 137, 150, 163
Danville, Indiana, 4, 58
Dayton & Western, 261
Dayton, Ohio, 151, 163, 182, 213
Delaware & Hudson Company, 253, 254, 255, 303
Delphi, Indiana, interurban photograph, 232
DePauw University, 88, 304
Detroit, Michigan, 10, 68, 152, 159, 170, 275
disruptive technologies, 7, 12–13, 14, 29, 58, 252
Dresser, Paul, 67
Dreiser, Theodore, 67, 185, 186
Dunreith, Indiana, 188
Duryea brothers, Charles and Frank, 116–117

Edison, Thomas A., 38, 44, 85
electric current: alternating versus direct, 88, 130, 238–239; voltage, 72–73, 74, 282, 283, 301
Electric Railway Gazette (formerly *Street Railway Gazette*), 13, 43, 268, 278. *See also* trade journals (electric railways)
Electric Railway Journal (formerly *Street Railway Journal*), 13, 39, 43, 45, 51, 55, 56, 80, 126, 127. *See also* trade journals (electric railways)
Electric Railway Review (formerly *Street Railway Review*), 13, 31, 43, 46, 52, 56, 79, 115, 122, 124, 145. *See also* trade journals (electric railways)
Electric Traction (formerly *Electric Traction Weekly*), 13, 147, 224, 243. *See also* trade journals (electric railways)
electricity, early applications, 6, 38, 276
electric versus steam railroads: parallel tracks, 159, 247; racing, 159; mentioned, 27–28, 56–57, 68, 70, 155–157, 274
Elkhart, Indiana, 69, 73, 132, 136, 163, 210
Elkins, William L., and Elkins family, 59, 280. *See also* Widener, P. A. B.
Elwood, Indiana, 27, 71, 190, 196
Emmons, Charles D.: biography, 198, 231, 272, 289; portrait, 198; mentioned, 128. *See also* *Fort Wayne & Wabash Valley*
Erie Railroad, 281
Evansville, Henderson & Owensboro: interurban ferry, 132; mentioned, 131
Evansville, Indiana: interurban history, 140, 146, 163, 170; mentioned, 9, 101, 131, 132, 134, 139, 177
Everett, Henry, 81, 282

Fairbanks, Charles Warren, 94, 95, 284
Fairmount, Indiana, 103
fare controversies, 220–221, 222
"Father of the Interurban," 24, 94, 113, 115, 225, 269, 293
Federal Electric Railways Commission (1919): testimony of Mortimer Cooley, 225–226; testimony of Charles L. Henry, 225; published results, 226–227; mentioned, 237, 299
First & Fastest, xiii, 303
Fisher, Carl Graham, 77

flood of 1913, 181, 182
Flower, Elliott, 182
Ford, Henry, and Ford automobiles, 11, 34, 204
Fort Benjamin Harrison, 215, 262; 270
Fortville, Indiana, 29, 275
Fort Wayne & Northern Indiana, 225, 292
Fort Wayne & Wabash Valley, 128, 136, 161, 192, 259, 289. *See also* Emmons, Charles D.
Fort Wayne, Indiana; interurban connections, 159, 262, 292; photograph, 84; mentioned, 26, 76, 134, 139, 155, 190
Franklin, Indiana, 57, 100, 136
French Lick, Indiana, 133, 145–146

Gary, Indiana, 132, 134, 135, 142
Gary & Interurban, 134
"Gas Belt": encouragement of early interurbans, 91, 92; final gas well, 103; source of interurban investment money, 85, 99–100, 102, 103, 106, 119; mentioned, xi, 22, 24, 25, 29, 48, 67, 71, 132
General Electric, 14, 41, 212
General Motors, 46, 155, 250
good roads, promotion of, 61–62
Gordon, Charles, 80, 260, 304
Goshen, Indiana, 64, 69, 71, 132, 136, 163
Grand Central Traction, 140
Greenfield Line. See *Indianapolis & Greenfield Rapid Transit*
Greenfield, Indiana: during 1950s era, 19, 25, 176; interurban history, 20, 172, 188, 189, 228, 265; mentioned, xi, 5, 24, 26, 29, 88, 141, 171
Greensburg, Indiana: interurban photograph, 240; mentioned, 5, 121, 124, 125, 136, 240, 283
Greenwood Line. See *Indianapolis, Columbus & Southern*
Greenwood, Indiana, 57, 58, 105, 136, 273

Hallidie, Andrew, 35
Hamilton, Ohio, 125, 197
Hammond, Indiana, 135, 155, 289
Hancock County, Indiana, 19, 21, 25, 29, 88, 187, 189, 257, 258, 275
Harding, Warren G., 233, 235, 237
Harlan and Hollingsworth (Delaware carbuilders), 152
Harrison, Benjamin, 285, 298
Haynes, Elwood: biography, 34, 46–47, 117; portrait, 34; mentioned, xii, 10, 116, 224, 287
Hemingray Glass Company (electric insulators), 48, 92
Henry, Charles Lewis: biography, 33, 86–87, 91, 92–93, 94, 95, 111–112, 124, 257–259, 284; business ventures, 87, 95, 131, 149, 234; death in 1927, 255–256; *Indianapolis & Cincinnati Traction Company*, 88, 106, 113, 120–122, 123, 234; friendship with Arthur W. Brady, 97–98, 127–128, 259; industry leadership roles, 127, 149, 153, 162, 193, 213, 230, 237, 256–257, 284; optimism, 213, 240, 273, 302; origins of interurban, 31, 91, 283; portraits, 33, 90; rehabilitation of *Indianapolis & Cincinnati Traction Company*, 1920s, 234, 259; role in launching *Union Traction*, 87, 103, 112, 113, 116, 148, 238; mentioned, xii, 13–14, 22, 23, 62, 74, 75, 102, 269, 288
Henry, George S., 258–259, 303, 304
Henry, Lewis W., 219–220, 258, 259, 304
Hernley, Charles S., 295
high cost of living (World War I inflation), 220–221.
highway competition with interurban railways, 4, 12, 241, 263–264
highway construction history, 47, 62–63, 209, 241, 250, 264
Hiner, Ward (Red Ball Lines), 243–245, 302
Holland, Harris F., 152
Holland Palace Car Company, 152
"Honey Bee and Wildflower Line." See *Indianapolis, New Castle & Toledo*).
"Hoosier Cabal," 7, 80, 128
Horseless Age. See trade journals (automotive)
horse railways, 35, 36, 38, 52, 276
horses and mules in transportation, 35, 36, 38
Huntington, Henry Edwards, 85

Illinois interurban history, 86, 163
Illinois Traction (later *Illinois Terminal*): sleeping car operations, 180; Staunton crash (1910), 193, 195; trans–Mississippi River connection to Saint Louis, 166, 170; unbuilt link to Indiana, 165–166; mentioned, 85, 91, 150, 157, 167
Indiana automobile industry. *See also* automobile; history
Indiana Capitol building, vi, 18, 27, 77, 81, 194
Indiana, Columbus & Eastern, 165
Indiana Electric Railway Association: evolves into Central Electric Railway Association, 283, 294–295; mentioned, 74, 77, 89, 127, 269
Indiana history and geography, 7, 21, 67, 76, 125, 131, 132, 165, 298
Indiana journalism, 27, 94, 97, 125, 138, 149, 186, 284, 287, 297–298. *See also* Indianapolis newspapers
Indiana Northwestern Traction, 197, 289. *See also* Purtelle, Eugene
Indiana pride in interurban railways, 19, 89, 272
Indiana Public Utility Association, 257, 284
Indiana Railroad, 106, 259, 261
Indiana Rail Road, iv, xii, 275, 294
Indiana roads and highways. See highway construction history.
Indiana Service Corporation, 259
Indiana University, 88, 132, 193
Indiana, "World's Greatest Interurban Center," xi, 3, 4, 16–18, 89, 273
Indianapolis & Broad Ripple Transit, 175, 272
Indianapolis & Cincinnati Traction Company: finances, 238, 284; freight traffic, 154; history, 96, 113, 126–129; pioneer of single-phase alternating current, 121, 122, 123, 283; receiverships, 130, 131, 187, 241; rehabilitation 1920s), 234, 235, 238, 241, 258, 279; role of Charles L. Henry, 88, 96–97, 114, 120–121, 123, 258; mentioned, 58, 74, 89, 95, 240, 301
Indianapolis & Eastern, 23, 178, 295. *See also Terre Haute, Indianapolis & Eastern*
Indianapolis & Greenfield Rapid Transit, 23, 53, 135, 155, 273, 274, 295. *See also Indianapolis & Eastern*
Indianapolis & Louisville, 282, 285
Indianapolis & Martinsville Rapid Transit, 174
Indianapolis & Northwestern, 152–153, 254
Indianapolis & Southeastern, 259–260
Indianapolis: automobile traffic, 105; bus stations, 244, 302; first interurbans, 57–58, 135, 273; industry, 154, 228; interurban freight, 144, 155, 237–238; interurban hub, 16, 19, 52–53, 76 135, 170, 231; population, 166, 170; urban growth, 49, 50, 103, 125, 272; mentioned, xi, 67, 75, 131, 137, 139, 151
Indianapolis Belt Railway, 177, 294
Indianapolis, Columbus & Southern, viii, 58, 100, 137, 282, 285, 301
Indianapolis, Crawfordsville & Western (Ben Hur Route), 2, 150, 179, 290–291
Indianapolis, Greenwood & Franklin, 57, 135
Indianapolis, Morristown & Rushville, 120
Indianapolis Motor Speedway ("The 500"), 75, 77
Indianapolis newspapers: *Indianapolis Journal, 36, 94, 95; Indianapolis News*, 4, 53, 84, 99, 111, 156, 241; *Indianapolis Star*, 95, 106, 107, 186, 232, 244. *See also* Indiana journalism
Indianapolis Northern, 136
Indianapolis, New Castle & Toledo, 136, 187, 295
Indianapolis Railways, 175
Indianapolis, Shelbyville & Southeastern, 119
Indianapolis Southern, 188
Indianapolis Stock Exchange, 52
Indianapolis, street railways of, 81, 84, 105, 115, 146, 155, 175, 272
Indianapolis Traction & Terminal, 53, 105, 172. *See also* Traction Terminal (Indianapolis)
Indianapolis Union Station, 27–28, 81, 169, 170, 294
inflation, post–World War I ("High Cost of Living"), 220–221
Ingalls, Indiana, xii, 247
Insull, Samuel, 24, 45, 98, 123, 261, 274

Interstate Commerce Commission (ICC), 86, 209, 237, 257, 264.
Interstate Public Service: acquisition by Indiana Railroad, 259; flood of 1913, 181; freight traffic, 235–236; Harry Reid, 233, 235; link between Indianapolis and Louisville, 120, 131, 136, 271; rollingstock (1920s), 238; sleeping car and dining car operations, 180, 229, 236, 240, 271; mentioned, 71, 74, 76, 114, 115, 154, 163, 282, 285
interurban access to central city, 73, 78, 79, 83, 103, 125, 126, 136, 157–158, 239
interurban apogee, 199, 296
interurban baggage handling, 30, 40, 179, 180, 222, 232.
interurban comeback illusion (1920s): undue optimism, 232–234, 237, 246; mentioned, 300
interurban construction, 137, 141, 167, 199, 213
interurban, definition of, xiv
interurban electric utility, 214
interurban employees, 22, 65–66, 172, 195, 221, 222, 226, 295
interurban enthusiasm: early years, 65–66; impact of Panic of 1907, 160, 185; mentioned, 3, 5, 6, 58, 137
interurban fares and tickets: methods of collection, 66, 160; three-cent fare controversy, 208; mentioned, 221, 222
interurban freight: traffic growth, 152, 153, 154, 155, 157, 229, 235–236; mentioned, 80, 124, 144, 145, 291
interurban hub cities, 5, 81, 84, 163, 178
interurban identity, 23, 66–67, 80
interurban impact on Indiana, vii, 3, 5, 10, 11, 52–53, 106, 272
Interurban industry, monetary value, 272, 274
interurban industry mistakes: analysis by Arthur W. Brady, 262–263; analysis by Charles L. Henry, 291; mentioned, 127, 153, 157, 158, 188, 196, 218, 219, 223
interurban infrastructure: bridges, 5, 171; trolley wire, 41, 56, 172, 213; track, 82–83, 157–158, 277; mentioned, 43, 48, 57, 181, 280
interurban investments: Indiana investors, 97, 110–111, 113, 137, 139, 185; stocks and bonds, 53, 54, 55, 57, 279–280; mentioned, 3, 44–45, 47, 49, 52, 59, 60, 84
interurban, local orientation ("localism"), 72, 76, 151, 153, 154, 158, 160, 162, 292
interurban, long-distance travel records, 151, 161–162
interurban, midwestern network: contraction, 167, 241; expansion, 26, 72, 73, 75, 76, 141, 150, 154, 163, 166; map, 161
interurban network gap closure: map, 164; symbolic significance, 159–161, 163–166, 241–242; mentioned, 30, 73, 74, 137, 148–149, 150, 159, 197, 275
interurban observers from outside Indiana, 181–182, 183, 294
interurban operations: floods, 181; lightning, 57, 181; winter ice, 181; mentioned, 56–57
interurban origins, 23, 31, 33, 34, 39, 40, 127, 276–277
interurban paper proposals ("hot air lines"), 54–55, 66, 115, 137, 139, 273, 284
interurban politics, 23, 66, 86, 92, 167, 186, 224, 264
interurban promoters; dishonesty of, 137, 140, 141, 197; mentioned, 55, 66, 107, 131
Interurban Railway Journal (Indianapolis publication), 77, 139, 290. *See also* trade journals (electric railways).
Interurban remnants, xi, 10, 23, 26, 152, 262, 265
interurban rollingstock: description, 178–179; sleeping cars, 151–152, 180, 271; mentioned, 41, 148–149, 158
interurban safety consciousness: heightened after 1910 crashes, 195, 248–249; "Safety First" movement, 213
interurban speed, 150, 157, 159
interurban stations and depots, 70, 79, 178, 216, 232, 234. *See also* Traction Terminal (Indianapolis)
interurban statistics: Indiana mileage figures, xvi, 7, 137, 218, 273–274; list by companies (1915), 217; significance, 167, 242, 272, 282,

295; traffic, 30, 65, 77, 198, 235–236, 299; mentioned, 160, 212
interurban, Sunday operation controversies, 71, 281
interurban suppliers, 14, 40, 41, 56, 57
interurban syndicates, 93, 101, 112, 113, 135, 185, 205
interurban track gauge, 73, 82. *See also* interurban infrastructure
interurban, word origin, 31, 33, 266, 267–270, 306
Irvington (Indianapolis Suburb), 78, 273
Irwin, Joseph Ireland: portrait, 101; mentioned, 58, 100, 103, 114, 139, 284
Irwin, William Glanton, 58, 100, 103, 114, 139, 284, 291, 301

Jeffersonville, Indiana, 26, 44
jitney competition with electric railways: definition, 201; illustrations, 200, 206; impact on electric railways, 199, 202–204; Indiana operations, 207, 209, 237; origin, 201; popular culture, 205–206, 209, 297; response, 205; word meaning, 201–202, 296; mentioned, 12, 13, 189, 198, 213, 218, 303
Johns Hopkins University, 117, 162
journalism, Indiana. See Indiana journalism

Kansas City, Missouri, 17, 82, 108, 109, 110
Kingsland crash (1910): details, 295; impact on industry, 192, 193; mentioned, 128, 181, 184, 198
Knightstown, Indiana, 6, 243, 271
Kokomo, Indiana: interurban station photograph, 216; mentioned, 24, 34, 47, 76, 92, 136, 190
Kosciusko County, 64

Lafayette, Indiana, vii, 101, 134, 153, 197, 254, 289
LaGrange, Indiana, 210
Lake Erie and Western Railroad, 104, 155, 156
League of American Wheelmen, 61
Lebanon, Indiana, 60, 254
Lebanon-Thorntown Traction, 280
Lee, Alfred Wilson (and Lee Newspaper Syndicate), 17, 183, 273
Light, R. C., 293
Logansport, Indiana, 5, 134, 190, 296
Loree, Leonor F., 253–255; 274, 303
Louisville & Northern, 285
Louisville, Kentucky, interurban connection to Indianapolis, 131, 236, 240; mentioned, 67, 74, 76, 100, 146

Madison County, Indiana, 248
Marion, Indiana, 24, 27, 62, 66, 71, 103

Marion, Bluffton & Eastern, xviii
Marshall, Thomas Riley: portrait, 194; response to Kingsland crash (1910), 194–195; mentioned, 99, 149, 295
"Martha" (*Union Traction* office car), 42, 148–149, 284, 303, 304
Martinsville, Indiana, 26, 131, 177, 286
Matter, Philip, 62, 103, 300
McAdoo, William Gibbs, 99, 215, 284, 289
McCarter, Thomas N., 75
McCulloch, George F.: biography, 94, 96, 149, 287, 300; portrait, 97; mentioned, 103, 105, 114, 138, 148, 259, 269, 302
McGowan, Hugh J.: alliance with Kesley Schoepf, 165; biography, 78, 79, 82, 106, 107–110, 146; death in 1911, 114; health concerns, 83, 108, 285–286; portrait, 107, mentioned, 17, 24, 76–77, 81, 87, 89, 102, 103, 112, 118, 172
McGowan, Joseph, xiv, 7–8, 65, 83, 112, 276
McKeen Cars, 211, 298
McKeen, William Riley, Jr., 211, 297
McKinley, William Brown: biography, 86; death in 1926, 177; interurban strategy, 165–166; portrait, 167; mentioned, 85, 91, 112, 150, 193, 286
Michigan City, Indiana, iv, 101; photograph, 102
Midland Utilities, 98, 261
Midwestern United States, 30, 34
Minton, Sherman, 4, 271

Missouri, Interurban History, 31, 41, 44, 90, 91, 92, 255, 283
Missouri Pacific Railway, 110, 286
Monon Route (Chicago, Indianapolis & Louisville Railway), 27, 70, 133, 281
Monroeville, Indiana, 156
Monument Circle (Indianapolis), 27, 52, 77
Morgan, J. P., 6, 111, 286
Morgan, Randal: biography, 111, 286–287, 297; criticism of, 54, 59, 84; interurban interests, 147, 185, 230, 239, 279; misspelled first name, 284; portrait, 51; mentioned, 24, 49, 51, 75, 83, 96, 108, 109. 110, 113
Morristown, Indiana, 120, 128
Mounds State Park, 174, 298–299
Muncie & Portland Traction, 138
Muncie, Indiana: interurban station, 81, 82; mentioned, 27, 48, 67, 71, 91, 92, 98
Munster, Indiana, 197, 289
Murdock, James: biography, 100–101, 114; sons James T. and Charles Michael, 101–102, 114; mentioned, 132. *See also Chicago, South Bend & Northern Indiana*

named trains, 120, 182, 189, 229
National Editorial Association, 17, 89, 90
National Road (also Cumberland Road): used by interurban tracks, 223; mentioned, 12, 20, 25, 53, 67, 182, 243, 265
New Albany & French Lick Valley, 133, 289
New Albany, Indiana, 301
New Castle, Indiana (also Newcastle), 23, 159, 187, 188, 295
New York Central System, 27, 69, 254. *See also* Big Four Route
Niagara Falls, New York, 87, 121, 122
Nichol, Harry A., 162, 172, 190, 245, 248, 301
Nickel Plate Road (New York, Chicago & St. Louis Railroad), 175, 176, 275, 281
North Shore Line. See *Chicago North Shore & Milwaukee*
Northern Indiana Commuter Transportation District, iv

Ohio interurban history, connections to Indiana, 106, 135, 151, 159, 163; mentioned, 7, 9, 55, 79, 81, 82, 83, 87, 163
Oregon Electric, 180

Pacific Electric, 85, 274
Paine, Albert Bigelow, 161–162
Panama Canal, 11, 204
Panic of 1907: impact on interurban industry, 160, 163–164, 165, 166, 187 189; mentioned, 83, 137–138, 152, 183, 213
Paris, Illinois, 163, 164, 166
Parry, David M., 295
Pendleton, Indiana, 88, 92, 190, 247
Pennsylvania Railroad: interurban competition, 136, 236; use of rail motor cars, 211–212; mentioned, 24, 27, 69, 70, 100, 135
Peoria & Eastern Railway (New York Central subsidiary), 166–167, 188, 275, 293, 295
Peoria, Illinois, 180
Peru, Indiana, 64, 70, 71, 73, 136, 159, 190, 252
Philadelphia finance: bankrolls Hugh McGowan, 108, 109, 110; criticism of, 54, 59, 84, 110–111, 137, 161; mentioned, 24, 49–50, 59, 82, 83, 96, 113, 239, 280
Philadelphia, traction history, 93–94, 113, 146–147
Plainfield, Indiana, 293
politics of Indiana, 92, 94, 98, 128
Portland, Indiana, 47, 117
power generation (powerhouse or power station), 121–122, 130, 172, 181, 213
Public Service Commission (Indiana), 4, 248, 260
Pullman Palace Car Company, 151, 152
Purdue University, 90
Purtelle, Eugene, 197, 296. *See also* interurban promotors

railroad motor cars ("doodlebugs"), 211–212
railroads, steam, 274, 274, 293
Reeves, Robert F., 22–23, 274
Reid, Harry: biography, 114–115, 233; portrait, 233; mentioned, 235, 236, 237, 272

Richmond, Indiana: interurban connections; 159, 197; mentioned, 26, 65, 66, 76, 101, 135
Richmond, Virginia, 38, 39, 147, 270
Ridge Farm, Illinois, 163, 164, 166
Riley, James Whitcomb, 24–25, 115, 171, 293
Roosevelt, Theodore, 62, 94, 208
Rushville, Indiana: headquarters of *Indianapolis & Cincinnati Traction Company*, 126; population, 240; mentioned, 5, 80, 96, 121, 122, 128, 239, 259, 283

safety conferences (1910). See Interurban Safety Consciousness
"Safety First" movement, 212–213. *See also* Interurban Safety Consciousness
St. Joseph, Michigan, 134, 163
St. Joseph Valley Traction, 210–211, 212, 218, 297
Saint Louis, Missouri: carbuilders, 277; connection to Midwest interurban network, 165–166, 170; population, 281; rivalry with Chicago, 68; street railway system, 43–44; mentioned, 20, 36, 37, 67, 137, 141, 253
St. Louis Car Company: construction of the "Martha," 148–149; mentioned, 41, 42, 44, 96, 124, 152, 178, 250
Saratoga Springs, New York, 146
Schoepf, Kesley: alliance with Hugh McGowan, 165; portrait, 112; mentioned, 75, 93, 106, 110, 112, 113
Scottsburg, Indiana, 236
Seymour, Indiana: interurban crash (1941), 251–252, 255, 303; mentioned, viii, 100, 136, 251, 301
Shelbyville, Indiana, 121, 240, 283
single-phase alternating current, 88, 129. *See also* electric current
Sloan, Alfred P., 46
South Bend, Indiana: interurban connections, 136, 160, 163; mentioned, 22, 27, 72, 73, 101, 132, 134, 139
South Shore Line. See *Chicago South Shore & South Bend*
Spanish influenza, 219–220, 227, 259
spatial relationships, 91, 134, 140, 141, 151, 159, 163–166
Sprague, Frank J., 38, 39, 44, 147, 270
steam, power of, 3, 6, 38, 41, 46, 51, 56–57
streetcar manufacturing, 41–42
Studebaker Automobile Company, 52
Sullivan, Indiana, 131
Sunday, Billy, 69, 281, 293

Tarkington, Newton Booth, 49, 50, 54, 111, 195, 278, 296
Terre Haute, Indiana: interurbans, 163, 166; track, 157; mentioned, 26, 131, 132, 135, 139
Terre Haute, Indianapolis & Eastern: accidents, 189; acquisition by Indiana Railroad, 259; bus operations, 245; formation of, 106, 110, 135, 161, 165; freight traffic, 154, 214, 228; map, 25; mentioned, 23, 29, 54, 71, 163, 188, 265
Tesla, Nikola, 44
Thorntown, Indiana, 58, 60
three-cent fare controversy, 208
timetables and guidebooks, 27, 28, 30, 69, 85, 104, 181
Tipton Indiana, 91, 190, 193
tinplate industry, 100, 103, 196.
Todd, Robert I.: biography, 128, 129, 162, 228; portrait, 129; mentioned, 75, 231, 272
Toledo, Ohio, 68, 76, 79, 83, 159, 188
Traction Terminal (Indianapolis): construction, 76–77; conversion into intercity bus station, 26, 244, 251; office tower, 50, 96; opening (1904), 80–81, 89, 169, 171; photographs, 80, 170, 173; train shed, 171, 173; waiting room, 170, 171, 177, 178, 183; mentioned, vi, 3, 24, 27, 29, 76, 78, 87, 110, 125, 273
trade journals (automotive), 34, 46, 61, 278
trade journals (electric railways): history, 278; spinoff of *Bus Transportation*; mentioned, xi, 13, 14, 31, 38, 43, 45, 77, 80, 99, 145, 147, 160, 267, 268
travel by interurban: described, 3, 5–6, 27, 71, 169, 178, 179, 182; long-distance, 6, 70, 159,

160 161, 182; outings and excursions, 168, 275; sleeping cars, 180, 236; Sunday operation controversies, 71; mentioned, 10
traveling salesmen, 30
trolley to interurban transition, 6, 23, 34, 39, 40, 43, 157–158, 163, 178, 263, 292
Turkey Run State Park, 164, 245

Union City, Indiana, 193
United Gas Improvement Company, 96, 110, 111
Union Traction Company of Indiana (also, *Indiana Union Traction*): access to downtown Indianapolis, 103, 105, 135, 136, 188–189; accidents, 192, 193; Anderson headquarters, 86, 93, 136; Brady as president, 98; bus operations, 245, 246, 260, 261, 302; early expansion, 87, 88, 92, 110, 112, 113, 116, 262.; freight traffic, 152; industry role model, 90, 260; origins, 300; parks, 174, 175; receivership, 250, 260, 261; rollingstock, xiv, 44, 148–149, 178, 238; safety matters, 213, 248–249; sale to Indiana Railroad, 1930, 98, 248, 259, 261; mentioned, xii, 5, 14, 22; 27; 29; 62, 70, 71, 81, 119
University of Michigan, 9, 98, 193, 225
University of Pennsylvania: Wharton School, 60, 297; mentioned, 51
Utica, New York, 161

Vandalia Line, 297
VanOsdol, James A., 238, 300
Vincennes, Indiana, 140, 146, 170, 177, 289
Vonnegut, Kurt, Jr., 177, 294
Vonnegut, Kurt, Sr., 174–175, 177

Wabash and Erie Canal, 68
Wabash College, 298
Wabash, Indiana, 151
Wabash Railroad, 108
Wabash River, 67, 166.
Walker, Guy Morrison, 52, 66
Warren, Indiana, xviii
Warsaw, Indiana, 64, 69, 71, 73, 159
West Baden, Indiana, 133, 146, 290
Westinghouse Electric, 14, 44, 88, 121, 130, 187, 241
Westinghouse, George, 44
Widener, P. A. B. (Philadelphia financier) and Widener family, 59, 280. *See also* Elkins, William L.
Wild, John Franklin (interurban banker), 54, 238, 279, 300–301
Wilson, Woodrow, 208, 225, 226, 227, 228, 237, 284
Winona Interurban: Sunday Operations, 71; traffic interchange, 136; mentioned, 64, 70, 72, 73, 132, 134, 281, 293
Winona Lake, Indiana, 69, 293
world fairs: Chicago, 1893 (World Columbian Exposition), 33, 34; Buffalo, 1901, (Pan-American Exposition), 148; Saint Louis, 1904 (Louisiana Purchase Exposition), 90, 110, 145, 178, 293
World War I: boosts interurban freight traffic, 144, 153, 155, 216, 228–229; impact on American railroads, steam, and electric, 214, 215, 227, 228; inflation, 221; mentioned, 71, 126, 167, 213, 219

Yale University, 87, 98
Yerkes, Charles, 45, 59, 110, 114, 117, 185

Zanesville, Ohio, 180

Railroads Past and Present

H. Roger Grant and Thomas Hoback, *editors*
Recent Titles in the *Railroads Past and Present* series

The Station Agent and the American Railroad Experience
H. Roger Grant

The Diesel That Did It
Wallace W. Abbey

Crossroads of a Continent
Peter A. Hansen, Don L. Hofsommer, and Carlos Arnaldo Schwantes

Narrow Gauge in the Tropics
Augustus J. Veenendaal Jr.

Amtrak, America's Railroad
Geoffrey H. Doughty, Jeffrey T. Darbee, and Eugene Harmon

The Panama Railroad
Peter Pyne

Last Train to Texas
Fred W. Frailey

Transportation and the American People
H. Roger Grant

American Steam Locomotives
William L. Withuhn

My Life with Trains
Jim McClellan

The Railroad Photography of Lucius Beebe and Charles Clegg
Tony Reevy

Chicago Union Station
Fred Ash

John W. Barriger III
H. Roger Grant

Riding the Rails
Robert D. Krebs

Wallace W. Abbey
Scott Lothes and Kevin P. Keefe

Branch Line Empires
Michael Bezilla with Luther Gette

Indianapolis Union and Belt Railroads
Jeffrey Darbee

Railroads and the American People
H. Roger Grant

Derailed by Bankruptcy
Howard H. Lewis

Electric Interurbans and the American People
H. Roger Grant

The Iron Road in the Prairie State
Simon Cordery

The Lake Shore Electric Railway Story
Herbert H. Harwood Jr. and Robert S. Korach

The Railroad That Never Was
Herbert H. Harwood Jr.

James J. Hill's Legacy to Railway Operations
Earl J. Currie

Railroaders without Borders
H. Roger Grant

The Iowa Route
Don L. Hofsommer

The Railroad Photography of Jack Delano
Tony Reevy

For Indiana University Press

Tony Brewer *Artist and Book Designer*

Brian Carroll *Rights Manager*

Dan Crissman *Trade and Regional Acquisitions Editor*

Samantha Heffner *Trade Acquisitions Assistant*

Brenna Hosman *Production Coordinator*

Katie Huggins *Production Manager*

David Miller *Lead Project Manager/Editor*

Dan Pyle *Online Publishing Manager*

Pamela Rude *Senior Artist and Book Designer*

Stephen Williams *Marketing and Publicity Manager*